ADDINGTON
THE LIFE STORY
of a
KENTISH VILLAGE

ADDINGTON
THE LIFE STORY
of a
KENTISH VILLAGE

by

PATRICIA RICHARDSON

ISBN No. 978-0-9574465-0-2

Design and Layout by John Hawtin
Published by Patricia Richardson,
St. Vincents, Addington, West Malling,
Kent. ME19 5BW

Printed by: Scarbutts Printers, Winsor Works, London Road, West Malling, Kent, ME19 5AN

Owing to the age of some of the photographs, the reproduction is affected.

Contents

Introduction and Acknowledgements

My family and I came to live at Addington in 1976, though I had known the village for much longer, having first visited my great aunts, May and Aline Cholmeley, during the 1950's. I began to research the history of St. Vincents, our home, partly because of its connections with Admiral Horatio Nelson. My interest quickly encompassed the whole village. In 1996, I wrote a short memoir about the village, as part of an "open village" weekend, and later studied modules of the Certificate in Local History from the University of Kent, to learn how to write a full history.

The village contains some of the most ancient monuments in Great Britain, described in all the county histories, but its later story has been largely ignored. From the Norman period to the 19th century, it was controlled by a single, but not wealthy, dynasty. The Wattons' opportunities for advancement were restricted by their enduring adherence to their Catholic faith. This life story is also about generations of Addington's families as they raised their children and crops, built and enhanced their church and administered their parish. It tells how the soil determined how the land was worked.

I have described the efforts and sacrifices that residents made in both World Wars and the housing development that brought new families to Addington after the break-up of the estate. I have brought the village story up to date by recording how the community created social, political, religious and recreational organisations. And of course the Life Story continues.

My first main source was "The History and Topographical Survey of the County of Kent", published by Edward Hasted at the end of the 18th century. My second was a series of articles written for the 1952 church magazine by James Gracie Maddan, of Aldon House. He transcribed Addington's manorial documents in meticulous handwriting into a foolscap book that he donated to the Kent Archives. I also transcribed material relevant to Addington. For instance, there have been seven further census returns since Maddan analysed that of 1851. My third source was the research undertaken by Cynthia Noble, and then by Audrey Marsh, for a series of exhibitions in the village since the 1970's. In this introduction it is impossible to thank everyone who gave me information, but I hope that they have all been acknowledged in the text.

However, I would like to specially thank Joan Scott for sharing her knowledge of the village with me.

I acknowledge with thanks the help given to me by the Kent Archive Service, now at the Kent History and Library Centre, Whatman Way, Maidstone, where I studied village and county wide material. At their library in Maidstone Museum, fellow Kent Archaeological Society members showed me original material. Their journal, the Archaeologica Cantiana, and books from the Kent Records series have been invaluable. My web sources, amongst others, included the National Archives, the National Maritime Museum, Ancestry.co.uk, the Times archive and the Kent County Library services. I would like to thank St. Margaret's Parochial Church Council and Addington Parish Council for their help. Lastly, I am indebted to my husband, Michael, for enduring the past two years of effort, and for proof reading each chapter at least four times. I am equally pleased to thank John Hawtin for designing the layout. John ran a graphic design studio at West Malling for many years, and it would have been impossible to produce this history without his expertise. His good humour and enthusiasm has forced me on when flagging.

This history is written for the general reader. However, references are given as endnotes to each chapter and I have placed a bibliography and index at the back. Although I have made every effort to trace the copyright owners of all illustrations, occasionally this has proved impossible. I have, however, acknowledged each source, where known.

Patricia Richardson
2012

5,000 BC to 1066 AD - The DISTANT PAST

When Addington is mentioned in any county history, it is not the mediaeval or modern village that is described, but its outstanding monuments from the distant past. Once they had been abandoned, well before the birth of Christ, there is no archaeological evidence that people made a permanent home here until Addington was resettled during the Saxon period. However, it is sensible to begin at the beginning, as it was the same soil, and the same topography that attracted both groups of people.

Within the boundaries of the modern village are two of the most ancient monuments in the county of Kent, if not in Britain. They may well date from about 3,700 BC, when Neolithic settlers first crossed the Channel. These people brought with them the knowledge of farming, a heritage of ancestor veneration and the desire and ability to create huge monuments at which to carry out their ceremonies. They may not have found an empty landscape. Earlier men had lived within the territory of the village. During an emergency excavation at Addington Sandpit during 1965 an unrolled, white, flint tool was unearthed. This was identified as having been made between 200,000 and 120,000 BC and is thought to have been a knife.[1] These first nomads vanished during one of the ice ages and for millennia the land was uninhabited until Mesolithic hunter-

gatherers crossed into Britain in about 10,000 BC. These families made their homes within the territory now known as Addington. In 1957, John Alexander (1922 - 2010),[2] from Cambridge University, conducted a field study of the area around the megaliths and found evidence of post holes and hearths pre-dating them at between 5,000 and 4,000 BC, confirming a settlement here. A huge amount of flint knapping debris from this period was also discovered

Mesolithic Microliths found by R. Burchell, 1965. Maidstone Museum. Photographed by the author.

suggesting that ceremonial flint knapping may well have taken place at the site. Alexander reported his findings in Archaeologica Cantiana, the journal of the Kent Archaeological Society, of 1961.[3] Unfortunately, although his finds were deposited in the Maidstone

Museum, a fire destroyed them before modern dating methods could be used on them. I visited the museum and was shown some similar material from Addington, but the flints I was able to photograph came from a later find nearer to the motorway.[4]

Whether the incoming farmers found an uninhabited region, or whether they drove away these hunter gatherers is unclear, but Alexander concluded that there was little time between the abandonment of the Mesolithic habitation and the building of the new chambered tombs. For a while both means of gaining a living may have co-existed. The incomers would have found un-cultivated land, covered in birch, alder and oak, with plenty of water from the many local springs as well as Addington Brook. They also found some key geological factors that encouraged them to settle nearby, though no sign has been found of post holes of this date to indicate that their homes were next to their monuments. The sand of the area, and in particular the silica within this sand, was crucially important to them. Between what are now the villages of Addington and Trottiscliffe lay great boulders of sarsen stone. This is a sandstone that was hardened during the ice ages by this silica. Silica sand remains an important component of the current mineral workings in the village and sarsen stone can still be found in the area.[5]

known as Addington Long Barrow and the Chestnuts, by Park Road, which slices through the Long Barrow.[6] They are the remains of two megalithic burial chambers, and of their associated mounds. The word megalithic refers to the huge size of the boulders that were used in their construction. The tumbled boulders of each structure were originally the upright stones that flanked them. Most of those of the Long Barrow are half buried, some are

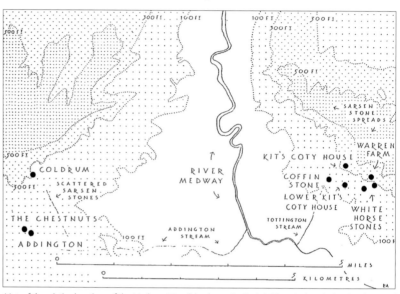

Map of the relative locations of the Medway Megaliths drawn by Paul Ashbee. Archaeologica Cantiana, Vol 120, p320 © Kent Archaeological Society.

flattened and others have been buried or moved. Those of the Chestnuts were re-erected during the 1980's to give a better idea of the shape of the chamber and its entrance. It is possible that the Addington megaliths were built as a pair, as they align with the winter and summer solstices respectively. They are part of a group of such structures. Others lie in the Aylesford area, where there are further sarsen stone deposits, and Coldrum barrow is nearby at Trottiscliffe. Together the structures are known as the Medway Megaliths. The people who used them probably had their homes on both sides of the Medway.

The Neolithic Structures

There are two distinct monuments close to the centre of the current village, near to the mound on which the church stands. From the village green one approaches the two structures,

After the megaliths were abandoned the site was lightly used over the centuries. In 1965 a mechanical excavator removing topsoil at Addington Sandpit uncovered a burial group from the Roman period. An emergency dig was conducted by D. Bartlett,[7]

who unearthed a cinerary urn containing bones and funeral artefacts, proving that there was at least one small community at Addington in the first centuries after the birth of Christ. Although not highly fertile, the soil was light and easily worked. Ground water and springs are prevalent in the area due to the juxtaposition of sand and gault clay, so it is not surprising that intermittent habitation continued. A Romano-British site was also identified during the 1930's next to East Street, to the north of the current motorway, but this is just inside the Ryarsh parish. No archaeological evidence has been found of a large settlement here during the immediate period following the withdrawal of the Romans. The village did not gain its name of "Addington" until the eighth or ninth century AD and is of Saxon origin.

There continued to be some interest in the nature and meaning of the huge stones, but a true understanding of their shape and purpose was not understood until late in the twentieth century. The process is still ongoing. Under Norman rule there was a revival of interest in megaliths throughout southern England, but only for plunder. During the thirteenth century many, including those at Addington, were excavated in an unsuccessful bid to find buried treasure. This was a systematic search instigated by the Crown, rather than the work of local grave robbers. It is doubtful that anything of value was discovered but, as a result of the excavations, the chambers of both megaliths collapsed inwards. Their shape became obscured, and their importance then lay once more un-recognised. John Harris visited them early in the eighteenth century, but in his "History of Kent",[8] he wrote that he considered the stones to be natural stone outcrops. However, by the end of that century the Kent historian Edward Hasted recognised their significance. In his "History and Topographical Survey of Kent"[9] he wrote that the stones were *of the same kind as those of Stonehenge*" and thought that they were placed in the same shape and for the same purpose. He found that "*The sandiness of the soil has covered many of them, which can, only by guessing their distances, be found by thrusting of a stick into the ground.*" Hasted counted seventeen stones at the Long Barrow and thought that its shape was an oval. He believed that some of the fallen stones had been "*carried away by*

Eighteenth century print of the Addington Megaliths.

the inhabitants for different uses." He could find only six stones at the Chestnuts and failed to recognise them as man-made. He described them as being just *"another heap of large stones, tumbled inwards one upon another."* A late eighteenth century print shows Addington church with the stones in the foreground. The caption reads that they are in the grounds of Leonard Bartholomew, Esq., of Addington. It is tempting to identify the gentleman in the print as Mr. Bartholomew himself.

The Medway megaliths are now accepted as having been built around 3,725 BC and as being connected to those in the Severn-Cotswolds area of the West Country, but pre-dating them. Brian Philp, of the Council for Kentish Archaeology, excavated both the Chestnuts and Addington Long Barrow in 1981 and established that their axes were remarkably similar to those at Aylesford and in the Cotswolds. The shape of retaining walls at both Coldrum and Addington resemble the truncated wedge shapes of those in the Severn-Cotswolds area, particularly at Belas Knap in Gloucestershire and at Waylands Smithy in Berkshire. Prior to the 1981 survey, the shape of the Long Barrow had been seen as either oval or at best rectangular and the connection had not been made, whilst that of The Chestnuts had completely vanished. The size of the Medway Valley barrows, particularly the one at Addington, fall into the same range as those in the West Country. Philp felt that as at Coldrum, the Chestnuts and the Long Barrow are so close to each other and to the three chambered tombs in the Aylesford area, they might well have formed a communal cemetery.

During the 1990's the material that had been amassed about the megaliths of Kent over the preceding centuries was reviewed by a number of archaeologists, using the information gained from systematic twentieth century excavations. Paul Ashbee (1918-2009), of the University of East Anglia, writing in the Archaeologica Cantiana in 1999 and 2000, came to the conclusion that the megaliths were foci for rituals involving human remains, rather than a final resting place for individuals.[10] Although human bones were found in a number of the Medway valley structures, including the Chestnuts and the Long Barrow, it seems that they were not those of a single chieftain and his family. From the type and number of bones, which were those of a number of individuals, including children, it is now generally accepted that these were from more than one family. The cremated bones were first buried elsewhere, and later brought to the chambers, to be used on important occasions. Those found by archaeologists were probably the last to be used in this way. Ashbee noted that as particular bones were favoured, such as skulls, arms, legs and hands, he felt that access to the sites was probably controlled. He concluded that usage was over a long period of time. Ashbee compared the chambers and barrows of the Medway Valley megaliths to those at the western end of the European mainland, as those in Kent have a similar, uniform, large size of chamber. However, they have similarities to those in countries bordering the southern North Sea, and the current thinking is that the Neolithic farmers came from this more eastern area of Europe, rather than from Brittany.

They are accepted as the first to be built in England. As I was completing this history of Addington in the summer of 2012, a new survey was being undertaken at Addington Long Barrow, led by Paul Garwood, Lecturer in Prehistory at Birmingham University. With the kind permission of Mrs. Bygrave, who owns the land on which the Long Barrow stands, and with the consent of English Heritage, Garwood led a team from Birmingham in a landscape scale study. This is part of a six-year project on the Medway Megaliths. The intention is to relate the structures within a context of lived landscapes. He confirmed that carbon dating at Kits Coty House, near Aylesford indicates that this was earlier than any other structure on the British Isles. It is likely that the farmers brought animals and improved cereals with them but, once settled, adapted their farming practices to the local terrain. The original number of settlers may have been quite small and they probably interbred with the indigenous Mesolithic population. As part of this study, test pits were dug in the field beside the Long Barrow, as this is a rare example of untilled and unaltered land, unlike the sandpits to the north west, or the manor estate and recreation ground to the south of the monument. Paul Garwood gave a short field talk on his and his team's work at Addington and the photograph shows his team of students at work in one of the test pits, observed by interested local people.

A test pit dug beside Addington Long Barrow, July 2012, by team led by Paul Garfield of Birmingham University. Paul Garfield is standing second from right.

involved selecting, shifting and raising substantial blocks of stone. They were not isolated, as they traded with other communities, both in this country and on the continent. Their understanding of the solstices suggests that they had an appreciation of time, place and history. Their ritual use of bones implies that they invoked their ancestors to help them with their present tasks.

The study involved a number of different surveys, including a 3-D laser scan, field, photographic, archaeological and ground surveys, including the use of magnetometry. The new methods were far more sophisticated than those available to earlier archaeologists. A particular discovery was that during one of the last ice ages a deep valley was gouged through this part of Addington. As the climate warmed this was infilled with sand and silt, so that unlike other parts of the village, the bedrock is deep below the surface, even below the water table. The megalithic structures were built on top of this great depth of sand. The team found at least a thousand pieces of knapping debris and tools in the field, dating from the Neolithic period. Those found at the Chestnuts between the 1950's and 1980's had been Mesolithic material. As this debris was clustered in certain parts of the field, Garfield suggested that these were where people would come up the hill from their settlement nearer to the water to gather communally and make their tools.

The current understanding is that Neolithic society was not entirely egalitarian, as it is most likely that the tombs were entered by only a few special individuals. They were, however, a skilled and co-operative people. Without such co-operation, they would not have had the ability to produce such large structures. The work

Addington Long Barrow

This is the megalith that one drives through on the way from the Village Green to the Recreation Ground. What one sees are a number of large, semi-rectangular stones rising out of the ground on each side of the lane. Although the mound of this long barrow is still obvious, its chamber, which was on the higher ground near the housing development, has vanished. Most of its stones are fallen and all are partly or completely buried. In 1828, when the track across the barrow was deepened and widened to make a proper carriage road, this work drove a deep channel through the Barrow. During the work some of the stones were laid flat and buried beneath the new track way and others were shifted aside. A few years after the new road had been cut, a Kent antiquarian, Rev. Beale Poste (1793-1871), recorded that two that had been moved out of the way now lay closer to the nearby wood. One of these can still be identified near to the track beside the Seekers' Trust wall.[11] Poste called the stones "Addington Circles" and thought they were a ceremonial henge, like Stonehenge.

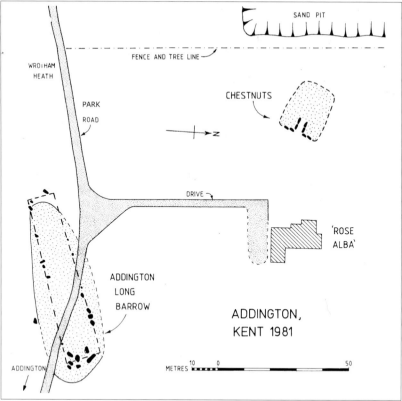

Map of Addington Long Barrow and the Chestnuts from The Medway Megaliths, Brian Philp, © Kent Archaeological Trust, 1981

John Evans, writing in 1951, ascertained its length to be about 60 metres but, like his predecessors, considered the shape to be an oval.[15] Before 1980 the maximum number of stones identified had been 22. However, when a detailed survey was undertaken in 1981 by an archaeological rescue team sponsored by the Kent Archaeological Trust and led by Brian Philp, it was finally ascertained that the structure was wedge shaped.[16] This survey confirmed its length and discovered three more sarsen stones in the peristalith, the standing stones that surround the mound, raising the number to 25. The stones had been raised by digging ditches either side of the mound. Although peristaliths are often in a circular shape, that at Addington was found to have straight sides, tapering in width from 14 metres to 11 metres east to west. The shape is of particular significance as it finally tied the megalith to those in the West Country, something that earlier researchers had refuted. Philp calculated that there may well have originally been 50 sarsen stones. Some still lie hidden. It is hopeful that the 3-D Laser survey will tell us how many were used in the Barrow's construction. One of these was discovered lying flat beneath Park Road as recently as 2007, when a rabbit hole caused the roadway to collapse, and another in 2010. The axis of the barrow is just north of east, at 75° (magnetic). This is similar to the other surviving barrows in Kent. From the position of the visible stones it is clear that the chamber had been at the eastern end of the structure. The mound of earth at Addington Long Barrow is still at least a metre high. 2,000 tons of earth must have been shifted during construction, and this would probably have resulted

In 1845 the Rev. Lambert Blackwell Larking (1797-1868),[12] the Vicar of Ryarsh, undertook the first archaeological excavations at Addington Long Barrow, where the chamber was then still identifiable, though he did not recognise its significance. He did not investigate the Chestnuts because, as had Hasted fifty years earlier, he saw only a pile of stones. This is strange as they were already called Druidical Remains in the Tithe Map compiled in 1843, so it was already appreciated that these stones had been moved in ancient times. Larking reported finding pottery and flints, but did a certain amount of damage during his excavations, through which the chamber collapsed completely. It was not until the end of the century that the Rev. C.H. Fielding identified the stones in Addington Park as a dolmen[13] or chambered tomb. However, Fielding also failed to record that there were two structures close beside each other.

During the twentieth century a number of archaeologists[14] visited the Addington Long Barrow.

in wide and deep ditches beside the mound. Material has now spread into these ditches and out beyond them.

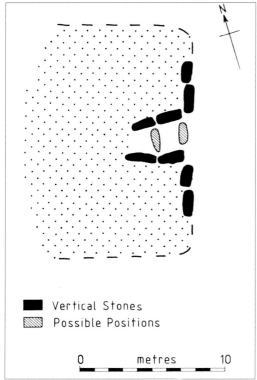

Plan of the Chestnuts drawn by Brian Philp. From The Medway Megaliths, 1981 © Kent Archaeological Trust

The Chestnuts

The Chestnuts chamber stands about 100 metres north-west from the Long Barrow. The field on which it stood was called Stoney Warren in the tithe schedule of 1843, as the area had been a mediaeval, managed, rabbit warren. The Chestnuts remained relatively unstudied until the mid 20th century, because of the very tumbled nature of its stones.

In 1953 Richard Boyle,[17] who had acquired the land on which both structures stand, cleared the scrubland and ploughed it for horticulture, at the same time protecting the stones. Although still only

in his twenties, Boyle became interested in the archaeology of his land, and conducted a field study of the area. He found a large number of flints and other material lying over a wide area, including where the recreation ground now stands. It was Boyle who invited John Alexander to make a survey of the Chestnuts. The stones were not then immediately recognisable as having contained a chamber. In fact a large holly tree was growing in the middle of them.

As has been said, Alexander published a record of the excavations he undertook that year in the Archaeologica Cantiana of 1961. He reported four distinct periods of occupation:

● *a primary, Mesolithic, level, including post holes and hearths*

● *a Neolithic level when a chambered tomb was built which was then used into the early bronze age,*

● *a Romano-British hut or settlement, and*

● *a Norman excavation and tomb robbery dating to the thirteenth century.*

He concluded that, as the Mesolithic material covered such a wide area, the site must have been in occupation over a considerable period. In all, 2,314 flints were found, of which only six dated from Neolithic times. These were in a variety of shapes, being used for different purposes. They included scrapers, microliths (miniature cutters), burins and gravers (chisels), awls (tools sharpened to a point for making a hole), saws and axes, although the majority were axes, chisels and microliths. The finds included 201 cores, from which the tools had been fashioned and 1,734 primary flakes – pieces which had been discarded during the work process.

He measured the axis of the Chestnuts as pointing to the east, like the Long Barrow but at 110°, slightly south. Of the artefacts found, some were in or near the tomb, but others lay as far to the west as Campions Bridge, by the village hall car park, and to the east for 200 metres into Chestnuts Wood.[18] The chamber was found to be four metres long and two metres wide, with a forecourt. This had a pavement of greensand stones set in white sand over yellow. Further small stones were of also of this material. As

The archaeological dig undertaken by John Alexander in 1957 Private collection of Alison and Andrew Linklater.

concluded that the mound may have been even longer than that of the Long Barrow.

Alexander found the cremated remains of a minimum of nine individuals of all ages, including children. The bones were on the forecourt and may have been thrown out of the chamber so that others could be brought in. He agreed with former archaeological evidence which suggested that bones were cremated and firstly buried elsewhere, to be brought into a tomb as a focus during ceremonies. It is now thought that bones may also have been removed by individual families for private veneration. Some grave goods were discovered and remains of the pots which had brought the cremated remains. At the time of this survey, some of the stones were re-erected, to give a better idea of the original structure. The result is a very impressive sight. What can now be discerned are the excavated chamber

these do not occur on the surface in this vicinity, Alexander speculated that they had been brought in. He identified the larger stones as sarsen and noted that the mound appeared to have been constructed first, to aid placing the upright stones. The trapezoid shape of the Chestnuts chamber was found to closely resemble that of Coldrum. Although the mound had disappeared, Alexander considered that it had been much shorter than that of Addington Long Barrow, possibly measuring only 20 metres long and 15 metres wide. However, when Paul Ashbee reviewed the previous studies in the 1990's, he

Photograph of the Chestnuts. With kind permission of Mrs. Joan Bygrave

and the façade, which has a line of four large upright stones and the central chamber with four more. There is also a noticeably large stone to one side which was probably a capstone. The plan on page 7 shows how the existing stones now stand.

The Intervening years up until 1066

The chambered tombs were in use for at least a thousand years, before falling into ruin. Why this occurred is unknown, but certainly later megalithic constructions such as Stonehenge were designed for different rituals. The Bronze Age came to Britain in about 1300 BC. There is some evidence that these people also altered the landscape around Addington. There is a particularly distinctive mound beside St. Vincents Lane. It appears to have an altered shape near its top, and a further mound in an adjacent field also shows signs of manipulation. It is feasible to suggest that one or both of these workings date from this time, as Bronze Age people also changed the shape of their surroundings, sometimes for use as burial mounds now called tumuli. However, these hillocks might simply have been used to corral cattle by making a "ditch" around the summit and driving stakes into this. Although no excavations have taken place on these, their shape suggests human intervention. Flinty material is scattered over the surface as if introduced from elsewhere.

The next direct evidence of men using the area that would become Addington dates from the Roman period. As has been noted above, in 1957 Alexander discovered a hut and some Roman pottery dating from the fourth century AD next to the Chestnuts megalith. He considered that this hut was an outlying hunting base for Romano-Britons living in the Aylesford area, rather than a permanent home. As the nearest major Roman road ran on the far side of the Medway, from Rochester to Hastings, this side of the river was not particularly accessible.

During the fifth century, without Rome's protection, Britain became vulnerable to invasion. Rising sea levels reduced available farmland in northern Europe, encouraging people to search out new places to settle. Hengist and Horsa, the first kings of Kent, are reputed to have been Jutes, from lower Denmark. However, the archaeological evidence gathered from grave goods points to the immigrants being a Germanic people with links to Jutland, rather than Jutes themselves.[19] There is some suggestion that they were encouraged to come to Kent. Their descendants became known as Anglo-Saxons and eventually ruled most of Britain, unifying the country under one king. They brought with them a tradition of chieftains leading a community, or manor. These chieftains owned some of their labourers, who could be bought and sold with the manor in which they lived. Other manor residents, although nominally free, owed many man hours of labour to their lords. Owners of small manors in their turn owed allegiance to overlords, i.e. the feudal system.

Before Addington was resettled, Kent was converted to Christianity under Aethelbert, King of Kent (d. 616). He allowed Augustine to found the monastery at Rochester in 597. There followed a highly Christian period, when kings gave grants and charters to found monasteries or to build minsters and churches, allocating adjacent land for their maintenance. In early days, preachers would go out from the minster into the community to preach, but once churches were built in manors the parish system came into existence, with a resident priest. These parishes are first recorded in the eighth century.

There is no direct evidence when the settlement of Addington began, and it may not have achieved the status of manor or parish until the turn of the ninth century. It is not mentioned in a charter of 788, by which Offa, King of the Mercians, and overlord of Kent, gave six plough lands in the parish of Trottescleva (Trottiscliffe) to the church, stating that the boundary for this land on the east and south was Birling, on the west Wrotham and on the north Meopham.[20] It seems likely that the church in Addington had not yet been built and that the settlement or manor then lay within the parish of Birling. Alternatively, it may not yet have existed.

The village acquired its name of Addington, firstly spelt with an "E", from its founder. It is accepted that this name sprang from a family chief, "Edda or Eadda" "inga" meaning people and "tun" meaning settlement enclosed by a fence or hedge. A book on Kent place names compiled by Canon Horsley in 1921 considers that Edda also founded a settlement near Woodchurch, Ashford. Great Engeham Manor, from Edda, ge and ham. Engeham farm still exists there. Canon Horsley also maintained that the letter "e" was pronounced as a short "a", as in cat, during the Saxon period, so Addington was always pronounced this way, unlike Malling which came from the name Maella. The spelling of the name changed over the centuries. It is called Eadintuna in the eleventh century Textus Roffensis. Other early spellings were were Eddingtune, Ed(d)intone and Eadintun. Adintone is a later version, with or without a "g" and the second "d" arrives later still.

Kent, which was part of Wessex, does not seem to have been settled by the Vikings, though they penetrated up the Darenth during the ninth century. King Alfred of Wessex rapidly won back the county and country and was succeeded by his son and later by his grandson, Aethelred. However, in 1016, on Aethelred's death, the country was seized by the Danish King, Cnut, who ruled until 1035. Cnut spent much of his time in Denmark, and divided the country administratively into four regions. He appointed Earl Godwine, Earl of Kent, to oversee Wessex. Godwine had three sons: Harold, later King of England, Tostig and Alnoth, and his family became immensely powerful. King Cnut was succeeded by his two sons, but their dynasty did not survive. In 1042 Edward the Confessor, son of Aethelred, returned from exile to be crowned King of England. However, he had no son. It was this succession that led to the Norman invasion 24 years later, when Harold, Earl Godwine's eldest son, seized the crown on the Confessor's death on 6th January 1066. The youngest son, Alnoth, then became the overlord of part of Addington, the settlement then being divided into two manors, until the Conquest.

During the Anglo-Saxon period, succession of land tenure in Kent became governed by the law of gavelkind which the Jutish or Saxon kings of Kent brought with them. Land holders paid their dues to their lord by service and rent, both in money and in kind, such as fowl or their eggs. They were permitted to make a will and to designate heirs, rather than their land reverting to the lord of the manor. Land-holdings became known as "heredes", or "hereditaments". The testator was expected to divide his land equally between his sons or, failing sons, equally between his daughters, unlike primogeniture which prevailed in the rest of England and whereby all the property was left to the eldest son (or, failing sons, the eldest daughter). Gavelkind resulted in small parcels of land where the holders were closely related to each other. More than one home often stood on a piece of communally owned land. It generated a bond between those working the soil.

Kent had a particular form of administration. Before England was unified, the kings of Kent established a complicated system of lay taxation based on large stretches of land called lathes. These centred on a "royal vill", which became responsible for collecting the taxes due to the King. From archaeological evidence, it seems that these were first established very shortly after the Anglo-Saxons arrived, as pagan cemeteries, containing grave goods, were found in their locality.[21] Addington was in the lathe of Aylesford, one of only two lathes in West Kent, whereas East Kent contained seven, being more densely settled. The highly forested Weald remained virtually unpopulated until the Middle Ages. To simplify administration the lathes were later subdivided into hundreds, so that people did not need to travel far to pay their dues, especially as these were in kind. The hundreds held a court where disputes that crossed more than one parish boundary were settled. Addington lay within the hundred of Larkfield. The Kentish tax system was based on sulungs and curucates. The carucate was the amount of land that could be ploughed during one day and the sulung was a figure based on the monetary value of this. These both varied with the terrain. These Saxon terms were used in the Domesday Book of 1085.[22]

A church was probably founded on its current site before the Conquest. The first structure may have been wooden, built on stone foundations. An archaeological evaluation was undertaken by the

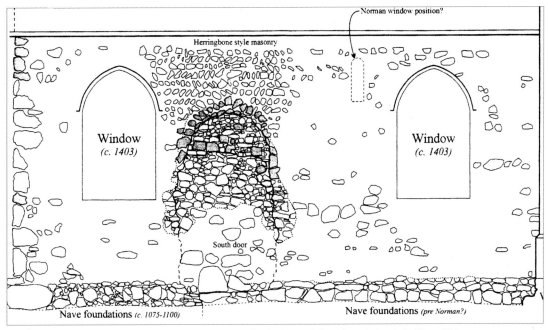

Linklater, Andrew, Archaeological Watching Brief at St Margaret's Church, Figure 4, © Canterbury Archaeological Trust, 2012.

Canterbury Archaeological Trust on the ground adjacent to the south side of St. Margaret's Church in 2010, before the construction of a new extension.[23] Andrew Linklater, who led the survey, noted that the widths of the early nave and chancel were typically Saxo-Norman. He considered that the south wall of the nave sat directly over pre-Norman foundations. The foundations on the southern side of the nave have a distinct change about half way along, as can be seen in the drawing above. The church's dedication to St. Margaret of Antioch could well date from its Saxon origins, as she was known to the West as early as the eighth century.

As the Saxon era drew to a close in the autumn of 1066, Edda's farmstead had grown into two small manors, each managed by a steward on behalf of his particular lord. The Domesday Book records that both manors were part of the King Edward's large Kent estate. The smaller manor, spelt Eddintone, had been held by Leftan (Leofstan),[24] and its rental value was slightly over £4. After the king's death Leofstan ceded it to Alnod Cilt (Young Alnoth),[25] Earl Godwine's youngest son. Addington was one of fourteen manors held by Alnoth. In this first manor there was a valuable mill, but no woodland. This

suggests that it lay in the southern part of the settlement, as northern Addington, beneath the Downs, is far more wooded.[26]

The second, and larger manor, spelt Eddintune, contained woodland, the church, two mills, meadows and arable land. This was held by Agelred (Aethelred) and had a rental value of £8. Aethelred held only one other manor in Kent. The prosperity of Addington, like so many others in the county and country, was then shaken by the brutal invasion of Duke William of Normandy, and both these manors lost value.

1.   Broadfoot, D.N., "*Flint Paleolith from Addington*", Kent Archaeological Review, 1967, 8, 13. The article continues: "The implement, rectangular and about 5" inches by 3" inches, is of the Levalloisian type, probably about 200,000 BC though some authorities might put it at perhaps 120,000 BC. It has been struck at one blow from a prepared core, with a faceted 'cupid's bow' butt and shows the negative bulb from a previous flake. It is probably a knife, with the broad edge retouched and typologically is Palaeolithic. The site is 9 miles south of the famous workshop site of such flakes at Baker's Hole, Northfleet."

2.   Alexander was the founder of the Cambridge Archaeology Field Group, and had a special interest in rescue archaeology.

3.   Alexander, John, "*Excavation of the Chestnuts Megaliths Tomb at Addington*", Arch. Cant 76, 1961, pp 157

4.   They originate from the emergency excavations undertaken by R. Burchell in 1965 before the motorway was built. Some were the gift of Professor and Mrs. D.T. Donovan, of the University of Hull. Others were donated by Dr. Jean Brown and are labelled Burchell, 1991 31/1. These may have come from the 1933 Burchell investigations in the Campions Wood area.

5.   Though it has been asserted that some of the boulders used in the Addington megaliths are dissimilar to that quarried locally. Wright, Christopher John, "*A Guide to Pilgrims Way and the North Downs*", 1971, revised 1982, 1987

6.   The housing development in Park Road is also called the Chestnuts, and the remnant of Chestnuts Wood stands to the north of this, having been mostly destroyed by the development and the motorway. I have therefore added "megalith" when describing the Neolithic structure in an attempt to avoid confusion.

7.   Bartlett, D, 1966, "*Recent Excavations: Emergency Excavation at Addington*", Kent Archaeological Review, 3, 41

8.   Harris, John, "*The History of Kent in Five Parts*", 1719, London

9.   Hasted, Edward, "*The History and Topographical Survey of Kent*" Vol. 4, pp 542548, 1798

10.   Ashbee, Paul, "*The Medway Valley megaliths in a European Context*" Archaelogica Cantiana, Vol. 119, pp 269-284, also Vol. 120, pp 319-345 Ashbee was born at Bearsted, Kent, but moved to Norfolk after being appointed the first archaeologist at the University of East Anglia in 1968. He was a co-director of the Sutton Hoo dig between 1964 and 1972.

11.   Poste, Beale, "*Military Antiquities of Kent, Sec. III*", mss, assessed by John H. Evans in Arch. Cant. Vol. 62, p 136.

12.   The Rev. Larking was the vicar of Ryarsh between 1830-1868. He was born at Clare House, East Malling. He became the founder of the Kent Archaeological Society in 1857 and wrote widely on Kent History.

13.   Fielding, Rev. C.H., "*Memories of Malling and its Valley*", 1893, p 5

14.   O.G.S. Crawford examined the barrow in 1924, John H. Evans, editor of Arch. Cant., visited in 1950 and measured structure as c. 200 feet, in an oval form, 22 stones. Evans also reviewed the notes of Beale Poste in Arch. Cant. and pointed out their inaccuracies. Ronald Jessup, renowned Kent Historian, visited in 1930 and 1970, and also thought the structure was oval. All these reports were recorded in Arch. Cant.

15.   Evans, J.H., "*Kentish Megalith Types*", Arch. Cant. 63, pp 63-81

16.   Philp, Brian, "*The Medway Valley megaliths*", Kent Archaeological Trust, 1981, pp 77-90

17.   Richard Gurney Boyle, (1930-1983), succeeded his brother as 4th Baronet in 1981, but died two years later, leaving three sons. He built Rose Alba, on Park Road. During the 1950's his mother, Lady Boyle, was the president of the Seekers' Trust but she never lived in the grounds.

18.   Most of this wood now lies under the motorway, but a remnant still stands behind numbers 1-12 The Chestnuts.

19.   Williams, J.H., ed, "*The Archaeology of Kent to AD 800*", Kent Archaeological Society, pp 187-248

20.   Fielding, Rev. C.H., "*Memories of Malling*", 1893, p 9 (Neither Addington nor Ryarsh are mentioned.)

21.   Christians were not buried with grave goods, and the bodies faced East, towards Jerusalem.

22.   In other counties the term used was "hide". These measures did not necessarily correlate to a particular acreages, but were based on the amount of land needed to support one or more families. Bede mentions the use of these terms. The sulung was later used purely as a monetary taxation method.

23.   Linklater, A., "*An Archaeological Watching Brief at St. Margaret's Church, Addington*", 2010/2012

24.   The first spelling is that used in the Latin Domesday, that in brackets the English translation.

25.   The Latin reads Alnod Cilt, meaning young Alnoth, to distinguish him from another man in the document.

26.   This part of the parish has now become part of Trottiscliffe.

2

1066 to 1499 - NORMAN RULE

The years following King William I's invasion were not at all pleasant for the native population. Although his passage through Kent had been unimpeded and Kent's traditions honoured, the Normans were harsh overlords. King William rapidly redistributed his new lands. Most were given to his Norman supporters, but a few Saxons who had become loyal to him were also rewarded. One of the latter, Ralf, became overlord of both manors in Addington, though these are not listed consecutively in the Domesday Book of 1085. Domesday records the effect that the Conquest had on virtually all small manors. From the information given to the compilers, it seems there had been a severe and lasting depression. The rental value of all land had fallen since 1066 and the two entries for Eddintone/Eddintune are fairly typical for Kent.[1] Right is a facsimile of the highly abbreviated Latin used in the book for the two manors, the smaller one being given first. Beneath this, in the translation, I have used square brackets where an earlier reference is omitted in the text. I have then used round brackets to give the Anglo-Saxon spelling of the Norman name.

Radulf⁹ ten̄ de ep̄o *EDDINTONE* . p̄ dimiđ ſolin.
Tra.ē.ı.cař.7 ibi.ē cū.ıııı.borđ 7 ıı.ſeruis.7 ibi.ı.molin
de.xxııı.ſoł.Totū M̃ app̄ciat.ıııı.liƀ.T.R.E.parū ualeƀ.
Leſtan tenuit de rege E.7 poſt mortē ej⁹ uertit ſe ad
Alnod.7 m̃ eſt in calūpnia.

"Ralf, [son of Turald (Thorold)], holds Eddintone, of the Bishop [of Baieux] for half a sulung. The arable land is one carucate, there are four borderers and two slaves, and there is one mill of twenty three shillings. The whole manor is valued at four pounds. In the time of King Edward it was worth a little more. Leftan (Leofstan) held it of King Edward, and after his death turned himself over to Alnod Cilt (Alnoth) and now it is in dispute."

Radulf⁹ fili Turaldi ten̄ de epō *EDDINTVNE* . p̄ . ıı . ſolins
ſe defđ | Tr̄a . ē . v . cař . In dn̄io ſunt . ıı . 7 vı . uiłłi cū
. ıx . borđ hn̄t . ı . cař . Ibi æccła 7 x . ſerui . 7 ıı . molini
de . xı . ſolid 7 ıı . den . 7 xıı . ac p̄ti . Silua . x . porc̄.
T.R.E.ualeƀ . vııı . liƀ . Q̃do recep̄ . c . ſoł . Modo . vı . liƀ.
Agelred tenuit de rege . E.

"Ralf, son of Turald holds Eddintune of the Bishop. It is assessed at two and a half sulungs. The arable land is five carucates, in demesne are two, and six villeins and nine borderers having one carucate. There is a church, and ten slaves and two mills worth eleven shillings and two pence, twelve acres of meadow and woodland for the pannage of ten swine. In the time of King Edward it was worth eight pounds. When received one hundred shillings. Now it is worth six pounds. Agelred (Aethelred) held it of King Edward."

Ralf owned a large number of manors in Kent including those in the Honour of Swanscombe, near Dartford. Addington would remain subservient to this Honour until the mid seventeenth century. Ralf's father, Thorold, came from Rochester, and was a powerful man and sheriff of Lincoln. Ralf's overlord was nominally Odo, half-brother to King William, the bishop of Bayeux, but by this time Odo had forfeited his lands, the former possessions of Godwine, Earl of Kent. The Bishop was a most unchristian cleric, being essentially a soldier. By 1085, he had already led a revolt against his brother and was in prison. The lands under the Earldom of Kent should therefore technically have been recorded as belonging to the King. King William was persuaded to release his brother on his death bed in 1087, but Odo quickly rebelled again against his nephew, King William II. He was permanently banished in 1088. His lands then reverted once more to the King.

The Domesday book gives a fairly precise view of the community of Addington. The entries record its ownership and extent, the number and type of residents, the land use and value. It uses the terms sulung and carucate, which, as described in Chapter One were Saxon terms based on plough land. It is suggested that in this area 120 acres would be a fairly accurate figure for these.

The smaller manor was valued at half a sulung, with one carucate. Ralf had no demesne land there, that is the land the lord farmed himself.[2] There was enough arable land to occupy one plough, four borderers (small-holders) and two serfs lived there. Although not a wealthy manor, its mill was worth a substantial 23 shillings. For comparison, two of Ralf's mills at Wateringbury were worth only 3 shillings together. This land had lost only a small amount of its value since the Conquest, so was still worth nearly £4. The reason for this may have been the value of the mill.

The second, and larger manor was worth two and a half sulungs, with enough carucates (arable land) for five ploughs, of which two were in demesne. There were six villeins (farmers), who would have farmed about 30 acres each, and nine borderers (small-holders) who farmed a carucate as a communal field. This manor may therefore have contained about 600

acres (242.8 hectares) of arable land, plus woodland and meadow. This manor was where the church stood. Its two mills were worth only 11s 2d between them. The mills in the village would all have been driven by water or animals, as windmills were not invented until the thirteenth century.

Other land included twelve acres of meadow and enough woodland to feed ten swine during the autumn (pannage). This land had lost quite considerable value during the troubled period after the Conquest, but its revenue was now recovering.

The six villeins, although more independent than borderers, were also obliged to do certain work for their overlord. Like the borderers and serfs they were not, except in special circumstances, permitted to leave the manor or work outside it. They continued to benefit from the Saxon custom of gavelkind, so were able to keep their holdings within the family. However, they had to pay a tax, known as a fine, to their lord if they sold their holding or when one of their children married outside the manor. Their heirs had to pay another fine, called a heriot, when they inherited. This might include their best four footed animal, and also a double year's rent to the manor. The thirteen borderers were, like the serfs, agricultural labourers. They worked most of the time for the lord, but had an acre or two of land to farm on their own account. This was however in their limited free time, and they still had to pay rent, mostly in kind, on their small-holding. The twelve slaves were at the bottom of the social scale and were a completely servile labouring class. The term is usually translated as "serfs", but it really applies to all three groups of inhabitants. They were later known as "nativi" as once born in the village they were expected to live their whole lives there. Should the lord of the manor transfer ownership, serfs were part of the bargain. To a certain extent, it was these families who benefited most from the fourteenth century disaster of the Black Death.

As mentioned in my introduction, during the middle of the twentieth century James Gracie Maddan conducted a great deal of research into Addington's history. It is his assessment, published in a series of articles in the parish magazine of 1952, that I have drawn on in my description above. He estimated that the information presented to the Domesday compilers gives an approximate census of the village that year. 32 heads of household are counted, suggesting a community of between 100 and 150. This would have been a fairly high population density for the time, compared to the whole country, but was typical for the fertile Vale of Holmesdale. It is interesting to note that the first census of 1801 gave Addington's population as 159, implying that until better farming methods took hold the land was unable to support more people. Maddan calculated that the extent recorded for these two manors is very similar to the acreage of Addington right up until the end of the twentieth century, when Aldon and the Coldrum area were transferred to Offham and Trottiscliffe respectively. Up to the 1980s this was recorded in different documents as being between 900 and 1000 acres.

In the early mediaeval period Addington had common open fields. The Domesday record refers to the nine borderers having one carucate of land between them. Manorial documents of the thirteenth and fifteenth centuries refer to work in these fields. All that now remains of the manorial common land in Addington is the Green and an area to the north of East Street, which is now divided by the M20 motorway. A map of Addington at the turn of the nineteenth century shows this stretched much more widely at the time, but the majority of Kent had been enclosed by the sixteenth century.

The Saxon gavelkind could have led to over-fragmentation of land-holdings. However, under Norman rule, the system changed in a way that this was avoided. The testator divided his holdings between his heirs from all his marriages, as before, but if his estate contained land-holdings in more than one place or manor, each heir would be designated a workable parcel, rather than separate small pieces. If no will was made, the courts would ensure that the property(ies) were divided in the same way.

In the case of Addington, the manor sometimes came to a daughter or grand-daughter. Under this law she would "carry" it to her husband, but if she

was widowed it would revert to her, to carry to her second husband in his turn. On her death the inheritance would pass to all her children. Addington manor followed this succession up until the beginning of sixteenth century and from existing wills it can be seen that some farmers continued the custom until later still.

The result of gavelkind was that holdings of land in Kent were continually being divided and reassembled, so that the county became made of many medium and small sized holdings, rather than single great estates. It also meant that the land was enclosed by hedges at a much earlier time than in the Midlands and elsewhere, and the open fields vanished at an earlier date. Eventually the practice was abandoned and inheritance passed to the eldest son, as in other counties.

The owners of the manor during the post Conquest period

The two manors of Addington that were recorded in the Domesday Book had probably been combined by the end of the eleventh century, having come back into the hands of King William II. It was granted to the de Gournay family, who held it of the Honour of Swanscombe until about 1250. Edward Hasted (1732-1812) is famous for his "The History and Topographical Survey of the County of Kent" that he wrote between 1780 and 1798. He stated that the manor passed into the ownership of William de Gurnay. (or Gournay)[3] shortly after the second disgrace of the Bishop of Bayeux. William de Gurnay's grand-daughter, Galiena, inherited the manor of Addington from him.[4] Galiena de Gurnay was born in Norfolk in about 1120. She lived with her husband, Manasser de Dammartin (pronounced Dawmartin) (d.1178) at Mendlesham, Suffolk, by whom she had two sons. Following instructions in her grandfather's will Galiena gave a charter to St. Andrew's church,

Rochester which confirmed his gift of the tithes of Addington church to them, payable yearly on the feast of St Andrew.[5]   By 1120 the Honour of Swanscombe, had come into the hands of Galfrid Talebot (Talbot), Baron of Swanscombe, as he is recorded as its owner in a document of that date. The Baron of Swanscombe, also called the Talbot Barony for many years after Galfrid's death, was responsible for providing men for the castle-guard at Rochester. Men from Addington, and from other manors owing service to the Honour, performed this duty.[6]   In about 1170 Galiena Dammartin predeceased her husband. Her grand-daughter, also named Galiena, was one of her heirs and inherited the manor of Addington. This second Galiena Dammartin married Ralph Mandeville, of Norton, later Norton Mandeville, Essex. Again she would have been a non-resident owner.

Her son, Hugh de Mandeville, inherited the manor. By this time the Honour of Swanscombe had come into the hands of the Montchensie family (in Latin Montecanis, and sometimes spelt Munchenesie). William de Montchensie (d. 1204) had come into the possession of the Honour of Swanscombe through marriage in about 1202, and he left the barony to his son, also William. By the time Hugh de Mandeville was lord of Addington, the grandson Warene de Montchensie had been the Baron for many years.[7] Warene was one of the most powerful men in the country.[8] He held the barony from 1213 to his death in 1253 and was succeeded by another William. The Montchensies were known as the capital lords of the fee, and de Mandeville did homage to them by knight service, castle-guard and rent.

Hugh and Galiena de Mandeville had no children and he sold the manor of Addington to Roger de Scaccario in about 1256. De Scaccario had been born Roger of Wallingford, in Oxfordshire. He had acquired his new surname by virtue of the position he held. In 1250, Henry III appointed him to the post of Usher of the Exchequer. This office was both lucrative and hereditary. The date he bought the manor is confirmed by a document of 1256, in which de Scaccario's name is given as head tenant of Addington manor, and this was probably the transfer. In this agreement Hugh de Maundevill

(confirming the long "a" in pronunciation) acknowledged that the Manor of Addington with all its appurtenances was held by de Scaccario. Although Roger owed the same service to the Honour of Swanscombe, in this document the three knights' fees and castleguard were commuted to 36 shillings for a payment, or "fine", of 200 marks.[9]

Roger de Scaccario was a person of note in the county. Besides his service in the Exchequer, he was Justice of the Assize and of gaol delivery at Tonbridge. In 1259, he was the arbitrator between the Archbishop of Canterbury and Richard, Earl of Gloucester over fairs at Cowden and Horsmonden. Nationally he was an important and far ranging servant to the king, who asked him to enquire into cases of trespass in Norfolk in 1260. Roger was married twice and lived to a good age. On his second marriage, in about 1260, he and his new wife, Lora, entered into an agreement with Lawrence, his adult son. By this Lawrence agreed that, when his father died, his young widow would have Addington as part of her dower. Should she have no children, as proved the case, Lawrence and his heirs would have the reversion.[10] When Roger died in 1271 she received a lucrative office as another part of her dower. This was the Marshalsy of the Eyre, which was associated with the Exchequer and included the duty to supply all (sealing) wax to the office and to carry its summonses around the country.[11] It is likely that Lora lived at Addington during her widowhood. If so, she was the first Norman owner to do so.

The long civil war led by the barons under Simon de Montfort was approaching its end. On regaining power in 1274, Edward I ordered an inquiry into his land-holdings throughout the country, to uncover any lost revenues or corrupt practices. The enquiry was based on the hundreds. The Hundred Rolls for Kent have been transcribed and are available on the Kent Archaeological Society's website. Jennifer Ward[12] published her transcriptions in Archaeologica Cantiana of 2007. The references to Addington make quite clear the hierarchy of payments, and indicate that Lora de Scaccario had been unwilling to pay her own share! Under the Hundred of Lauerkefeld (Larkfield) the first entry below tells who the overlord is, i.e. the King, and the value of the Hundred, the second section gives information on Addington, then spelt Adinton, and shows that Lora de Scaccario's debts accounted for 4% of the value of the Hundred:

Item dicunt quod hundredum de Lauerkefeld est in manu domini regis et valet per annum Cs

Then they say that Larkfield hundred is in the lord king's hand and it is worth 100s[hillings] each year

Item dicunt quod Adinton et Otles que Lora de Scercio* nunc tenet in dotem subtraxerunt sectas hundredi predicti per potestatem Willelmi de Montecanis a tempore belli de Evesham ad dampnum regis iiijs per annum

Then they say that Addington and Eccles, which Lora de Scercio (Scaccario) now holds in dower, have withdrawn suits from the aforesaid hundred through the authority of William de Montchensie from the time of the battle of Evesham [1265] with loss of 4s. each year to the king

* (Alternative spellings of this name are numerous: de Scercio, de Saccio, del Escheker, L'Ascheker Lescheker(e) and Lescheke being some of them).

Under the Toltingtrough Hundred William de Montchensie's holding is confirmed:

Item dicunt quod dominus Willelmus de Montecanis tenet baroniam de Talebot ad Swaneschamp de domino rege in capite et inde reddit annuatim custodi castri Roff' xviij libras set nesciunt quo warento

Then they say that the lord William de Montchensie holds the Talbot barony at Swanscombe of the lord king in chief and he pays rent of £18 each year for this to the keeper of Rochester castle, but they do not know by what warrant

The Montchensie family remained capital lords of the fee for Addington for many years more, and the de Scaccario family were lords of the manor for the next century. Lora de Scaccario was still in possession of the manor, and that of Eccles, in 1284. She paid 36 shillings in lieu of two knight's fees for Addington, 6 shillings in lieu of half a knight's fee for Eccles and 14 pence in lieu of a quarter of a knight's fee for Tottington, also near Aylesford. By the time of her death, her step-son had predeceased her. Lawrence de Scaccario, like his father, had been a man of great substance. He inherited the post of Usher to the Exchequer, for which he did homage after his father's death in 1271. He was sheriff of Essex and Hertford, and constable of Colchester Castle. At the time of his death in 1283 he held land in Oxfordshire, Buckinghamshire, Essex and Suffolk. Lawrence left a widow, Gunnora and was succeeded by his son, Simon, then aged fifteen. It was probably Simon who inherited the reversion of Addington on Lora's death, but in the event, although married, he died in 1290 without heirs. Simon's estate went to his three sisters: Maud, (sometimes called Matilda) wife of John de Dagworth, Lora, wife of William Peyforer and Beatrix, wife of John Peverill. The post of Usher was shared equally between the three sisters. Maud seems to have been given Addington as her share, and eventually the post of usher came to her son, who was born in 1276, but not after three sisters had died.

John de Dagworth died in 1290, when his son, also named John, was only fourteen. As John was then still a minor, he became a ward of the Crown. King Edward I, because of the good services that his former servant, William Fitzwarin (d. 1285) had given him, granted the gift of John's marriage to Fitzwarin's eldest daughter, Alice.[13] The grant then stated that if John were to marry *"elsewhere without her will"* she should have the forfeiture due to the king. The Escheator, the public official who administered such estates on behalf of the King, was told *"to deliver the body of John to the girl's mother to be married on 4th July 1292."* Alice's mother had by then remarried so was by then Alice de Beaumont (or Bello Monte).[14]

John de Dagworth, who was born in Suffolk, inherited Addington from his mother and reunited the post of Usher of the Exchequer in 1329.[15] He then took the name of de Lescheker, spelt in the Norman French way. He held the post of Usher for less than three years. As he was buried in St. Margaret's Church in 1332, it is feasible to suggest that he and Alice had made the manor house their home. She survived him for only a year. His gravestone is now in the south chapel, in three pieces, having been moved from the chancel when encaustic tiles were laid there in the early 1880's. The inscription was in Lombardic lettering, filled with metal. Having lost this, the stone has degraded and it is illegible. Some words (in Norman French) were deciphered in the past as: *"Johane de:Leschek...est mercy Amen...chekere gist ic....Dieu de la al...".* They can be roughly translated as *"here lies John de Lescheker, God have mercy on his soul Amen"* (the al fragment is alme meaning soul).[16]

John had come into possession of the manor just as life was becoming very difficult. The thirteenth century had been a period of growth and prosperity in the country as a whole. The economy had expanded and improvements were made in husbandry. The mediaeval population in England grew rapidly and reached a zenith of between five and six million, a figure that would not be matched for three hundred years. During the fourteenth century the number of

taken some time to recover and although there are no manorial rolls for the century, the number of names in those of the fifteenth century is much reduced from that of 1270. However, John did not live to see the first outbreak of the Black Death.

When John de Lescheker died in 1332 his heirs were Roger and Robert de Lescheker. Although probably his son(s) I have not been able to confirm this. When a lay subsidy was demanded of Kent[17] during 1334/5 a Roger de Saccio, was recorded in the list for the Larkfield Hundred and was assessed at eight shillings. This was amongst the higher assessments, as most were in the range of one to three shillings, so the manor must then have been productive. The highest assessment, at £1, was for Lady de Alyntone (i.e. Allington). It is unlikely that he was a resident landlord, as John de Lescheker appears to have been the only member of the family to be buried in the church. Roger probably spent most of his time in the City of London. Many lawyers, administrators and holders of royal positions owned manors in this part of Kent, but their homes were mainly in London.

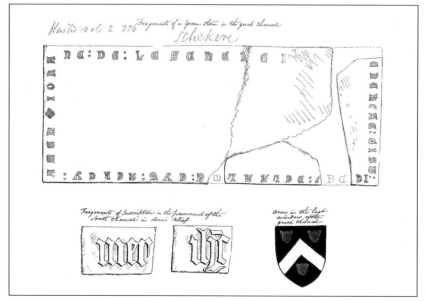

The gravestone of John de Lescheker, which is now in three pieces in the Watton Chapel of St. Margaret's, and two other fragments of gravestone which are also in the chapel. The arms are those of William Snayth as seen in the East window by John Philipot, Rouge Dragon Pursuivant, in 1619.

From evidence of the patronage of the church, Roger de Lescheker seems to have been succeeded by Robert, but the manor then changed hands. By 1346 it had been leased to their cousin, Sir Nicholas de Dagworth. In that year Edward III raised a tax for "aid" to knight his son, the Black Prince. The Addington entry reads: *"De Nicholao de Dagworthe pro uno feodo quod Robertus de Scaccario tenuit in Aldyntone (SIC) de Warino de Monte Caniso xi s"* (*"From Nicholas de Dagworth for one feoffment that Robert de Lescheker holds in Addington of Warin de Montchensie. 11 shillings"*)[18] This

people in England fell dramatically. Both 1315 and 1316 brought famine, due to devastating rain and harvest failure. The village economy would have assessment confirms that the manor still owed allegiance to the Montchensie family of Swanscombe. Although de Dagworth was in possession of the manor, a Robert del Escheker remained the patron for the church until 1349 as he installed two rectors during the dreadful year when the Black Death ravaged England. After this de Dagworth came into full ownership as it was he who installed Robert de Custone in 1350.

Like his predecessors at Addington, Sir Nicholas de Dagworth was a powerful London magnate. Addington was just one of his possessions. In 1377, he was made a Privy Councillor, the Steward of the King's Household, Keeper of the Great Seal and Treasurer of England. However, prior to this he had sold Addington.

The table below summarises the succession of Addington between the de Lescheker/de Scaccario family and the de Dagworth family. The names in bold were the Lords of the Manor.

1. **Roger de Scaccario,** born Wallingford (d. 1271) Owned a number of manors. He bought Addington from the de Mandevilles.
Roger married firstly an unknown lady by whom he had a daughter who became a nun and a son named Lawrence.
He married secondly **Lora** (c. 1244 - after 1284) (who held Addington and a third of Eccles as her dower). She died without issue.

2. Lawrence de Scaccario (d. 1283), who inherited his father's other manors, and lands, including 2/3 of Eccles, predeceased his stepmother.
Lawrence married Gunnora. They had four children, a son named Simon, Maud/Matilda, Lora and Beatrix.

3. **Simon** b. 1269 was married but died without issue in 1290. His inheritance was then shared between his sisters, **Maud/Matilda de Dagworth** (d. 1308), Lora Peyforer and Beatrix Peveril
3. Simon's eldest sister, **Matilda**, held Addington as her share. She married John de Dag[ge]worth (who also d. 1290), their son was

4. **John de Dagworth**, (24th April 1276-27 July 1332)

who took the name of **de Lescheker** in 1329 when he reunited the three parts of the Usher-ship. John married Alice de Fitzwarin.

4/5. **Roger de Lescheker** was either John's son, or his cousin. Probably died in 1346/7.

4/5/6. **Robert de Lescheker** (d. 1349-50) who leased the manor to Sir Nicholas de Dagworth about 1346 (Roger's son or brother?)

Sir Nicholas de Dagworth acquired Addington from his cousin Robert del Escheker, in 1350. He transferred it to John de Cologne in 1356 and died after 1377.

Addington left the de Dagworth/de Lescheker family in 1356 when Sir Nicholas de Dagworth conveyed the manor to yet another Londoner, John de Cologne (de Colonia), reputedly in payment for a debt.[19] John de Cologne was an elderly armourer of the City of London, and was the supplier to King Edward III.[20] de Cologne presented three rectors to the living of Addington between 1356 and 1359. He was succeeded by his son, Roger, who held the manor only briefly. Roger de Cologne presented John atte Felde to the living early in 1361 but died on 15th July that year. By this time, after a succession of absentee landlords, the land and buildings had fallen into decay. Roger's Inquisition Post Mortem (IPM) of 8th December 1361 (35 Ed III) gives a damning assessment of the care and nurture given to the manor.

This IPM states that Addington was held of the infant heir of Roger Mortimer, Earl of March as of his manor of Swanscombe by the service of one third of a knight's fee and payment of 36 shillings per annum. The manor house was rated as being of no value, due to it requiring extensive repairs. Its dovecot was worth only 3s 4d per annum as it was not well stocked. The watermill, which should have been a money spinner, had a value of just 13s 4d as it was broken, ruinous and unable to grind properly because of a defective stone. The demesne held 60 acres of arable land of which two thirds were sown each year. If well cultivated it could be worth 4d per acre per annum after deductions and when fallow and grazed the value could be 2d per acre. Two parts had been sown before the death of de Cologne and the *"third part, namely, 20 acres, was fallow but nevertheless was worth 1d per acre, being in pasture for sheep–it was not worth more because the land is dry and sandy."* Since his death twelve acres had been sown with winter seed and were worth 4d per acre after deductions.

Outside the demesne, the lord held six acres of meadow, from which hay would be taken. This was worth 12d per acre at time of mowing, but at other times of year was worth only 3d. Twenty four acres of very poor pasture covered in heath (bruera) and broom (scobis) would be used as cattle food and fuel, and there was a further 120 acres of separate pasture-land. This was worth only 1d an acre *"and not more because it is dry and sterile as appears by looking"*. The profits of the manor court were 18 shillings per annum. One feels sorry for the tenants, as despite this poor land and bad management, the collective rent for their holdings was 60s 8d.

Manorial Life in Addington during the middle ages

Although for most of this period the owners of manors such as Addington were non resident, life in a mediaeval manor was an ordered affair. Villagers were regulated by the manorial court whose president was nominally the lord, but in practice his steward. All the landholding tenants were required to attend to its administration.[21] The business of the court was recorded in two Court Rolls: the Court Baron and the View of Frankpledge. Where these survive a good picture can be obtained of the inhabitants of the village and their concerns. As in the county as a whole, land was held in roughly three ways, and followed the customs that had been established by the Saxons, albeit honed by the Normans. The divisions were as follows:

a) land held in demesne, that is kept in the hands of the lord of the manor and farmed by him with the aid of his steward, serfs and customary tenants;

b) land held by customary tenants. These were the villeins and cottagers who paid a small fixed rent and also rendered agricultural and military services when required. They were also known was copy-holders.

c) land held by free tenants. This was land let to tenants for monetary rent only. Some might be churchmen or great magnates, and others later became known as yeomen. These were more numerous in Kent than elswhere in the country. Some families began to own property in more than one manor.

The manorial court was a system for payment of rents and agreement of services between the tenants of the manor and their lord, rather than a criminal court, which took place at the King's Assizes. However, the court also dealt with minor infringes of duties or manners, such as failure to pay rent or fines, failure even to attend the court, blocking paths, causing an affray or allowing animals to stray, but only if these offences took place within the parish boundary.

The manorial roll known as the Court Baron dealt with the customary tenants who, despite having some independence, were subject to the customs of the manor as well as paying rent to their lord. These customs included suit of court, which was the duty to attend the manorial court and serve on the jury, services in the Lord's fields and the payment of fines and heriots on the transfer of their land. In the early years after the Conquest their fealty (allegiance) to the lord of the manor could mean physically going to war beside him. Records in Courts Baron refer to punitive fines for infringements of the customs.

So life in Addington under the Normans was harsh for customary tenants and serfs, but it was not desperate. Both men and women understood and largely fulfilled their obligations to the lord, their family, their neighbours and their church. Very few were serfs, even before this form of personal restriction vanished from Kent. The climate was reasonably benign and, on the whole, Kent people were better fed and housed than those living in the harsh north of England. However, the local soil was, and still is, sandy and dry. It was less fertile than in Kent's coastal regions or on the nearby gault clay. This soil, however, strongly favoured the breeding of rabbits (coneys), which the Normans introduced as a managed food source. Coney warrens were built with "pillow mounds" into which stone built tunnels were inserted for the does to establish themselves. The sand here was very easy to excavate. Addington's warren stood near to the megaliths and was managed for centuries. Some warrens were surrounded by a moat, as rabbits do not like swimming, but no evidence for one remains here. Rabbit meat was a welcome addition to the diet, but the warren was the property of the lord, who also owned all rights to take game: deer, birds, fish, hares etc. from his lands. The village still houses a multitude of rabbits, particularly near where their managed warren once existed.

Maddan deciphered what he called "crabbed and contracted Latin" in the transcript of a trial of an Addington man that took place at Canterbury in 1241. This succinctly recorded the facts of a case held before the King's itinerant justice, William of York, Provost of Beverley Minster. At this period few surnames were used, and people were referred to by their first name, with a qualifier to distinguish them. The proceedings were against a man named Pagan (or Payn) of Aldon, who was accused of harbouring a criminal. William, the son of Arnold of Addington, had killed his brother, Peter, one night and had fled across what was then marshy land to the homestead of Pagan at Aldon. This sounds as if he came from the Westfields area across the stream where the golf course now lies. After this he disappeared. Pagan was brought before the justices accused of harbouring a robber, but was acquitted. William was outlawed, and exiled from the village. This was a particularly harsh judgement as settlement was the only means for survival in those times and he would have been hounded out of other villages. William of Addington must have been a man of some means as his chattels were recorded as being worth 16 pence and these, together with his house and two and a half acres of land, were forfeited to the Crown. Even so, he got off lightly, as *Christina, wife of the said William, was taken*

for that death and hanged at Canterbury in the presence of the justices assigned for gaol delivery." One can only hope that she did, in truth, share in the guilt of her husband for this crime.

The manorial roll of 1270

The first record of a manorial court in Addington comes from a roll of 1270 shown by John Dudlow, a nineteenth century solicitor from West Malling, to his friend, Rev. Lambert Larking, who transcribed it. The roll gives the names of the jurors of the court, all of whom owed rent and services to the lord of the manor, Roger de Scaccario. It states that the jury consisted of Walterus de Burgo (Walter de Burgh), Rogerus de Corulo (Roger Hazel), Radulphus Campium (Ralph Campion), Ricardus Lotelyn, Egidius de la Done, Thomas Ricard, Robertus Burel (Robert Burel), Walterus de Monte (Walter Mount), Simonis Bolle (Simon Ball) and Adam de Campo (Adam Field) *"et per alios Juratores."*

These identifications would later become full surnames. One of these was that of Ralph Campion. He and his three brothers had a messuage of six acres of land on which stood three cottages, implying that the family had lived in the village for some time. Their tenement was probably in the area where Campions Wood now lies, beside St. Vincents Lane. Between them they paid rent of six shillings, a ploughshare (the metal cutting edge of the plough), a cock, two hens and 24 eggs. They were also required to give service in the grain field on half a rood and reap one rood, to provide one man at the lord's hay meadow and two men hay making for the lord. This was one of the more substantial pieces of land in the parish, as the largest was only ten acres.

The roll records the names of over seventy men and five women who were liable for rents and manorial services to the Lord of the Manor on just less than fifty parcels of land. Some were simply agricultural land known as tenements, whilst others were called messuages, meaning that they contained cottages. As with the Campion family, other messuages had more than one cottage standing on them, the result of shared inheritance under gavelkind. Some of the agricultural tenements were also jointly owned. The average holding was 3¼ acres, the range being from one to ten.

Two types of ploughshare.

The roll, which is in Latin, uses the terms "acras", "virga" and "perticata" to measure the land. The virgate (or rood) was a quarter of an acre, and there were 40 square perches to a virgate. In all about 180 acres of tenanted land are accounted for in this document, but only 5¾ acres were held by seven free tenants. The names of these were Roger atte Hesele (2 acres), Walter Godwyne (2 roods), Joanna de Burgo and Bartholomew atte Broke (jointly holding 2 acres), John de Burgh and G[iles] Alyndon (jointly holding 1 rood) and John le Webbe (1 acre). These free tenants paid scutage at a hefty price of 11s 1¼d per acre. Scutage was the tax paid in lieu of providing knight service. Some of these families, including the Hasylls and Goddens would still be resident in the village two hundred years later.

Amongst the 76 names in the roll, only 26 surnames occur. This is partly because of the proliferation of brothers, sisters and cousins, but some tenants are referred to as son or daughter of their parent. The only Anglo-Saxon name that I can distinguish is that of Aldred (formerly Ealdred) Textor, and even then his brother had the name of Galfrid. A fairly typical entry translates as: *"Thomas, Richard and John, sons of Ranulph le Bealde, hold one messuage and four acres of warland.[22] And they owe 27½ pence per year. And three hens and half a cock. And sixteen eggs. And they*

must work one virgate in the arable field and reap one virgate of land." The reference to "the arable field" infers that this was a large field, worked in strips. One name still survives as Westfields, and East Street may well have had a communal field nearby. Other documents refer to a Northfield, probably in the Woodgate area. The word "Gate" does not mean a gate in the modern sense, but was a corruption of an Anglo-Saxon word "gazza" for way or street, similar to the Norse "gata" which was used in the north of England. Therefore, Woodgate is the road towards the large wood lying beneath the North Downs, rather than a gate into it.[23]

The services owed by tenants were "arr[ur]are", which meant working in the arable field, "metere", reaping, "ad fena domini collegenda", harvesting the lord's arable field and "vomerus", a ploughshare, referred to earlier. It seems that these had to be presented at either the Nativity of St. John (24th June) or the feast day of St. Michael (29th September) and must have been quite an expense as they had to be made each year. In addition to the individual rents, there was a communal obligation on behalf of both the lord and his tenants. This document states that *"the tenants promise to bring 8 men and 8 lost rents to the lord at a later date and the lord will bring 2 wagons, or 4 at a later date. And they owe the lord 52 men at harvest time and 52 men in the hay meadows."* This high number of men suggests that the population had grown quite considerably since the time of Domesday. The loss of some of these families in the next century would have been devastating.

A woodcut showing the different services owed to the Lord of the Manor

Misdemeanours

Although the manorial court dealt with minor breaches of protocol, more serious misdemeanours were referred to the court of the Hundred. Ralph Campion and one of the free tenants were indicted in 1274, and their names occur in the Hundred Roll of Larkfield that year. In this document the two men are accused as follows: *"and that Walter de la Broke and Radulfus Champun have obstructed a certain path leading from Addington church towards Luke Speche's house."*[24]

Another, more serious, case heard and recorded in this Hundred Roll states: *"Then they say that Reginald de Cokkeshale (the gaoler) took one mark to release Edward the miller of Addington who had been imprisoned because Agnes of Wilton, who had been imprisoned for her robbery at Addington, had escaped."*

The verdicts and sentences, however, were not recorded.

The Fourteenth and Fifteenth Centuries

The population in England as a whole had grown during the thirteenth century, as it had been a time of plenty. During the first half of the fourteenth, the picture changed dramatically. Famine followed bad harvests caused by atrocious weather, but it was the Black Death that affected the entire management of the village. When Sir Nicholas de Dagworth came into possession of the manor in 1350, the rents he received would have been dramatically reduced, due to the death of many tenants. His work for the King would have become a far higher proportion of his total wealth. The recovery was slow as plague returned a number of times and then, in 1381, Kent was rocked by the Peasants Revolt, led by Wat Tyler. The emancipation of the serfs gathered pace as their labour gained a higher value. The cost of of a day's work in 1380 has been assessed at three pence and it was now necessary for lords to pay wages, as land holdings had been amalgamated and there were no longer enough customary tenants to do the work as a service. This further reduced the value of the manor, as serfs were no longer barred from seeking work outside their native village. Although suppressed, the Peasants' Revolt of 1381 led to greater personal freedoms, and changes to land leases. Serfdom had largely collapsed by the end of the fifteenth century, but was not formally abolished until 1574.

From the second half of the fourteenth century, surviving tenant farmers acquired land farmed by families who perished in the successive plagues, or for other reasaons. These men were more likely to commute their manorial service to monetary rent. As a result, the business at the manorial courts changed. The Court Baron rolls for Addington of 1472 and 1473 are more concerned with sales than services. Rather than a list of services owed to the Lord of the Manor, these two documents record the actions required after the "alienation" (sale or transfer) of land, the non payment of rent and encroachment issues. Some order the "fines" that must be paid after sales. The exact Latin wording is: *"Ideo preceptum est distringere eos erga proximam curia in pro secta curie, relevio et fidelitate domino faciendis." "It is ordered to distrain them before the next court for suit of court, relief (i.e. the fine) and fealty to the Lord of the manor."* As a result, these court rolls demonstrate the increasing status of some of the villagers.

By the fifteenth century, surnames had become ubiquitous, but the tenants bearing them no longer felt the old obligation to do their duty. Ricardus Eggeyock was fined for failure to attend the Manorial Court in both 1472 and 1473 – Hedgehogs on St. Vincents Lane is probably a corruption of his name, and where he lived. The items in these two rolls give a picture of the continuity of families within the village. Some surnames in the 1472 and 1473 rolls are those that appeared in 1270. John Hasill was living at Woodgate, (spelt as Johannes Hessill. and also as Hassil). His forebears were called "atte Hesele" and "de Corulo". Three others were Ricardus Borgh (formerly "de Burgos") and Johanni Serch (Pirich or Spirich in the 1270 roll) and the Desye or Deysey family, who held land in both Trottiscliffe and Addington. Addington church benefited from bequests that a widow, Alice Deysey, made in her will. Both she and her husband also left legacies to Trottiscliffe church.

The 1472 and 1473 rolls also record the names of wealthy outsiders who held land within Addington's boundaries. The 1472 document begins with the names of three landowners who preferred to pay a fine rather than attend the court. These were the Bishop of Rochester, who held a small parcel in the parish for many years, probably near to his church at Trottiscliffe, Sir George Browne, a wealthy London merchant who lived at Betchworth Castle, near Dorking but owned land throughout the South East,[25] and John Clerke of Ford, in neighbouring Wrotham, one of the Barons of the Exchequer.

The rolls were written in Latin, but in 1472 John Elyott sold a $1^1/_2$ acre piece "in Northfield", written in English, to Richard Partrych.[26] That particular open field was therefore not yet enclosed, though this process was by then accelerating. An encroachment recorded in the second roll, of 1473, deals with meadowland with a place name that still survives, albeit in a corrupted form. Thomas Tersse of Offham was brought to the court to answer for his encroachment upon the Lord's meadow at Frowdeford mede (which is now the lowest part of the golf course next to Plowenders Bridge), and for erecting a hedge between Cuddewelle meadow and this meadow.[27] As another spelling of this place was Frowenders, the name suggests that it was the furthest arable field in the parish, i.e. the furrow's end. It was a much later misreading of a map that replaced FR with a PL.

The shape of the village was tall and thin in the north and broad in the south. The reason for this was the rights that Addington villagers had to access the

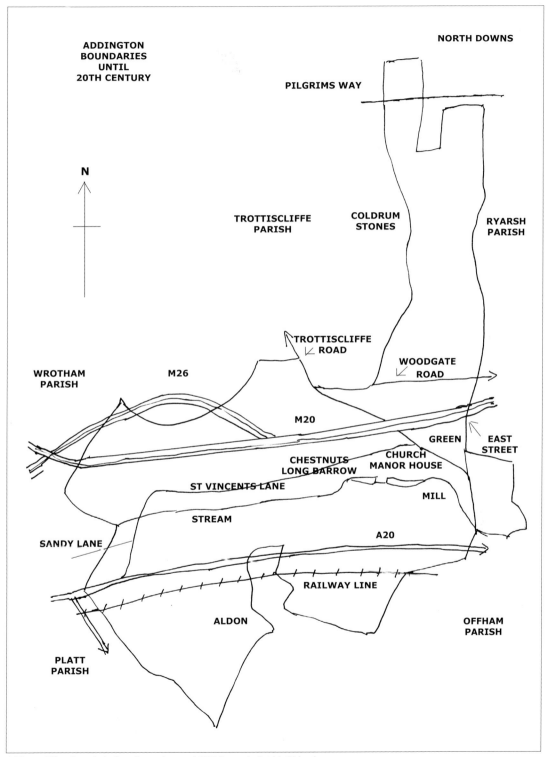

ADDINGTON
BOUNDARIES
UNTIL
20TH CENTURY

NORTH DOWNS

PILGRIMS WAY

N

TROTTISCLIFFE
PARISH

COLDRUM
STONES

RYARSH
PARISH

TROTTISCLIFFE
ROAD

WOODGATE
ROAD

WROTHAM
PARISH

M26

M20

GREEN

EAST
STREET

CHESTNUTS
LONG BARROW

CHURCH
MANOR HOUSE

ST VINCENTS LANE

MILL

STREAM

A20

SANDY LANE

RAILWAY LINE

ALDON

OFFHAM
PARISH

PLATT
PARISH

Addington Village Boundaries from Saxon times until 1985. Drawn by Patricia Richardson materials they needed for successful husbandry. They had rights to reach the chalk of the North Downs and further rights to take clay from the Aldon area. The territory also contained ample water from the stream and from numerous springs. Its indentations are probably to give other parishes rights of access to resources as well. The boundaries remained the shape below until 1985, though a few alterations were made a century earlier.

The church during the early Norman period

The East Wall of the church showing the original height of the roof.

The nave of the church was constructed shortly after the Conquest, though the archaeological survey of 2010 confirmed that it had been built partly on the foundations of an earlier Saxon structure. Andrew Linklater, the project manager, reported that *"the positioning of huge roughly hewn boulders at the structure's principal corners and infilling between along the line of each wall with large rough square stones is a typical foundation configuration associated with churches of the late Saxon-early Norman period."*[28] Linklater's estimate of the date of construction was between 1070-1100. The end of the nave is contained by large tufa quoins (the corner stones). This stone ran out locally shortly after the end of that century.

When looking at the exterior east wall of the church one can clearly discern the height and width of the original chancel, which was narrower than the nave. The north and south walls of the nave from the west of the porch survive of this first church, the western end of the south wall being clearly visible within the new extension. The original entrance was on the

south. This had been blocked up during the fifteenth century but was re-opened for access into the Geoffrey Grimes room. The original south door contained tufa in its semi circular door head.

Although the first written evidence of the church's dedication to St. Margaret of Antioch can not be found until 1409, she was a particularly popular saint of dedication for churches of the early mediaeval period. Alan Everitt, the Kent historian, found 239 churches in England with this dedication, 22 in Kent alone. One of the very earliest was St. Margaret's at Cliffe, near Dover, which is mentioned with that dedication in the Domesday Book.

Very few facts survive about St. Margaret's life, but there is a great deal of legend. Antioch, now called Antakya, lies at the southern tip of modern Turkey, close to the Syrian border. It was associated with

Christianity at a very early date. It was at Antioch that St. Paul and St. Barnabas shocked Jewish Christians by preaching to the gentiles as well as to them. Tradition says that Margaret was the daughter of a pagan priest, living some three hundred years after St. Paul's death. She had a Christian nurse, who brought her to the faith. Because of this, her father banished her from his house. She was very beautiful, so a Roman prefect called Olybrius determined to make her either his wife or his mistress. She refused, and this led to her imprisonment and martyrdom. Legend goes that she was publicly put through the ordeal of fire and water, but survived. Recognising this as a miracle, thousands of spectators were converted to Christianity. Unfortunately, as a result, they were killed in a mass execution. Thrown back in prison, Margaret was swallowed by a dragon, but as she was carrying a cross the beast spat her out. So she was brought out to be executed, upon which a dove bearing a golden martyr's crown lit upon her head. Even this did not protect her. She was beheaded, but after doing the deed the executioner fell dead beside her. St. Margaret very quickly became venerated in the East, where she was known as Marina. As her fame spread westwards her name was interpreted as Margaret. Her name was already in the calendar of saints by the seventh century, her saint's day being 20th July. The Crusades brought a fresh wave of devotion to her in Western Europe, but it seems that the church at Addington was built even earlier than the First Crusade of 1090.

The chancel was widened and its roof raised at the end of the fourteenth century. The chancel arch was remodelled in the perpendicular style at that time and the windows of the nave were also remodelled. This was when the wealthy William Snayth was Lord of the Manor, and it is known that he was a very pious and generous man. Incorrectly, Edward Hasted

St Margaret's Church showing 1400 chancel arch and new height of roof.

Apart from the walls, a small architectural feature survives from this early period. It is the the piscina on the north side of the nave. This was constructed to pour away any dregs of sanctified water. There are also signs that there was once a hole in the wall nearby for providing bread to beggars and lepers, who were not allowed within the church.

inserted a doggerel poem into his entry for Addington stating that the church was actually built between 1400 and 1403. This rhyme sadly continues to be relied on in history and guide books to this day. In fact the verse refers to the house of a John Lee at Addington, Surrey, and it seems that Hasted confused his notes!

This was a period when a number of other local churches were extended and altered, taking advantage of the extra light that the Norman or "decorative" style of architecture brought into the building. The work involved changing the Romanesque (round) arches into Norman pointed ones. These allowed the roof to be raised. The new windows at St Margaret's were flanked by a small head on either side of the arch, one of a king and one of a cleric. William Snayth then set his coat of arms in the new East Window.

The church remained a simple nave and chancel structure until the south chapel, a north transept and the tower were built between 1450 and 1453, on the instructions of William Watton. The porch, with a carved oak verge board was added during the sixteenth century at the expense of a parishioner.

The Rectors of St. Margaret's Church up to 1400

In the early days, the patronage (the term used was advowson) of parishes was often in the hands of monasteries. This was the right to appoint the Rector or Vicar to a living. However, Lords of the Manor, who in many cases had built the church on their land, and who certainly maintained it, acquired this right. The Lord of the Manor of Addington appears to have bought the advowson in 1259 as: "On the morrow of St. Martin" (twelfth November) Roger de Scaccario entered into an agreement with Peter, Prior of Pritewell[29] in respect of "half an acre of land in Adington and the advowson of the church of the same vill." Roger agreed that he and his heirs would present to the Prior yearly at Easter a pair of white gloves, or one half-penny, for this privilege. He also paid a fine of a sparrow-hawk![30]

The annual payment of white gloves appears to have been given for long enough to establish a precedent,

and Addington possesses a list of its rectors and their patrons, compiled by Rev. Frampton, rector of Platt, towards the end of the nineteenth century, who gave biographical details where known.[31] The first entry records that in 1327 Lawrence de Polle was installed by Roger de Leschekere, and the list continues to the present day. The patronage remained the privilege of the Lord of the Manor of Addington until, in 1934, it was transferred by the last Lord, Colonel Sofer-Whitburn, to the Bishop of Rochester.

It seems that de Polle remained in situ until 1349, the year of the Black Death. Whether or not Lawrence died as a result of this, the village, and indeed the whole district, was particularly badly hit. Three more rectors were installed that year, the first two by Robert atte Chekere (yet another spelling of the family name) and the third by Nicholas de Dagworth. These were Wymunden Conyntone (27th April), John Mounte (17th May) and Robert de Cuxtone (2nd November). Just six months later, on 2nd May 1350, Squire de Dagworth installed Richard Gerveys and he, in his turn, was rapidly followed by John de Wynchecombe. There was therefore a succession of six rectors in two years. This must have been very unsettling for Addington's inhabitants, both socially and spiritually.

By the end of 1350, the plague had run its course and de Wynchecombe remained in service for six years. He then took up the post of Precentor (the music director) of St. Paul's, London which he held until 1370, after which he became rector of Snoreham, Essex. The merry-go-round of rectors had sadly returned to the village. Two were installed during 1356, followed by a third in 1358. It was not until 1361 that stability returned to the parish, when the Rev. John atte Felde was installed by John de Cologne, who had just acquired the manor.[32]

Rev. atte Felde gave 35 years' service to the parish, perhaps staying until his death in 1396. Late in life, on 7th January 1395, he was admitted as rector of Wanstead in Essex, but this living was perhaps given to him as a pension, and he may have handed over the day to day service of the living to a younger man. When the IPM of the younger Richard Charles took place in 1387 it was conducted by Robert Faryndon, who was named in the document as the parson of the church of Addington, so it is possible that by then John atte Felde was an absentee priest.

Rev. Frampton recorded that the de Cologne family installed the rectors until after 1400. However, Richard Charles took possession of the manor in the 1360's and evidence shows that he also acquired the advowson. On John atte Felde's death in 1396 John Graunger came to the parish, but stayed only a short time, as he was shortly afterwards appointed the prebend of the High Mass at Malling Abbey and later became the Dean of Malling. Graunger was followed by John Marshall (1400-1411) and Thomas Clerk (1411-1416). Both men moved to new positions. Clerk became the vicar of St. Nicholas, Rochester and later was rector of St. Michael's, Lewes. These brief biographies show how itinerant the priests were, seeking promotion, moving between parishes and even to new dioceses.

How the Watton family came to own Addington

After the death of Roger de Cologne Richard Charles (sometimes spelt Charlis) bought Addington manor from his heirs. Charles founded a dynasty that would endure for over five hundred years. He is reputed to be descended from Edward Charles, who was admiral of the fleet *"from the Thames mouth northwards"* in 1305,[33] towards the end of King Edward I's reign. Edward Charles owned the small manor of Charles, near Dartford, though it is not known whether Richard was born there.

Richard Charles was a soldier, and a

Brass of Richard Charles, d. 1378
Drawn by E.H.W. Dunkin (1871-1915)

member of the order of chivalry. His arms were *"Argent, a chevron between three eglet heads erased sable."* An approximate translation is "a white field (the heraldic term for background) on which is a chevron with three black eagle heads roughly cut off at the base around this. He spent a number of years abroad and probably spent little time at Addington, which he leased for a while to a consortium. However, on his return to Kent in 1373, he became a Knight of the Shire (i.e. member of parliament), one of only two for the county. This shows his standing in the community. He held this position until 1376. He took back his manor of Addington and may well have made it his home, as when he died on 1st June 1378 he was buried in St. Margaret's church, where he is commemorated by a very substantial brass which originally stood over his grave. This is the earliest brass at Addington and one of only ten fourteenth century brasses of men in armour to survive in Kent churches. Unfortunately only the upper half remains, within a broken frame.[34]

The IPM for Richard Charles's manors of Addington and neighbouring Paddlesworth took place at Aylesford on 14th June 1378.[35] A number of the jurors may have from this village, as some of the surnames appear on manorial rolls. The jurors were Thomas Rote, William Godwyn, Ralph Partrych, Stephen Smyth, John Julk, Roger atte Hasele, Richard Julk, Thomas Holeweys, William Chapman, John atte Hasele, William Mory and Richard atte Pette. Witnesses stated that Charles had *"transferred the manor and advowson to Hugh Segrave, Sir Walter Alderberry, Sir Richard Astone and Robert Corby, to hold at his will. Subsequently he entered into the manor and took the profits thereof during his lifetime, and died seised of such estate therein."*

This document therefore contradicts Rev. Frampton's assertion that the advowson of Addington church had continued in the hands of the de Cologne family.

The manor of Addington is described as follows: *"Adynton. The manor, with the advowson of the church; whereof the lands of the manor in the parish of Adynton are held of the earl of March, of his court of Swannescompe, by knight's service and payment of 36s yearly for ward of Rochester castle, and the residue of the lands of the manor, which lie in the towns of Ryerssh and Ofham, are of the tenure of 'gavelekend' and are held of the lord de Moubray, of his manor of Ryerssh, by fealty, suit of court every three weeks and a rent of 33s 9d." "And they say that the said manor is worth 6 pounds and 12 pence, 63 cocks and hens given, and is worth by year in all its extent £10 8s."* These extracts confirm that the fee for knight's service at Rochester castle had not increased for nearly a century and that Addington manor contained land in both Ryarsh and Offham, a situation that would endure for centuries to come. The Ryarsh parish land was in the form of "islands" within Addington's boundaries, some in the Coldrum area and others near to the manor house in what later became Addington Park. In 1368 Charles had instructed his agents, Roger Digge, John atte Felde (the Rector of Addington), James de Pecham, Nicholas Heryn and William Topclife to hold the manor of Padelesworth (Paddlesworth) and its advowson on his behalf, but on his return, had demised it at farm (i.e. leased it) to Thomas Rote for six years, of which four had elapsed.

Richard Charles was clearly a wealthy man, as he owned a number of manors in addition to Addington:

- Iclesham, near Rye in
    Sussex, (inquest at Iclesham)

- Palstre, near Tenterden,
    with *"a moiety of the ferry at Smalelyde (Small Hythe)"*, (inquest at Wittersham)

- Paddlesworth, near Birling, (inquest at Aylesford)

- Nashenden and Little Delse, both near
    Rochester, plus a number of tenements in the city of Rochester (inquest at Rochester)

One of these, Palstre, near Tenterden, later passed to the Peckham family, who may have been connected with James de Pecham, above. Another manor owned by Richard Charles was Goddington, a small manor later also known as Wattons, lying in the parish of Frindsbury, near Rochester. This manor would pass through William Snayth to the Watton family, who would retain it until the 1660's.[36]

Richard Charles was married, but left no surviving offspring. His estate was therefore administered under the custom of escheat, which dealt with estates without direct descendants. He left a widow, Alice, who married secondly Walter Colpeper and had children by him. In fact she remarried so quickly that, when the IPM was conducted, only fourteen days after Richard Charles' death, she was denied some of her dower under the terms of gavelkind. Her remarriage was not unusual at that period, as a widow with property was very vulnerable and her guardians would try to find her a new protector as quickly as possible. The escheator assigned a third part of Richard's manors to her, except where the parts of such land of were of gavelkind tenure *"whereof in accordance with the custom of 'gavylkende' she will have no dower because she married after Richard's death."* Alice lived until 1385. Her IPM was held at Rochester on 1st December that year. It confirms that her dower reverted to one of her first husband's heirs.

The escheator determined that these heirs were Richard and John Charles, the sons of his brother, Roger, who had predeceased him. They were then aged 18 and 10 respectively, so their lands *"were seized into the king's hand."* until they came of age. Richard, as the eldest, inherited the *"tenements held by knight's service"*, i.e. Addington, but he had to share those held of gavelkind with his younger brother. Although Richard inherited Addington he had to wait for his aunt's death to come into possession of it. During her absentee tenure the manor appears, once again, to have been very badly managed.

This second Richard Charles married Alice Caune, daughter and heiress of Sir Richard Caune of Ightham Mote. The couple had three children, a son and two daughters. It is probable that they remained at the

Mote even after he came into his inheritance at Addington, as he is not buried at St. Margaret's. He was only 27 when he died on 21st April 1387, just two years after his aunt. Witnesses at his IPM described the manor as being in a ruinous state. The mill was valueless, perhaps it had not been brought back into use since the death of Roger de Cologne in 1361. Much of the rest of the land seems to have been under cultivated and making very little money. Even so the tenements were bringing in £5 4s 1d, plus 24 cocks and 52 hens at a joint value of 13s 10d, 200 eggs at 10 pence and seven ploughshares at 8s 2d. One hopes that the tenants were making a better job of husbandry than their lord. After Richard Charles' death his widow remarried. Her second husband was Nicholas Haut, and the couple also lived at Ightham Mote, where she died in 1400. Their descendants continued in possession there.

Richard and Alice's son, named either Robert or James,[37] died without issue and so their two daughters, Alice and Johanna, became his co-heirs. Alice Charles married William Snayth (pronounced Snette) and Johanna married William Repoun. A fine dated 1398/9 states that William Snayth and two others purchased the reversion of the manors of Palstre, Addington and Parva Delse from William Repoun and Johanna his wife, formerly Charles. On 10th April 1400 Snayth was fined again, this time for acquiring the reversion of Palstre without the King's licence. Maddan was therefore not prepared to state categorically how Robert Watton came into possession of Addington manor. It would appear from the fine above that Snayth was concerned to safeguard his family's share of the manor, and therefore bought his sister-in-law out. Otherwise on his wife's death these three manors might have had to be shared equally between the heirs of her sister as well as her own.

Like the first Richard Charles, William Snayth was a prominent man in Kent, but he was not a soldier. He was a businessman, whose family had origins

in the North of England. The name Snayth is Saxon and comes from a manor in the West Riding of Yorkshire, a Henry Snayth being a Freeman of York at the end of the twelfth century. William Snayth continued to have connections with Yorkshire.

He was High Sheriff for Kent in both 1407 and 1409. John Philipot, Heraldic Rouge Dragon Pursuivant, came to the church in 1619 as part of his "Visitation of the County of Kent".[38] He recorded that the East window contained Snayth's coat of arms, *"sable a chevron between three leopards faces, or"* (A golden chevron between three golden leopards' faces on a black field). Philipot pointed out that these were virtually identical to those of Richard Charles. It seems that William Snayth adapted the arms of his wife's family for his own use, and he was afterwards referred to as "armiger". The couple made their home at Addington. The only surviving child of the marriage was a daughter, named Alice after her mother.

William Snayth seems to have been a rich, generous, kind and practical man. His practical side is demonstrated by a bequest in his will, whereby he left 40 shillings towards repairing the road between *"Adynton and Mallyn"*. His piety was manifest. Apart from improving his manor church at Addington at great expense, he left 6s 8d to the High Altar and 6s 8d to the work of St. Margaret's, plus clothing for the priest – a chasuble with alb and apparel.[39] He left generous bequests to other parish churches in Kent. 19 chalices, the price of each to be 26s 8d, and 19 corporals (the cloth which was used with the chalice) with their covers were to be given *"where there was the greatest need."* His financial interests seem to have be wide ranging, as he also left legacies to churches in Norfolk, Lincolnshire and Yorkshire and asked that his executors *"arrange that a mass of requiem shall be celebrated with all solemnity in the Monastery of Bythorne, in the Diocese of Ely, satisfaction being made to the canons, vicars and other ministers."*[40]

Chasuble

Alb

Illustration of an early fourteenth century priest wearing a chasuble and alb

Brass of William and Alice Snayth, Watton Chapel, St. Margaret's Church

He also left large sums of money to Aylesford Friary, Boxley Abbey and West Malling Abbey.

He lived to see his daughter, Alice, marry Robert Watton, a local man whose family had held land at Ridley, near Stansted, during the thirteenth and fourteenth centuries.[41] Robert may also have been a relation. When Snayth wrote his will on 6th March 1409/10,[42] his executors were his wife, to whom he left half of all his goods, his son in law, Robert Watton, whom he called *"consanguineous meus"*, (my cousin), the Rev. John Thost, rector of Elmele,[43] William Manware and *"Robertum filium meum"*, (Robert, my son). This suggests that Alice Charles was his second wife. As Robert Snayth is left no money, he had perhaps received his portion at the time of his father's second marriage. Snayth left Robert Watton and his brother, Thomas, the manor of Palstre to hold jointly. This seems to confirm a family relationship.

William and Alice Snayth were buried in St. Margaret's Church. They were given a joint brass, originally set with coloured hatchments at each corner.[44] The brass was moved to the east wall of the south chapel towards the end of the nineteenth century but lost its coloured inserts through theft during the twentieth.[45]

The first Wattons

Robert and Alice Watton made their home at Addington. In addition to his wife's inheritance and his share of Palstre, Robert Watton had received Goddington. This manor remained within the family until at least 1617.[46] A second manor he owned was Caustons, in the parish of Hadlow, which he bought from Hugh Causton. According to Hasted, Robert's son sold Caustons to Thomas Peckham in the reign of Edward IV, which began in 1461. In 1433, Robert's brother, Thomas, bought Carews (later known as Callis) Manor in Ryarsh from Nicholas Carew of Beddington, Surrey. Thomas left this manor to his nephew, William. In this way Callis manor came into the ownership of the Watton family and would remain so until the second half of the seventeenth century.[47] During the sixteenth century the family acquired the advowson of St. Martin's church, Ryarsh, which, before the dissolution of the monasteries was part of the possessions of the priory of Merton.[48]

The Watton family arms were *"Argent, a lion rampant, gules, debruised with a bend, sable, charged with three cross-croslets fitchee, argent"*. A rough translation reads: A white field on which is an upright red lion, with a black diagonal stripe across the lion, on this are three white crosses which have subsidiary crosses on their upper three arms. Their crest

The Watton family's arms From Arch. Cant. Vol IV, p 258 © Kent Archaeological Society.

St. Margaret's Church as it looked from 1450 to the mid 19th century. Sketch by Henry Petrie,, c. 1803
© Kent Archaeological Society

was a helmet on which was an angel bust with wings outstretched. It was an important distinction to be "armigerous" and one which was proudly held. As has been mentioned, William Snayth "took" the arms of his wife for himself as he himself did not hold this honour. The Watton arms can still be seen in their chapel in the church, on their flamboyant seventeenth century memorial.

The Watton family were unusual in that each generation lived exclusively at their manor house. They were also unusual in that not one member of the family held a major position in public life, whether as administrator, priest or soldier. Perhaps this accounts for why they held their land for so long, as they were not ambitious enough to inspire envy and were not themselves covetous. There is no record that Robert Watton fought

Brass of Robert Watton, d. 1444, who married Alice Snayth. He was the first of the long line of Watton Lords of Addington Manor

at Agincourt in 1415, even though there was a general call to arms from every able bodied squire that year. He and Alice had a son, William, who succeeded him. After his first wife's death, Robert Watton married Elizabeth Bacon (or Chaworth), but there were no children from this second marriage.[49] Her cousin, Thomas Chaworth, became Rector of Addington.[50] Robert Watton, enjoyed a long life. His tenure as Lord of the Manor of Addington lasted for 34 years, until he died on Ascension Day (17th May) 1444. He was buried within the church at Addington. His single brass depicts him as a man in armour, standing on a grassy mound.

Extensions to the church

Robert and Alice Watton's son was named William. He married Benedicta atte Towne. Benedicta was the middle of three daughters and co-heirs of Thomas Towne. Towne had built a mansion at Throwley, near Faversham, which he named Towne Place. It was constructed on land inherited by his wife, Benedicta Detling. William and Benedicta Watton had three children, a son, named Robert, and two daughters, but she died in about 1440, before William inherited Addington manor. Through Benedicta, William acquired a second manor in Hadlow, called Crombury. Like Caustons, this later came into the hands of the Peckham family. William and Benedicta's grand-daughter, Katherine, received it as part of her marriage settlement to William Peckham.[51]

It was not until after his father's death that William seems to have remarried. His second wife was Anne Arderne, who, like her predecessor, came from the Faversham area. Anne was from a prestigious family, and it is very probable that she brought with her a generous dowry, as the marriage seems to have inspired a major building programme at the church. This began in 1450, the year that their first child, John, was born. A substantial tower was constructed at the western end of the church, and the first bells were installed. The nave was extended three metres. It can be seen from the joins in the brickwork, especially within the new extension, how the tower was first built separately, and then joined to the extended nave. There is a short bridging piece of stonework between the original Norman quoins and the tower, and this now forms part of the inside wall of the Geoffrey Grimes room. The south door was closed up, and a new entrance made in the extended north wall.

Extensions were then made on each side of the chancel, accessed by arches in the same style as the main chancel arch. A chapel for the use of the Watton family was built to the south of the chancel, and was called the Chapel of the Assumption of the Blessed Mary. A small transept was added to the north of the chancel, presumably for the use of the priest. The work took up to three years. During this period the young priest, Thomas Dyne, died. He left a generous legacy to complete the tower steps. In a way this was a remarkable building project, as it took part during one of the most troubled times in Kent. In 1450 there was considerable unrest due to unreasonable taxes being levied by an unpopular and incompetent King, Henry VI. His corrupt chamberlain, the Duke of Suffolk, was murdered in January that year off the coast of Margate. Jack Cade, a yeoman from the Hawkhurst area, was unjustly blamed for his murder, and this was the spark that ignited a violent rebellion in Kent, under his leadership. Tax collectors throughout the county were attacked and parochial records destroyed. The rebellion spread to London and beyond before being suppressed. Although I can find no record of Addington's inhabitants being involved, there was considerable unrest in the area and men from both Trottiscliffe and Wrotham took part. Henry VI retained power after the rebellion, but he

was usurped by Edward IV in 1461. He was restored to power in 1468, but was deposed a second time three years later and murdered in 1472. It was a perilous time for William Watton and his family to live through, let alone oversee such an important project for their village. The basic shape of the church then survived until the mid nineteenth century. The illustration on page 33 shows the size of the original north transept.

The succession of Addington Manor during the fifteenth century

The line of succession was as follows:

1. **Robert Watton (1)** (d. 1444) married firstly Alice Snayth. They had one son, called William, who succeeded to the manor, and two daughters
Robert married secondly Elizabeth Chaworth (or Bacon), but had no further children.

2. **William Watton (1)** (d. 1464) married firstly Benedicta atte Towne. They had a son, Robert, who succeeded to the manor, and two daughters.

3. **Robert Watton (2)** (d. 1470) married Alice Clerke and had a son:

4. **William Watton (2**) (d. 1496) leaving no children.

2. **William (1)** married secondly Anne Arderne, who gave him three sons, and two daughters. His second son,

3. **Edmund Watton (1)** (d. 1527), half brother to Robert (2), succeeded to the manor in 1496, on the death of his nephew, William (2) and left descendants.

William Watton (1) was able to enjoy his new chapel for at least ten years. During this period his second wife died, and he remarried, but had no further children. His health was probably poor when he dictated his will on 17th May 1463, but it was not proved until 1465, as he survived until 29th December 1464. In his will be asked to be buried in his new chapel the *"capella assumpcionis Beata Marie de novo constructa"* and then instructed his widow, Joan, to erect a marble monument above his tomb in the new chapel. She should place his effigy (ymagine) on this monument with his first wife, Benedicta, on his right with her son and two daughters and his second wife, Anne, on his left with her three sons and two daughters, together with their respective arms. Because of this monument, no brass was made for William Watton and his tombstone has been lost. The monument stood in the chapel until 1652, when it was replaced by the current Watton Memorial. At his visitation of 1619, Philipot noted that *"in brass eschuchens (escutcheons) on the tombstone"* were five coats of arms: Detling, Towne impaling Sherland, Watton and Towne quarterly, Watton impaling Arderne and finally Snayth. These same hatchments are on the Watton memorial.

William Watton owned land in Trottiscliffe and Wrotham (at Coldrum and Ford). By his will he left items to both these churches and to the monastery at West Malling. Edmund, the second son, did not receive a legacy and his older brother, John, received some curious items, but no money. These were three skewers, two skewers called trussing needles, two basins, one pot, one pan, one chafing dish, two andirons and one lantern! William's widow subsequently married Sir Richard Frogenhall, a connection of the powerful Beaufort family. Frogenhall was one of the leaders of the Readeption Government of 1468 set up after the Earl of Warwick and the Duke of Clarence forced Edward IV from the throne and briefly restored Henry VI as a puppet ruler.[52]

William Watton was succeeded by his son by his first wife. Robert Watton (2) married Alice Clerke, daughter of John Clerke of Ford Manor, Wrotham. This was another prestigious marriage as Clerke was one of the barons of the King's Exchequer. It was also a very local one, especially as Ford manor included

land within Addington parish itself. Robert and Alice had two children. William Watton (2) succeeded to the manor and Katherine married William Peckham of Hadlow.

Robert was Lord of the Manor for only six years, as he died at the end of 1470. He and his family had been accumulating property. His will, dated 6th Nov 1470, gives an indication of the extent of this. By it he stipulated that his executors, Alice, his wife, and John Clerke, her father, should sell a messuage and land at Palmerstrete in Hadlow to pay legacies and to complete the sale of two further properties. One of these was in East Street *"formerly called Bukherstys"*.[53] His wife, Alice, was to have the profits of a piece of land in Offham called Prestislande (Priest's Land) so that she could maintain his anniversary in the parish church of Addington. After her death their daughter, Katherine Peckham, and her heirs were to receive the land for the same purpose. He left legacies to his two surviving half-brothers, John and Edmund, though one benefited more than the other. To his older half-brother, John Watton, Robert left a wood knife, perhaps to complement the variety of household goods left to John by their father. Edmund, on the other hand, received a horse, saddle and bridle, worth 20 shillings and a further 20 shillings in ready money. Robert and Alice Watton were commemorated by a double brass. This shows how the fashion in dress had changed in only sixty years. Alice's clothes look far more flowing and casual than those of her great grand-mother in law, Mrs. Alice Snayth.

Brass of Robert Watton (2) (d. 1470) and his wife, Alice Clerke.

There is no record that Robert's heir, William Watton (1460-1496) married. He was a child when his father died, but he reached maturity and installed two rectors to the living, Richard Smith and Thomas Gooddale.[54] His time at the manor was peaceful to start with, but then he and his family lived through another turbulent period. Once he had regained the throne in 1472, Edward IV enjoyed an unchallenged reign until his death in 1483. However, Richard III then seized the throne from his nephew, the child King Edward V, and reigned for two years, until defeated at the Battle of Bosworth, in 1485. By the time of William's death, however, Henry VII had been on the throne of England for over ten years, and the country was again at relative peace with itself. As William had no children, the succession moved back a generation to his uncle, Edmund Watton (1454-1527), John having already died. Edmund was only six years his senior.

Later mediaeval life in Addington

The fifteenth century manorial rolls are more specific than those of the thirteenth, so it is easier to identify where residents lived. However, although some general areas have retained the same name, such as the Green, East Street and Woodgate, all the field and house names have changed, with the exception of Hedgehogs and Westfields. None of the actual field names survived to be recorded in the tithe map and statement of 1843. Some family names show continuity since the thirteenth century. One of these was the Hazel family (called de Corulo in the earlier Latin form). The will of Thomas Hasyll, a yeoman, was proved at Rochester on 14th April 1452.[55] He left his sons, John and Thomas, his lands at Woodgate. Thomas may have been still a child, as the will stipulated that if either or both did not reach the age of twenty, half their share would become the property of the vicar of Ryarsh, whilst the other half would be given to his two daughters. To his wife, Johanna, Thomas Hasyll left a field called Edwardsfield at East Street, and another called Claygate, lying at Woodgate.[56] She also received four parcels of land containing sixteen acres called *"Spyrelys at a place called Skeme".*

This name seems similar to Kyme. A few years later, In 1471, a William Kyme[57] left a "mansion" in East Street called Pyt(c)hystenement in his will, plus Brueryfield, indicating that ale was brewed in that part of village,

and Brokefield, presumably down near the stream. John Hazell later owned "Pytcheners", but this came into the hands of the Godden family during the sixteenth century, either by sale or marriage.[58] A family that lived in a different part of the parish was called Elyot. In 1474, Robert Elyot bequeathed *"my whole mansion and lands called Kychenfeld, Westfeld and Spokefeld"*, indicating that these lay near to what is now St. Vincents Lane.

The Goddens lived for generations in the village, though their name was spelt in a number of ways. Its origin seems to have been Godwin, which was a Saxon name. A John Godyn appears to have owned land close to what is now the London Road. His will of 20th July 1466[59] gave to each of his daughters twenty shillings from his land *"called South Field"* payable after the death of his wife, Margaret. Meanwhile she would have the use of all his lands in both Addington and Ryarsh, implying that they lay to the east of the village. The Goddens became substantial freeholders of the manor, and also owned land in neighbouring parishes, so they played a social role beyond its boundaries. John Godyn's will gave six pence for the new bells that were being made for Birling church. He also gave twelve pence to repair the bridge of Frowdeford (Plowenders). His descendant, Thomas Godyne, who died in 1528/9, still held land at Southfield, but he had by then acquired some of the Hasyll property, as he left Birchett, Southfield and Edwardesfield to his son, John, after providing for his wife. It was not until the mid seventeenth century that their name disappears from parish records.

One particular will, written in 1474, is somewhat tongue in cheek. John Galon of Addington left to William Wyberd, carpenter, *"my best chipping axe upon this condition, namely that he pays and delivers to each of my executors five shillings."* He then named two executors, so receipt of this axe would cost the carpenter ten shillings, or about three weeks' wages, whilst the axe itself was probably worth only six pence![60] Perhaps William Wyberd had pestered John Galon to leave him the axe, and this was John's way of reproving his neighbour's covetousness.

Very few of the buildings that stood in the village

during the fifteenth century still survive, as virtually all houses at that time were wood framed, filled with wattle, and daub. Although there are still oak framed homes standing in the village, both around the Green and in outlying areas, most were built after 1500. The Angel public house, though, is reputed to be of fifteenth century construction, if not earlier. Hedgehogs is reputed to be the oldest dwelling house in the village. Without dendrochronology assessments and a proper survey, their age cannot be accurately ascertained. It is likely that some current buildings stand on ancient foundations. The manor house at the time would have been timber framed. It was rebuilt in brick during the early seventeenth century, but was demolished in 1950. Two further timber framed buildings, later known as The Vale and St. Vincents, had new brick fronts put on them and their cores encased in brick at the end the eighteenth century.

By the fifteenth century, manorial rents paid on properties had become insignificant. They did not increase over the centuries, so their value to the manor gradually whittled away. From the thirteenth century onwards, a house, garden and eighteen acres might be held for a yearly rent of only seven shillings, seven acres for two shillings and four pence and two

cottages for just one penny. That was if any money changed hands at all. Even during this late period eighteen tenants paid rent only in kind. In 1472, the Lord of the Manor, William Watton, received in rent 42 hens, 5 cocks and 405 eggs, plus a number of ploughshares. It was not until the seventeenth century that all rents were paid in cash. Most tenants were still expected to give manual service for their holding, but this was not onerous, unlike in other counties. It was, at the most, a day's work per week. Even the fines when a property was sold had diminished in value. As these were by custom a doubling of rent for the first year of a new tenancy, they were constrained in that such rent did not increase. The heriot that must be paid on a death, that had been the finest agricultural animal owned by the deceased, was now often commuted to a monetary payment.

So Addington's residents, like those elsewhere in Kent, were not overburdened with service to their lords of the manor, and lived their lives in relative freedom. They were able to sell their holdings, or dispose of them as they wished, as long as they paid the small fine or heriot, as the law of gavelkind continued to prevail within the county. By judicious agreement between heirs, land holdings did not become too fragmented. However, most husbandmen and yeomen farmed only between five and thirty acres. Fifty acres was a substantial holding, due to the need for labour. The main hazards farmers faced were bad weather, sickness, the death of their heirs and unrest.

Hedgehogs By kind permission of Mr & Mrs C. Reader

The Angel from a postcard by Stedman in the early 20th century. This shows the narrow access to the village green.

The Angel Public House

The Angel is reputed to have been constructed to house the masons who were building the tower and chapel at St. Margaret's Church between 1450 and 1453. However, some evidence points to the building being earlier than this, perhaps dating to the end of the fourteenth century. Its name could have three origins. Firstly the building stands on a crossroads, or angle in the village and the name may be a corruption of this, pointing people to its location. Secondly, at the time it was built there was a gold coin in circulation known as the angel, originally the angel-noble. This had a value of between a third and half a pound and had as its device the archangel Michael and a dragon. As public houses were places where workmen were paid and deals were done, it is possible that this was how it took its name. However, my preferred hypothesis is that the pub was named after the crest of the Watton family who built it. This was, as has been

mentioned earlier, an angel's bust with wings soaring upwards. Within the family chapel in the church four angel heads guard the corners of the roof, the funerary helmet once bore a wooden angel on its spike,[61] and an angel's bust crowns the Watton arms at the top of their monument. Near to the public house is a cottage called the Laurels,[62] in which Tudor wall paintings still survive. Some of the motifs are angel heads, suggesting that the Watton crest was once much evident in the village.

The Rectors from 1410, under the patronage of the Wattons

Six rectors served Addington during Robert Watton's life in Addington, of whom he certainly appointed four. These were John Marshall, Thomas Clerk, Edmund Webley, Simon Stoke, Robert Bradley and Thomas Chaworth. Little is known of the first five, who stayed only briefly, exchanging parishes with each other as they sought a living, as had their predecessors. Robert Watton's final appointment, however, was of a distinguished civil servant. Thomas Chaworth was the cousin of his second wife, Elizabeth, and rector of the parish from 1438 until his death in 1446. Chaworth was the first relative of the patron to be rector of this parish. He was buried at Addington, suggesting that the village was his main base. However, he was more of a public servant than a rector. His father, Sir Thomas Chaworth had been an active royal officer in Nottingham and Leicester and the Rev. Chaworth's first parish, which he joined in 1437, was at Stonesfield by Wodestoke in the nearby diocese of Lincoln. He came to Addington within a year of this appointment, so may have held both at the same time. Certainly he was rector of at least one parish concurrently with Addington, as he was instituted to the rectory of Long Melford in Suffolk on 14th July 1441. However, his main occupation was as one of the clerks in the King's Chancery, which would have brought him significant wealth. It seems likely that he spent much of his time in London. His memorial brass hangs beside the reredos. It is a fairly standard brass of a priest in vestments holding a communion cup. This would have been filled with red enamel.

Robert Watton's son, William, was the patron of six rectors in less than twenty years. Thomas Skelton (or Dalton) was the first. The second was a wealthy

The fifteenth century tower steps, partly funded by Rev. Dyke.

young man, Thomas Dyne, who came to the church in 1451 and died only two years later. We know a certain amount about Dyne from his will. He firstly asked to be buried in Addington Church, so he had intended to make the parish his home. It seems that the work on the tower was not yet finished, as he left forty shillings to complete the "vise" (screw) of the steeple, i.e. the circular stair. Perhaps it was because the church was being enlarged that he came to this small parish. He left valuable items and rich clothes to his friends and family. His brother received his sword and a gown of many colours, his father received his blue gown with cap to match. He had made friends locally. John (his executor) and Johanna Hasyll, of Addington received a doublet and pair of hose plus a silvered bedspread and canopy and a stained tester with three curtains of red worsted, which were then still at his rooms at Oxford. He left a book called "Pupilla Occuli" to a second executor, Marmaduke Skelton, rector of Trottiscliffe and another, covered with red leather and beginning "Qui amicum" to a third executor, John, vicar of Ryarsh.

The next rector was Robert Watton, presumably a cousin of his patron, but he moved away after only two years. Robert Stoke had an even shorter tenure, less than a year, but then Addington was blessed with a rector who committed his life to the parish. Alexander Broun was installed on 24th January 1455/6. He was well respected locally and in 1460 was elected Proctor for the clergy in the Canterbury province. This was an important position, as he was the representative of his fellow clergy at convocations and would have voted nationally for changes in church liturgy and practice. It implies that he was a good speaker, and probably an excellent preacher. Others who held this position went on to become bishops. Alexander Broun remained until his death nearly forty years later, in 1494.

In all, 24 rectors served Addington between 1327 and 1500. Nine remained less than two years whilst two gave over 30 years' service. These two were John atte Felde (1361-1396) and Alexander Broun (1455/6-1494). Rev. Broun was the final presentment of William Watton. His grandson, also named William, would make the next appointment.

During the fifteenth century the church would have been highly decorated. Saints were venerated, and their coloured images were painted on the wall or installed as statues in parish churches. In Addington church there was a statue of the patron saint, St. Margaret, one of the Blessed Mary of Pity, which stood in her chapel, a third, of St. Anne, the Virgin's mother and a fourth, of St. Mary Magdalene. On the high beam stood the crucifix with a light in front of it. The windows were decorated with stained glass coats of arms. In the west window were the arms of William Watton, impaling those of atte Towne and Arderne, representing both his wives. Those in the East window were those of William Snayth. The walls were also decorated; one of the paintings, it seems, was an depiction of the Trinity. All these items were described in wills written by Addington's residents. These images would be swept away within fifty years

St Margaret's Church 1500. Painted by T.A. Liverton, Maidstone Polytechnic for Addington P.C.C.

by the Reformation, though the family arms in the windows would remain until the nineteenth century.

Religious Dissent

In fact, there had already been religious dissent in Addington. Before printing was introduced, literacy was in the hands of the church and very few others. All church services and the bible were, of course, in Latin. Priests were the only people who could interpret God's law. Even so, a number of the yeomen and husbandry class were taught to read, some being educated by the emerging grammar schools. Led by John Wycliffe, from the end of the fourteenth century they began to challenge some of the doctrines of the church, including transubstantiation, whereby it is believed that the bread and wine of the mass are changed physically into the body and blood of Christ. They particularly abhorred the worshipping of images and the movement. This became known as Lollardy, was a precursor to the protestant faith.

Lollardy was heartily repressed by the Catholic church. Those who persisted in their beliefs were burned at the stake. Despite this, there were a number of Lollards in Kent, as the movement had spread from Sussex. Although it is unlikely that many of Addington's citizens were followers, one resident stood trial on 26th August 1426 before John Langdon, the Bishop of Rochester, at his manor in Trottiscliffe.[63] The defendant was John Burgh, "Wedetman" of Adyngton, who may have been a descendant of Walter de Burgo, whose name appears in the manorial roll of 1270. The proceedings took place, and were recorded in English. John Burgh admitted the error of his ways, and disowned his heresy. In particular he promised that he would *"ne teche nor afferme errour ner hersey agaynst the law of god and of holy cherch"* and that *"Moreover I shall not hydd no have wyth me no english bokys ne non latyn boke no serre no I may knowe that conteynynge errour or other heresi."* He promised to remain within the boundaries of the village until Michaelmas when he would come to do penance.

1   Morris, John, "*Domesday Book, Kent*", 5, 4 and 5, 51, Phillimore, 1983. "5" is the section of lands belonging to Odo, Bishop of Bayeux.

2   The word demesne is associated with a hand. Later documents refer to land as being kept "in hand".

3   These notes are from James Gracie Maddan's researches, Hasted's history of Kent, and my own researches through the web.

4   The Honour of Swanscombe remained with a male line of the family. Her inheritance shows how gavelkind worked to give all heirs a share of an estate.

5   Register Ecclesis Roffensis (Cotton. MS. Domitian X. p 91) The Feast of St. Andrew is on 30th November.

6   Addington paid this same amount for many years, well after Rochester Castle itself had become derelict.

7   Hasted, E., "*History and topographical survey of Kent*", Swanscombe – states that William de Montchensie died in the 6th year of John, i.e. 1204, having held it for only a short while and that he was succeeded by his son, another William, who died in fifteenth year of John, (1213) and then by Warene de Montchensie, died 38th of Henry III (1253).

8   He was the "Capital Lord of the Fee" of a large number of parishes, both within Kent and further afield. He was therefore owed almost a large army of knights from all his feoffees. The Montchelsea as in Boughton Montchelsea, is a corruption of his name.

9   Kent Feet of Fines 41 Hen III, 1256-7, 97. 41.808, KAS Kent Records, p 285

10   Kent Feet of Fines 44 Hen III, 8 July, 1260, KAS Kent Records, pp 312-3

11   The Marshalsy of the Eyre, Cam, Helen. M, Cambridge Historical Journal, Vol. 1, no.2, 1924

12   Ward, J., The Kent Hundred Rolls, Arch. Cant. 127 pp 57-72

13   Patent Rolls

14   J.G. Maddan was confused by this issue, as he stated that John had married Alice de Beaumont, rather than Alice Fitzwarin. I have now confirmed the true identity of his wife.

15   Close Rolls 12 Dec 1329

16   Edward Hasted, in his "*History and Topography of Kent*" of 1798, appears to have slightly muddled the generations.

17   Subsidy rolls had originally only been called when the country was in danger of war, but by the fourteenth century they had become a general way to raise taxes.

18   The Latinised spelling "Scaccario" was still in use for legal documents.

19   According to J.G. Maddan. Edward Hasted mistakenly stated that before the end of Edward III's reign Daggeworth conveyed the manor to Sir Hugh de Segrave, and that it was he who sold the manor to the Charles family. In fact, it was Richard Charles who granted a lease to Sir Hugh and others, seemingly when he was away on the continent.

20   This is well documented. The goods de Cologne supplied also included silk hoods, pennants, etc. during the war against the Scots of 1334.

21   Much of the information in this section is drawn from J.G. Maddan's articles of 1952.

22   This is another term for agricultural land. It was written "wareland" or "warland" in English, even within the Latin text. The term is Anglo-Saxon and refers to land on which geld (tax) was paid.

23   Another path in the village is referred to as "Clay Gate", The road to the clay.

24   In other documents this man was called Luke Pirich.

25   Sir George Brown(e) (1438-1483) was an active player during the Wars of the Roses, and like his father, was eventually executed. His life is described in Arch. Cant. Vol. 131, 2011, pp 65-85. His connection with Addington probably stems from landholdings at Swanscombe, to which Addington was long affiliated.

26   Whose forebear had been a witness at Richard Charles' IPM of 1378.

27   The name Cuddewelle may later have also been corrupted, to Godwell, as the land of Godwell farm lay in Offham, Addington, Ryarsh and West Malling. Godwell Farm was sold at the auction of Addington Manor in 1923.

28   Linklater, A, 2010, "*Archaeological Evaluation at St. Margaret's Church, Addington*", Canterbury Archaeological Trust, Sub Section 3.12

29   Pritewell Priory (now called Prittlewell) is near Southend, Essex. It was a Cluniac Priory founded in the twelfth century, with links to the Priory at Lewes, Sussex.

30   44 Hen III, p 306 (1259-1260), 97.44.890, from KAS Kent Records, Feet of Fines

31   The list was compiled by the Rev. T. S. Frampton, F.R.S., Rector of St. Mary's Platt, in July 1889.

32   The de Colognes are recorded as lords of the manor and patrons by J.G. Maddan. However this family is not included in Hasted's history of the manor.

33   Dartford Town Archive: The manor of Charles was a sub-manor within the manor of Dartford rectory. The manor was later acquired by Adam Bamme, a goldsmith, who was lord mayor of London in 1390 & 1396. A Rose Bamme later married into the Watton family of Addington. Arch. Cant. Vol. 21, p 214, gives a short biography of Richard Charles as a knight of the shire, calling him a chivaler, or member of the order of chivalry.

34   99 brasses of men in armour, either with or without their wives still exist in Kent.

35   Calendar of Inquisitions post mortem, Vol. XV, 1 - 7 Richard II (1378) K 942 PUB

36   Hasted, E., "*History and Topographical Survey of Kent*", Vol. 3, pp 525 - 546 – Frindsbury

37   Depending which document one looks at!

38   *Archaeologica Cantiana, Vol. 4*, 1861, p 258 Transcribed from a copy in the hand-writing of Sir John Dering, then in the Library at Surrenden House, near Tunbridge Wells. Philipot copied the Watton Arms, and gave their genealogy from St. Margaret's registers.

39   The alb is the robe and the chasuble is the tunic that priests wear. Apparel is no doubt the other items of clothing, such as the cincture, or belt.

40   Lambeth Wills, Arundel II 43a. Translated from the Latin. www.kentarchaeology.org.uk

41   Bartholomew Watton is mentioned in the Hundred Rolls of 1274 which have been quoted from earlier in this chapter.

42   Until 1755 the new year started on Lady Day, 25th March, and dates from January to that date were written in this form.

43   Elmele is now spelt Elmley. Elmley Marshes are at the bottom tip of Sheppey, Elmley Island nearby has a single building on it, and was once cut off from Sheppey by the river Dray. It was a sparsely populated area, and Hasted himself noted that the church had long been in decay.

44   Coats of arms.

45   Information from Mrs. Joan Scott, who remembers seeing these in the brass.

46   Edmund Watton, who died in 1527, left this manor to his eldest son, George. His will also said "and the landes lying under the Darent[h]", which were connected to this manor. The manor is mentioned in a settlement of 3rd December 1617 between Thomas Watton, (d. 1622), Thomas Dabitoll, of Ridmarly Dabitoll, Worcs. and Edmond Attwood, of Trottiscliffe, Kent. Hawley papers 2/Hawley/1/B/1, Lincolnshire archives.

47 Sold during the reign of Charles II. Hasted, E. 1798, "History of Kent, Ryarsh", Vol. 4, pp 488-496
48 In 1608 the advowson of the vicarage came into the hands of Thomas Watton II (1547-1622), and remained with the family until the 19th century.
49 Elizabeth's arms on the Watton monument are those of Bacon.
50 His brass is in the church.
51 The Peckhams sold both manors to the Vane family.
52 Griffin, R., *Kentish Items, Wrotham*, Arch. Cant. Vol. 131, 1915, p 71 - mentioned during an article on the life of Sir George Brown.
53 This property is mentioned two years later in the manorial roll of 1472 when the sale of of a messuage and croft .by Thomas Frere to John Cherch is recorded, adjacent to land "formerly called Bokehurst," implying that the property was renamed after its sale.
54 In 1494 and 1495 respectively.
55 Rochester Lib. II 173 a. b
56 Clay was used for building up the sandy soil, in wattle and daub, and later for making tobacco pipes. These were still being made in the Woodgate area during the nineteenth century.
57 It is probable that Skeme was once owned by Mr. Kyme. The land is called "Keme's land" in a roll dated 1560.
58 Statement of services to the manor of c. 1560 states that "Old John Godden" owed services on Pychener's tenement "sometime one John Hasell". It is possible that "Spyrelys" was a corruption of this property's name.
59 Also proved at Rochester.
60 Dyer, Christopher, "*Standards of Living in the Later Middle Ages*", Cambridge University Press, 1989 – the average daily wages at the time were about 5 pence.
61 This is still kept in the church.
62 The Laurels is now two homes, and must have been one of the substantial buildings of the village when it was built. The date on the wall paintings is 1586.
63 Rochester Diocesan Register, Langdon, folio 76a (transcribed by J.G. Maddan)

3

1500 to 1700 - TUDOR and STUART ADDINGTON

As the sixteenth century dawned, Addington was a small Catholic community, governed by its manorial court and by the church at its centre. The population had recovered from the devastation of the series of plagues and the yeomen of the village were comfortably off. Agricultural practices had not changed dramatically, but experiments were being made to improve yields. The fields were fertilised with chalk from the nearby Downs, and clay from beneath them. About thirty families lived within its boundaries, in simple wood-framed homes, most of only one storey.

The residents felt secure. Bequests were made for tapers to burn before the statues and other images in the church "for ever". Alice Deysey, a widow from Trottiscliffe, owned land in both that village and Addington, and left legacies to both churches. Her will of 1509 contained a request that her executors give "a cow to keep a taper burning before the Image of the Blessed Mary of Pity for ever" at Addington church. John Mylner, dictating his will in 1517, used the same terminology: "I bequeath a cow to fynde a taper of wax to bern afore St. Margaret for ever." John Grove left 20 pence for the provision of a new chalice in 1522 and it was possibly his son, Richard Grofe, who in 1537 left 7 pence "to the paynting of the clothe of the roode lofte if the parysshe painte it." All these testators seem to have been unaware that the storm clouds of the Protestant reformation were already beginning to form over the Channel.

The Lord of the Manor was now Edmund (or Edmond)[1] Watton (1454-1527). Edmund had come into his inheritance in 1496 after the death of his nephew, though as the son of a second marriage he was only six years the senior. Edmund Watton's early life as a younger son had been spent quietly, but he was now a wealthy man. His manor at Addington contained two messuages–parcels of land with a home on them, a mill, 300 acres of arable land, 60 acres of meadow, 200 acres of pasture and 20 acres of woodland. He owned a further twenty acres of woodland in Leybourne, Ryarsh and Offham, plus the manor of Goddington (spelt Godyngton), in Frindsbury. His wife was Sybill Howton (or Houghton), by whom he had a son, George Watton, born in about 1484. He appears to have been close to Sybill's relatives as his IPM recorded that he had appointed three of that surname amongst his trustees to hold the parish and advowson for the benefit of Sybil and George, presumably should he die whilst George was in his minority. In 1505, he appointed John Houghton, who was most likely one of Sybill's relatives, as priest in the parish. When John left (or died) in 1514, his successor was the Rev. Sir Robert Houghton, who remained priest for the next twenty years.

Edmund was widowed in about 1516, but he remarried. His second wife was Elizabeth Arnold, daughter of Robert Arnold of Gillingham and granddaughter of Richard Bamme, an extremely wealthy merchant from the City of London, whose country home was in north Kent.[2] It was their son, Thomas, born about 1520 when Edmund was in his sixties, whose descendants carried the family by the male line through to the eighteenth century. Edmund and Elizabeth also had a daughter, who married Richard Rutland. A new trust was made after this marriage, with new trustees, to look after the interests of Elizabeth and her children, but this trust also protected the rights of his elder son, George.

Edmund enjoyed over thirty years as squire of Addington, though it seems that he was in poor health during the last few years. He dictated his will in October 1524, but survived for three more years, dying on 13th October 1527, aged 73. His piety is apparent, as he asked to be buried in the *"Chapel of our Lady"* at Addington Church, for thirty masses to be said and sung on the day of his funeral–he used the term *"my burying"*, and a solemn dirge the night before. These had to be paid for, so he directed three friends to oversee the masses (probably to check they were in fact conducted). He asked for a further thirty masses to be sung a month after his funeral as well. His will was made in accordance with gavelkind. This was the last time that Addington manor would be passed down under such terms, as the lands were disgavelled after Edmund's death and would from henceforth pass to the next generation by primogeniture. His widow, Elizabeth, was given Addington and all his lands in Kent as her dower. After her death his estate was to be divided between his two sons. George received Goddington and, as the eldest male, had the advowson of St. Margaret's church. Thomas was left the manor of Addington which also possessed land in neighbouring villages. Thomas was only seven at the date of his father's death and no doubt grew up at Addington, living with his mother and sister.

There may have been some ill feeling between Elizabeth and her stepson, as his inheritance of Godynton Manor and *"all the landes lying under the Darenth which both togider are to the yearly value of*
xx li (£20) by estimacion", would only come to him if he *"nor noon other by his procurement shall not trouble nor vexe nor interopt the said Elizabeth my said wife of her said interest for her lyfe nor any parte of this my last will."* There is no record that George Watton married, and he predeceased his step-mother. When he died, on 28th August 1534, Goddington came into the possession of his half-brother, Thomas Watton, again under the terms of his father's will. George Watton appears in Addington's records only once, when he instituted James Goldewell to the parish in 1533.

The outline tree below gives the names of the sixteenth century Watton family members, those in bold type inherited Addington manor.

---

1. Edmund Watton (1454-1527)
married firstly Sybill Howton (or Houghton)
(d. about 1516)

    2. George Watton (1484-1534)

Edmund married secondly: Elizabeth Arnold
    2. Daughter, who married Richard Rutland

    2. Thomas Watton (1520-1580)
married, in 1545, Margaret Sheffield

        3. Thomas Watton (1547-1622)
married firstly Marie Rutland (who died childless in 1583)
married secondly Martha Roper
(c. 1568-1600)

            4. William Watton (1592-1651)
– the heir

            4 John, Edmund, Francis and Thomas – all died young

            4. Anna Watton, survived to adulthood.

        3. Margaret

        3. Anna, married Richard Hynde, 2 sons

        3. Elizabeth, married Thomas Dedicote, 2 sons

The Reformation, counter reformation and Queen Elizabeth's reign

King Henry and Anne Boleyn were married in 1533 and this event set in train the Reformation of the Church of England and the break with Rome. The Watton family would not forsake their Catholic faith, and this must have been a devastating blow to their authority within the village. Research has shown that the Reformation was mostly welcomed in Kent, by a population which had grown restive at high church taxes and a lax priesthood. From the start, the Wattons were going against the tide of local opinion. In 1534, all priests were asked to acknowledge the supremacy of King Henry VIII as head of the Church of England. James Goldewell had recently been installed as Addington's rector. It seems that Goldewell had no hesitation in signing the declaration that "*the Bishop of Rome hath no greater jurisdiction committed to him by God in this realm of England than any other foreign bishop*". He remained at Addington for many years. He was made Commissary to Bishop Holbeach, the Protestant bishop of Rochester and, on 4th January 1546/7, he was appointed one of the Bishop's domestic chaplains. Goldewell left the parish in 1549 to become vicar of Holy Trinity, Dartford. By this time the monasteries had been closed, and the ministry at Rochester Cathedral was led by secular priests, i.e. those who had never belonged to a religious order.

King Henry ordered that bibles written in English be introduced into churches, but the liturgy and the layout of the buildings remained unchanged. However, when King Edward VI came to the throne in 1547 a Protestant form of worship was enforced on parish churches. The Book of Common Prayer became the required form of worship and wooden communion tables replaced the stone altars. The chalice was now a communion cup and rood screens were torn down. During Edward's short reign, statues and images were removed or painted over and the lighting of tapers was banned. When people faced death they were even forbidden to start a will by asking for the intercession of the Blessed Virgin Mary.

This may have been when the porch was added to the church, as the new religion empowered the congregation.

The porch has an interesting verge board with motifs such as oak leaves and fleurs de lys. Photograph; Patricia Richardson.

Thomas Watton came into his full inheritance on the death of his mother. In 1545, at the age of 25, he made an advantageous marriage. His wife was Margaret (though she is named Eleanor on the Watton memorial) Sheffield.[3] She was the granddaughter of Sir Robert Sheffield of West Butterwick, in the Fens. Sir Robert had been knighted for his support, aged only 17, for King Henry VII. He married one of the great heiresses of the time, Helen Delves.[4] Sir Robert's son, of the same name, died leaving a family by two wives. Margaret was from the first marriage so must have been older than her husband. Her half brother, Edmund Sheffield, (1521-1549) was the ward of Lord Rochford, Anne Boleyn's brother. Edmund served King Henry VIII well, and was created Baron Sheffield by the King's will of 1547.[5]

Thomas and Margaret Watton's children were born between 1547 and 1553, during a period of change and turbulence. Their son was named after his father, and their three daughters were called Margaret, Anna and Elizabeth. All the children lived to adulthood. As a staunch Catholic, Thomas Watton may well have been at odds with Rev. Goldewell and been somewhat relieved when he left the parish at the end of the decade. The Rev. Goldewell was followed briefly by Richard Taylor, but he may have been only the curate, as, on the death of James Goldewell in 1551, Robert Goodey (or Goodaye) was installed as rector by the Archdeacon of Rochester, suggesting that Thomas had forfeited the patronage. It did not return to the family until they had conformed to Anglicanism in 1616, though in 1570 Thomas Watton (2), was the patron who installed the rector of Addington, Robert Salsbery, as vicar of Ryarsh. The advowson of Ryarsh church was purchased at some time during the sixteenth century.

In 1554, King Edward VI died and the Catholic Queen Mary came to the throne. Although probably welcomed by Thomas and his family, her four year reign would prove very expensive for Addington church, as for many others in the country. Now communion tables were in their turn cast out, a new chalice had to be purchased and stone altars reinstalled. It was an unhappy reign, full of tension and persecution, during which Calais was lost for ever to France.

And then, once more, all changed when Queen Elizabeth became the monarch in 1558. One of her first decisions was to reimpose the Protestant religion and, in 1559, the Elizabethan Book of Common Prayer was brought into churches. Queen Elizabeth was the patron who installed Robert Salsbery at Addington in 1561. The Rev. Salsbery was an interesting character, who knew how to bend with the prevailing wind. He was installed as rector of Trottiscliffe by the Bishop of Rochester in 1554, implying that he was a good Catholic, but he retained his living under Queen Elizabeth, who went so far as to give him Addington in addition. Thomas Watton then ensured that he became vicar of

Ryarsh in 1570. Rev. Salsbery was therefore respected by Squire Watton and may well have quietly administered Catholic sacraments to his patron. There is a broken slab set into the floor of the Watton chapel with cross shaped incisions typical of a Catholic altar. Was this used by the family during this period? Rev. Salsbery remained at Addington until his death in 1579, one year before his squire. During the last year of his life he was made the stipendiary curate of Birling. He was, it seems, the first incumbent of the present day joint ministry of BART (Birling, Addington, Ryarsh and Trottiscliffe). He may have married, as an Alice Sallisburie was buried at Addington church on 24th February 1571/2.

After Robert Salsbery's death in 1579 it took four years to replace him. There was a general shortage of ordained men during the late sixteenth century. The mid century had been a very dangerous time for clerics and a new disease, influenza, also took its toll. Visiting the sick and dying made the clergy particularly vulnerable. In 1580 the squire, Thomas Watton, died and his will directed that his executors should pay *"to a learned preacher xxLi (£20) for a Sermon to be made at my ffunerall."*

Queen Elizabeth, "by lapse", appointed the new rector, Henry Silliard (Syllard), in 1583. He was a young man, ordained just three years earlier, and he would live at Addington until 1605. He continued as rector of Addington after he moved to Ightham, where he was buried in January 1615/6. The Queen's appointment no doubt reflected her reluctance to re-appoint the Watton family as patrons of their local church. Equally, it seems that the Wattons did not care for Henry Silliard as they did not attend church until he died. It was perhaps at this time that a passageway was constructed which led from the manor house to the church. Such passageways were built by Catholic families so that they and their priest could celebrate the Mass without being seen. It was a dangerous time for the priests who served such families, though a number of young ordinands came to England from the continent specifically to do so. About 130 priests and 60 lay Catholics were executed during the 1580's and 1590's. Did the Wattons have their own priest?

The Babington Plot

Rev. Salsbery may have been related to Thomas Salisbury who was implicated in the Babington Plot of 1586. This was a conspiracy which touched Addington. Thomas Watton's family was not the only Catholic family in the village. Christopher Dunn, a wealthy man, came with his family to the parish in about 1560. During the 1570's three of his children were married here, but it was one of his unmarried sons, named Henry, who brought disgrace upon the Dunns. In the spring and summer of 1586, a plot was led by a young man called Anthony Babington. He had been approached by John Ballard, a Jesuit priest acting for Queen Mary of Scotland's friends in France, and had been asked to attempt her rescue from imprisonment. The plot later extended to planning the murder of Queen Elizabeth herself. Henry Dunn, who was working as a Clerk in the Office of First Fruits and Tenths[6] in London, was drawn into the conspiracy through his friendship with Anthony Babington.

Sir Francis Walsingham, Queen Elizabeth's Spy Master. © National Portrait Gallery, London

Francis Walsingham, the Queen's spy master, had, of course, been following the action throughout and eventually made his move. In early August Henry Dunn was one of the first to be arrested, together with Babington, Ballard, Chidiocke Tichborne, Thomas Salisbury, Robert Barnwell and John Savage. On 10th August 1586 Henry's father, Christopher Dunn of Addington, was examined, but was exonerated of any involvement or knowledge of the affair. The conspirators were quickly condemned to be hung, drawn and quartered. Henry Dunn made an impassioned speech on the scaffold, in which he used the word "sorrowful" four times. This final address and a description of his execution on 21st September 1586 were both recorded.[7] The young man was described as *"of middle stature, a broad visage, broad sette blacke eyes and black bearde which grew somewhat thicke; of speeche he had a reasonable good deliverye and was of a melancolicke complexion, as it seemed."*

Amongst abject apologies and sorrowfulness Henry declared: *"I lyved here joyfullie and pleasantlie under her majestie, and tenne weeks agoe I mette with Anthonie Babington, who toulde me of all his treasons and devises, and he urged me thereunto to give my consent, but I refused and disswaded him also. Then he toulde me that I was one whom he loved well, & therefore he woulde bestowe me wem (SIC). And soe urged me againe. And to confes a truthe, I saide I would doe the best I coulde and consented."* Finally, he begged: *"Last of all I hastelie aske my prince forgiveness and I praie she and one and all maie be eternized with eternall blessedness."*

Perhaps his contrition had some effect as it seems he was not cut down quickly in order to be drawn whilst still alive. Instead he was *"thrown off the ladder where he hanged until he was thoroughlie dead."*

The Spanish threat

Although Thomas and Margaret Watton had been relatively unmolested as they clung to their Catholic faith, their son, also Thomas, had a more onerous time. Fortunately, his loyalty to the Queen would be rewarded. Thomas Watton (2)

(1547-1622) was married twice. His first wife may have been his cousin, as her name was Mary Rutland and Thomas's aunt had married a Richard Rutland. No children of the marriage survived and she died in 1583, probably during childbirth. Thomas's second wife was Martha Roper, daughter of William Roper of Faversham and a grand-daughter of Sir Thomas More. The families would have been drawn to each other by their common adherence to Catholicism. Thomas and Martha had a large family but only one son, William, and a daughter, Anna, lived to adulthood.

Despite remaining a Catholic, Thomas was always staunchly loyal to his Queen. The Armada of 1588 had been driven away by English ships and the weather, but the King of Spain continued to pose a real threat to the security of the realm. On 31st August 1590, Queen Elizabeth, having learned that King Philip was building ships once more, ordered a general muster in the counties. Thomas Watton responded positively to the request for aid and made himself responsible for mustering the men at arms. This muster took place on a large field near to the village green, bounded by the road to the church and Trottiscliffe Road. This was still called Troop Field at the Tithe Assessment of 1843 and now forms part of the Seekers' Trust property. The following year, on 6th July 1591, Roger Twysden of Roydon received a letter from an unidentified writer, but possibly Thomas Watton, stating that *"he will be glad to have their companies and assistance on Thursday, 17th at Addington Green where he intends to muster the soldiers of the hundreds of Larkfield and Wrotham."* This large event took place, as a further memo, dated 15th September 1591, stated that, at Addington, the order had been taken for watching the beacon at Ringmer Hill (a point above Birling where the fire could be seen from Frindsbury, Ightham and Coxheath).[8] Thomas Watton seems to have incurred considerable expenses in this work, but these were settled in his favour in 1595. His support, and that of Addington, as it lay in the centre of the county, seems to have been crucial and the village was called to play yet another part in national affairs. In April 1596, the Spanish, who already controlled Flanders, captured Calais from the French, and once again threatened England. On 25th May, the Queen

ordered a levy of 180 men within Kent to be sent to Boulogne. The Justices met with Lord Cobham, who was raising these troops, at Addington Green on the 27th *"before 9 o'clock of the morning"*.[9] Subsequent to this meeting the Justices of the Peace issued orders on the 28th to the Constables of the Hundreds to provide men so urgently that armour, weapons and coats were to be taken from the trained bands of the county and the men instantly conveyed to Dover. The order made a levy on lands and goods to meet the expense. The fleet sailed and victory was achieved by the sacking of Cadiz in July that year.

A well-known contemporary rhyme confirming the wealth in the county relates to this incident.

A knight of Cales,
A gentleman of Wales,
And a laird of the North Countree,
A yeoman of Kent,
With his yearly rent,
Will buy them out all three.

"Cales" was the old English name for Cadiz. The commander of the army, the Earl of Essex, knighted 66 men who were with him, even though they were mostly of humble origin and few means—hence the ability of a comfortably off yeoman of Kent to buy out a knight, a gentleman and a laird.

Recusancy laws

The general hatred of Catholics during these troubles and alarms prompted Queen Elizabeth to introduce a new act specifically targeted against them. "An Act for restraining Popish Recusants" was confirmed by parliament in 1593. Recusants were those who refused to attend church or chapel in their community or the *"usual place of Common Prayer to hear Divine Service there"*. In doing so they were effectively refusing to acknowledge the monarch's supremacy as head of the Church of England. Further acts were introduced during the reigns of James I and Charles I, and these recusancy acts, although no longer prosecuted, were not repealed until during the regency of George III.

Catholics would not be fully emancipated until 1829. The recusancy laws laid down a series of heavy fines on recusants, which could rise to as much as £20 per month. As part of the proceeds fell into the hands of the collectors, wealthy Catholic families were pursued with relish! In fact, those of little means seem to have been left alone, according to the few families whose record of indictments survive.

Thomas Watton's generosity in her adversity was acknowledged by Queen Elizabeth, who intervened to protect him. In February 1602, the Vice Chamberlain and Secretary, Lord Cecil, wrote from Whitehall to the Justices of Assize at Maidstone: "*We signified Her Majesty's pleasure that you should forbear proceedings against Thomas Watton of Addington, Kent, for recusancy, but you have not accomplished her meaning because you have taken bonds of him to appear before you at the next assizes, and thereby he continues in trouble: being informed that in other respects he demeans himself well as a dutiful subject, she directs forbearance of any proceedings against him; you are therefore to order that he be discharged of the said bonds.*" With the accession of James I there was no such forbearance. A stay of proceedings took place in 1605,[10] but in 1606 His Majesty "*was pleased to confer on the Clerk of the Peace at Maidstone the benefit of Mr. Thomas Watton's recusancy as refusing the communion and the oath of his Majesty's supremacy*" and the letter proceeds to direct that legal proceedings be commenced against him. Three years later on 22nd February 1607/8 a grant was made to "*James Fenton and Anthony Witherings for the benefit of the recusancy of Thomas Watton of Addington, Kent, John Wells of Hoarcross and Richard Fleetwood of Calwich, Stafford and Thomas Kerry of Sutton, Berks.*"[11]

In his old age, Thomas Watton relented and attended church. His conformity appears to coincide with the death of the rector of Addington, Henry Silliard. A certificate of his attendance was recorded by the Quarter Sessions at Maidstone on 20th February 1615/6 and 21st September 1617 respectively, the latter also being a certificate for his son, William.[12] Having obtained his certificate, Thomas Watton regained the advowson of the parish and was permitted to install Edward Drayner

to the living in April 1616. Drayner, who was already the vicar of West Peckham, would serve the village until 1635. At last the family were no longer burdened by fines and they celebrated by renovating

The four bells at St. Margaret's church. The three that were renovated in the early seventeenth century are at the rear

two of the church bells. These were taken down and recast by John Wilner, an excellent bell maker whose foundry was at Borden, near Sittingbourne. The work was done between 1620 and 1622. Thomas Watton died in September the year the second bell was rehung, at the very good age of 75. His coffin was topped with a funeral helmet as it was taken to the church for burial. He was succeeded by his son, William. William Watton (3) (1592-1651) renovated a third bell in 1635, again using the Wilner foundry. The fourth and final mediaeval bell did not need recasting until the next century. He also began to rebuild the manor house.

The manor under the Tudors and Stuarts

The Wattons continued to owe fealty to the Honour of Swanscombe. The manor also remained liable, with its neighbours, for the maintenance of Rochester bridge. This duty was not enforced and became much neglected. In 1561, to prevent the bridge collapsing, Queen Elizabeth appointed a commission for its repair and asked for contributions. Among those received was 100 shillings from Thomas Watton, described alternatively as a "benevolence" and a "loan". This system of maintenance became obsolete during the Commonwealth, but was not abolished until the Restoration, when the Tenures Abolition Act of 1660 was passed. This also took away the knights' service and other legal rights of the mediaeval barons.

During these two centuries a number of timber framed homes were built in the parish . One of these was Westfields Farm, seen below in a photograph taken during the early 1920's. Although its oast was built in the nineteenth century, it was during the sixteenth and seventeenth centuries that hop growing established itself in this area. The original farmhouse is on the left, with a later addition on the right. A second house that is known to have been constructed at the end of the sixteenth century is now called numbers one and two The Laurels, and stands on the north side of the Green. Other contemporary buildings that survive relatively unchanged are the White Cottage and Old Carolcot in East Street, Woodgate and Woodgate cottage. Some were later clad in brick, such as Overlea Cottage, which most likely dates from the seventeenth century. The Vale and St. Vincents were substantially rebuilt at the end of the eighteenth century. The largest example was the Manor House, which was demolished and replaced with a Jacobean mansion at the beginning of the seventeenth century.

Here are three of the properties that were standing at Addington by the end of the seventeenth century.

Westfields Farm. Photograph from the auction catalogue of the sale of the manor in 1923. Reproduced by kind permission of Knight Frank LLP

The Laurels, The Green. A wall painting in number two gives the date 1586 and shows the Watton insignia of an angel's bust. This property still retains its wattle and daub infilling.

Woodgate, showing the fine herringbone brickwork. Reproduced by kind permission of Mr. and Mrs. John Noble

Rents, services and laws of the manor

Land holders in Addington continued to pay their rent in service to the manor, in money and/or in kind, such as cocks, hens and eggs, though a great percentage now paid only in money. The roll of 1560 counts the number of days' service owed by each tenant, but specific duties are not itemised, as in earlier documents. Sometimes this is just half a day's work. The steward had visited each piece of land to ascertain who was living there, and some place names are given, if spelt phonetically. Alycander Fulckain owed a man's work for a piece of land called Palleyzheyrs, seemingly land held by the heirs of a man called Palley. This surname occurs in the parish records as Pawley, but not until the next century. The "z" in the spelling is evocative of the Kent accent right into the twentieth century. The succession of land was clearly important, as each description mentions who held the land earlier. Thus Thomas Godyn owed one man's service for the Upperhouse lands, and another *"for the tenement att East Street and the landes thereunto belonging sumetyme [to] one John Amphell."* Richard Clark, George Clark, Nicholas Howell, Thomas Godyn and old John Godyn had already commuted their services to money so that it is recorded that *"all these pay no services for that they have agreed with Mr. Watton to paye for their land after iiij pence the acre by the yere as long as hytt shall please hym."* The 1560 statement of services due to the manor of Adyngton names only about twenty people, and some of these were giving services as sub-tenants. Thus the statements read: *"Wymble for old John Godyn (ii men)"* and *"Willard for old John Godyn (i man)",* though "old John Godyn" himself provided one man *"for the ii Brokefields"* and another *"for the tenement that he dwelleth in."*

A lay subsidy was granted by Parliament in 1592 when yet another invasion was threatened. This gives the names of just ten people to be charged. The village was assessed at £47 10s 0d; the sum payable being £5 6s 4d. Thomas Watton (2) paid the lion's share of this, (£2 13s 4d). Three other men were assessed on the basis of their land. These were Reginald Balmer, John Fayreman and Edmund Linke (in other documents known as Lynche). The others: Christopher Dun[n], George Shawe, Robert Fletcher, Thomas, Anthonie and John Godden were assessed on the basis of their goods alone. Most villagers' payments were about five shillings, the highest sum being 8s 4d, showing the relative size of holdings compared with that held in demesne. Within a century, only two of these families would still be resident in the village—these were Wattons and the Goddens.

A "fine" to the manor was still due on the transfer of land, either by sale or inheritance, as in the past. These quit rents, as they became known, had not increased since the Middle Ages, so by the end of the seventeenth century were nominal. Even double rent for the first year was so low that this was not much of a burden. Ralph Petley, Esq., who purchased Woodgate Farm from the Godden family at the end of the seventeenth century, had to pay rent of only

£1 2s 8d, four hens, 24 eggs and the service of six men *"att all workes",* so his quit rent would have been only £2 5s 4d. The reference to six men's work implies that this land was already an amalgamation of a number of mediaeval holdings.

By 1600 five cottages had been erected on the common land next to East Street. The annual rent for these was twenty eggs collectively, four per cottage, suggesting that they had been built with the squire's consent. The process of enclosing this land would continue into the nineteenth century.

The manorial court sat right up until the end of the seventeenth century, but no longer as frequently as in the mediaeval period. They had then been held three weekly, but by the end of the seventeenth century only one or two were held each year, sometimes even fewer.[13] The last record that survives for Addington is dated as late as 1692. The roll continued to record the rents and services owed to the Wattons, and also set the manorial bye laws. Much of its business was to do with infringements of manorial customs and poor management of the public areas. By 1600, many farms had been amalgamated, so there were fewer tenants to draw upon for the work that needed doing under the system of manorial services and in most cases these involved only a few days per year. The open fields had become a thing of the past, and yeomen now held over fifty acres in the manor, and more in other parishes.

A long serving steward of the mid seventeenth century was Laurence Byng. He came to his post during the reign of Charles I, stayed during the years of the Interregnum and, although he had to conduct business in English during the Commonwealth, on the restoration of the Monarchy he reverted to recording the proceedings in Latin. He proudly signed himself: *"Senescallum manerii predicti".* (Steward of the aforesaid manor)

A manorial rent roll of about 1680 lists only 31 man days of service on the lord's demesne, far less than had been the case during the mediaeval period. Some service was a general obligation of "all workes", but other duties such as harvesting corn or rye, cleaning the watercourse of the mill, carrying and spreading dung on the demesne and turning, collecting and cocking hay were still specified in this document. Twenty two landholders' names were recorded, though not all owed services.

The View of Frankpledge or Court Leet, as it was otherwise known, continued to set local bye-laws and acted as a minor magistrates' court. The jury heard disputes over unlicensed drinking, obstruction of the highway, allowing animals to roam, public nuisance etc. More serious cases continued to be referred either to the Hundred Court at Aylesford, or the Quarter Sessions at Maidstone or Canterbury. During his tenure as the steward, Laurence Byng unearthed a number of these old laws, made by the village jury, and consolidated them. The village bye-laws of 1603 had set fines for villagers who allowed their animals to stray on the King's highway and the Green (nowadays it is cars that cause the trouble). Between 1603 and 1620 some of these had been refined, and Byng set them down as follows:

1. If any person after All Saints' Day (1st November) allows his pig or pigs without yoke or un-ringed to stray on the road, he shall after three days' warning pay for each pig a fine of two shillings.
2. Any person allowing his animals to stray on the King's highway in the summer time shall be fined for each animal so straying.
3. If any person allows his animals and their young to stray on the King's Highway or on the Green, he shall be fined for each animal twelve shillings.
4. If any person allows his animals and their young to stray on the King's highway or on the Green, he shall be fined for the first offence 4d. and for the second offence five shillings and for each subsequent offence twelve shillings.
5. Any person breaking hedges or fences, taking away wood thereof or stealing from wood heaps shall be put in the stocks for four hours and immediately afterwards he shall be whipped.
6. Any person breaking hedges or fences and carrying away wood thereof shall be fined for each offence 3s 4d or he shall be put in the stocks for six hours on the next day of worship.
7. If any person permits anyone in his house to be drinking or offending in any other manner after 8

o'clock in the evening, he shall be placed in the stocks on the day of worship next following until evening prayers have been said in Addington Parish Church.

This last bye-law suggests that the parish constable, known in Addington as the borsholder, would creep around at night and peer in through cottage windows to check whether its inmates are quaffing beer. However, it was probably directed against informal beerhouses. Some cottage women brewed surplus beer and offered it for sale to their neighbours. These establishments were later licensed through the Beerhouse Act of 1830, but this was primarily to counteract excessive gin drinking. A licensed beerhouse later existed at May Hill.

The View of Frankpledge of 1657 starts with a long list of essoynes, or excuses for absence from persons whose duty or holding required their attendance as a juror. The length of this list presages the eventual demise of the manorial court system. As years passed fewer landholders actually lived within the village boundaries, and they preferred to pay a fine, rather than take time off from business to attend the court. Gradually the number of people available for jury service dwindled away. This particular document does give the names of twelve men sworn as a jury, implying that it was still possible to find them. The jury found that *"the footway adjoining the orchards of Thomas Godden, gent. lying in the highway leading from Trottiscliffe by Woodgate towards Ryarsh is derayed (SIC) to the annoyance of passengers"*, and ordered him to mend it before midsummer or forfeit 20 shillings. They also found that two others had failed to comply with an order to scour and amend a pond of water lying in Woodgate Lane, so each was fined 10 shillings and warned that if the nuisance was not abated by Ladyday, each would have to pay a further 10 shillings. These powers were rather greater than the current Parish Council possesses.

The jury appointed Richard Jackson as the Borsholder, John Lorkin and Thomas Hardy to be Pinders (in charge of the pound for stray animals) and John Stephen to be Ale-taster. The last man had the right to enter the Angel public house and any other beer house in the parish and check the quality of the product! There was a close relationship between civil and church authority. Apart from the manorial bye-laws given above, the church's jurisdiction over its parishioners had been widened under Thomas Cromwell, who introduced civil powers to the church vestry, including poor law administration. Later, the vestry was also empowered to pass the local bye-laws and appoint the parish officers in addition the churchwardens and overseers of the poor, such as the borsholder, ale-tasters, waywardens, etc. One of the borsholder's roles was to enforce the poor laws, which later included accompanying paupers back to their village of "settlement".

Agriculture

The dry, somewhat infertile land meant that farming remained a mixture of animal husbandry, arable and field crops and woodland. Only at Woodgate and Aldon was clay to be found, and these were the areas that fruit was grown. Wheat was the principal crop, followed by barley. Oats, rye and field peas were also grown, mainly as fodder, and a few acres were planted with the newly introduced hops. Inventories refer also to orchards, a term that included top fruit, nut and cherry trees.[14] No probate inventories exist for Addington from the sixteenth century, but those for nearby parishes indicate that each farm owned cattle. These animals would be a few cows, some sheep and a pig or two. Because the land was easy to work, horses rather than oxen were used for draught purposes. The number of animals on each holding was not high, less than ten sheep and perhaps twenty chickens on average.[15] This partly reflects the size of the holdings, as each sheep required about half an acre of grazing, and a cow needed one and a half. Addington still possessed a good sized heathy common north of the Green to the west of East Street, a small part of which survives, but cottages were being erected on this, and gradually the communal area shrank.

Land was cultivated on a three yearly rotation. As the seventeenth century dawned, improvements were made to grazing land through the introduction of forage crops of the pea family such sainfoin (onobrichis), lucerne, also known as alfafa (medicago sativa) and tares, another name for vetch (vicia sativa). Nine varieties of rye grass (lollium), sometimes also called tares, were developed. This type of grass is particularly nutritious. Hay was cut so that a larger number of animals could be grazed on these improved meadows and pastures, especially during the fallow year of rotation. These new plants would have been particularly beneficial in enriching the local soil, and all can still be found growing around the modern village. Lucerne, a tall plant with pink, white or mauve flowers, is still abundant in the sandpits opposite the recreation ground and the village boasts a wide variety of vetches. Dung was also applied to increase fertility. As about 30 loads per acre were needed, this was a fairly major undertaking and this duty is mentioned in the manorial rolls. The land needed to support a family dropped by five to ten acres because of these improvements. Fifty acres was now considered a large farm. Most animals still had to be slaughtered in the autumn, as there was not enough feed to keep them through the winter.

Another way of improving the poor, acidic, soil was to apply lime. This was readily available from the nearby chalk downs, and led to the cultivation of two other plants. These were gorse or furze as it was more often called, (ulex europaeus) and broom (cytisis scoparius). These grew abundantly on the sandy heathland of the parish, and were used not only in the lime kilns, but also for fuel and as winter fodder for the breeding cattle. In the tithe map of 1843 one field was still known as "Furze Field" and another as "Broom Field". Both plants still grow on any available rough ground and along the lanes.

It was in this scarpfoot area, which stretches to Ashford, that hops were first grown in Kent during the sixteenth century. Prior to this only ale had been drunk, the malt being flavoured and preserved with wormwood. Beer flavoured with hops was a European brew. The plant also has an antibiotic effect which furthers the activity of brewers' yeast so, once introduced, beer rapidly gained in popularity. By 1577 hop-growing had become fairly widespread in Kent. The hops were heat dried in divided rectangular buildings that were already used for malting. The word "oast" is derived from a word meaning "heat" and was used long before roundels were invented. Inventories of the seventeenth century refer to hoppegroundes.

Farm leases lasted about seven years, but sometimes stretched up to twenty one, and these could be passed to the next generation. Rents rose until about 1640, but then the population stagnated, so they remained fairly stable for the rest of the century. Crop values rose and fell, but returns for sheep remained low up to and beyond 1700, as wool prices were depressed.[16] The last ten years of the century saw particularly poor harvests, due to bad weather.

The following inventories give a good idea of crops grown and animals husbanded in Addington at the end of the seventeenth century. Both the estates were clearly of wealthy men.

family ate from thirteen pewter dishes and eight pewter porringers. He had a dairy and also brewed his own beer, as in his "Drincke House" were ten drincke wesels, two brase killetes thre brase botels and warmingpanes. (i.e. drinking vessels, brass skillets, brass bottles and warming pans) He owned fewer animals than Mr. Miller, but amongst these were six working horses (worth £15), eight cows, seventeen sheep with six lambs, five hogs and all the farm equipment needed for these. His arable land covered 67 acres, and he had a further twenty acres of pasture for his cattle.

The mill on Addington Brook was occupied for two generations by a family called Knight. In 1649, Thomas Knight left legacies to be shared equally between his son, Richard, and his daughter, Mary. When Richard died in 1691, his goods at the IPM, valued at £170 8s 8d, included 3 bushels of lime, oats, wheat and hops, suggesting that in addition to being the miller, he was also a farmer.

Even a husbandman could make a reasonable living on an acreage that to-day would be completely insufficient to support a family.

Henry Miller, brewer (1691)	Sale value	John Elbye, farmer (1690)	Sale value
5 quarters of mault (from barley)	£3 0s	3 quarters of wheat, 1 quarter of pease (plus other items)	£5 0s
4 bagges of hoppes	£10 0s	11 acres of wheat on the ground	£13 15s
10 quarters of wheat	£12 0s	15 acres of barley on the ground	£15 0s
a stock of hoppolls upon the ground of 4 acres	£22 10s	19 acres of oats on the ground	£13 0s
14 acres of wheat upon the ground	£21 0s	10 acres of pease on the ground	£10 0s
37 acres of corn upon the ground	£30 0s	12 acres of clover	£6 0s
Totals for arable produce	**£99 0s**		**£62 15**
Totals for all his goods	**£192 1s 2d**		**£143 5s 10d**

Henry Miller the brewer, farmed about 60-70 acres of land, of which 51 were arable.[17] He owned a ten roomed, four bedroomed house. In addition to the bed chambers, there was a hall, parlour and service rooms. However, the main value of his estate was in his land, crops and animals, which included seven horses, nine pigs with piglets, eight cows, four budds (young steers), twenty sheep with twenty lambs, plus waggons, carts, ploughs and harrows. The animals he kept were typical for the area. In the second example, Mr. Elbye's house was slightly smaller, with only seven rooms, of which three were bed chambers. The largest of these contained two beds. His house was well furnished, with feather and flock beds, plenty of linen, chairs, cushions, tables, stools and chests. His

Richard Buggs, who called himself this in his will, died in 1691. He had lived in a two bedroomed cottage, and his goods amounted to only £26, but his property included a yard, barn and orchard. His cattle were three hogs and three sows, a cow with calf, six sheep and a colt, and his barn held wheat, oats, pease and hay. There was, however, little furniture in his home. His bedrooms held only beds, bedding and chests.

The small number of lambs in each of these inventories suggests that these were the hoggets or tegs, older lambs and yearlings kept for winter food or for breeding stock, rather than the full yield from the ewes themselves.

Settlement and Poor Relief

Relief of the Poor was gradually codified as this period rolled out. Although the better off had always left bequests for the poor of their parish, during the sixteenth century there was great concern about the number of itinerants in the realm. Laws were introduced for the control of *"sturdy beggars"*, who were moved on after three days. The concept of the deserving poor came into being towards the end of the sixteenth century. Queen Elizabeth's Poor Relief Act of 1601[18] consolidated previous legislation and allowed parishes to charge a levy on residents to care for their paupers. Thus the first "settlement" laws were introduced, as parishes certainly did not want to pay for any paupers who did <u>not</u> live within their boundaries. These gradually became more proscriptive. Farmers could no longer take on workers for seasonal jobs such as the harvest unless they carried a certificate from their home parish to prove that they would be accepted back afterwards.

There was an instant attempt by the overseers at Addington to rid it of potential *"strangers"*, as they were known. Edmund Lynche, a yeoman, was a kindly man, who had taken on labour from elsewhere and given shelter to the needy. This led to him to be one of the first to be prosecuted under the new law. At the Quarter Sessions held at Maidstone on 21st April 1601 he, *"being the owner of a cottage in Addington, on the 1st June, 1597, received into his cottage certain inmates, to live there, that is Francis Danke with his wife and children from the 1st June, 1597 to the 20th April, 1601, and from the 20th May, 1598, Henry Neate, clerk, with his wife and children until 20th April, 1601, and from the 1st November, 1600, [blank] Fuller with his wife and children until the 20th April, 1601, and from the 12th March, 1600/01 [blank] Turner, widow, until the 20th April, 1601."*[19] However, it seems that Lynche's kindness was successful in establishing a settlement for at least one of these couples. Francis and Joan Danck remained in Addington for the rest of their lives. Francis became

the sexton,[20] and clearly gave good service to the parish. On his deathbed in 1625, when he dictated his will to Thomas Godden and to Edward Drayner, the rector, he had money and goods to leave to his unmarried daughter and housekeeper, Frances.

Under the Poor Relief Act of 1662, also known as the Settlement Act,[21] the overseers of the parish were given the power to forcibly remove any stranger from the parish who might become a burden on the funds available for poor relief. A further Settlement Act of 1697 had similar aims but, in addition, it laid down that people wishing to move to another parish to live would require a document stating their home parish, as a safeguard against their future poverty. A child whose parents were not married took the settlement of his mother, and therefore could become a charge upon the parish. This led to some women being driven from their homes when visibly pregnant. However, it seems unlikely that Addington's overseers were this cruel. There seem to have been very few children born out of wedlock during the 200 years preceding 1700, even before the acts were passed. Only four were baptised. The first was Francis Easborne, baptised on 21st September 1589 noted as the *"child of one Susan Carter."* Marie Palmer Easeborne, baptised 14th May 1592, was simply recorded as child. Were these two children a brother and sister? The two born in the seventeenth century were both girls. Frances, the daughter of Marie Tunbreag, was baptised on 6th April 1622. Anna, the daughter of Eliza Martin, who was baptised on 29th December 1670, was recorded as *"base born,"* a new terminology. Eliza later married William Harvey, a widower. The couple had a family of six children, one of whom was baptised Ann, implying that Anna Martin had not survived.

The overseers of Trottiscliffe seem to have taken advantage of their new powers. A case came to court on 15th November 1698 that clarified which of two parishes should look after a baby girl. An order was made as follows: *"Order made by two justices of the peace within the South Division of the Lath of Aylesford for the relief of the parish of Addington for the keeping of a female bastard begotten by Edward Stone of Trottiscliffe on the body of Elizabeth Misson of Addington, single woman."*[22]

Wealth and possessions

Most residents were not paupers, and the homes of the better off may have been highly decorated, even though sparsely furnished. As mentioned above, No.2 The Laurels, on the Green, contains wall paintings, including a frieze with the Watton motif of an angel's bust repeated along the wall and the date 1586. The wooden beams, both upright and in the ceiling, were also decorated with painted patterns. It is likely that other homes in the village were also adorned in this way.

A fragment of wall painting at 2, The Laurels, The Green. Note the repetition of the angel motif. Taken by the author with kind permission of Mr. and Mrs. P. Annis

Fifty two wills survive for Addington over this two hundred year period and from them one can confirm that a number of yeomen owned land in more than one local parish, or even in other parts of Kent. They show the relative importance of household items we now take for granted. Bequests included beds and bedding, specific items of furniture, clothes, household utensils and linen. At the start of this period, in 1518, Thomas Dunton left one of his best sheets to be sold for the reparation of

the high altar. In another will from the sixteenth century a man who described himself as a labourer left two separate pieces of land. Most of these wills ensured that each son received his portion of land but, towards the end of the seventeenth century, it was more likely that younger sons and daughters would receive a monetary bequest. Although, surprisingly, gavelkind was not formally abolished until 1926, it had by then been abandoned. If possible, the chidren were entrusted to the widow, who was frequently made the executrix. In some wills an unmarried daughter was made executrix, even though there were sons of the marriage. Farmers' wives and daughters, it seems, were literate and had a good standing within the family. Widows were provided for. Hugh Davy, in 1513, left his lands to his son, but his will provided that the son *"shall suffer Marjorie my wife to have and occupy the space of ij (2) years after my decease the chamber with the chimney."* In other words, she should have the best and warmest chamber. Where she was to sleep after that was not specified! Thomas Godyne in 1528 wrote *"I will that Jone my wyf have her chamebre within my house and all the movenbylle stuff that I have the terme of her lyf."*

One of the wealthiest residents was Anthony Attwood (or Atwood), a City merchant, who lived in East Street at the property that was later called Addington Vale. He purchased this during the late sixteenth century and also owned land at Woodgate and in Trottiscliffe parish. His home may well have been the "Pythystenement" that William Kyme lived in during the fifteenth century. He died in December 1610 and his will was proved in early 1611. It is typical of the period. After leaving a legacy of ten shillings annually to the poor of both Addington and Trottiscliffe, he bequeathed his daughters, Frances and Elizabeth, £350 each. They would receive this at the age of 21 or at their marriage, if this were earlier. His son, also named Anthony, would inherit the rest of his estate, which included properties in the City of London and its suburbs, in the county of Kent and *"elsewhere in the realm of England."* His wealth had been managed by two "scryvenors", who were appointed executors in addition to his wife, Margaret. The value of woodland was stressed. Mrs. Attwood, although fully responsible for the young children, must not cut more wood or underwood than was sufficient for the use and repair of the estate, its buildings, etc. This was to ensure it passed intact to his son at his majority. The ownership of this property can be traced from the Attwoods to the twentieth century through manorial and other records.[23]

Their elder daughter, Frances, became the wife of Augustus Moreland of Strood, near Rochester. Three of Frances' children would later marry into the Watton family. Margaret Moreland became the Lady of the Manor. The Woodgate land was later divided between Frances' sons, Christopher and Augustus Moreland.[24]

A number of wills survive for the Godden family, who were based at Woodgate and East Street. This was a large and wealthy family, with relatives in the surrounding villages. Robert Godden, a contemporary of Anthony Attwood, left by his will of 1624 a messuage and land in Addington whose adjoining land was in Ryarsh. He also owned a tenement called May Hill in Offham. His properties in Addington were left to his elder son, John, whilst John's younger brother, Robert, received all his messuages and land in Staplehurst, Wateringbury and Teston. Robert's widow, Mrs. Mary Godden had the care their daughters, Parnell and Frances. She was given the marital home as her dower. The two girls were left £60 each, to be given to them at the age of 21, or at their marriage if this took place sooner. Again, the importance of woodland management was emphasised. She was instructed, that she should *'hot free or cut down any timber or wood growing in or upon the same or any profit thereof but by the assigns of my own sonne herein after mentioned."*[25]

When a Thomas Godden, who may have been

Robert's father, died a few years later, he held land in both Addington and Leybourne and lived in a two storied farmhouse.[26] He willed *"that Frances my wife shall have a fine roome in some low roome and the use of her chamber in my mansion house where she now lyeth and the bedding and other stuffe and household stuffe fitting to her."* He then left bequests to his grandchildren. Another Thomas Godden is recorded in the Hearth Tax return of 1664. His home contained five hearths, so was certainly a substantial building.

During the second half of the seventeenth century, once the practice of primogeniture was being followed, entailing property became popular, not only for the gentry, but also for the yeomanry. As a consequence far fewer wills were lodged with the courts from this period onwards. The entail on the manor itself would cause a scandal at the end of the century.

Misdemeanours

Yobbish and violent behaviour is not a modern phenomenon. Such cases were too severe to be dealt with by the manorial court. In 1602 a case came before the Justices at Maidstone of an unpleasant incident involving an Addington man. The report goes *"Giles Allyson of Addington, labourer, riotously assembled together with other people unknown to the number of three, armed with staffs and knives on 21st September, 1602, at Maidstone, and broke and entered into a close of John Brooke, gent., and assaulted him."* It seems that Allison may not have attended that court, as he was brought before them in April 1603, when he pleaded guilty and was fined five shillings. This was not the first time Giles Allison, also referred to as a husbandman, had a brush with the law, as in July 1602 he had been bound over on the surety of £10 put up by Robert Lynche, yeoman, having had an argument with John Soman, a fellow villager.

A slightly earlier case introduces the surname "Whiting" as a resident of Addington. Following the verdict at the county court of 27th October 1594, comes the following instruction:[27] *"Thomas Whighting of Addington, husbandman, in £10 to appear, do and receive and to keep the peace towards Edmund Lyon of the same, weaver."* Cloth had become one of the major exports from Kent and it seems that at least one such craftsman was then working in the village. Thomas Whiting learned his lesson and went on to become a responsible resident. He and his wife, Isabel, raised a family in the village, and their descendants, who were later millers as well as farmers, would live at Addington until the mid nineteenth century. There are no church records under the name of Lyon, so perhaps Edmund spent only a short while here. The yeomen of the parish were frequently asked to stand surety for their rowdy neighbours. Indictments give the occupations of the Addington residents as butcher, tailor, yeoman, husbandman, labourer and tanner. The Tithe Map of 1843 shows Butcher's Field as being near Aldon, whilst Tanyard Meadow lay next to Woodgate. In the nineteenth century census returns all of these occupations except labourer would have vanished.

William Watton (3) and the years of the Civil War

William Watton (3) inherited the manor of Addington in 1622, by which time relative prosperity had returned to the family. William was aged thirty and had married Elizabeth, daughter of John Simonds of Essex. Having lost their first son, the couple already had a healthy daughter, Elizabeth. William and his family now belonged to the Church of England and the family had every expectation of a peaceful life. He finished rebuilding the manor house in local red brick in the Jacobean style. The resulting building, nestling beneath the parish church, was a pleasing edifice of about thirty rooms, with a galleried hall.

However, not only would the 1640's unsettle the

The Jacobean manor house. Apart from the addition of the glass houses, this is how it would have looked for nearly three hundred years. Late 19th century print. © Kent Archaeological Society

family, this would, be the last full century that the male line of the Watton family would live at the manor house.

The squire's family was as follows. Again, the names marked in bold inherited the manor and estate.

1. **William Watton (3)** (1592-1651) married Elizabeth, daughter of John Simonds of Essex

> 2. Thomas (died young)
> 2. Elizabeth, (1622-before 1660) m. Christopher Moreland (left two sons)
> 2. Margaret, (1623-after 1660) m. Augustus Moreland (left one daughter)
> 2. **William (4)** (1625-1661) m. Margaret Moreland
>> 3. Elizabeth (1645-1711) unmarried
>> 3. **William (5)** (1649-1703) m. Mary Fane (six children who all predeceased their father)
>> 3. Martha (died young)
>> 3. Thomas (1651-1685) unmarried
>> 3. **Edmund (2)** (1652-1716) m. 1 Sarah
>>> 4. Mary (1699-1714)
>>> 4. **Elizabeth** (1703-1775) (married twice and left children by both husbands)
>>> 4. Margaret (1705-1714)
>>> 4. Anne (1706-1707)
>> (Edmund m. 2 Anne [Miller?], and had 1 daughter who died young)
>> 3. Robert (1653-1674) unmarried
>> 3. Frances (1661-1739) unmarried
> 2. Thomas, Martha and Susan (all died young)
> 2. Anne (1631-before 1660) m. William Brewer (left a son and a daughter)
> 2. Thomas, born 1635, died young

As can be seen above, three of the children married members of the Moreland family, and four left descendants.

William and Elizabeth Watton were typical of the lesser gentry in Kent of the seventeenth century. Their family had been established in the county for over two hundred years, and played little part in London life. Their estates were on the whole concentrated around the home in which they lived, though they owned holdings in a number of parishes adjacent to Addington. Alan Everitt, who wrote about Kent during the Civil War, assessed that in 1640 the rents received by this group of parochial gentry were on average £270 per year, about 28% of the total rental income of Kent landowners.[28] Through careful husbandry and good marriages, the Wattons had conserved their wealth and, although now Anglicans, their Catholic bias was not out of balance with their immediate neighbours. The powerful Nevills at Birling had their own private chapel within their mansion and were still recusants during the Civil War.

The Civil War

As early as 1630, storm clouds were brewing at Court, and these would eventually lead to thirty years of strife and change. Whether William Watton was an out-and-out Cavalier is hard to assess. Cavaliers tended to be the younger and more hot headed members of his society. It is more likely that he was a moderate, part of a group who were naturally for the king but also longed for good government. His estates were not sequestered by the County Committee, though a number in the locality were, including those of Sir Roger Twysden of nearby Roydon Hall. This implies that he was not heavily involved in defending the King's interests. On the other hand, his memorial in the church shows him in a flowing Royalist style wig, William signed the second petition to the King of 1647-8, described later, and he protected his Anglican rector, John Smith, who retained his living throughout the Commonwealth and was still in post at his death in 1660. William Watton was certainly not a puritan. The main support in Kent for the Commonwealth seems to have stemmed from families who had moved to the county from London within the century. These were involved in business or were lawyers, clerks and liverymen, rather than long standing landowners.

Addington emerged relatively unscathed from the Civil War, even though an action took place nearby.

In 1645, Ford Place was the scene of a mutiny of recruits into Cromwell's Model Army, when they realised that they were to be asked to fight outside their own county borders. A year earlier, Ford's owner, Sir John Clerke, had died fighting for the King at Copredy Bridge. Ford Place, where Lady Clerke was in residence during the riot, was badly damaged during the fighting. A wing had to be demolished and subsequently its status diminished considerably.[29] Although skirmishing probably took place on parish land, there is no record that any of Addington's residents were amongst the recruits or rioters.

Addington's rector, John Smith, had been installed in 1635. At that period the Bishop of Rochester, John Warner, was firmly continuing to install Anglicans, even though the tide was running against him. After the King's execution in 1649, the government forced bishops out of office and many cathedrals fell into decay. Rochester was still functioning on a limited scale in 1652 as Bishop Warner installed Edward Archbold at Trottiscliffe that year. However the cathedral building was later used as a store yard for builders' materials.[30] Warner was later deprived of his see, but regained it at the Restoration. He then held it till his death six years later.

Strangely, for a conventional Anglican incumbent, the Rev. Smith's first wife was called "Be Thankful". However, none of their six children were given puritan names.[31] William Watton and he were staunch allies. Perhaps the fighting around Ford Place, and the unpopularity of the leader of the County Committee, Sir Anthony Weldon, firmed up their opposition to what was happening in London. At Christmas 1647 there had been a riot at Canterbury, and in the spring of 1648 a petition was raised in Kent which attracted 27,373 signatures and led to the last local rebellion of the Civil War. The petition was organised on a local basis in each corner of Kent. A rendezvous was arranged at Coxheath under the pretence of a horse race. Everitt recorded that *"Thither the squire and rector of Addington in Holmesdale sent their tenants and relatives, furnished with arms and money, persuading the villagers both in public and private to support the petition."*[32]

This petition asked to settle the King's and Parliament's rights, to disband the army, to ensure that government should be by known and established laws and, lastly, for taxes to be abolished! Not surprisingly, it was rejected. A somewhat motley Kentish army, led by both Cavaliers and moderates, neither party liking the other, met at Blackheath, led by an outsider, the Earl of Norwich. They then marched back to the Burham area. In response, Thomas, Lord Fairfax, entered the county, came down the North Downs at Ryarsh and avoided the heavily defended Aylesford Bridge by crossing the Medway at East Farleigh. He then approached the rebels, who were by then at Maidstone, from the south. A running battle took place up Gabriels Hill and along Week Street before ending with the Royalists' defeat in St. Faith's churchyard, near to County Hall. This was a decisive victory for the Parliamentarians and 300 Royalists lost their lives. It is unlikely that William Watton was involved in this, though, as support for the petition did not translate into outright rebellion amongst the smaller gentry. He was also by then aged 56. The failure of the uprising was blamed more on the disunity between the community and the Royalists than the outstanding leadership of the New Model Army.

The Watton Memorial

William and Elizabeth Watton then had to endure the trial and execution of their King, and William died two years after this, in 1651, aged fifty nine. Although by now Cromwell and Parliament were in full command of the country and it seems that many Kent gentry were struggling under a great weight of debt, William felt confident that his dynasty would survive and prosper. By his will, he asked his wife to erect a new monument in the family chapel, replacing earlier ones to his family. This new monument was to be so large that it was necessary to block up the East window of the chapel. On it are alabaster portrait busts of William and Elizabeth, with their children beneath them. William is shown looking very much like Charles I. His wife is wearing a Catholic matron's veil. Beneath them are swags of plentiful fruit. Above them black stone plaques record William's great grandfather, grandfather and father, and also give the pedigrees of their wives. The inscriptions were taken from the earlier monuments, but strangely give the wrong Christian name to Margaret Sheffield, naming her Eleanor. Each marriage is marked with a delicately sculpted pair of clasped hands and an armorial shield. William Watton's own arms are at the top, surmounted by the Watton's angel crest. The work was undertaken by Joshua Marshall (1628-1678), son of Edward Marshall. Father and son were master stone masons. Joshua succeeded his father as master mason to Charles II. His work can be seen in a number of cathedrals, including Lincoln and he worked with Hawksmoor on his new London churches after the Great Fire. Despite the horrors of the past ten years, it seems that the Watton family were confident in their own environment.

The Watton Memorial in the south chapel at St. Margaret's Church.

Mrs. Elizabeth Watton survived for another nine years. She was a wealthy woman in her own right, and therefore made a will. It was unusual at the time for a widow to do so. It is possible that the family finances were still fairly stretched, as she absolved her eldest son, William, who had inherited the manor, from a £50 debt and specifically gave him a further £20 to be paid within a year of her death. She gave gifts of £20 to each of her five grand-children, and a further £20 to her surviving daughter, Margaret Moreland. Her female descendants were all left items of linen in addition. She may have lived at Callis Court, as it was after her death that the property was sold by her son, but this is not borne out by her will. She left money to the poor of East Malling and Addington, but not to those of Ryarsh.

William Watton was succeeded by his second son, his first, named Thomas, having died as an infant. William Watton (4) (1625-1661) had married Margaret Moreland in about 1644, when he was aged only nineteen. Margaret, as has been mentioned, had close connections with Addington through her mother, born Frances Attwood.[33] William and Margaret eventually had a large family. She bore seven children, four sons and three daughters. All four sons survived childhood, as did two of the daughters, but only two of their children married. In such a period of unrest, the family's finances began to suffer once again.

The Commonwealth

Cromwell took full power in 1653 and the 1650's saw heavy taxation and a rigid system of government. Any form of entertainment was banned, including dancing and horse-racing. Traditional holidays, such as Christmas, were not to be celebrated and in 1655 marriage became a civil, rather than a religious contract. Marriages had to take place before a judge, the banns having been published at the local market, rather than in church. Despite this, in the three years between

1656 and 1659 Rev. Smith celebrated five marriages at Addington church. Couples must have sought him out as four of these ceremonies were of non-residents. Research has shown that couples would approach sympathetic Anglican clergymen where their own parish now had a puritan, or godly minister. The first, however, was of a couple from Addington, who underwent two ceremonies as follows: *"1656 Sep: 24 Thomas Hatch and Margaret Hatch were married by Justice Meacox of Boxley and by the minister of Addington."*

A year later the following note was made in the marriage register: *"1657 Sep: 15 John Kender of Stansted and Mary Wells of Meopham having 3 several market daies their banes published in Rochester,"* whilst the banns of another marriage had been published *"in the market of Tonbridge by the Register there."* The number of marriages celebrated at Addington during this four year period was actually higher than during the previous ten years.

After the Restoration of the Monarchy, fifteen marriages were celebrated at Addington church before the end of the 1660's. Six of these couples came from outside the parish, suggesting that a number of puritan ministers had retained their livings.

The 1650's was a difficult and unhappy decade for Kent. During the Civil War Sir Anthony Weldon had been the harsh leader of the County Committee, but he had been a Kent man and had protected his county's interests. After Weldon's death in 1648 an outsider replaced him. Thomas Kelsey was a soldier who ruled with an impartial iron fist. Kent families were even more heavily taxed and yoked under central rule. It is probable that this was the reason that the Watton fortunes declined so badly. Having recently been relieved from paying recusancy fines, they were again on the wrong side of the argument. In 1659 William Watton was forced to sell some of his property. One sale was of Smytherne Mills, part of his Callis Court estate, to Samuel French of West Malling. The amount raised was £230.[34] The two water mills, together with a house and five acres of land, straddled the parishes of Ryarsh and Leybourne, behind what is now the Wheatsheaf public house, on London Road.

The Restoration of the Monarchy

After Cromwell's death in 1658 his son, Richard, known as Tumbledown Dick, proved unable to run an effective government. The younger Cavalier "hotheads" and the older moderates in the country came together in unity and invited King Charles II to take the throne. King Charles arrived at Dover on 26th May 1660. One of his first acts was to bring to an end the feudal system. By his Tenures Abolition Act of 1660 Addington manor ceased its liability to pay service or rent to the Honour of Swanscombe. In other ways the Restoration of the Monarchy must have been greatly welcome to the Watton family, though their financial position did not improve greatly. William Watton died the following year, aged only 36, leaving a widow and six young children. Frances, the baby, was only six months old. He left four sons, so it appeared that the dynasty was assured. His will was written to ensure that the name of Watton survived at Addington, as he gave instructions that if each son in turn failed to produce a male heir, on that son's death the estate would pass to the next son, and so on in turn. Only if all sons died without leaving a male heir would the estate pass to *"the right heirs of me the said William Watton,"* in other words to a grand-daughter by one of the sons, or to the issue of one of his daughters. In the event, there would be just one grand-daughter to take the dynasty forward. Neither daughter married, though both women lived to a good age. Elizabeth was 67 at her death in 1711 and Frances, the youngest child, outlived the last of her siblings by 25 years. She was buried at Addington church on 29th May 1739, aged 77.

William entrusted the care of his large family to his wife. One of Margaret Watton's first challenges was to preserve her children's inheritance, which was difficult after so many years of heavy taxation. This burden did not end at the Restoration.

The Hearth Tax

King Charles II swiftly realised that he needed to raise funds. He turned to a hearth tax as a means to supplement his tax intake as this was considered easier than taxing individuals. A bill was introduced in 1662, but the first Hearth Tax in Kent parishes was not levied until Lady Day 1664, by which time a number of exemptions had been introduced. Householders were exempt if they owned or inhabited homes with a rentable value of less than £1 per year, if their personal estate was less than £10 or if they were not liable to contribute to local rates for the church and poor. The last category included officers such as the parish clerk. The tax was fairly onerous, as one shilling was demanded for every fire, hearth or stove within a dwelling and the tax was payable twice yearly.

The record for Addington gives a snapshot of the parish that year and shows a fairly affluent village. Only thirty two homes are itemised, showing a very small community. A church census held ten years later also suggests this. Of these homes, seven were not chargeable–just over one fifth. This was quite a low proportion, even for a country parish. Ryarsh, for instance, contained 40 homes, thirteen (32.5%) of which were exempt. In East Kent the percentage was higher still. Dr. D.C. Coleman made a study of the economy of Kent under the Stuarts and ascertained that in rural Kent as a whole some 33% of households did not have to pay this tax.[35] Another surprising fact is that although six cottages in the village with a single hearth were exempt (and one with two hearths), five families living in one hearthed homes were liable.

At the other end of the scale the manor house, then occupied by Mrs. Margaret Watton and her children, possessed ten hearths, implying a nice warm house. However, to demonstrate its relative size, Bradbourne Park in East Malling, contained 23 and Wateringbury Place 22. 27% of homes in Addington held four or more hearths. These nine houses were occupied by freeholders, yeomen and clergy. A yeoman's house at the time generally held about 8-10 rooms, though some were service areas. The homes of William Bing, Rev. William Polhill, Rector of Offham, Thomas Godden and Anthony Brabson had either five or six hearths. A further four householders, including the rector, Peter Davies, contained four each.

Church records

The sixteenth century was the first in which accurate church records began to be kept. On 5th September 1538, Thomas Cromwell, King Henry VIII's chief minister, issued an important edict. This was that every parson, vicar or curate must enter into a book a record of each wedding, christening and burial in his parish. This book was to be kept in a chest with two locks. The key for the first would be retained by the incumbent and the other would be kept by the churchwardens. However, the parish records for Addington do not start until 11th March 1561/2 for baptisms, 30th November 1563 for burials and 9th May 1568 for marriages. The reason for this was that, in common with other parishes, the early entries were probably made on sheets which were later bound together. In 1598 an order was made to copy the original records, at least from the start of Elizabeth's reign in 1558, into a new book made of vellum. Some of the early sheets or books may by then have been lost, or become illegible.

The first baptismal record reads: *"Thomas Booreman, soone of John Booreman the 11th Day of March was baptised."* John Booreman was a wealthy yeoman farmer, who died in 1566. It seems that the child survived as his descendants were still living in the parish a hundred years later. No further baptism was recorded for that year, suggesting that something had prevented transcription. From then on until the end of the century 215 christenings were conducted, an average of just under six a year. During the same period there were 121 burials, of which only 41 were of infants or children. This does not necessarily imply that the village population was growing, though, as young people had to leave the village to seek employment, a trend that continues to this day. The marriage registers record 50 marriages for the first thirty years, up to the end of the sixteenth century. No marriages at all were celebrated between 1578 and 1582, but the parish was without a rector during those years.

It has been suggested that, taking a period of years, an approximate population number can be made by multiplying the average number of marriages by 125. This would give a population for Addington of about 213 for the second half of the sixteenth century.[36] However, this figure seems too high, as it would imply nearly fifty homes in the village, which is not confirmed by the Heath Tax. Even by 1841 there were only forty.

However, some families _were_ large. Thirty one children with the surname of Godden were baptised at Addington between 1597 and 1667. Twenty Goddens were buried, the last in 1657, after which the family disappeared from parish records. By the end of the period Mr. Godden was styled _"gentleman"_. This family may well have been related to the Godynes who were resident during the fifteenth century, but there seems to have been a break, as otherwise their baptismal records would have occurred earlier. Only a handful of families stayed in the village for more than a century, so if this is the case they would have been exceptional. The Tudor and Stuart reigns saw the names of Allyson, Buggs, Bowerman or Booreman, Crowhurst, Godden, Hatch, Lynch, Sandcocke, Whiting and Young appear in the baptismal records, but of these only the Whiting family remained as the eighteenth century dawned. Even the Wattons at the manor house were about to vanish. The last baptism of a Watton child took place in 1715.

The population of Addington grew very slowly, if at all. It may have mirrored Kent as a whole, as this grew sharply until the mid seventeenth century, before falling back, due to poor harvests, plague and other diseases such as influenza. However, the growth was mainly an urban phenomenon and, when disease struck, it was more devastating in towns. Rural parishes were less affected by this boom and bust.

The population of Addington was fairly typical for a rural parish, over half of which contained less than fifty families. Examination of the burial records suggests that there were no major epidemics in the village during this two hundred year period. The seventeenth century saw 460 baptisms and 284 burials. In 1676, a census was taken to ascertain the number of conformists (Anglicans), Catholics and non-conformists living in the country as a whole. This document, known as the Compton Census, is used by historians as a rough and ready calculator of the relative size of parishes. Addington is recorded as having 25 conformists, no Catholics and no dissenters, implying only twenty-five inhabited buildings, eight fewer than at the time of the Hearth Tax return of 1664. This is borne out by from the christening records as there are a limited number of surnames involved. Between 1640 and 1659 94 baptisms took place. This number shrank to 69 between 1660 and 1679. Both Ryarsh (95 conformists) and Trottiscliffe (76 and one Catholic) were then much more populous. From the figures for Malling Deanery it would seem that there was little dissent in this locality, and this was confined to one or two communities. 70 non-conformists lived in Offham and 165 in West Malling. [37]

The table below compares Addington with some of the local parishes:

The Compton Census of 1676			
Parish	Conformists	Papists	Non-conformists
Addington	25	0	0
Birling	159	1	2
Ryarsh	95	0	0
Trottiscliffe	76	1	0
West Malling	239	0	165
Offham	79	0	70

The church and manor from 1660-1699

Addington's rector, John Smith, lived to see the Restoration of the Monarchy, but died about a month later.[38] Mr. Smith left to his second wife, Mary, his _"house and tenement called_

Birch Hall with its lands, hoppegrounds and orchards" and his *"piece of land called Westfields"* for the term of her life. After her death Birch Hall would pass to his elder son, George and the second, Abell and his daughter, Phoebe, would share Westfields, with about 18 acres. Phoebe was appointed his sole executrix. According to manorial records, Phoebe, who did not marry, appears to have made Westfields her home. Although Birch Hall appears in the manorial rolls, it does not appear to have been the Vale, as that property was by then in the hands of Rev. William Polhill (spelt Polley in the document), then rector of Offham. Birch Hall came into the possession of William Watts at the end of the century. A John Watts had married Jane Smith at Addington in 5th February 1649/50. She may have been the sister of Rev. John Smith. William Watton (4) installed Peter Davies as rector of Addington on 4th August 1660. Where Rev. Davies lived at Addington is unclear. When the Hearth Tax return was made in 1664 he was living in a home with four hearths. As the name "Smith" or "Watts" does not appear in this document, it is quite likely that he leased the home of his predecessor. John Sellars' map of Kent dated 1686 shows Addington Parsonage standing at Aldon. Although rebuilt in the eighteenth century this may have been Birch Hall. Rev. Davies was buried in the chancel on 22nd October 1673 and his successor was installed within a month. Mrs. Davies moved away, but was buried here in 1716.

Rev. Davies' patron, William Watton (5) (1649-1703), was a minor until 1670 and the the church appears to have been kept in poor condition. Bishop John Warner, on his return to office after the Restoration, sent out emissaries to ascertain the state of the parish churches in Rochester Diocese. One of their duties was to note whether each church was properly equipped for the restored Anglican services. Addington church was not unique in its state of repair, though the report was pretty damning. When the visitation took place on 22nd August 1663, the churchwardens were told to to repair:

> the gutter between the chancel and the church, the roof of the church, the floor and pavements of the church and belfry;

In addition:

> the porch should be tiled and paved, and both the chapels "that belonged to Mr. Watton" were to be leaded and floored.

The churchwardens were then told to provide a linen cloth and carpet for the communion table, a chalice, a paten, a poor man's box and a new register book. They were ordered to provide a plug for the font, a shovel and spade, to repair the church clock and set it going, repair the seats where defective, set up the Lord's prayer, creed and ten commandments and provide a canopy for the pulpit. All these repairs and purchases were to be effected by 16th October—just six weeks later. Of the four parishes in the current BART United Benefice, only Trottiscliffe appears to have been in a worse condition.

As the parson, Rev. Davies was instructed separately to repair the tiles in the chancel and to white its walls. He must also repair his parsonage, particularly the buttresses in the garden, the paling and fences in the yard and the outhouses *"where need is"*. Ryarsh Church was also in the patronage of the Watton family, the patroness being Mrs. Margaret Watton, the mother of the juvenile squire. The vicar of Ryarsh in 1663 was Mr. William Deane. His parsonage also appears to have been in poor condition as this note accompanies the assessment: *"and that the Churchwardens doe make request to the Patronesse to add a new Chimney to the house the which wile be taken as a worthy acte and soe represented to the Lord Bishop."* It is to be hoped that she complied with the request.

After the 1663 visitation, the churchwardens of Addington seem to have been somewhat lax about carrying out the instructions. A second visitation took place in 1670 and the orders were very similar to the first, but even more was asked of the churchwarden. Richard Hasell was told *"to repair the roof; the church to be whited; to provide a new door entering Mr. Watton's aisle and the same aisle to be repaired in the roof, shingling, walling and paving."* However, they had purchased the cup and paten cover, as these date from 1666-1667. The Anglican church was by now returning to a more formal liturgy, and Mr. Hasell was told *"to place the*

Communion table and rail it in as at the Cathedral Church of Rochester; to provide a carpet." He must also: "provide a chalice with a foot, a poor man's box, a hood for the minister, a book of homilies, a book of common prayer and a table of consanguinity." That wasn't all. Even the parish chest appeared to have gone missing. The churchwardens were told to provide a chest with three locks. They also had to "repair the seats in the church in the bottoms." From these instructions it seems that St. Margaret's had remained in a poor state since the first inspection. Once again, only Trottiscliffe was in as bad a state of repair, but as that parish was also told to provide the King's Arms, it seems that Addington must at least have had those displayed.

On Peter Davies's death, William Watton (5) installed William Polhill, at Addington on 9th November 1673. Polhill was already rector of Offham. He had been living in Addington parish since 1660. His substantial home was charged in the Hearth Tax of 1664 for five hearths. From a manorial roll it seems that this property was near the common and had previously been held by by Anthony Attwood. In January 1666/7 Polhill had been married at Addington Church to Margaret Deane, possibly the sister, or daughter of the vicar of Ryarsh. His tenure at Addington was to be very short, as he died two years later and was buried at Offham church on 15th October 1675.

William Watton appointed a further five rectors during his forty years as squire of Addington and patron of the living. Rev. Polhill was followed by Robert Topp who, like his predecessor, arrived at Addington promptly, just a month after Polhill's death. Rev. Topp stayed for thirteen years, after which he moved to the Chichester diocese and died there in 1701. His replacement was the only one not to be presented by William Watton. The reason is unclear, but the institution was undertaken by a James Hickford "for this turn."[39] It seems that Andrew Frederick Forneret came from Lausanne, in Switzerland. He studied at Oxford where he published a dissertation in 1673 with an impressive title, "Dissertatio Theologica de Personna et Officio Christi Medatorio." Shortly after arriving at Addington in October 1687 he petitioned the bishop of Rochester for a dispensation to be non-resident so that he might visit his parents "who are very aged, and

living at Losanna." Whether he ever returned to the parish is unclear, as he died two years later. He was followed as rector by Abraham Lord. Rev. Lord was also appointed vicar of West Malling in 1695 and held both posts concurrently for three years.

In June 1698 William Watton presented Rev. Samuel Attwood to the living, but this was yet another short service rector, as he moved to the larger parish of Ash, near West Kingsdown, in 1701. Rev. Robert Worlidge, already vicar of Ryarsh, then served Addington for a year. William Watton made his last appointment on 6th August 1702. This would, in fact, be the last time a member of the Watton family would install a rector at Addington church. The choice was a particularly fortunate one. The Rev. John Boraston, son of the rector of Hever, would become very much loved, and would remain in the parish for very nearly forty years. I have given his biography in the next chapter.

All these rectors appear to have been reasonably well off, unlike the majority of clergy of the seventeenth century. Alan Everitt, who wrote a number of books on society in the seventeenth century, calculated that most tithes brought in an income of little more than £40 a year, much of this in kind, and often difficult to collect. A number of clergy were forced to increment their income by teaching. Those who served Addington, on the other hand, seem to have led fairly easy lives, so may have had other income.

The final years of the seventeenth century

Although King Charles II had been greeted with relief and joy, all was not well with the House of Stuart. Charles died in 1685 leaving no legitimate son, and his brother, King James II came to the throne. The new king was a committed Catholic and a stubborn and unyielding man. His reign came to an abrupt end when William of Orange and James's daughter, Mary, came bloodlessly into the country in 1689. One of their first decrees was to rescind the Hearth Tax.

This was much welcomed. It is possible that some of the village homes were now extended. There was little incentive when the Hearth Tax was in operation, but homes perhaps now also became warmer. The miller, Richard Knight, was assessed as having only two hearths in 1664, but when he died thirty years later his house had four chambers (bedrooms) alone.

However, as the church records confirm, the country continued to suffer from disease. The great plague of 1665 was followed by further outbreaks. Influenza also took a heavy toll. The weather was particularly bad, so poor harvests brought starvation. It was not until the eighteenth century that further improvements to husbandry increased agricultural production to a level that could sustain people through such tribulations. The result was that the population stagnated from about 1640 right up until the mid eighteenth century. The figures for Addington show that the village did not escape this. Additionally, on a personal level, the final years of the seventeenth century were stressful and unhappy for the Watton family.

William Watton (5) (1649-1703)

The third William Watton to live at Addington Manor during the seventeenth century was also the last of that name. He came into his inheritance in 1661 when still a child. One of the first things he, or his mother on his behalf, seems to have done was to sell Callis Court to Edward Walsingham. This manor had been in the family for two centuries. Although a wrench, the sale of the property would have released some much needed money, after a decade of austerity and high taxes under Cromwell. He also disposed of another property that had been in the family for generations. This was the Goddington Manor in Frindsbury that had been George Watton's inheritance, but which had returned to the main branch of the family. In his entry for Frindsbury, Hasted states that William Watton, Esq., of Addington *"in the reign of king Charles I, alienated it*

(Goddington) to Francis Barrell, esq. serjeant at law, and recorder of the city of Rochester."

At the end of that decade, whilst still a teenager, William married Mary, a childless widow. She was the daughter of the Hon. Robert Fane, and granddaughter of Sir Francis Fane, of Mereworth Castle,[40] who later became 1st Earl of Westmorland. Mary's father was one of seven sons (and six daughters), so it is unlikely that he was wealthy. However, Mary brought with her a dowry which included properties in Bampton, Devon, possibly through her mother. This was an advantageous marriage, as it gave William a family connection to one of the great families of the locality. Sadly, the union was blighted by the death of all three of their sons as infants. Two baby daughters also died and only their eldest daughter, Rachel, born in 1671, survived her mother. By the terms of his father's will, William's inheritance was entailed. Should he fail to leave a male heir the estate would go to each of his younger brothers in turn. Only if none should leave a male heir would the estate pass to a female Watton. Mary Watton died in 1695, taking William's hopes of a son, and also her dower, which died with her.[41] This was a particular blow, as the estate was struggling to provide an adequate income. The weather was particularly bad during the 1690's and they became known as the barren years. Tenants were hard to find and rents fell. However, he did have one living daughter, Rachel, who was in her twenties. By this time two of William's brothers, Thomas and Robert, were dead. The third son, Edmund, although over forty, was still unmarried. Edmund's income was modest, an annuity of £40 and the tithes and profits accruing from Ryarsh vicarage, which had been left to him by his father. This may have prevented him attracting a woman with a dowry.

However, towards the end of the century, Edmund married a young woman named Sarah and their first child, Mary, was born in the spring of 1699. Sarah is reputed to have been one of Edmund's servants, a fact that would have scandalised his older brother. In 1700, William's daughter, Rachel, died. At the turn of the century William decided to void his father's will. He was determined to deny Edmund and his children their inheritance of the manor of Addington.

1   This is how the name is spelt in his will of 1527.
2   Richard Bamme's will is translated on www.kentarchaeology.org.uk. Charles manor, the home of Richard Charles (d. 1378) was also near Dartford, and this later came into the hands of the Bamme family.
3   Thomas's wife is called Eleanor on the Watton memorial, and described as the daughter of the 1st Lord Sheffield. However, this lady was not born until 1537 and married Denzil Holles. Lord Sheffield's two half sisters were called Margaret and Eleanor, but the latter married James Ducie. It was Margaret who married Thomas Watton, according to Philipot. The Sheffield family website also gives this information.
4   Sir Robert Sheffield was a prominent barrister as well as being as wealthy landowner and held the office of the Recorder of London. He later became the Speaker of the House of Commons, sitting as the member for the county of Lincoln.
5   Two years later, during the Kett rebellion which took place under Edward VI's rule, Lord Sheffield was brutally murdered outside Norwich by insurgents. Source: Burke's Peerage, and an online history of the Sheffield family.
6   From "A brief account of the many Rebellions & Conspiracies against Queen Elizabeth etc. etc."
7   Calendar of Scottish Papers, 1547 - 1603, edited by William K. Boyd. (Vol. IV, 1586-1588).
8   From Twysden Lieutenancy Papers examined by J. G. Maddan, and recorded in his Material for a History of Addington.
9   I have deduced the date from the letter which went to them asking them to meet "on the Thursday next before nine o'clock of the morning."
10   Calendar of State Papers Domestic, James I 1603 - 1610
11   As above. James Fenton and Anthony Witherings seem to have received fines from a number of recusants in the country.
12   Kent Archives catalogue no. K.H.L.C. Q/M/SB/1199 and 1287
13   Chalklin, C.W., "Seventeenth Century Kent", John Hallewell Publications, Rochester, 1978 – This includes general information about quit rents and manorial services in this late period.
14   Some specifically itemise cherry trees, no doubt because of their value.
15   Zell, M., ed., "Early Modern Kent 1540-1640", Kent County Council 2000, pp 83-86 on Agriculture in Kent, Joan Thirsk
16   Armstrong, A., "The Economy of Kent, 1640-1914", Kent County Council, 1995 pp 56 - 57
17   K.H.L.C. Drb/Pl5/82
18   Calendar of State Papers: 43 Eliz. I c 2
19   K.H.L.C. Q/SR/2/m4 1601
20   This was a paid position. The holder looked after the graveyard, and was responsible for digging the graves.
21   Calendar of State Papers: 14 Car II c 12
22   K.H.L.C. Q/SB/25/212: 15 November 1698
23   Rev. William Polhill was resident at the Hearth Tax of 1661. The property belonged to another rector, Thomas Buttonshaw, during the eighteenth century and then passed via the Davis family to Mrs. Style, before becoming part of Addington manor estate in the mid nineteenth century.
24   Information from manorial rolls of the late seventeenth century.
25   Rochester CC. Pl/21.99
26   Rochester CC. Pl/21/210
27   Kent Archives: Quarter Sessions QM/SRc/1594/78
28   Everitt, A. "The Community of Kent and the Great Rebellion 1640 - 1660", 1969 p 41
29   John, F.D., "The Royalist Rising and Parliamentary Mutinies of 1645", Arch. Cant. Vol. 110, 1992 pp 1 - 15.
30   Newton, D. Papists and Puritans 1596 - 1714, Cambridge University Press, 1998
31   Addington baptismal records: George, Phoebe, William, Abell, another Phoebe and Elizabeth were born between 1636 and 1647. Be Thankful died the following year and was buried at Addington.
32   Everitt, as above, p 246 (from The Clerke Papers, i-iv. Ed C.H., Firth, Camden Society 1891, 1894, 1899 and 1901)
33   The Moreland family were from Strood, Kent and are noted in Philipot;s Kent Visitation of 1663-68. Margaret's mother was the daughter of Anthony Atwood, a wealthy London merchant who lived in Addington.
34   Hawley papers Bargain and Sale 2 HAWLEY/1/B/7 16 Sept., 1659 These documents are held at Lincolnshire Archives. Smytherne Mills later came into their possession.
35   Coleman, D. C., Thesis on "The Economy of Kent under the Later Stuarts", London Ph.D. Thesis, 1951 (manuscript)
36   I added 3 to the 50 recorded as people may have married elsewhere between 1578 - 1582, then divide by 31 (the number of years between 1568 - 1599) then multiplied the figure by 125. This gave Addington's population as 213.
37   Whiteman, A, Clapinson, M. "The Compton Census of 1676: A Critical Edition", p. 407, British Academy, 1986
38   His will was written in June 1660 and proved in August. The burial records for that period are incomplete, but he asked to be buried in the chancel of Addington church.
39   Rev. James Hickford was Rector of Ightham in 1664, according to Hearth Tax records.
40   Mereworth Castle was then a mediaeval building. It was transformed in 1723 into a Palladian Mansion by John Fane, the younger brother of the 6th Earl of Westmorland.
41   A lease held at the Derbyshire record office refers to a property in Bampton held by William Watton through his wife, which would run for 99 years from 1636, or be terminated on the death of Mrs. Watton. Gell family papers - [no title] D258/34/85/6 1636î

4

1700 to 1799 - FAMILY CHANGES and NAVAL CONNECTIONS

The year 1700 was an extremely unhappy year for the head of the Watton Family. The squire, William Watton, was a widower, his wife having died five years earlier. Surprisingly, though he had been aged only 46 at his wife's death, and having no living son, William Watton had not remarried. This was despite the fact that, under the terms of his father's will, should he leave no male heir, the manor would pass to his next brother. The second son, Thomas had died, as had, in fact, the fourth. The third son, Edmund, therefore stood to inherit the manor and its estates, despite William having a daughter. The two brothers were inimical to each other. Edmund was married to his former servant, Sarah, and had one child. This was Mary, who was baptised at Addington church on 16th April 1699. It was highly likely that he would have more children.

William Watton's daughter, Rachel, then died unmarried at the age of 29. It is surprising that she had not found a husband, and suggests that the contents of her grandfather's will were known locally. William, in his bitterness, determined to overthrow his brother's rights by subverting his father's explicit wishes. On 9th April 1702, he wrote a new will. After bequeathing annuities of £15 each to his sisters, Elizabeth and Frances, he left another annuity of only 20 shillings to his brother, Edmund, whom he deprived of the rights to Ryarsh parsonage that he

had already received under the terms of their father's will. William Watton then bequeathed the manor of Addington to his contemporary, Reginald Peckham of Yaldham Manor, Wrotham. Apart from being a friend and neighbour, Reginald Peckham may possibly have been a distant cousin, as during the fifteenth century Katherine Watton had married into that family.[1]

The bequest of Addington's estate included *"all its Messuages Barnes Stables Buildings Gardens Orchards Lands Meadowes Pastures Woods Underwoods Warrens Commons Mills Rents Services Tenements and Hereditaments whatsoever with their appurtenances situate lying and being in the severall parishes of Addington Ryarsh als Raish Layborne and Offham or elsewhere in the said county of Kent together with the Advowson of the Rectory or Church of Addington aforesaid. And the Advowson of the Church of Ryarsh als Raish aforesaid and all Tythes arising or growing due to the same."*

William's sisters, like their brother Edmund, appear to have had a very limited social life. His will specified that if his younger sister, Frances, were to marry John Willoughby, who was formerly his personal servant, she was to forfeit her legacy. In the event, this match did not take place and Frances died unmarried at Addington in 1739.

On 3rd April 1703, William Watton died at the age of 54. He was buried in Addington church. His will was proved by Reginald Peckham, but not until 8th June 1705. Not surprisingly, William's younger brother, Edmund, challenged it, on the grounds that it countermanded their father's wishes. Edmund Watton obtained two verdicts in his favour, one at Kent Assizes and the other in the Queen's Bench. (Queen Anne, James II's daughter, had succeeded to the throne two years earlier) Eventually he and Reginald Peckham came to an agreement whereby, in consideration of £700, the will was "wholly avoided." This cost Edmund Watton very dearly. In February 1705/6, he was forced to mortgage Addington manor, together with its mansion, to Richard Goodhugh and George Hooper, both of Tonbridge, and Thomas Tomlyn, a close friend who lived at East Malling, for the full amount of the settlement. The two Tonbridge men both built up significant estates through acting as mortgagees, and their names recur in other documents relating to property nearby. Luckily, Edmund kept up the payments and the estate remained in his hands and passed to his descendants.

Edmund and Sarah had four daughters, Mary, Elizabeth, Margaret and Ann, but 1707 was another sad year for the family. The baby, Ann Watton, died just before her first birthday. Sarah Watton died only two months later, most likely due to another pregnancy. Her burial took place on 17th December. During the summer of 1714, Edmund remarried. His new wife was named Anne, and she is reputed, like Sarah, to have been a former servant. The following extract comes from a letter written by Miss Isabella Twisden, in which she recounted a number of local scandals to her correspondent, about gentlemen who had formed alliances with servants.

"Watteringbury, 22nd November 1714
To Mary Hammond
About 2 months agoe a gentleman of about 3 or 4 hundred pd a year – his name's Watton, a neighbour of Cosen R. Twisden's – thought fitt to marry his maid. He had 5 daughters by a former wife, the eldest a woman;

but there mother was but of just ye same ranck, so it is not so much to be wondered at, for I sopose the poor man was born for the binifitt of the Cookmaids.
                                    Isabella Twisden"[2]

This letter was particularly unkind, as a joint tragedy had just struck the family. Mary Watton, aged fifteen, and her sister, Margaret, aged nine, died within days of each other. They were buried on the same day—3rd November 1714. Two other Addington children, Jane Penury and Mary Wells, were also buried that week, suggesting that an outbreak of infectious fever struck the village. It was a very sad beginning to the second marriage. Anne was already pregnant. In July 1715, she presented Edmund with a fifth daughter, but the child only lived for a few weeks. When Edmund himself died, on 16th April the following year, only one of his five children remained alive. This was thirteen-year-old Elizabeth. Her grandfather's will had stipulated that should his sons leave no male heirs, a daughter could inherit. She became the sole beneficiary of William Watton's estate. Two further plaques were later added to the Watton memorial, the first showing the families of her grandfather and her uncle William with the names of their families and the second plaque recording her father and herself:

SVB HOC MARMORE ETIAM DEPOSITÆ SVNT EXVVIÆ EDMVNDI WATTON, FRATRIS ET HÆREDIS GVLIELMI WATTON - ET SARÆ VXORIS EIVS·QVIBVS NATÆ FVERVNT QVATVOR FILIÆ, ELISABETHA, MARIA, MARGARETA, ANNA E QVIBVS ELISABETHA, TANTÆ STIRPIS ET TOT PROGE-NITORVM VNICA HÆRES PARENTES SOLA SVPERSTITIT

Under this marble also are deposited the remains of Edmund Watton, the brother and heir of William Watton - and Sarah his wife by whom were born four daughters, Elizabeth, Mary, Margaret and Ann And of whom Elizabeth, out of so many relations and all progeny was the only one and sole heiress who survived her parents.

An Inventory Post Mortem was taken after Edmund Watton's death. He had not needed to make a will, as his inheritance passed to Elizabeth by entail. The appraisers were John Miller of Addington and George Elliott of Wrotham, both yeoman and William Hartridge of West Malling, an iron monger. The contents of twenty-four rooms are itemised in this inventory. Those used for public entertainment were the great parlour and the little parlour, the hall and the withdrawing room, all overlooked by a gallery. Eight bedrooms (chambers) are catalogued, including one, surprisingly, for the carter. Only four of these bedrooms contained chairs and fireplaces, but all had feather beds. Some had bedsteads, curtains and valences, mats and cords (presumably implying carpeting). The two largest bedrooms, the best chamber and the knighton chamber (probably Edmund Watton's room), each contained a looking glass and window curtains, those of the best chamber being made of satin. The nursery—alas by this time occupied only by Elizabeth—was also a bedroom, but within it were stored "one pair of Pistolls and blunderbuss"! There was just one upstairs room in which the maids slept. The kitchen chamber downstairs was most likely for the men servants as it contained a carbine and a musket. Two more guns were kept in the kitchen. Overall, 59 chairs were placed around the mansion. Twelve of these were in the great parlour and eight stood in the hall, but a further seven were in the "Knighton chamber" and eight in the best bedroom. Even the nursery contained six chairs. The implication is that meals were at times taken in these rooms.

The standard of furnishings was high, compared with contemporary inventories of local yeomen, though frugal in comparison with Victorian homes. There were no comfortable upholstered chairs or sofas, very few silver items and no porcelain at all. However, all the beds were feather, not flock, even those of the maids, and many luxury objects were itemised such as eleven pictures (three in the great parlour and eight in the hall), sconces, books, a brass hilted sword, a silver hilted sword, a silver headed cane and, in the "long closet", six silver spoons. These last items are the only ones made of silver, as this did not come into wide use until later in the century. The kitchen was extremely well equipped and, no doubt, it was a help

to have an ironmonger record the 202 items within it, plus "some earthenware." The list of its contents is the largest in the inventory. The items in the kitchen and in the long closet demonstrate that the family ate from pewter plates, whilst the staff used wooden trenchers. Cooking was done in brass or copper pots and pans. The Wattons had begun to partake of new beverages, as four coffee pots stood on a shelf in the kitchen and there was a copper teapot in the long closet. Surprisingly, no cutlery, apart from the silver spoons, is recorded. The kitchen inventory noted only two chopping knives and no stirring or mixing implements. The long closet held no cutlery, despite containing 71 items, including the family's pewter, specialist items such as a cheese plate and pastry plate, two pewter salts and the copper teapot mentioned above. Perhaps the cutlery was in the closet amongst "some small things."

As would be expected, the mansion house contained a number of service rooms. The manor produced all its food and drink, so it contained a kitchen, a small beer buttery, a dairy, a lather (larder?), a brew house, a "cyder" room, a strong beer cellar and a bake house.

The mansion's curtilege contained barns, yards etc. The wheat barn contained unthreshed wheat and rye and also some wheat that had already been threshed. These were together worth £38 (over £5,000 in today's terms). There was also an oat barn, a cart lodge, a yard, a stable, a granary, a further yard adjoining the stable and a garden. The garden was probably a kitchen garden, rather than pleasure grounds. The animals were eleven hogs and fourteen "little Piggs," four horses, four mares, two colts, four cows, a steer, three budds (young steers), two calves (probably female) and sixty sheep with their lambs. The picture is of a relatively comfortable, but not wealthy squire, self-sufficient in produce, living on the proceeds of his husbandry and selling his surplus, but mainly dependent upon his rents. Unfortunately, the picture was not as rosy as this and young Elizabeth's future was fairly grim, especially as her father's widow must be provided for. The goods in the inventory totalled £690 11s 4d, and his personal estate was valued at £715 10s 4d, but Edmund Watton's debts amounted to £1,470

Elizabeth Watton (1703-1775), later Mrs. Bartholomew and Lady Twisden

Elizabeth was put under the wardship of Thomas Tomlyn, her father's friend. Tomlyn ascertained that the annual rents on the manor amounted to about £230 per annum. On his ward's behalf, he came to an agreement with Anne Watton, the widow and administratrix,[3] whereby Mrs. Watton would have an annuity of £30 in lieu of a dower, and that she would sell her husband's goods to pay his debts.

Elizabeth remained unmarried until she was 23. Her position was somewhat of an anomaly. She was heiress to a comfortable inheritance and her father came from a long and respected line of minor Kent gentry. Her mother, on the other hand, had been a servant and in any case was long dead. Her stepmother was not in a position to promote her interests, either. It must have been a great joy to her and to her guardian when, in November 1726, she became the wife of Leonard, the second son of Leonard Bartholomew Esq., of West Peckham. Leonard had been born in 1695, so was eight years her senior. The Bartholomews were a long established and wealthy Rochester family.[4] Leonard Bartholomew, senior, had married Elizabeth, the sister and heiress of Sir Borlase Miller, of Oxonhoath, an historic manor in West Peckham. After the death of Sir Borlase in 1714, the family moved to Oxonhoath. Philip Bartholomew was the eldest son. His first wife was Mary Knowe, heiress to Ford Place, so the two families would have been well known to each other. By 1726, Mary was dead and Philip had recently remarried.[5] The youngest son, Humphrey, who remained unmarried, was a long serving and much respected physician at West Malling.

Elizabeth's stepmother, Mrs. Anne Watton, was still alive at her marriage. On 14th November 1726, Mrs. Watton reached an agreement with Elizabeth's new husband.

She had been receiving rents in lieu of the annuity agreed in 1716, and was £71 9s 6d in hand. It was agreed that Leonard Bartholomew would pay her a further lump sum of £230, after which he and Elizabeth would be released "of all claim to annuity, dower, moiety or thirds out of Addington." When or where Anne died is not known, but she was not buried at Addington.

Elizabeth's marriage settlement with Leonard Bartholomew covered both their estates. Her land lay in Addington, Ryarsh (including the parsonage), Leybourne and Offham, whilst Leonard owned land in further Kent parishes; Rainham, Halstow, Hartlip, Upchurch, Iwade, Birling, Detling, Bredhurst and Wrotham. It was agreed that all would pass to their children, the trustees being John Willis of Lincoln's Inn, Charles Paine of Otterden and Francis Brooke of West Malling. Should both parents die during the children's minority their guardians, Dr. Humphrey Bartholomew and the Rev. Thomas Tilson of Aylesford, were instructed to raise portions by sale for the maintenance of such children. Leonard and Elizabeth settled at Addington and their first daughter, named Elizabeth after her mother, was born in June 1727, but the baby lived for only three months. On 15th June 1728, they had a healthy son, Leonard,[6] who was followed by Edmund (1729-1743), who drowned in the River Medway whilst at school at Rochester, and Jane (1730-1735). Elizabeth was widowed just three months after Jane's birth. Her husband, Leonard, was buried at Addington on 8th October 1730, aged 35.

She remained a widow for nearly six years, and during this time lost her second daughter, Jane. Elizabeth was not a particularly attractive "catch", as she had two sons by her first husband, and the inheritance of her manor would descend to one of them. Even so, in 1736 she caught the eye of Roger Twisden.

Roger, at 30, was two years her junior. He was, like her first husband, a second son, so Addington Manor was an attraction as a place in which to live. His father was Sir Thomas Twisden, 3rd Baronet, of Bradbourne Park, East Malling. It is said that he "courted Mrs. Bartholomew from his carriage", which suggests a curious scenario of him parked outside her home and her having to come to the door to speak with him. The couple were married at Addington church on 23rd October 1736 and made

Sir Roger Twisden, 5th Baronet, Husband of Elizabeth Watton.
© Kent Archaeological Society

their home at the manor house. Their first child, a son whom they named Roger, was born there on 7th November 1737 and was baptised at St. Margaret's church on the 14th of that month. However, just before Roger's birth, news came to England from Granada, in Spain, that three months earlier Roger's older brother, Sir Thomas Twisden, 4th Baronet had met a very sticky end. Sir Thomas, who was a bachelor, had been killed by the jealous husband of a lady he was courting. Roger and Elizabeth's lives were transformed as, when the news was confirmed, he inherited the title as the fifth baronet. His infant son's baptism at Addington was noted in the East Malling parish records, so there should be no doubt as to the succession at Bradbourne.

Bradbourne House

Sir Roger and Lady Twisden moved to Bradbourne House. The manor of Addington was then let for the following 35 years, until she moved back during her widowhood. Elizabeth bore five more children, her last when she was approaching 40. Roger was the eldest, next came female twins, Elizabeth and Jane, and they were followed by Thomas Philip (but these three all died young). Their last two children were sons: William (1741-1771) and John Papillon (1743-1810).[7] Elizabeth's children who lived to adulthood were, therefore, all sons: Leonard Bartholomew, Roger, William and John Papillon Twisden.

Elizabeth's progeny were as follows (again, the names in bold inherited Addington manor):

1. Elizabeth Watton (1703-1775)
  married firstly Leonard Bartholomew
  (1695-October 1730)
    2. Elizabeth Bartholomew (June-Sept 1727)

    2. Leonard Bartholomew (1728-1810)
    m. Frances Thornton, born Wildash

      3. Frances Bartholomew
        (m. John Wingfield-Stratford)
        Their son inherited at Addington.
    2. Edmund Bartholomew (1729-1743)
    2. Jane Bartholomew (1730-1735)
  1. Elizabeth married secondly Sir Roger Twisden,
    5th Baronet
    2. Roger (Sir Roger Twisden, 6th Baronet)
      (1737-Oct 1779)
      m. Rebecca Wildash (1758-1833)
        3. Rebecca Twisden (Jan 1780-1843)
    2. Elizabeth and Jane Twisden – twins
      (1738-1738)
    2. Thomas Philip Twisden (1740-1740)
    2. William Twisden (1741-1771)
      m. Mary Kirk
        3. Captain Sir John Twisden, R.N., rightful
          7th Baronet, (1766-1853)
          m. Mary Hammond. Two grandsons
          inherited the title in turn.
    2. Sir John Papillon Twisden (1743-1810)
      usurped title from his nephew
        3. Sir John Twisden (1784-1841) also used
          the title, married, but dsp

As the wife of one of the major landowners in Kent, Lady Twisden's life at Bradbourne would have been extremely comfortable. Her husband was a straightforward countryman, happiest when on a horse or with a gun in his hand. He hunted regularly, was a member of the local militia, and fulfilled his local obligations as Justice of the Peace and trustee of the local highways board. His portrait, which still hangs at Bradbourne House, shows him in a relaxed pose, wearing hunting pink and reclining on a grassy bank. Sir Roger and his wife were a frugal and competent couple. They managed their joint estates well and, unlike his Twisden predecessors, repaired their finances rather than falling deeper into debt. Although fundamentally kind, Sir Roger was short tempered and known to use extremely bad language if thwarted. His sense of family honour led him to reject and abandon one of his sons. The result was a grave miscarriage of natural justice.

As her husband, Sir Roger Twisden appointed two incumbents to the Addington living. The first was Thomas Buttonshaw, who came to the parish in 1741, following the death of John Boraston. The second was Daniel Hill, already the vicar of East Malling, who also became rector of Addington in 1768. Elizabeth's relationship with Mr. Hill appears to have been cordial, but the care of Addington was principally undertaken by his curate, the Rev. James Thurston, who was vicar of Ryarsh, with whom she appears to have had a warm friendship. Both men would still be undertaking their respective roles at the beginning of the nineteenth century.

Although this is the story of Addington village, I am including the story of Elizabeth's second family. Her surviving Twisden sons had complicated personal relationships with each other and all failed to fulfil their parents' expectations. Sir Roger and Lady Twisden made career plans for each of their three sons. Sadly, not one of these came to an expected outcome. The eldest son, Roger, was destined to inherit Bradbourne, to run his estate, marry well and to continue the dynasty through providing a male heir. The second son, William, would enter the Navy and thus make his fortune from prize money. The third son, John Papillon, was to become a clergyman, and they would find him a comfortable living. Roger

and John Papillon were duly sent to public school and university, whilst William entered the Navy, under the patronage of Admiral Francis Geary, a family connection of Elizabeth. Roger and John Papillon were educated at Westminster School and Trinity College, Cambridge, where Roger gained an M.A. In 1759. John Papillon obtained a B.A. in 1766.

William Twisden's early naval career began reasonably smoothly. He passed his exams and attained the rank of Lieutenant. However, he had a wild, and somewhat uncouth character. His career went disastrously wrong. It was prematurely cut short in 1763, when the Seven Years War was ended by the Peace of Paris. He was then only 22, but had already formed an alliance with Mary Kirk, having sustained a wound in a naval skirmish. She was a woman who nursed wounded naval officers. The couple made a home together and were married in 1764. Sir Roger Twisden refused to accept the validity of the marriage and shunned William, his wife and their children, of whom there were many, though just one son, born at Portsmouth in 1766, survived. William's patron, Admiral Geary, stood by him and acknowledged the marriage, and its validity was not challenged by the wider family. Although Lady Twisden and her other three sons, including Leonard Bartholomew, helped William financially from time to time, they followed Sir Roger's lead and refused to speak to their brother. It is probable that Elizabeth never saw William again.

Sir Roger demanded that William return to his naval career before he would forgive him, though he did continue to give a small allowance to his wayward son. It seems that William preferred to live in poverty, and the family moved between Portsmouth, Essex and Southwark, where William died on 30th December 1771, predeceasing his father. Sir Roger remained adamantly opposed to meeting or acknowledging William's family and, when he died a year later, left no legacy to either the widow or to John, his only living grandchild.

Sir Roger had a reasonable relationship with his other two sons, though John Papillon Twisden did not become an Anglican priest. Roger succeeded to the title, as his father had expected, but left no male heir. Lady Twisden's tenure at Bradbourne came to an end on her husband's death on 7th March 1772. Both she and Sir Roger had been in very poor health for a number of years and, as a widow, she moved back to Addington Place. She lived there as an invalid until her death on 5th March 1775, at the age of 72. She was buried at East Malling church, beside her husband, the ceremony being taken, at her request, by the Rev. James Thurston, to whom she left £5. By her will, she left £10 to the poor of both Addington and East Malling and was particularly generous towards her nurse, Sarah Swaseland, who received £50 and the remainder of her mistress's clothing. She also left legacies to her other servants. It seems, from the way her will was drafted, that her relationship with her eldest son was cool. His inheritance of Addington Manor was already secure, but Lady Twisden simply left to him and his wife a mourning ring, her wedding ring and a hoop ring. She referred to her two other surviving sons, Roger and John Papillon Twisden, as "beloved" and made them her executors. She left John Papillon Twisden her household goods and the residue of her personal estate went to both sons equally. Because of her husband's intransigence, Elizabeth does not appear to have met her grandson, John, and left him no legacy.

Despite her long life, two marriages and many children, Elizabeth remains a hazy figure. No portrait of her survives. This is surprising, as that of her husband is one of the most striking in the Twisden collection at Bradbourne House. It is possible that hers was given to Leonard Bartholomew, and thus removed from the Twisden archive. She seems to have been dominated by the irascible Sir Roger, although there is no suggestion that the marriage was unhappy. It is sad that she did not use her influence to restrain her three youngest sons, who all seem to have inherited volatile characters from their Twisden forebears. Certainly, Leonard Bartholomew seems to have had a much calmer personality. This would be to the benefit of Addington.

During her widowhood, Lady Twisden had regained control of her Watton inheritance. This allowed her son, Leonard Bartholomew, by then aged 45, to marry a young widow, Frances Thornton, of West Malling Abbey. The ceremony took place at West Malling church on 19th August 1773. Frances was the

daughter of Isaac Wildash, a wealthy brewer and businessman from the Sittingbourne area, who held property in Chatham and in the Malling locality. As a brewer, he owned a number of public houses, including the Swan at West Malling. Frances, who was the child of his first marriage, was the widow of George Thornton, who had died in 1767. Frances Thornton had already borne two sons, but neither had survived. By her husband's will, she had retained the lease of the house at West Malling Abbey, and the couple made their home there. They remained at the Abbey for a while after Lady Twisden's death, as their daughter, Frances, was born at West Malling and baptised at St. Mary's on 27th December 1775.

Elizabeth's son, Roger Twisden, had by then succeeded his father as the 6th Baronet. He was well educated. He increased the library at Bradbourne, asking the Rev. Daniel Hill to make a proper catalogue of it for the first time. It is said that he alone of all his relations possessed a bookplate! In 1774, he modernised Bradbourne Place in the style of the Adam brothers, though he did not alter the external aspect. Elizabeth did not live to see him marry. Sir Roger remained a bachelor until 22nd February 1779, when he was over 40. His wife, Rebecca Wildash, was the half sister of Mrs. Leonard Bartholomew. She quickly became pregnant, but three months before the child was due, on 4th October 1779, Sir Roger Twisden died suddenly, leaving no will. Even the baronetcy remained in doubt until, and in the event beyond the day when his daughter, another Rebecca, was born, 5th January 1780. By right, it should have passed to John Twisden, a child of eleven, as the legitimate heir of the second son. The story is much murkier than this.

John Papillon Twisden, had gone up to Cambridge in 1761, but the following year he was left a comfortable inheritance by his childless godfather, Philip Papillon. The inheritance would have been more comfortable still if Mr. Papillon's nieces had not contested the will, as some of the funds disappeared in protracted litigation. However, in 1765, judgement was made in his favour and he received an income of about £450 a year. He returned to Cambridge and gained his bachelor of arts before setting off for France and Italy, where he spent the next few years, returning to England in about 1770. He bought Abbot Meads, between New Hythe and Snodland, and settled down to the life of a country squire. He was a kind man, who had a good relationship with his nephew, John, and when John's mother died in early 1779 accepted the role of guardian to the child. However, this did not prevent him from doing him a great disservice.

Once it had been ascertained that Sir Roger's child was a daughter, John Papillon Twisden seized the baronetcy and held it throughout his lifetime. He moved into Bradbourne House, whilst his sister-in-law moved to Jennings, in Hunton. William's son does not appear to have challenged the raw deal he was handed. He stayed at Bradbourne on a number of occasions and appears to have had a good relationship with his uncle. "Sir" John Papillon Twisden became known as the "benevolent usurper", as he acted as guardian to his nephew and arranged for his entry into the Navy, under the patronage of the redoubtable Admiral, now Sir Francis Geary, who had earlier helped the boy's father. Sir John was extravagant, but most of his problems arose through the need to provide a jointure for his brother's widow and a marriage portion for his niece. This led him to sell off a large proportion of the land around Bradbourne House. He married Admiral Geary's daughter, Elizabeth, and the couple had one son. This was another John, who took the title in turn on the death of his father in 1810. This next Sir John Twisden was quite mentally fragile and was tricked out of more of his inadequate inheritance. He was briefly married, but left no living issue and the estate was reduced to just a few hundred acres when his cousin, Captain John, finally inherited the title as the rightful 7th Baronet, in 1841.

John Twisden, the son of William, had risen slowly in the ranks, but was wounded and unable to return to active service. He retired from the navy with the rank of Commander, which entitled him to be known as Captain. He married and had a large family, which he supported through acting as secretary to the Grand Western Canal Company. Despite being nearly twenty years his senior, he outlived his cousin. Captain Twisden enjoyed the baronetcy for the last twelve years of his long life. He died on 22nd June

1853 at Bradbourne House, at the age of 85. By then the Bradbourne estate had shrunk even further. Sir John Twisden, 7th Bart. was succeeded by two of his grandchildren in turn, through different sons. Sadly, Elizabeth's Twisden descendants continued to squabble, further dissipating anything that remained. The line ended with the death of the bachelor 12th Baronet, Sir John Ramskill Twisden, in 1937. Bradbourne House is now run by a trust.

Leonard Bartholomew (1727-1810)

Elizabeth Watton's most successful child was her eldest son. In early 1776, Leonard, Frances and their baby daughter moved into the manor house at Addington. The delay may have been that work was needed on the ancient building, following years of tenanted occupation and his mother having been an invalid when she returned to her childhood home.

Leonard Bartholomew seems to have been a self-sufficient, perhaps lonely man, who had a somewhat cool relationship with his half-brothers, and also with his mother, but he could not avoid being troubled by and involved in their problems. When Sir John Papillon Twisden seized both the title and the estate, Leonard's sympathies lay with the young widow, Lady Twisden, especially as she was his wife's sister. He gave Rebecca good advice, thereby conserving her inheritance and the marriage prospects of her daughter. The child, Rebecca Twisden, later married Thomas Law Hodges of Hemsted House, Benenden, (now the main building of Benenden School, the girls' public school), who also fought hard for her interests. As has been commented on above, the finances of the Bradbourne estate suffered greatly, and never recovered.

Addington estate, on the other hand, began to enjoy a period of good husbandry under its sensible new squire. During his tenure of the manor, Leonard Bartholomew rarely enlarged his land holdings. He kept the same amount in hand until his death and appears to have made only one major purchase. According to the Land Tax returns for Addington and Trottiscliffe, in 1790, he bought the Addington mill and land at Woodgate from the Petley family of Rochester, whose tenants were the Whiting family. The Whitings then continued in occupation as Leonard Bartholomew's tenants.

Including tenanted land, Leonard Bartholomew's Addington estate was assessed at 34% of the monetary value of the parish. His son-in-law, John Wingfield-Stratford, would be more expansionist during the next century. Leonard Bartholomew had not only inherited Addington manor from his mother, he also had a significant inheritance from his father. His holdings included Old Soar Manor and Burton's Bourne, at Crouch, plus land at Roughway, between West Peckham and Dunton Green. At that time, these were all part of the extensive Wrotham Parish. The land remained in the family for many years. The 1843 Tithe Schedule for Wrotham indicates that they covered about 536 acres. Other possessions included the tithes from Ryarsh vicarage, two other small parcels of land in that parish and detached pieces within Addington itself. He owned

the part of Offham Wood that lay in Leybourne parish. After a long wait, he had come into a substantial inheritance, and because of his mother and stepfather's good management, it had not been dissipated. Leonard's wife was also wealthy, as she enjoyed an income from her father's land and rents in north Kent.

Leonard Bartholomew became an established public figure in Kent during the last quarter of the century. He was High Sheriff of Kent during 1790. During his period of office, the first contested election for Parliament for many years took place. As High Sheriff, he was responsible for the design and erection of a polling booth at Penenden Heath, just outside Maidstone, and ensuring that this was accessible to all electors, however lame, and secure against riots. It is interesting to note that disability access was of importance even at that early date, but it was appreciated that a number of the landowning electors were of an advanced age. A note at the front of the Poll Book for Kent of that year gives him great credit for the speed and efficiency with which he carried out his duties, and the event passed without incident.

Andrew, Dury and Herbert's Map, 1769

The toll roads through and near the village were developed during the eighteenth century. Some turnpikes were built or extended and existing roads were brought up to their standard by deviation and improvement. The extension of the Farningham to Wrotham Heath turnpike passed through Addington's boundaries on its

The Land Tax. First page of the entry for Addington, 1796 showing how Leonard Bartholomew had taken in hand land from earlier proprietors and tenants. KLHC-Q/RPI/445

way to Maidstone. This is now the A20. Spurs were then created at Wrotham Heath. One was Seven Mile Lane, leading to Tonbridge via Mereworth, the second was Teston Road, which was the start of a southern route to Maidstone via Offham, Teston and Barming.[8] Highway Trust boards included all the major landowners as their trustees, one, of course, being Leonard Bartholomew. Unlike some of his fellow trustees, he was an active member of the board. His father had been an early trustee.

On 25th April 1797, Leonard and Frances Bartholomew celebrated their daughter's marriage at St. Margaret's church to the Hon. John Wingfield. The ceremony was conducted by Rev. James Thurston, the curate, but effectively the rector of Addington. Mr. Thurston by then had served the parish for 27 years. Frances' new husband was a 26-year-old Captain in the Coldstream Guards. He was the second son, and the elder of twins, of Richard Wingfield, 3rd Viscount Powerscourt, of Powerscourt House, County Wicklow, which still stands about ten miles from Dublin.[9] The family had been elevated to the peerage through their involvement in politics. John's father had died in 1788, and he was a landowner in his own right in Ireland. A clue to how the young couple met comes from the names of their witnesses. Two of these were John and Dorothy Larking of Clare House, East Malling, a paper

maker and banker and his wife. She was the daughter of Sir Charles Style, 5th Baronet, of Wateringbury. Dorothy's mother had been Isabella Wingfield, John's aunt. A third witness was Miss Frances Davis of The Vale, whose sister was married to Rev. Robert Style.

Captain Wingfield returned to active service, and eventually rose to the rank of Colonel. As their family of three children were not born until well into the next century it is possible that he served abroad. The new Mrs. Wingfield may well have remained with her parents at Addington. As the eighteenth century drew to a close, the future looked bright for the family at the manor house.

Addington Village and its residents during the eighteenth Century

From studying the Land Tax records, which begin in 1780, it seems that most of the houses around Addington Green were built by the end of the eighteenth century. Park Cottage and a terrace of four brick cottages now known as School Row had already been built.[10] Next to these, according to information given in a Tithe Amendment of 1882, stood a workhouse. After Workhouse Unions were created in 1834, Addington's residents were sent to West Malling Union House and this building was replaced by a school. Across the track lay Overlea Cottages (now one house) and the Old School House, which was then owned by an educational trust. Next to these was an empty plot that became a shop, the wooden cottage and the Laurels. The plot on which now stand Stone Cottages was vacant, but across the track to Lane Farm was the Angel Public House, as it had been for over three hundred years.

end of the seventeenth and beginning of the eighteenth century. These give an idea of the relative values of household goods versus agricultural produce and equipment. Both houses described below are likely to be of holdings of only a few acres, as no arable crops are mentioned. The two houses are of a good size, but Wells lived in greater comfort than Paise.

Date	Name and occupation	No. of rooms	Value of household goods	Value of husbandry
7th August 1714	Thomas Paise, husbandman, (burial record gives the spelling as Pace)	8 rooms. 3 chambers plus hall, bake house, milk house, brew house, and woodhouse	£4 6s 0d	£14 10s 0d incl. 2 cows, a mare and colt and 2 young sheep, but no grain.
10th July 1719	Thomas Wells	9 rooms. 3 chambers plus hall, kitchen, buttery, wash house, cellar, dairy and barns	£18 1s 10d	£15 0s 2d incl. 2 cows and 2 mares, 2 hogs, 2 pigs, a wagon, plough, cart and harrow. (Again no grain)

Behind the Green and in the outlying areas were some ramshackle buildings that have since vanished. Their presence is known because they were shown on the 1843 Tithe map and schedule. From inventories, the larger homes, both in the centre of the village and further out, by now had two stories, and service rooms were attached, such as the buttery, milk house, brew house, etc. Most bedrooms were now on the upper floor, though a few remained downstairs, as they were named in inventories the "hall chamber" or "the kitchen chamber". Some yeomen's homes contained eight to ten rooms, and even those of husbandmen had six or seven. Most householders continued to earn their living from the land. There were few professional men living in the village, though a few annuitants were tenants or owners of the more substantial buildings. Agricultural labourers had tiny plots by their cottages and worked for hire either for the manor or for other farmers in the area. Farms now stretched to about 60 to 70 acres. Apprentices lived in the farmer's home as servants learning their trade.

A number of inventories from IPMs survive from the

The goods in Paise's house were not itemised, but his home contained two stories, as all its chambers were on the first floor. The main chamber, described as "over the hall", had goods within it to the value of £1 5s 0d, those in the other two were worth 15 shillings and 10 shillings respectively. The bake house may have served as a general kitchen, though at that period it was quite usual for cooking to take place within the hall. The goods in this hall, however, were valued at only £1 5s 0d. This suggests very simple furnishings, and probably no cooking utensils. In contrast, Mr. Wells' home contained at least twenty chairs, including ten in the best chamber, which was probably used as a living room. This, again, was quite usual for the period. The goods in this chamber were valued at £3 4s 0d but it was still quite sparsely furnished, containing only *"One old featherbedd and all things thereunto belonging one table one cupboard and tenn Chairs."* Although a kitchen is recorded, in this home the main hall was clearly used for cooking, as it contained: *"One old clock a cupboard too old tables two fformes (benches) eight chairs a turnspit jack two spits two panns Andirons tongs fire shoo pothookes and other small things."* Value: £2 10s 0d.

Wells' main luxury item would seem to have been his old clock.

Whilst Thomas Wells lived in greater comfort than Thomas Paise, the value of their animals and farming equipment was remarkably similar, being £14 10s and £15 respectively. In addition, both men had a similar amount of money and wearing apparel, at £1 5s 0d, and the same number of bedchambers. It is the furnishing that differentiates them, though neither home remotely approaches the standard of luxury within the manor house. As their inventories survive, these two homes must have been occupied by the better off members of the community. Most labourers' homes would have had, at the very most, two flock beds, (or even straw palliases) a bench or two, a table and cooking equipment.

One particular inventory is worth mentioning, as it is of a craftsman who, like many other skilled artisans, worked at home. Nicholas Newstead was a basket maker who died in January 1705/6. He was clearly a successful man. His estate was valued at £104 8s 7d. Like his neighbours, he appears to have combined his kitchen with his main living room, but there was an inner room behind this. The house again had three bedrooms. However, the best chamber was more lavishly furnished than those of the two farmers above.

Moreover, it was warm! It had *"two feather beddes two bolsters two pillows two Blanketts two Ruggs two Bedheades one pair of curtaines one old curtaine and Vallance two cords two matts one Chest of Drawers two chests one trunk one box two chairs one stoole one pair of Bellowes one paire of tonges one fire pann and beddpan one paire of creepons(?)"* Value: £6 7s. 0d. He even provided a comfortable (but not warm) room for his servants, with *"two flock beds two Bolsters six feather pillows two blankets two ruggs one curtaine and Rodd."* Newstead's real worth was in his basket making materials and the tools in his workshop. Even the white and brown rods were worth £20. His unsold stock of white and brown baskets were valued at £1 5s. He was also a farmer and brewer, his animals being valued at £8, his corn in the barn at £13, and his apples, beans and farming gear at a further £18. His occupation was given as farmer in the church burial records. Basket making continued at

Addington into the nineteenth century, when the osier beds that lay opposite the modern village hall were harvested by itinerant workers from the East End of London.

The village families

No taxation records survive for Addington for the first half of the eighteenth century, but the size and composition of the village can be estimated through church records. It seems that during the century the village population shrank. Although baptisms increased by 23–from 460 to 483, there were 458 burials as opposed to only 284 during the previous hundred years. Infant and child mortality, not surprisingly, continued to be a major problem. 104 out of these 458 burials were of children of thirteen and under, 93 of these children were under the age of five, and a shocking 70 had failed to reach their first birthday.

During the first half of the century, 240 children were baptised at St. Margaret's, 118 boys and 122 girls. 257 burials were recorded up to 1750, so it seems that this was the sharpest period of population decline. Just nine people are known to have lived to more than 70, the oldest being Mary Crowhurst, a yeoman's widow, who was 83 when she died in 1740. Between 1751 and 1800, the number of baptisms was very similar, at 241, but only 201 burials took place. Over the whole century, 179 marriages were celebrated at the church. Taking the formula suggested in Chapter Three,[11] the population should have averaged about 223 people. As 102 of these marriages took place in the second half of the century, it should also imply that the village was growing, but the first census figure of 1801 gives the number of residents as only 159. Childhood mortality, remained stubbornly high, at 27% of burials.

Due to the rigid settlement laws, itinerant workers were not welcome. Only nineteen baptisms were of children born to "travellers" or "strangers". These children could, in certain circumstances, have become a charge on the parish. Most had no surname, and in only one case was the name of the father given. A family with a pregnant wife was probably moved on pretty quickly. During the century, nineteen travelling people were buried. Most of these died during the harvest period, from July to September. With one exception, these deaths were of women and children.

Land ownership in the parish was in very few hands, and a high proportion of landlords lived outside the parish. The manor house owned the largest portion, but gentlemen, yeomen and husbandmen controlled well over half the acreage between them. Many families who had lived here for generations vanished from the parish records towards the end of the seventeenth century, mainly through lack of sons. By 1700, no Goddens, Hasells, Knights or Brabsons remained resident at Addington. With one last exception, the Watton name vanished in 1726, when Elizabeth married Leonard Bartholomew. Her Aunt Frances was buried here in 1739. New families moved into the yeomen's and cottagers' homes, either through purchase, through marriage to the female heirs or through taking a tenancy. These families were not as stable as during the mediaeval and early modern period. A few families, such as the Broads, Capons, Danes, Elliotts and Whitings remained for over two generations, but most were transient. Scarcely any were resident in the village for more than fifty years and a large number of couples moved on after a year or so. This shows that the settlement laws did not wholly prevent freedom of movement, especially as 44 couples baptised only one child here, but the practice of annual service contracts may have some bearing on the figures. Fear of censure seems to have ensured a moral society, as only 18 children from the settled families were born out of wedlock, six in the first half of the century and twelve during the second.

Of the 481 baptisms that took place, 127 surnames were given. 32 families accounted for 287 of these births, just less than 60% of the total number. As has been shown, it was rare for all to survive infancy. Five children were born to Thomas and Ann Colgate between 1717 and 1729 but all died. Female twins followed, in September 1731, but Anne died within a month. Although the twins' burial is not recorded, it is unlikely that they lived. Thomas Colgate, however,

remained for the rest of his life in the village and was 73 years old at his death on 4th September 1758. Five of the fifteen children with the surname of Cheesman failed to live beyond their second birthday. Cheesman's farm was later called Coldrum Farm. Of those baptised here between 1700 and 1799, 137 were also buried at Addington, but only 37 of these were adults.

The most enduring and numerous family had the surname Whiting, spelt also as Whighting or Whitting. The family came to the village during the last half of the sixteenth century, as the first baptism is recorded in 1572. Annis Whiting was married to William Petley in 1594, the first of a number of such contracts with their neighbours. No less than 33 Whiting baptisms took place during the eighteenth century, the parents being seven couples amongst this cousin-hood of yeomen and gentlemen. They intermarried with local families, such as Smith, Edmead, Hills, Rofe, Capon and Mills. Thomas Whiting (1764-1827), who was the local miller as well as being a substantial tenant farmer,[12] was married to Sarah Hills, daughter of Thomas Hills, the butcher. In 1821, she inherited land from her father, further extending their farm. Their son and grandson, also named Thomas, followed at the mill. The family's association with the village ended when the third Thomas Whiting left the village during the mid nineteenth century.[13] The 71st and last baptism of a Whiting child was that of Lot Whiting, son of Thomas and Harriet, in 1853, but they were at their most numerous during the eighteenth century. The final burial of a Whiting at Addington was that of a widow, Marie Whiting, aged 79, on 7th October 1862. She had been living at West Malling.

The parish continued to be financed through church rates. During the 1770's, over twenty families were liable for these, though others were exempt. Their names included Alchin, Featherstone, Pawley, Smith, Hills, Sutton, Bing, Brooker, Whiting and Wickenden. By 1800 only the Whitings and Smiths would still remain. As families died out, their homes were taken into the manor and occupied by its employees, rather than farmers in their own right.

Politics

The eighteenth century was not a democratic period, except at parish level. Firstly, very few people had the right to vote in national elections and secondly, scarcely any of these elections were contested in Kent. At the poll of 1734, only four men had the vote in the parish. Even the lady of the manor, Elizabeth Bartholomew, was denied this right, by reason of her sex. All four electors were termed "yeoman", and three were owner/occupiers of a freehold house and land at Addington: William Bing, George Hooker and Richard Pace (Paise), who had clearly improved in status since the death of his father only twelve years earlier. William Whitehead, the fourth elector, was listed as living at Boughton Malherbe, near Canterbury. Twenty years later William Bing was still an elector, but had moved to Boughton Monchelsea. However, a William Bing was buried here on 6th September 1769. In 1754, the franchise had grown to eight:

- William Bing, of Boughton Monchelsea. Tenant: William Harvey
- Rev. Thomas Buttonshaw, of Addington, by virtue of his tenure of the parsonage.
- Richard Whiting, of Trottiscliffe. Tenant: Richard Edwards
- James Edmead of Boughton Monchelsea. Tenant: Richard Mills
- William Whitehead, of Boughton Monchelsea. Tenant: T. Cheeseman
- George Pawley of Hadlow. House and land in hand.
- Philip Saxe and William Phillips, who were the only two voters who qualified as owners and occupiers of a freehold house and land in Addington.

Elizabeth, now Lady Twisden, and still the major landowner, remained debarred and her son, Leonard, though adult was not an Addington voter, as her land was under the control of her second husband. In the next century, the son of the house gained a vote, as his father made sure he held land within the parish in his own right.

By the time of the third contested election of the century, which took place in 1790, Leonard Bartholomew was the squire. He was, of course, by now a qualified elector and he was also the High Sheriff of Kent. That year the franchise had retreated again. Only four other men were entitled to vote, but they were now more locally based. Thomas Featherstone, yeoman, farmed at East Street, Stephen Capon farmed at Woodgate, James Lewis, gentleman, owned land in the parish but lived at Ryarsh. The fourth was the butcher and farmer, Thomas Hills. No reliable indication of the population of Addington can therefore be gleaned from the democratic process.

The new turnpikes

By the beginning of the eighteenth century, arrangements for the repair of roads were breaking down (as were the roads themselves). By the Statute of Highways of 1555, each parish was made responsible for road maintenance and repair, under the supervision of a reluctant and unpaid surveyor. He was expected to force local labour to give their time, and to pursue landowners if their hedges encroached on the highway or their ditches were not scoured. As the volume of long distance goods and human traffic increased, this system collapsed. Packhorses could not cope with the amount of freight being transported, but wagons and coaches bumped and sank on the dreadfully rutted or soggy roads. Landowners and local tradesmen petitioned Parliament for powers to create trusts to maintain stretches of road between towns. These became known as turnpikes. Each was run by a board of trustees with the ability to charge tolls for their use. The landowners advanced the original funds to pursue the Act of Parliament. They, as trustees, then improved, straightened and/or built the road and levied a mortgage on the Trust to recoup their costs.[14]

The first Kent turnpike trust was created in 1718 for

improving the road from Sevenoaks to Tunbridge Wells. By the end of the century Kent had 100 of these trusts, on average the length of road maintained being about 13 miles. The first Act of Parliament in relation to the road through Addington was presented in 1728.[15] This act created the Rochester to Maidstone turnpike and also included improvements to the "Lower Road" from Maidstone to Wrotham Heath. The petition asked for a 21 year lease for repairing and improving these two roads which: *"By reason of many heavy Carriages, and Passengers frequently passing through the same, are become very deep and ruinous (especially in the Winter Season) and many Parts thereof are so bad and narrow, that Passengers cannot pass and re-pass with danger."* 61 trustees were appointed, including Leonard Bartholomew, husband to Elizabeth Watton, and his brother, Philip Bartholomew of Oxonhoath. Other trustees were the main landowners along the two routes, plus the Mayor and Recorder of both Rochester and Maidstone. This was similar to contemporary and future petitions, though trustees could number up to 200 on a long stretch of turnpike. Luckily, the quorum that was needed to conduct business was between five and nine. Even so, as time went by, many meetings of this and its subsequent trusts could not raise a quorum and meetings were frequently postponed.

The 1728 Act allowed gates to be placed across the road, toll-houses to be constructed and tolls to be charged for every coach, berlin, chariot, calash, chaise or chair—the sum being one shilling if drawn by four or more horses, with reductions if fewer. A shilling was also charged for every wagon, wain, cart or carriage drawn by five or more horses or oxen, again with a reduction if

drawn by fewer. A penny was charged for every horse, mule or ass, laden or unladen, and appropriate amounts for driven oxen, cattle, calves, hogs, sheep or lambs. However, the intention was to charge passers through, rather than local people, who were exempt. Other exemptions were for soldiers and for those going to an election! The trust had fairly draconian powers to obtain the materials needed to mend the road and could dig gravel, chalk, sand or stones or cut furze from any nearby waste or common without paying for such materials. The power to charge neighbouring landowners who refused to maintain their trees or ditches remained as before. They were allowed to appoint salaried officers– treasurer, clerk and surveyor. These clauses were fairly standard for such a turnpike trust. A toll-gate was placed opposite the Royal Oak at Wrotham Heath and the beginning of this stretch of road.

It was expected that such roads, once built or upgraded, would look after themselves, and trusts were given a finite life of about 21 years. Not surprisingly, this was not the case, and the new roads rapidly began to fall into disrepair. Parishes no longer gave direct statute labour, but commuted their labour requirements by payments to the trusts. Quite soon, this became quite a contention as

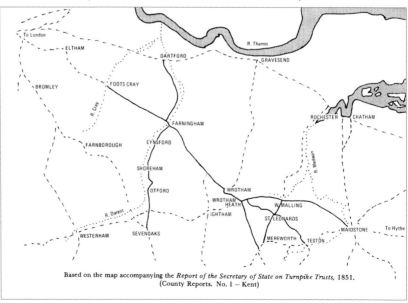

Based on the map accompanying the *Report of the Secretary of State on Turnpike Trusts*, 1851. (County Reports. No. 1 – Kent).

Key: ——— *Wrotham & Maidstone, Dartford and Sevenoaks* – – – *Other Kentish turnpike roads.*
From "Farningham Crossroads, A Study of two Kentish Turnpike Roads", p 6, by Shirley Burgoyne Black, Darenth Valley Publications, 1984

demands began to spiral. The obligation was eventually repealed by an Act of 1835.

As the years passed, this first trust came to the end of its permission and was replaced by means of a new Act. The heyday for trust creation was the 1750's and 1760's. The Maidstone to Wrotham Trust, which was created in 1752, (with 105 trustees, but still with a quorum of only five, seven or nine, depending on what business was discussed) applied to maintain and improve the road from Foots Cray to Wrotham Heath.[16] In 1759, a further Act allowed them to continue this road to Maidstone Bridge via Larkfield. During the 1770's this particular trust substantially built what is now the A20, bypassing the village. The attractive milestones along this road were installed at that time. A boundary map of 1810 shows that the road originally meandered into the park. It was later altered, as by the time of the 1843 tithe map, the entrance gate had been moved, a lodge built, and the road straightened at this point.[17] In 1795, the renewal act for this trust authorised the first part of Seven Mile Lane and in 1817 Teston Road began, as a southern route to Maidstone, through a further renewal.

Trustees changed as the years passed, but by virtue of his position, the squire of Addington was a trustee. Thus, Leonard Bartholomew was replaced by Elizabeth's second husband, Sir Roger Twisden, who was followed by the younger Leonard Bartholomew. He was, in turn, replaced by his son-in-law, Col. the Hon. John Wingfield-Stratford and lastly by his grandson, John Wingfield-Stratford Esq. The toll-house at Wrotham Heath, called the Royal Oak gate, was rebuilt in red brick in the early nineteenth century. It was later a private house until demolished in the late twentieth. Other gates were at Farningham, Comp, Yotes Court (at Mereworth crossroads), and Larkfield, but a traveller did not have to pay twice, as having obtained a ticket he passed freely through the all the gates. The road from Wrotham Heath to Sevenoaks was also turnpiked, so communications to and from Addington had improved dramatically by the end of the century. The Treasurer and Clerk of the Wrotham to Maidstone trust were, for well over fifty years, John Dudlow and his son, John Noble Dudlow, solicitors at West

Malling. They also served other local trusts. The surveyor, John Collis, of Birling, came from a family who acted as surveyors for a number of Kent highway trusts. He gave 27 years personal service to this particular one.

An Act of 1822 stipulated that public accounts should be produced and those for the Wrotham and Maidstone Turnpike Trust have been preserved at the County Archives. The first half year of this set of accounts was signed by an Addington resident as its chairman. This was the Rev. John Bosanquet Polhill, J.P., of St. Vincents. A chairman was appointed at each meeting from amongst those present and the accounts show that Addington's trustees regularly attended meetings, which were held at the Swan, West Malling. Both the Wingfield-Stratfords and their steward, William Brown of Westfields Farm, chaired meetings. When the trust was finally wound up in 1870, the final accounts were signed by John Wingfield-Stratford, the younger.

The demise of the trusts came through lack of business and/or debt, although the Wrotham to Maidstone trust was always solvent and had repaid all its borrowings. In fact, there was a residue and this was distributed amongst the parishes along the route. By the second half of the nineteenth century, mail and other freight had begun to be transported by rail, though the Bromley to Maidstone line did not open until 1874. However, these roads remained, and still remain the principal means of access to the village.

The church

The church building was not altered internally during the eighteenth century, except possibly by the installation of box pews, since lost. This was partly through having an absentee lady of the manor fron 1737 until she returned in 1772. Services concentrated on preaching, the rector would be in his pulpit, and the clerk would sit below. The system of paid for, allocated pews became common.

The treble bell that was recast by Matthew Bagley in 1710.

The treble bell was repaired in 1710, having survived since mediaeval times. It was sent to Matthew Bagley's bell foundry at Upper Moorfields, London. Bagley was not a Latin scholar, and he was notorious for failing to read old lettering correctly. He excelled himself over this one. It now reads: **ARISTVS : PARPATVA : DA : NOBIS : TAVDIX : VITA : MB FECIT 1710,** rather than: **CHRISTUS; PERPETUAE; DET; NOBIS; GAUDIA; VITAE (May Christ give to us the joys of everlasting life).** In 1732, a new foundation frame for six bells was installed at the church, but two extra bells were never purchased.

Some new memorials were added to the church, all installed in the second half of the century. A marble plaque was erected on the north wall, commemorating John Petley of Rochester, who had inherited land at Addington, Meopham and Nonnington from his father, Ralph Petley. Although it is unlikely that he spent much time here, he asked for his body to be buried in Addington Church *"in or near the seat which belongs or is appropriated to Woodgate Farm."* As this plaque is on the north side of the nave, this must have been where he sat. The family sold their large holding around Woodgate at the end of the century, but it is probable that Mrs. Petley lived in the village during her widowhood. A second, oval plaque was installed on the south wall of the nave in memory of Admiral William Parry (1705-1779), who spent his retirement in the village and had built a new home here. Given the previous

instruction, one might assume that Parry's seat was below this. It may have been after Lady Twisden's death in 1775 that her son, Leonard Bartholomew, arranged for the final tablets to be added to the Watton memorial at Addington church.

The church ministry

For almost the entire first half of the eighteenth century, Addington church was blessed with having John Boraston (1663-1741) as its rector. Rev. Boraston came from a clerical family. His grandfather and namesake was rector of Ribbesford, Worcester and a canon of Hereford Cathedral. George Boraston, his father, was rector of Hever, Kent. He inherited land in that parish. Boraston attended University College, Oxford, going up when only 16, and gaining his M.A. in 1687 at the age of 24. He remained at University College as one of its Fellows for a number of years. During this period, he was tutor to the historian John Thorpe, later a surgeon at Rochester, who collected ancient documents. These he edited and published as the Textus Roffensis. After a period as curate of Penshurst, Boraston was appointed rector of Addington by William Watton, in 1702. He was then 39. He subsequently served William's brother, Edmund, and Edmund's daughter, Elizabeth.

Rev. Boraston remained a bachelor and held no other benefices. In 1721, he presented a silver flagon to St. Margaret's, on which he placed his family's coat of arms and the inscription: *"Gloriae Dei Opt' Max'. In usum Ecclesiae Parochialis de Addington. Dat dicet Dedicatque Johannes Boraston A.M. Predictae Ecclesiae Rector Anno Dom' 1721"*[18]

It is reputed that John Boraston built the handsome rectory at Aldon. However, this is shown on a map of 1686, so perhaps he rebuilt an existing property. He became part of the local gentry and was a particular friend to Sir William Twysden of Roydon Hall, a cousin of Elizabeth's husband. (The Roydon family used a "y" in their name.) By his will of 6th September 1733, proved 26th October 1742, Rev. Boraston left

£5 to the poor of both Addington and Ryarsh. His will somewhat resembles that of the Rev. Thomas Dyne (d. 1453). Like Dyne, Boraston left books to his friends, a generous donation of £50 to his old Oxford college, and remembered his long-standing servant, May Varge, giving him £20 and his wearing apparel.

A handsome chest tomb, now a listed monument, was built over his grave in the churchyard. The eulogy inscribed on this in fine and deeply incised lettering

Addington churchyard. The chest tomb is beneath the yew tree, near to the obelisk memorial to Captain William Locker, R.N.

reads: *"Here lieth interred the Body of ye Revd J. Boraston, Fellow of University College in Oxford, and many yy Minister of this Parish. A Man truly learn'd, Charitable and Religious, Of a Temper Mild, Cheerful and Humane, For which while living he was beloved By all that Knew him. And when he died was by All lamented. He dyed June 9th 1741 aged 78 yrs."* He sounds a really nice old gentleman.

His successor was Thomas Buttonshaw (1707-1768), who was installed by Sir Roger and Lady Twisden. Rev. Buttonshaw did not move into Boraston's rectory at Aldon. Instead, he is known to have lived at The Vale on East Street. This had been the home of Rev. William Polhill during the seventeenth century, and the two men may have had a family connection. Thomas Buttonshaw came from a scholarly and clerical family. His ancestor, Rev. Robert Gunsley (d.1618), rector of Titsey, in Hampshire, had endowed four scholarships at University College, Oxford. The stipulation in the legacy was that the scholars should have attended either Rochester or Maidstone Grammar School and that preference should be given to his relatives. Both Thomas and a William Polhill, who was the headmaster of Maidstone Grammar School during the mid eighteenth century, were such scholars. Thomas was born at Cobham, Kent in 1708 and attended Maidstone Grammar School. After gaining

his M.A. at University College in 1731, he was ordained and became the vicar of St. Stephen's, Hackington and Holy Cross Church, Westgate, both in Canterbury. Whilst in Canterbury he served as a minor canon of the Cathedral. He came to Addington in 1741 and was given the living at Ryarsh the following year, both parishes being under the same patronage. He held both posts concurrently. His wife was Jane Wilkes, the daughter of a wealthy London merchant. The couple lived extremely comfortably, but had no children. By his will of 1763, proved with a codicil in 1768, he bequeathed land in Addington, Ryarsh, Shorne and elsewhere in Kent.

When Rev. Buttonshaw drafted his will, his wife was still alive and his bequests to her give an inventory of her bedroom. In it were

- bed and window curtains made of linen,
- a mattress, a feather bed, a bolster and two pillows,
- four blankets and a quilt,
- a carpet, five chairs and a close stool chair,
- a chest of drawers, a dressing table and looking glass,
- a washing stand, a stove, fender, fire pan, tongs and poker and
- the little chest of draws in the closet.

He also bequeathed to her his fire screen, his best set of china, a Japan (lacquered) tea board and tea chest and their silver plate. These last items show the increase of foreign trade. The English middle classes were now enjoying tea, china, silver, linen and lacquered ware.. Their food was no longer presented on pewter dishes.

Mrs. Buttonshaw died four years before her husband, so he wrote a codicil to benefit both their relatives. Numerous nephews and nieces received generous monetary bequests, jewellery and silver items such as sauceboats, mugs, candlesticks and a silver salver. His wife's jewellery was itemised in this codicil as a gold watch, diamond earrings, diamond buckles and two diamond rings. These bequests confirm that the couple were related by marriage to the Whitings, the Tomlyns and the Alchins, three well-established local families. Their chest tomb stood near to the obelisk. Inscribed on the top slab was a fulsome elegy noting his educational achievements and those of his forebears. Sadly, it fell into dangerous decay at the end of the 1980's and now only the top slab still remains, and its inscription is no longer legible. Without the work of amateurs who went to churchyards and transcribed such inscriptions during the twentieth century, we would have lost much of the heritage of tombstones.

The third, and final rector of Addington during the eighteenth century was Rev. Daniel Hill. He had been appointed vicar of East Malling in 1764 and four years later was given the living of Addington by his patrons, Sir Roger and Lady Twisden. He remained incumbent of both parishes until his death in 1805. Rev. Hill was a Fellow of All Soul's College, Oxford and came from another distinguished clerical family, his namesake having been Dean and Prebendary of Rochester Cathedral during the late seventeenth century. However, he rarely visited the parish, unless to be given a dinner (at a stable cost of 3s 6d) when he presided over the annual vestry meeting. The care of his parishioners was undertaken by his almost equally long-serving curate, James Thurston, the vicar of Ryarsh. Rev. Thurston, who attended Tonbridge School and King's College, Rochester, was a Fellow of Queen's College, Oxford. His institution at Ryarsh was at the same time as his rector's at Addington, and he took over as curate in 1760. Rev. Thurston was

a conscientious minister, conducting every wedding but one during his tenure. He died in 1802.

Parish administration

The churchwarden's accounts survive from 1763/4. Each warden served one year and the post was undertaken in rotation by the gentlemen and yeomen of the parish. The warden had to account for all his expenditure, and make up any deficiencies at the end of the year from his personal pocket. In 1763/4, the churchwarden was William Bing, perhaps a relative of the seventeenth century steward, Laurence Bing. His vestry consisted of Richard Whiting, George Pawley and Thomas Whiting. The next year Nicholas Lambert took over from Bing, who reverted to being a vestry member. Richard and Thomas Whiting then took the post in succession, but Thomas Featherstone then joined the group. And so it went on. As there were so few educated men in the village, this was a necessity and some had to serve more than once during their lifetime.

The receipts from the assessment (or Cess as it was known) for 1765/6 were £9 12s 6d, but by 1782/3 the figure had risen quite substantially, to £16 1s 1$\frac{1}{2}$d. Regular expenditure was typical of a small parish of the time, the bells had to be oiled, bell ropes purchased, bread and wine provided for three masses a year, and even writing up the assessment for levying the taxes cost one shilling. New prayer books were bought, *"a hook on the church gate"*, and in 1787/8, a Mr. Comfort was paid for painting the church. The following year prayer books were again purchased, this time "for His Majestie" at a cost of two shillings. A special thanksgiving service appears to have been held to celebrate his recovery from his long bout of illness, as two shillings more were paid *"To thanks given to his Majestie".*

The salary for William Smith, the long serving Parish Clerk was £5 per annum, plus minor disbursements. In common with other parishes, national legislation had to be taken into account. The churchwardens recorded payments for hedgehogs and sparrows, in accordance with a directive whose origins lay in the sixteenth century. The heads had to be presented and payment must be made from the church rate. These payments continued into the nineteenth century, and seem to have been a source of income for boys. In 1798, payments were made for 27 hedgehogs (including 8 young) and 251 sparrows.

The Poor Laws meant that travellers must hold a pass to show that they would not become a charge on the parish they were passing through. Thus in 1765/6 six pence each was given to *"a Wooman With a Pass"* *"A Man with a Pass"*, and a *"Great Beled Wooman"*. However, *"Brushon (sweeping) the church lane"* cost a shilling and *"mendon (repairing) the church windos"* 1/7d—these jobs cost a shilling more between them than charity to strangers. Addington does not appear to have been a soft touch, as such payments are recorded only rarely. The accounts of the Overseers of the Poor are unfortunately long lost, as these would have given a better picture of the care given to people when they fell on hard times in the parish that century.

Periodically, the church needed repairs, and an extra amount was put on the Cess to pay for these. In 1768/9, 800 roof tiles were ordered at a cost of £6 15s 0d, and John Oliver then installed them for a further £4 0s 4d. The mortar for these required lime, sand and two bushels of charcoal for burning the lime. The Cess of 1769/70 gives the names of only seventeen resident householders who were chargeable for church rates, fifteen men and two women. A further eleven people were charged as "out-dwellers" and the amount raised in total was £14 6s 1d. Only four of these landholders paid more than £1. The tenant at the manor house was Admiral William Parry, who had arrived in the parish shortly before the accounts begin. He paid £2 12s 6d, which was the largest amount.

That year, repairs were made to the church, as the churchwarden

"paid for lime, sand,
fetching a load of timber,
one day's work with a teame,
a fetching of timber and another day's work,
paid myself for beer for massions (masons)
paid for new bell stops."

3,500 plain tiles, 20 ridge tiles and 12 corner tiles were needed in 1781/2, plus lime, sand, water etc., implying a major refit. The actual materials must have been paid for by Mr. Bartholomew, the squire, as the accounts only write of "fechin" them. Even so, the charge that year rose to £19 4s 1d.

Addington's naval connections

During the eighteenth century, the Royal Navy became a major industry in the north of Kent. Many of the nation's ships were built at Chatham, benefiting from the Thames Estuary and the plentiful supply of oak in the Weald. Naval wars generated significant capital for senior officers, as they were entitled to a share of the "prize money" from captured enemy vessels. There was a great incentive to go for merchant vessels instead of confronting warships. There was some justification, of course, as they were carrying supplies to aid the enemy. By the time they retired from active service, many captains and admirals had accumulated enough wealth to build a pleasant home and many chose to remain in Kent. Admiral Sir Francis Geary was one of these. Through marriage, he and his descendants came into possession of Ford Place and Oxonhoath, and he played an important role in the lives of Lady Twisden's family. Another incomer was Admiral William Parry, whose son-in-law became a lifelong friend of Admiral Nelson.

Admiral William Parry (1705-1779)

Whilst Lady Twisden was living at East Malling, Admiral Parry, who had recently retired from active service in the West Indies, leased her manor house and lived there with his wife and daughter, Lucy. Mrs. Parry was one of

Vice Admiral William Parry, (1705-1779), by J.F. Rigaud. © National Maritime Museum, London

two daughters who were co-heirs of Commodore Charles Brown, Commissioner of the Navy at Chatham.[19] For most of his career Admiral Parry was a fairly undistinguished naval officer, who failed to be present at any of the outstanding battles of the mid eighteenth century, through illness or mischance. He was one of Admiral Byng's captains when Byng drew back from decisive follow on action after the Battle of Minorca in 1756, and Parry's career was blighted by this.[20] He was denied promotion for many years and was the longest serving captain in the fleet for some time. Eventually his career progressed and, in 1762, he attained the rank of Vice-Admiral and became Commander in Chief of Jamaica and the Windward Islands. This position entitled him to a portion of any prize money won in that theatre of war.

His family joined him in the West Indies and it was there that Lucy met another naval officer, Lieutenant William Locker. Locker was not a wealthy man, as he came from a literary and professional background. His father, Stephen Locker, was Clerk to the Leathersellers Livery Company. His maternal uncle, Benjamin Stillingfleet, was a writer and intellectual. Stillingfleet had lived at Felbrigg Hall in Norfolk as companion to the Wyndham heir, and when William expressed a "violent" desire to go to sea at the age of

fifteen, Stillingfleet found him the patronage of a Wyndham relative. However, his career had taken some time to progress, partly because at the end of the Seven Years War there was a period of peace in Europe, during which he was forced to join the merchant navy. William was sixteen years older than his wife, a cheerful man, described by his family as apple cheeked. He was lame from a leg wound sustained in a successful assault on a French ship in his early career. Despite the difference in their ages, the couple were drawn to each other, and her family supported a potential alliance. However, William and Lucy's courtship lasted eight years, being dependant on Lucy having an independent income, and/or Locker gaining promotion. These two events happened in the summer of 1770. The first catalyst was a happy one, as William gained his promotion and his first independent command. The second was sadder, as Mrs. Parry died and her marriage portion devolved upon her daughter. William and Lucy Locker were married at St. Margaret's church on 20th October 1770. Locker then returned to sea, and Lucy remained at Addington Place with her father. Their first child, named Lucy after both her mother and grandmother, was born in Addington and baptised at St. Margaret's on 11th August 1771.

When Lady Twisden was widowed and returned to her old home, she sold a piece of land to Admiral Parry near to Addington brook on which stood an old farmhouse. He converted this into a classic Georgian home, which he named Addington Brook House. Whilst this was being constructed, between 1773-1775, James Maddan thought that the Admiral rented a house called the Mount, and that this stood due south of his new home, but I cannot identify this. Admiral Parry moved into his new home in 1775, as this date is recorded on its first fire insurance certificate from the Sun Insurance Company. He enjoyed four years at Addington Brook House and died there at the end of April 1779. He was buried in St. Margaret's and commemorated by the marble plaque on the south wall mentioned earlier. Meanwhile Captain Locker pursued his career, and his family increased by five more children, of whom four survived. They were William (1773), John (1774), Elizabeth (1776) and Edward Hawke (1777).

On their inheritance of St. Vincents, Captain and Mrs. Locker commissioned a painting of their family home by a distinguished naval artist, Dominic Serres. This shows the couple and their children standing on the driveway. Serres had already painted Locker's portrait in 1768 when he gained his first command.[21] Locker had also commissioned a family portrait in 1779 by Jean François Rigaud that shows Mrs. Locker to have been a very attractive woman. She also seems to have had a kind and loveable personality. She certainly made a very good impression on young Horatio Nelson, who described her as "amiable" in the true sense of the word.

Addington Brook House, as it was called until renamed St. Vincents in 1798. By Dominic Serres, R.A. © the Yale Center for British Art, New Haven, Connecticut

Their marriage was shattered only a year after they had moved to Addington Brook House. In April 1780 Mrs. Locker died in childbirth, leaving five children and a distraught husband. She was buried in Addington churchyard. Although Locker was naturally a man of cheerful disposition, this was a devastating blow. He took Lucy's death very badly,

and, years later, tears would still come to his eyes as he spoke of her. He also lost his home through her death. By the terms of Admiral Parry's will, Locker was forced to grant a lease on Addington Brook House, to provide for the upbringing of the children. However, he remained a very stable force in their lives. They were put into the care of his unmarried sister and lived at East Malling. When in Kent, he took lodgings in Swan Street, West Malling so that he could be near them.

The Locker family, painted in about 1779 by J.F. Rigaud. From "Conversation Pieces" by Sacheverall Sitwell, Batsford Books, 1936

Locker's friendship with Admiral Nelson

A few years earlier, in 1777, Lieutenant Horatio Nelson, then aged 18, joined Captain Locker's ship, the H.M.S. Lowestoffe, when it was being kitted out for a voyage to the West Indies. The two men became firm friends, despite the twenty-seven year difference in their ages. William Locker widened young Nelson's horizons and introduced him to art, literature and politics. He encouraged Nelson to have his portrait painted whilst the young man was in London organising the impress of men for the ship. This painting, by Locker's preferred portraitist at that time, J.F. Rigaud, now hangs at the National Maritime Museum. However, on its completion three years later, following Nelson's return to London, it was given to Locker. By then the uniform had to be changed to that of a post-Captain, but the face remained that of a teenager.

Just after they arrived in the West Indies, Locker fell seriously ill with malaria and had to be put ashore at Port Royal, Jamaica. He asked Nelson, rather than a senior officer, to deal with his affairs should he not survive. The following letter shows the friendship and mutual esteem that the two men had already established.

"Lowestoffe, at Sea, August 12th 1777

My most worthy friend,

I am exceedingly obliged to you for the good opinion you entertain of me, and will do my utmost that you may have no occasion to change it. I hope God Almighty will be pleased to spare your life, for your own sake, and that of your family: but should anything happen to you (which I sincerely pray God, may not) you may be assured that nothing shall be wanting on my part for the taking care of your effects and delivering them safe to Mrs. Locker such of them as may be thought proper not to be disposed of. You mentioned the word "consolation", in your letter – I shall have a very great one, when I think I have served faithfully the best of friends, and the most amiable of women.

All the services I can render to your family, you may be assured shall be done, and shall never end but with my life; and may God Almighty of his great goodness keep, bless, and preserve you, and your

Post-Captain Horatio Nelson, R.N., by J.F. Rigaud. © National Maritime Museum, London

Captain William Locker, R.N., by Gilbert Stuart © National Maritime Museum, London

family, is the most fervent prayer.
Of your faithful servant,
HORATIO NELSON

p.s. Though this letter is not couched in the best manner be assured it comes from one entirely devoted to your service. H.N."

Once he had recovered, Locker encouraged Nelson to hone his skills. On their third sortie out of Port Royal, the Lowestoffe captured a schooner, a small sleek type of ship of about 100 tons, capable of carrying about 75 men and eight guns. Locker renamed the schooner the Little Lucy, after his wife and daughter and gave Nelson command of it, showing his confidence in the young man. Nelson was delighted and took full advantage of this opportunity to command men, and as navigator. However, Captain Locker's health was still poor, and having recommended Horatio Nelson to Admiral Peter Parker, the new commander-in-chief for Jamaica, in 1779 he returned to England, where he lived in semi-retirement. From then on, the two men never sailed together again, but they corresponded for the rest of Locker's life. As Locker kept all these letters, an insight has been preserved into Nelson's early life at sea. Their correspondence spanned Nelson's wilderness years in Norfolk, when he would supply Locker with turkeys, and Nelson visited him at West Malling.

Locker was brought out from retirement to head the impress service at Exeter during 1787 and he was appointed commander-in-chief at the Nore, off Sheerness, in Kent, at the age of 62, in 1792, holding the rank of Commodore, a temporary title just under the rank of Admiral. He retired from active service in 1793 and was fortunate to be appointed Lieutenant Governor of Greenwich

Hospital. From this position he introduced Nelson to his political friends, many of whom were naval officers. For a time, Nelson considered whether to enter parliament himself. However, naval duties reclaimed him, for the greater benefit of the country. Locker continued to follow his career from Greenwich and rejoiced as Nelson became involved in the great victories of the time. Another of Locker's close friends was his contemporary, Admiral Sir John Jervis (1735-1823). In February 1797, Admiral Jervis wrote to him delightedly from his stateroom in the great "Victory", then lying off the coast of Portugal:

> "Victory" Lagos Bay, 11 Feb 1797
> My Dear Locker,
> I know you will be desirous of a line from me, and though I have not time to give you anything like details I cannot resist telling you that your "élève" Commodore Nelson received the swords of the Commander of a first-rate and eighty gun ship of the enemy on their respective quarter decks.
> John Jervis"

This was the great battle of Cape St. Vincent, when Nelson disobeyed orders and broke the line to cut between the enemy, to great effect, securing the victory. He carried out the amazing feat of personally capturing two ships in one action. Jervis was elevated to the peerage as Earl St. Vincent because of this victory and Nelson received promotion. It seems likely that it was in honour of this that Locker's Addington house was renamed St. Vincents, as it is called this a year later by Edward Hasted in his history of Kent, whilst its former name is also given.

Later that year Nelson sustained the loss of his arm at Tenerife and, whilst he was recovering in London, Locker persuaded him to sit for a second portrait. The public by then was clamouring for a new likeness, and a print made from Locker's early portrait of Nelson by Rigaud had sold well, despite being very inaccurate, as the print maker had simply guessed how the years had changed the hero's face. Nelson came to Locker's rooms at Greenwich Hospital to sit for Lemuel Abbott, a somewhat eccentric portraitist, but one who produced a number of iconic portraits from this sitting.[22] The first of these, which was

Admiral Horatio Nelson by Lemuel Abbott. © National Maritime Museum, London. Nelson sat for this portrait at Locker's rooms at Greenwich Hospital. This is the triumphant version.

given to Locker himself, depicts a man suffering from the pain that came from the slow healing wound. As the portrait was reworked, signs of this pain were erased, the costume became more elaborate and, in the final version, the hero emerged triumphant. Locker's daughter, Elizabeth, was by then his housekeeper and she was very pleased to be able to help the great man to remove his heavy coat for the sitting.

Nelson continued to correspond with his ageing friend. In Locker's penultimate year, he wrote a letter that shows the bonds of affection between them:

> "Palermo, 9 Feb 1799
> Dear Friend,
> I well know your own goodness of heart will make all due allowances for my present situation, and that truly I have not the time or power to answer all the letters I receive at the moment. But you, my old friend, after twenty-seven years acquaintance, know that nothing

can alter the attachment and gratitude to you. I have been your scholar. It is you who taught me to board a French man-of-war by your conduct when in the Experiment. It is you who always said "Lay a Frenchman close, and you will beat him." and my only merit in my profession is being a good scholar. Our friendship will never end but with my life, but you have always been too partial to me...."

Locker died in London on 26th December 1800 and his body was brought down to Addington for burial. Nelson attended his funeral, rising at 5 a.m. in Mayfair to travel to Greenwich and then follow the coffin down to Kent. The following December, in a letter to a friend, Nelson wrote how low he felt as it was the anniversary of Locker's death. A striking obelisk was later installed in Addington churchyard in memory of Captain William Locker, which incorporated the gravestone of his beloved wife, Lucy. Locker's youngest son, Edward Hawke Locker, became Civil Commissioner to Greenwich Hospital in the early nineteenth century. He took forward a proposal that Locker had made to the governing body of the Hospital, that a collection of naval paintings be hung in the Painted Hall there. This collection was founded with the support and generosity of King George IV, who presented paintings from his own collection. Locker's paintings were also amongst the first to be donated. This collection eventually became part of the National Maritime Museum. William Locker, resident of Addington, left a broad and important legacy to the nation.

A snapshot of the parish at the end of the century

K ent is fortunate in having a very detailed description of its communities at the end of the eighteenth century. Edward Hasted, the county historian, was a gentleman of leisure who published his first edition of the History and Topographical Survey of Kent between 1778 and 1780. Unfortunately, his efforts bankrupted him.

When he later enlarged this between 1797 and 1801, he used the help of researchers, as he himself was in the debtor's prison for part of this time. The second edition contains detailed topographical descriptions of the villages and towns in the county. Addington is described as a pleasant and comfortable community, on poor sandy soil, underlaid by quarry rock, with a stream (which still contains numerous trout) and some interesting buildings, including the church. It mentions the new turnpike road and how the land rises past the manor house (now gone) to the church and village green.

"The Parish of Addington is not unpleasantly situated, for the greatest part on high ground, adjoining to the northern side of the Maidstone road, at the twenty-seventh mile stone, at a small distance from which is the small rivulet which rises at Nepecker, in Wrotham, and flowing through this parish is here called Addington brook, whence the new built house takes its name of St. Vincents, alias Addington Brook. ..... At a small distance above it is the mansion and garden of Addington place, pleasantly situated on the side of the hill, having a lawn and avenue down to the road, from which it is a conspicuous object, behind it still higher stands the church and village, built round Addington green, over which the road leads from Trottescliffe, to which and Wrotham, this parish joins towards the west. The soil is sand covering the quarry rock, but the land is most of it but poor and infertile, especially towards the north and west parts of it, where the sand is deepest; in the latter is a small green called Addington common.

"Here is an eelbourn, which breaks out with great impetuosity once in seven or eight years, which then directs its waters along a trench, dug for this purpose, till it flows into the Leybourne rivulet, the trout of which it makes of a red colour, which otherwise are white.

"In a place here, called The Warren, about 500 paces north-eastward from the church on a little eminence, there are the remains of several large stones... The sandiness of the soil has covered many of them. ... About 130 paces to the northwest of the above is another heap of large stones, tumbled inwards one upon another."

After a lengthy discourse on the history of the manor,

which I have drawn on when researching the mediaeval period, Hasted gave the value of the rectorial tithes at £61 6s 8d., with the yearly tenths at 12s 8d. For comparison, Trottiscliffe was valued at only £10 2s 11d but its tenths were higher, at £1 0s 3½d.

The village today is easily recognisable from Hasted's description. The soil remains so infertile that no crops are now grown upon it, though the sand is a bonus as an industry and for the golf course. The mansion house is sadly no longer the "conspicuous object" described above, but the church, the green, the streams and the stones still survive and the open aspect has been maintained. The future would have looked reasonably bright for the elderly resident squire and his wife, for their daughter and her husband, and for the thirty other families living in the village. The nineteenth century, however, would see the disappearance of the last small freeholders, and the new squire would take their land into his manorial estate. There would be crop changes and further improvements in agriculture. The village population would slowly grow and, towards the end of the century, a fundamental change in ownership would take place, as a descendant of the Watton family sold his five hundred-year-old inheritance.

---

1   Katherine Watton (b. 1461) married a William Peckham, and had left issue. An earlier William Watton had conveyed the manor of Caustons to a Reginald Peckham during the fifteenth century, and a Hadlow rental roll of 1581 confirms that the Peckham family were in possession of the manor at that date. Hasted notes that the two families were of the same root as those in Wrotham. In the event, Reginald Peckham (d. 1713) was the last of his line at Yaldham, leaving only two daughters and his mansion house deteriorated into a farmhouse. When William Watton died, Peckham signed the affidavit for his burial.

2   Arch. Cant Vol. V, p 95. The article starting on p 87 is headed: A Chapter of County Gossips. Isabella Twisden was daughter of Francis Twisden, a younger son of Thomas Twisden of Roydon. The letter is also quoted in "The Family of Twysden and Twisden", by Sir John Ramskill Twisden, 12th and last baronet of Bradbourne, 1939

3   As the succession was by virtue of his father's will, Edmund Watton did not write one himself. Anne Watton was therefore granted the administration of his estate by the courts, so was called the administratrix rather than the executrix.

4   At the Hearth Tax return of 1664 a Philip Bartholomew was living at Middle Borough, Rochester, in a home with 12 hearths, two more than the manor house at Addington possessed at that date.

5   His second wife, whom he married in 1725, was Mary Thomas. They had one daughter, who became the wife of Admiral, Sir Francis Geary.

6   Leonard was baptised on 7th July 1728 at St. Margaret's church, Addington.

7   John was named after his godfather, Philip Papillon, of East Malling, a close friend of his father. He inherited his godfather's estate in 1762. It was worth £400-450 p.a. Not a huge amount, but enough to encourage him not to take up employment.

8   During WWII Teston Road was stopped up when West Malling airfield came into operation, so the road to Maidstone now turns south down the A228 before turning east again on the A26.

9   Powerscourt House and Gardens are now open to the public. The house was gutted by a fire in 1974, and was restored as a tourist attraction. It boasts 47 acres of gardens, shops, etc. and is open for weddings and other events.

10   It is possible that these were built by Mr. Tomlyn. In 1780, he held two parcels in this area, and within a few years, he had one tenant, Joseph Selby, liable for £3 rent and four further tenants liable for only £1 each.

11   Average the number of marriages over a period, then multiply by 125. However 223 seems too high a number.

12   Land Tax records show that he was the tenant at Woodgate of the Petley family of Rochester, but this land was later incorporated by Leonard Bartholomew into the Addington estate. This is probably where he lived.

13   Thomas Whiting 3rd, (b 1822) moved with his young family to North Kent where he worked in the cement industry. Both he and his son were designated, rather appropriately, "cement miller" in the censuses.

14   Lucas, K., Kentish Turnpikes, Arch. Cant, Vol. 100, 1984, pp 345-369

15   1 Geo II chapter 12, pp 515-539, 1728. A copy of this is held at K.L.H.C.
     1625 Geo II c[hap].8 (1752) and that called 33 Geo. II c40 (1759)

17   This was probably done in the early 1830's when Colonel Wingfield Stratford was establishing his park. This gate was closed when the golf course was built during the 1970's and the lodge house was then enlarged.

18   To the Glory of God on High: Property of the Parish Church of Addington. Given and dedicated by John Boraston, M.A., and Rector of the said parish. AD 1721.

19   A post that Samuel Pepys had held in the seventeenth century. The position was also lucrative, as the Commissioner had the use of the build money before ships were completed. Mrs. Parry and her sister inherited a number of properties in the Chatham area.

20   Admiral John Byng was subsequently court-martialled. He was executed on the deck of HMS Monarch six months later for "failing to do his utmost" to prevent Minorca falling to the French after the battle. In practice, his ships had badly needed repair and he had been relieved of his command before he could secure the extra forces he required.

21   These two paintings are unique in the work of Dominic Serres, as all his other paintings are of ships and naval battles. This demonstrates that the two men must have also been friends. Serres was a founder member of the Royal Academy, the only naval painter to be given this privilege.

22   Lemuel Abbott (1760-1802) rarely agreed to leave his studio, so he was giving Nelson a special honour by coming to Greenwich for the sitting. His mental health was a problem, and, in 1798, the year after painting these outstanding portraits, he was declared insane. He never fully recovered, and died in 1802.

5

1800 - 1850 - The late GEORGIAN and early VICTORIAN PERIOD

Col. William Mudge conducted the first ordnance survey of England at the end of the eighteenth century, and despite inaccuracies his map of Addington shows clearly the road network and buildings in the village. The roads and footpaths differ slightly from the modern layout, but the layout of the buildings is recognisable. The turnpike ran through the south of the village and each milepost is marked on Mudge's map. A bend in its line formerly veered into the Park and a road then led in a northerly direction across the park towards St. Vincents Lane/Park Road. One access to the mansion house was via an avenue and a small bridge over Addington brook.

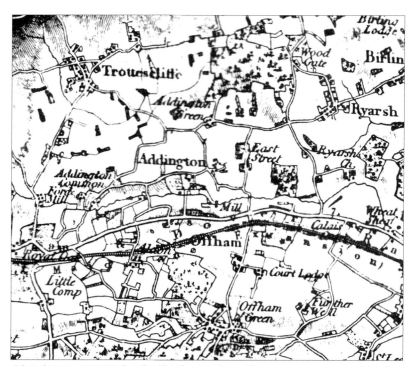

Col. Mudge's Map 1819, 1" to the mile with Railway as a later edition.

St. Vincents, Hedgehogs and Westfields can all be seen on this map, as can the group of houses and cottages on the Green. More are drawn at East Street, Woodgate and Aldon. There are some discrepancies, though. Addington Common is marked in the wrong place, north of Westfields, rather than to the west of East Street. Addington Green is in the correct place, but its logo is too far north.

An almost contemporary map, sketched by Rev. Elers in about 1806, as an adjunct to a perambulation of the parish bounds, shows a similar road pattern. The perambulation, no doubt with boys beating each tree, stone or bridge, started opposite the Vale in East Street and, heading south, crossed the turnpike road. Then, in a somewhat jerky manner as it took in the vagaries of the bounds around Aldon, it continued round the parish, up to Woodgate Road, then to the Downs, and thence back to the Vale. 123 trees and distinctive features were recorded. The road northwards across the park is clearly marked on this map. A second access to the mansion house from the turnpike road is designated a "walk". This "walk" follows the present line of the footpath from Hernewell to the recreation ground. It was for centuries the main route that people took from Aldon to the centre of the village.

Map sketched by Rev. Peter Elers for a perambulation of the bounds in 1806.

The succession of the manor

In 1800, Leonard and Frances Bartholomew celebrated their silver wedding, but Mrs. Bartholomew died in September the following year. Mr. Bartholomew was aged 73, an elderly widower, with no grandchildren, although his only daughter, Frances, had been married to John Wingfield for two and a half years.

The Hon. John Wingfield was the second son, and the elder of twins, of Richard, 3rd Viscount Powerscourt and his wife, Amelia Stratford. He was a man of property. In 1788, aged 15, he inherited from his father the Wingfield estates of Robertstown, Co. Limerick, and Wingfield Lodge, Ennistimon, Co. Clare. In 1802, he came into possession of further land in Co. Wicklow and London through the death of his eccentric and quarrelsome maternal uncle, Edward Stratford, 2nd Earl of Aldborough.[1] Aldborough, a bachelor, thoroughly disliked most of his family and in particular his younger brother, who would inherit the earldom. He therefore willed away all his "unsettled" estate to his nephew. This included a new town called Stratford-upon-Slaney[2] in Co. Wicklow and a small development just north of Oxford Street, London, that he named Stratford Place. Aldborough had built himself a London mansion on this, Stratford House.[3] In recognition of this dubious generosity, and in order to benefit from the bequest, in 1803, John Wingfield took the additional name of Stratford by deed poll. It is likely that he and his wife used Stratford House as their main residence until they inherited

Addington manor, and it remained their London home. All three children were born there, though each child was brought in turn to St. Margaret's to be christened.

Leonard Bartholomew celebrated his eightieth birthday on 15th June 1808. By this time, the Wingfield-Stratfords had a daughter. Frances Amelia was born on 9th January that year, ten years into their marriage. Perhaps, as a serving officer, Wingfield-Stratford had been out of the country for much of this time, especially as the period was one of European conflict, though I have been unable to confirm this. Their second daughter, Isabella Harriett, was born on 28th October 1809, by which time Wingfield-Stratford had achieved the rank of Colonel. Leonard Bartholomew died less than a year later and was buried on 27th October 1810 at Addington. His short will left a specific legacy of £1,000 to his *"eldest grand-daughter"*, Frances Amelia, but Isabella got nothing.

Having specified bequests to his housekeeper and his bailiff, Mr. Bartholomew left the residue of his real and personal estate to his son-in-law, whom he appointed his sole executor, and thereafter to John's heirs, assigns, etc. This shows that the entail that began with William Watton (4)'s will had finally ended. Leonard Bartholomew did not live to celebrate the birth of his grandson and eventual heir. John Wingfield-Stratford was born on 10th December 1810, two months after his grandfather's death, and was named after his father.

In early 1811, Col. Wingfield-Stratford, his wife and three small children settled into the manor house. His first priority, it seems, was to enhance the environment around Addington Place. He began to purchase more land within the village, as this became available. When one of his tenant farmers moved or died, he took that land in hand. The Land Tax records demonstrate this. Although they are missing for the years between 1808 and 1811, by 1812 Col. Wingfield-Stratford's liabilities covered fifteen parcels of land, as opposed to the nine charged to his father-in-law. Land Tax records show that the liabilities of Leonard Bartholomew had amounted to just over a third of the value of Addington, being principally the

park, home farm, the mill, the Angel public house and land at Woodgate. His holdings only covered 167 acres, about a fifth of the land area, according to another source, a rectorial tithe book kept by the rector, which is described below.

Three holdings were now brought "in hand", annotated as *"himself, late Golding"* (at Aldon), *"himself, late Hooker"* and *"himself, late Sutton"* (both at East Street). Wingfield-Stratford also acquired the complex of cottages in East Street, now known as Lomar, Carolcot and White cottages, from John Larking, of Clare House, East Malling.[4] Larking had bought these from the Tomlyn family, who inherited the Vale from Rev. Thomas Buttonshaw. Later in the decade, Col. Wingfield-Stratford extended the park, by purchasing some land near Plowenders Bridge (then known as Frowenders) in Offham parish. It was perhaps at this time that the mansion became known as Addington Park. During the 1820's, he continued this process, as yeoman farmers died or sold up. More acreage came under the direct management of the estate, including land in the East Street area, previously farmed by Thomas Whiting, senior, and James Pankhurst.

Addington Village

The area of the parish remained approximately 940 acres. Some small pieces of ground within its bounds were still detached parts of Ryarsh. The Land Tax for 1807 gives the names of 22 land-holders liable for this tax in the parish, including the squire. Only four of these, Thomas Hills, Thomas Featherstone, William Smith and John Wells were resident farmers. Some of the non-resident proprietors were major landowners in the county. Thomas Whittaker, of Barming Place, owned land near Coldrum, as part of his holdings in Trottiscliffe. Sir William Geary, of Oxonhoath, owned Ford Place and its farm.[5] Although this lay mostly in Wrotham, some of its land stood in Addington parish. Hedgehogs Farm was also in Sir William's ownership. Henry Nevill, 2nd Earl Abergavenny, held woodland in north Addington, adjacent to Ryarsh wood. The

Nevill family still hold this, but it is now part of Trottiscliffe.

The population was recorded in the first census of 1801 as 159. At that time the village probably contained about 30 houses and cottages. From the steady number of people liable for the Land Tax, it seems that little building had taken place over the past quarter century. Cottages were clustered around the Green, or stood at East Street, Woodgate and Aldon. Others were associated with the outlying farmsteads. During the first half of the century, new homes were built or extended. Some, though, were little more than huts, and have since been demolished. The shop on the Green opened, and a carpenter was working nearby. By the time of the 1841 census, 44 homes lay within the parish boundaries.

Population growth

The census table below shows that Addington's population grew from 159 to 228 by 1821, before dropping back. It had recovered to 220 in 1851. The 1841 census, the first to give personal names and occupations, recorded 208 residents, living in 43 homes, with another cottage standing empty. However, the true figure may not have declined significantly. Both Addington Park and St. Vincents housed only caretakers that night. Ten years later, at the 1851 census, the Wingfield-Stratford family were at Addington Park with fourteen servants, but the same caretakers, Joseph and Sarah Danes, remained at St. Vincents.

Year		Male	Female	Totals
1801	32*	NK	NK	159
1811	32*	NK	NK	203
1821	?	113	115	228
1831	?	NK	NK	206
1841	44	113	95	208
1851	44	107	113	220

*Estimate from the 1819 tithe survey by Rev. Elers

Land use in the early 19th century

From taxation records, it is possible to ascertain the crops grown in Addington during the early nineteenth century. In 1805, Rev. Peter Elers began to record the rectorial tithes due to him, and his small book has survived as part of the material on Addington in the Kent History and Library Centre.[6] It notes the names of tithe payers, the crops on which the tithes were based and the charge per acre. The Tithe assessment of 1843 also records the crops grown in each field.

The first entries in the rectorial tithe book show a parish where most of the land was put down to arable and pasture, hops being grown on only a small acreage, 30 out of 553. However, the value of hops to the rector was much higher than all cereals, except for wheat, at twelve shillings per acre. About four hundred acres are unaccounted for, so must have been woodland, waste, roads, houses and gardens. Credit was given where land was unproductive. Rev. John Bosanquet Polhill, of St. Vincents, paid only four pence an acre *"his land being bad."* Later in the century, about twelve acres of St. Vincents land were planted as woodland.

The statement that went with the boundary map that Rev. Elers drew at the turn of the nineteenth century notes eleven types of tree and shrub that were boundary markers. These were alder, ash, beech, blackthorn, buckthorn, hawthorn, hazel, holly, maple, oak, whitethorn and willow. All these still grow within the current village. Missing from these markers were both sweet and horse chestnut, and any conifer. Sweet chestnut, however, would soon be widely planted, because of the burgeoning hop industry. Those most likely to have been pollarded were ash, maple and willow.

When Mr. Henley and Mrs. Sheaf were about to quit their land, Rev. Elers agreed that each should "compound", i.e. give him the monetary value, rather than a tenth of the actual crops. From these two records, it is noticeable that the two farms were very similar, but that Mrs. Sheaf grew more hops and wheat on her land, so she paid a slightly higher rate.

Name of farmer	Crop	Acreage	Tithe per acre	Total payable
Mr. Henley	Hops	4	12 shillings	£2 8s 0d
	Wheat	3	10 shillings	£1 10s 0d
	Barley	18^1/$_2$	7 shillings	£6 9s 6d
	Beans	2^1/$_2$	7 shillings	£0 17s 6d
	Clover	4	5 shillings	£1 0s 0d
	Pasture	7	2 shillings	£0 14s 0d
	Total	39		£12 18s 6d
Mrs. Sheaf	Hops	5^3/$_4$	12 shillings	£3 9s 0d
	Wheat	10^1/$_2$	10 shillings	£5 5s 0d
	Barley	8	7 shillings	£2 16s 0d
	Beans	3^1/$_2$	7 shillings	£1 4s 6d
	Oats	2^1/$_2$	7 shillings	£0 17s 6d
	Clover	12^1/$_2$	5 shillings	£3 2s 6d
	Pasture	2^1/$_2$	2 shillings	£0 5s 0d
	Total	45^1/$_4$		£16 19s 6d

The crops on both these farms show that cattle were kept, as barley was used to feed them as well as to make ale or beer. Hops and wheat were the most valuable cash crops. Mrs. Sheaf seems to have kept horses as well, as these were generally fed on oats. Mr. Henley owned land in adjacent parishes, so oats may have been grown on his other holdings.

Farming practice was changing, especially with the introduction of steam driven machinery. Root crops would be grown more widely and fruit was increasing in acreage. In 1809, Nicholas Ellis, who farmed 81 acres near Coldrum, was given an allowance in his tithe assessment *"for the ground that the young fruit trees take up."*

In 1819, Rev. Peter Elers conducted a detailed survey of the village.[7] He estimated its extent as only 823 acres, which seems shy of the actual total. Col. Wingfield-Stratford had by then increased his father-in-law's holdings to 267 acres and 3 roods of this.

Rev. Elers accords the title of "mansion" only to Addington Place and St. Vincents. Rev. Elers noted tithe charges for nineteen houses, ten cottages and two lodges, a total of 31 homes, plus a further nine parcels

of land. Some landholdings were part of larger farms that spanned more than one parish. For instance, Mr. Thomas Woodger held 56 acres at Hernewell as part of his farm at Aldon, which lay in Ryarsh parish. Thus, individual wealth cannot be measured from a survey of Addington alone. As has been mentioned in the previous chapter, Thomas Whiting, Senior, lived at Woodgate, where he farmed 68 acres, but he also held land in Trottiscliffe.

Although it was not until after 1850 that most oast houses were built, in 1819 there were already two in the parish. One was in the centre of the village and the other was at Coldrum. It is possible the former was on the site of the oast that still stands behind the Green. Oast houses were often converted farm buildings. On the later tithe map, it seems that there were no roundels on the oast at Coldrum. There were four barns and many other agricultural buildings, stables and yards standing in the village. It is this document that first records the grocer's shop on the Green and the carpenter's business. The shop was owned by Richard Luxford, one of the few men in the village eligible to vote. The miller was Thomas Whiting, Junior, and the publican was Thomas Capon. The butcher and the nearest forge were at Trottiscliffe.

Rev. Elers' rectory tithe book was continued by his successor, Rev. Thomas Bowdler, who came to the parish in 1821. A new crop was turnips. Eight acres were being grown by Mr. Woodger (also spelled Woodyer) that year at Aldon, for which three shillings per acre were charged. This crop appears regularly from then on, together with podded peas and tares, another legume. The charge on the mill was only three guineas, indicating that this was a fairly small concern.

By the 1830's, fruit was grown extensively, particularly cherry and nut orchards. Woodland also brought in significant revenue for the rector, being charged at 3s 6d per acre. In 1835, Col. Wingfield-Stratford's land contained 110 acres of woodland, so he had to pay £19 5s 0d. However, during the 1840's, the tithes were fully compounded, so the rector's book from then on only the noted the payment due from each land holder. The major farmers can still be identified, as they were paying the largest share. In 1848, these were William Brown (Westfields), James Fremlin (East Street), William Ledger (Hedgehogs), John Luxford (Coldrum), Thomas Woodger (Hernewell and Aldon) and the late Thomas Whiting (Woodgate).

The final Land Tax was levied in 1831. Col. Wingfield-Stratford paid over 50% of the total taxation of the village. That year only 14 other people were liable and only two of these could be termed resident farmers. The retired carpenter, John Wells, held a few acres adjacent to Lane Farmhouse, and Thomas Whiting, the miller, farmed at Woodgate.

Style of Wateringbury.[9] Mrs. Style is recorded as living there on the Land Tax records of 1802, and it seems likely that the property was rebuilt and extended at this time. Hasted's late eighteenth history of the village makes no mention of this building, implying it had not then been rebuilt. Mrs. Style lived with two daughters, Charlotte and Clara and, by her will of 1832, she directed that they should have use of The Vale until their death or marriage. They may, however, have left the village during the late 1830's, as The Vale was occupied by Abraham Sugden and his family at the 1841 census. Clara married at Addington church in 1844, but was widowed in 1850. The two sisters remained together, in Tunbridge Wells. The Vale was sold to the Wingfield-Stratfords, but was unoccupied at the time of the 1851 census.

The Vale and St. Vincents

A ddington now held two substantial properties in addition to the manor house. At the turn of the nineteenth century, The Vale, a Georgian style house, was built on East Street. This property had been owned by Anthony Attwood in the sixteenth century. From the footprint on the 1843 Tithe Map, it seems that Attwood's mediaeval property still lurked behind the flat late Georgian frontage of this building. The photograph shows the additional wing that was added after 1850, but Georgian glazing bars can be seen in the windows that flank a Victorian central door.

There is no paperwork to confirm who undertook the conversion but from this point the house was known as Addington Vale, or simply, The Vale. Ann, the widow of Rev. John Davis, vicar of West Farleigh, had leased the property since 1776.[8] She subsequently bought it, and on her death in 1791, it became the home of her unmarried daughter, Frances Davis. In 1802, Miss Davis, bequeathed the property to her sister, Priscilla, widow of Rev. Robert

The Vale, Addington. Photograph from the Auction Brochure of 1923.
© Knight Frank LLP

Rev. John Bosanquet Polhill, J.P., curate of West Kingsdown, had bought St. Vincents from the children of William and Lucy Locker in about 1802. Rev. Polhill came from an old Kent family. His father had been rector of Goudhurst. Polhill was an active Justice of the Peace. He assisted at St. Margaret's church, as on three occasions he was the officiating minister at marriages and he conducted burials after Rev. Elers' death. He was married to Elizabeth May, the sister of Walter May, who later built Hadlow Castle. Rev. Polhill died in 1821 and was buried at Hadlow Church.

Mrs. Polhill continued to live at St. Vincents. In 1825, she was clearly trying to improve her poor land, as her rates included 13 acres of sainfoin at 7s 6d. per acre. Sainfoin is a plant of the pea family and was then used as a fodder crop. It was also grown to improve the land, by fixing nitrogen in the soil. Six years later, she was courted by William Twysden, of Roydon Hall, East Peckham, the future 8th Baronet. She made the disastrous decision to marry the handsome, but impoverished rake. Sir William was a gambler and a man of despicable character, who saw Elizabeth's fortune as a solution to his pressing money problems. Fortunately, she was well advised by her friends and her money was tied up inextricably. William Twysden failed to acquire the settlement of £350 per year that he had sought. As a result, the couple immediately separated, and the future baronet wrote a scurrilous pamphlet about his bride that he finished by stating :

"Mrs. Twysden's sole motive for marrying me was to obtain a rank in society which neither her late name nor her family could claim for her, the latter never having been anything more than yeomen of the County." [10]

Mrs. (later Lady) Twysden moved to London, where she lived very quietly until her death at an advanced age. She had fortunately retained most of her wealth. She was buried next to her first husband at Hadlow. When her death was announced in the press this came as a great shock to Sir William's second 'wife'! [11]

St. Vincents was acquired by a Maidstone farmer, William Scoones (1771-c1842). Scoones had leased Hedgehogs farm for some years. Sadly, in 1839, he was declared bankrupt. [12] At the 1841 census, he was living in Wheeler Street, near the prison, aged 70. St. Vincents then became part of the manor, and was given to John Wingfield-Stratford, the squire's son, to use as his country home. At the 1841 census, as has been noted above, the property was in the care of servants.

Village Administration

The prosperity of Addington's residents was based on agriculture and the maintenance of the manor house, except for the few who were of independent means. Four of the fourteen men who left a will during the first half of the nineteenth century, gave their occupation as "farmer" or "yeoman". These were Thomas Hills (d.1815), George Fishenden (d.1820), Thomas Whiting, Senior (d.1827) and John Wells, (d.1848), who was also a carpenter. They had all given good service to their community. However, the land farmed by these yeomen then came on to the market and Col. Wingfield-Stratford was the main purchaser, depriving the village of new independent volunteers for public duties. There was a much smaller pool to draw on, and the posts of churchwarden, overseer of the poor, way-warden, etc. began to rotate between very few men. Thomas Whiting, Junior, held the post of churchwarden a number of times, eventually in consecutive years. Two other names recur: Stephen Capon of Woodgate, who died in 1834 and Thomas Lemmey of Westfields Farm, who left the village in 1836. [13] Other farmers, such as William Ledger, at Ford, and William Scoones, at Hedgehogs and St. Vincents, were non-resident, so were ineligible to act as village officers.

Wealth and comfort

The legacies in the yeomen's wills point to a comfortable standard of living. However, one man who termed himself a gardener in his will, was also a wealthy man. Clement Elliott's will of 1833 included the legacy, of a property in Borden, near Sittingbourne, with a coach house, garden, stable and appurtenances. It is probable that Clement was head gardener at Addington Park. His home was very comfortable. He left *"plate linen china wines liquors books household furniture goods chattels and effects whatsoever"* to his widow. His property, stocks, funds and other securities, were to be sold to provide for her, and would later be divided equally between his eight children by two wives. Ann Elliott survived her husband for over thirty years, living with her bachelor son, William, also a gardener, in one of the School Row cottages. It is possible that she and her husband were at Park Cottage at the time of his death, because of the lavish description of their goods. It was perhaps after Elliott's death that a retired farmer, Richard Luxford, took over the tenancy.

Richard Luxford (1777-1847) was for many years the tenant farmer at Coldrum, but he also owned freehold land and cottages. He and his wife were living at Park Cottage at the 1841 census and when the 1843 Tithe Schedule was drawn up. He was an almost exact contemporary of the squire. He owned the shop and the wooden cottage beside it, and probably the Laurels behind these. They would have come to him through his wife, Mary, who was also his cousin. Mrs. Mary Luxford was a native of Addington, the daughter of William Smith, the long serving clerk to the parish. Her mother was born Elizabeth Luxford. Mr. and Mrs. Richard Luxford lived very comfortably. By his will, he specified that she should receive *"absolutely all my wines liquors fuel and other stores and provisions"*, plus the income from his estate. After her death, his estate was divided equally between their three children. These were John, who had taken on the lease at Coldrum, William, the butcher at Trottiscliffe, and Elizabeth, wife of Thomas Woodger, the farmer at Aldon.

With the exception of one cottager, the remaining wills of the first half of the century were those of professional people, or those of independent means. These testators were the squire, Leonard Bartholomew (1810), Rev. Peter Elers (1820), Rev. J.B. Polhill (1822), Miss Frances Davis (1801) and her sister, Mrs. Priscilla Style (1832), both of the Vale, and Mrs. Sarah Whiting (1827), who died just one month after her husband, Thomas. The last will was that of Col. Hon. John Wingfield-Stratford.

Church records

Only 57 marriages were celebrated at St. Margaret's church between 1800 and 1850, compared with 103 during the previous half century. These were overwhelmingly local marriages. Only four grooms came from outside the county and all the brides were from Kent. 43 brides gave Addington as their parish, and none came from further afield than Maidstone. In 19 cases, both bride and groom were from Addington. It was a time of young couples. Very few had been previously married and only two of marriages were celebrated between a widower and a widow. The most disastrous marriage was, of course, that of William Twysden and Mrs. Polhill.

Despite the low number of marriages, cottages were becoming more crowded. 328 christenings took place between 1801 and 1850, over 80 more than during the last half of the eighteenth century. As only 227 burials are recorded for the same period, it is not surprising to see the population figures grow. 49 residents lived to be more than seventy years old. Sixteen reached eighty, and George Ridges and John Wells lived to celebrate their 90th birthdays. John Wells, of Lane Farmhouse, was 95 years old at his death in December 1848.

The christening figures reflect increasing fertility, and a lessening of childhood mortality. Only 36 children were buried before their first birthday, though eleven of these died during their first month of life. Altogether sixty children died before the age of thirteen (26% of burials, but only 18% of baptisms). Most childhood deaths were still of the very young, as 53 out of the 60 were aged less than five.

The boys that did survive were able to make a few pennies catching sparrows and hedgehogs, the first were supposed to eat grain and the second to annoy the milking cattle by drinking from their udders. These they brought to the churchwardens for payment. Although the numbers seem high (two dozen hedgehogs in 1807-8), it is most unlikely that any advantage was gained by farmers of the parish. Both sexes joined their parents at harvest time.

From 1805, all Addington's rectors were resident and this meant that records were now kept more assiduously. In addition, legislation ensured that these become more informative. From 1813 the books for baptisms and burials are printed forms that include a box for the occupation of the father in the case of baptisms and the date of death and age of the deceased in that of burials. Thus, we learn that Thomas Ridges, whose seven children were baptised between 1815 and 1832 was the village shoemaker, Clement Elliott was a gardener, John Norton a (horse) team-man and Jesse Ottway a gate-maker. As the census records tended to call all these occupations "labourer", the baptismal records are more helpful. Obviously, though, most fathers gave their occupation as "labourer" (153).

During the first half of the century Thomas and Mary Whiting, the miller and his wife, had eight children. The carpenter, Thomas Millhouse and his wife, Jane, had a further eight (and they had already started their family before moving to the village.)

Colonel Wingfield-Stratford

As one of the significant landowners in the county, Col. Wingfield-Stratford was a magistrate and highways board trustee. He served as Sheriff in 1813, and on the grand jury at the assizes at Maidstone in 1822. His arms, which can be seen on his memorial plaque in the church were quartered. The Wingfield quarter was *"Argent on a bend gules three pairs of wings conjoined in lure of the field."* This translates as a red band across a white field, on which are three following angels' wings." The angel theme was rather fortunate, and the shield on his plaque is held by an angel. The two quarters containing the Stratford arms include a black rampant lion, which, again, mirrors the motifs in the family chapel.

The Arms of Col. The Hon. John Wingfield-Stratford, on the memorial plaque in St. Margaret's Church.

John's first marriage ended with the death of his wife on 18th July 1827. Frances was aged only 51. Their two daughters were young adults but their son, John, was 16 and still at school. Col. Wingfield-Stratford remained a widower for five years, and began a series of major landscaping works. In 1828, he lowered the track across the ancient megaliths to make easier access to his mansion, as described in the first chapter of this

history. It was probably that year that the fine rag stone wall was built along the London Road, as he enclosed the park. This work brought him into conflict with his rector, Thomas Bowdler. At the perambulation of the bounds on 8th April 1828, Rev. Bowdler complained that the road through the park had been closed to the public to create a carriage drive, and demanded that it be opened once more. The squire sat tight and the Park became a private enclave, albeit still crossed by footpaths. Col. Wingfield-Stratford also enclosed part of Addington Common to bring it into agricultural use.

Col. Hon. John Wingfield-Stratford, (1778-1850) Portrait by John Partridge. Image © National Portrait Gallery of Scotland These portraits were in the collection of the Malcolm family, but after a fire at Poltalloch House they were lost.

He seems to have become more right wing during his widowerhood. In September 1828, he chaired the inaugural meeting of the Kentish Brunswick Constitutional Club. This was an ultra conservative and Protestant association set up in support of the Hanoverian monarchy. He was a leading member of the Club, which met for patriotic dinners at the Star Inn in Maidstone.

In 1830-1831, there was intense and general agitation amongst the agricultural population in Kent. The insurgency became known as the Swing Riots, named after the mythical signatory of inflammatory letters, Captain Swing. The rioters were not motivated by politics, but by distress. One of the causes was the fear of unemployment as machines began to replace men, both in growing and in harvesting crops. Other complaints were about low wages and high tithe charges. Although there are no records that workers at Addington downed tools or burned hayricks, disturbances took place in neighbouring parishes, particularly Wrotham and Ryarsh. Ryarsh had no dominant landowner, and the population there was growing rapidly, from 162 in 1801 to 435 in 1841. At the census of 1841, there were 85 houses in Ryarsh, as opposed to 41 in Addington. This growth may have led to competition for work and greater poverty. Farm labourers burned ricks and smashed the threshing machines in the district. The situation remained tense for months. There had been little incentive for John Wingfield-Stratford to build more cottages, as he had enough for his agricultural workers. If new families were to move into the village they might struggle to find work, and become dependent upon the parish. A combination of self interest and benevolence prevented unrest.

Just after this unsettled period, on 21st July 1832, the Colonel had the pleasure of seeing his daughters married at a double wedding. This took place in London, at the parish church of St. Marylebone. The ceremony was conducted by Rev. W. Waldegrave Park, curate of Addington. Frances Amelia's husband was Rev. John Cecil Hall, who was a widower with one son. He had been serving as the curate at Offham. He later became Archdeacon of the Isle of Man. The couple had no children. Ven. Hall died in 1844, having caught a fever from a parishioner he was visiting.[14] Mrs. Hall remained based on the Isle of Man for the rest of her long life. She played an active and charitable role there. She purchased land at Cronk-e-Voddy and paid for a church to be erected on this. In 1860, she, purchased more land for a Grammar School at Douglas, even providing a home for the headmaster. She died at Douglas on 3rd August 1888 at the age of 81.

Isabella Harriet became Mrs. John Malcolm, 14th of Poltalloch, Argyll. John and Isabella Malcolm had a family of five, and lived near to her father, as their main home was at Lamb Abbey, Bexley. Mr. Malcolm was a magistrate for Kent. Isabella died in 1858, but her husband survived her for 35 years. After his wife's

death, he became an eminent and prolific art collector, whose collection is now in the British Museum. This eventually contained 970 drawings and engravings, amongst which were works by Michelangelo, Titian and Rembrandt.

On 1st August 1832, less than a fortnight after the marriage of his two daughters, Col. Wingfield-Stratford himself remarried. The wedding took place at Neath, in Glamorgan. His second wife was Miss Harriette Grant (1783-1863), the second child, and eldest daughter, of Henry Grant, a very wealthy India merchant. On his retirement in 1811, Grant had purchased Gnoll House, at Neath, near Swansea, which had been the home of the Mackworth family, an important industrial family of South Wales. Henry Grant died in early 1831, leaving each of his unmarried daughters well provided for. Harriette was 49 when she married. She would become a good friend to her adopted family, and a generous benefactor to the village.

Hon. Mrs. Harriette Wingfield-Stratford, (1780-1863) Portrait by John Partridge © National Portrait Gallery of Scotland

Despite her geniality, Mrs. Wingfield-Stratford could not prevent her husband from incurring the wrath of Rev. Bowdler's successor, Rev. George Paulson. In

1840, the colonel incorporated yet more land into the Park. He somewhat redeemed his reputation by helping the church to install central heating by paying for the pipes, but was only partially generous. The parish had to raise an extra rate to cover the costs for the installation.

Because he had taken common land from the villagers, the Addington Freeholders' Charity was established. In November 1840, the churchwarden's accounts recorded the following.

"The sum of £33 6s 8d, (which was an amount given to the parish by Col. Wingfield-Stratford in lieu of land incorporated into his park), was vested in 3 per cent consolidated annuities in the trusteeship of the Rev. George Paulson, rector, and Mr. Thomas Whiting, miller, the interest of which it was agreed by the freeholders of the parish should be annually distributed at the discretion of the rector and churchwarden to one or more persons with large families being good attendants on the public service of their parish church, the first distribution of which took place 17 January 1841, viz

10 shillings to Stephen West, 5 children

10 shillings to William Barnden, junior, 8 children

George Paulson, rector

J. Wingfield-Stratford Junior, churchwarden

Memorandum: to check whether one or two trustees should anything happen to either of them."

The following year Thomas Millhouse, 7 children, and Thomas Pankhurst, 6 children, received 10 shillings each, but the third distribution was not made until 1846 when similar amounts went to James Baldwin, "2 children, but has had 5", and again to Thomas Millhouse, now with 8 children.[15]

The interest in non-distributing years was added to the principal. From 1847, the charity seems to have struggled to find claimants and, by 1849, the principal rose to £39 16s 2d. The trustees that year were John Wingfield-Stratford, Esq. and William Brown, of Westfields Farm. No further notes were made about

this charity, but it still existed until the end of the twentieth century, when it was wound up. During the final years of its existence, the interest was used to buy harvest gifts for senior citizens in the village.

Col. Wingfield-Stratford's holdings in Kent, which came from the Watton and Bartholomew families, brought him a substantial income. They included land in Addington, Trottiscliffe, Ryarsh, Offham, Leybourne and Wrotham parishes. In 1840, his liabilities for rectorial tithes rose suddenly from £48 to £64. He had just purchased St. Vincents with its thirty acres, which had come on the market following William Scoones' bankruptcy. The property was then loaned to his wife's brother, Col. Turner Grant.

On 10th December 1844 the Colonel's son married, and after Col. Grant's death in 1845, John and Jane Wingfield-Stratford moved into St. Vincents. Two of their many children were born there.[16] That year, Col. Wingfield-Stratford invited Rev. Lambert Larking to undertake excavations at Addington Long Barrow. He had appointed Rev. Larking to the living at Ryarsh. The two men were cousins.[17]

In addition to these local properties, Col. Wingfield-Stratford received rent from his lands in Ireland. However, in 1845, the disaster of the Irish Potato Famine struck, returning and worsening the following year. As the majority of his tenants farmed less than five acres, their situation rapidly became untenable. From correspondence between Col. Wingfield-Stratford and his land agent, William Ormsby, which were auctioned by Messrs. Adams at Dublin in May 2010, it seems that they were in constant touch. One response of responsible landowners such as he was to fund infrastructure projects to give work. A letter put a proposal to him to start up a woollen mill at Robertstown, at a former distillery. However, even these projects caused problems. His agent wrote to him in 1845 referring to the difficulty of *"ejectments of tenants along a new road."* By the end of that year, hunger had become a stark reality, and rents were going unpaid. His agent wrote to him on Christmas Eve, telling him *"The potatoes are getting worse every day. In a short time, they will have none. What am I to do about the arrears, as from day to day I am put off without getting it."*

In 1846, Col. Wingfield-Stratford built new homes for tenants who could no longer stay on their land. He instructed his agent to *"give them some indulgence over the rents."* However, the situation continued to deteriorate. On 19th July 1846, Ormsby wrote to him *"We will not have a potato in this country, a good part of mine are going already, bad news for the children."* In September, he wrote, *"Patrick McHale called on me for one hundred pounds as part payment for the meal Col. Wingfield desired to give the tenants. I got from McHale £163 worth, and as he is anxious to purchase new oats next week he wants the £100 as soon as possible."*

In 1846, Col. Wingfield-Stratford paid for a number of his tenants to emigrate to America, but he remained a man of his time and upbringing. When a suggestion was made, in 1848, for harbour works to give employment, he expressed his reluctance to fund the project, as it might bring some of these "idle" tenants back! The letters show a robust concern for his tenants, but a fear of Catholic ascendancy and Irish insurrection. He also professed a total abhorrence of the Chartist Movement of 1845, as their adherents planned to raise funds to buy estates and parcel them out to individual small-holders.

Col. Wingfield-Stratford did not survive to see his estates in Ireland recover. He died at his London home on 3rd August 1850, the day after his 78th birthday. He was buried on the 10th in St. Margaret's churchyard. He had, however, lived to see the birth of five grandchildren to John and Isabella Malcolm, and three more grandchildren, including a son, to John and Jane Wingfield-Stratford.

He left a long-term legacy to the village. The rector would have £30 to spend on the poor of Addington at his discretion. Rather than spending this immediately, the £30 was invested in 3% Consols, so that the interest would be available each year. In the short term, each poor man within the parish was given a suit of mourning clothes.

John's widow, Harriette, was given St. Vincents as her dower. Its land then included part of what is now the golf course. This was a field adjacent to the wood, on the south side of St. Vincents Lane, opposite the sand workings. However, Mrs. Wingfield-Stratford continued to reside at Addington Park with her stepson and his family, so St. Vincents was leased to a series of tenants until her death in 1863. After this, it was brought back into the main estate. Col. Wingfield-Stratford left his estates in Ireland to be shared between his three children. Mrs. Frances Hall received those in County Carlow, Mrs. Isabella Malcolm those in County Wicklow and John Wingfield-Stratford those in Queens County. John also received the Stratford Place Estate, the Addington estate and all the residual real and personal estate One particularly charming bequest was of his *"little pony called Whiskey"*, which he left to his eldest grand-daughter, Isabella Malcolm, then aged eight.

By his will, Col. Wingfield-Stratford directed that a marble plaque be installed in the chancel at St. Margaret's church commemorating his first wife and the Bartholomew family. His widow, instead, installed two. These were made of brass, with sculpted stone surrounds. The first commemorates the Bartholomews and its pair commemorates the Wingfield-Stratfords. The executors were his son, John, his son-in-law, John Malcolm, and his beloved twin brother, Edward Wingfield.

Agriculture in 1843

During Col. Wingfield-Stratford's tenure at the manor house, the financing of the village underwent a radical change. Paying tithes in cash, rather than in kind, had become quite usual by the 1830's. The Tithe Commutation Act of 1836 ensured that in future all tithes would be paid this way, rather than by private arrangement with the rector. A series of accurate maps of parishes was drawn up, showing each parcel of land and any buildings on it, together with an accompanying schedule. This schedule gave the name of the owner, the occupier, the crops grown and the acreage of each parcel. The final sheet gave the acreage used by roads and waste.

Addington was surveyed in 1843. The acreage of land and its use was calculated by the surveyor,

Thomas Smith Woolley.[18] He stated that the taxable area was 934 acres, 3 roods and 36 perches, though his detailed figures actually add up to 940 acres 3 roods and 39 perches. He stated that:

"I find that the total estimated quantity in statute measure of all the lands of the said Parish the whole of which are subject to payment of all manner of tithes in kind to the Rector of the said Parish for the time being amounts to Nine hundred and thirty four acres three roods and thirty six perches which are now cultivated and used as follows that is to say Exclusive of the Glebe lands of the said Parish Four hundred and four acres one rood and one perch as Arable land including the Hop grounds of the said Parish
Two hundred and seventy six acres one rood and two perches as Meadow or Pasture land exclusive of the Glebe lands aforesaid
One hundred and sixty four acres one rood and twenty perches as Woodland
Twenty acres three roods and nineteen perches as Orchard and Fruit Plantation
Ten acres three roods and five perches are the sites of Houses and Buildings and the Homestead Yards and Gardens and
Thirty eight acres one rood and eight perches are the Roads and Waste land.
Twenty six acres and twenty four perches are the Glebe lands of the said Parish."

Mr. Smith Woolley then estimated the monetary value of the crops owed to the Rector, as follows:

"Now Know Ye that I the said Thomas Smith Woolley Do hereby award that the annual sum of Two hundred and twenty three Pounds and four shillings by way of Ordinary Rent charge subject to the provisions of the said Act shall from the first day of October next preceding the confirmation of the Apportionment of the said Rent charge be paid to the said Rector for the time being instead of all the tithes, except the tithes of Hops arising from all the lands of the said Parish except the Glebe lands thereof

And that a further annual sum of Five shillings per statute acre and a proportionate sum for any quantity less than an acre by way of Rent charge subject to the provisions and to commence from the time aforesaid shall be paid to the said Rector for the time being instead of all the tithes except the tithe of Hops arising from all the Glebe lands of the said Parish or from such part of the said Glebe."

The tithe statement recorded the amount of grain harvest. Barley was the most valuable crop, oats the least, but the largest. It is probable that the sandy soil was responsible for making the last the heaviest crop in the parish.

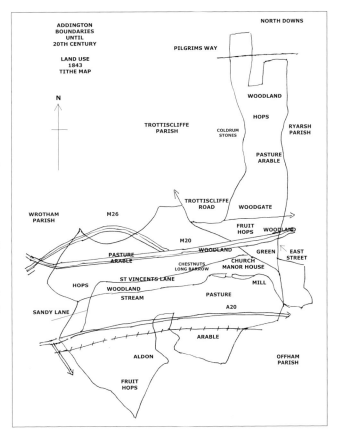

The map above is similar to that in Chapter Two, but I have added captions to show where the different crops were grown. It is worth describing more fully three of these, as they indicate how the parish might have looked during the middle years of the nineteenth century.

Hops

In 1843, only 31 acres were under cultivation with hops. However, this was the most valuable crop, and was taxed heavily as a result. The acreage for hop grounds in Kent doubled between 1800 and 1878. The earliest roundel oast was built at Benenden in 1812, having been invented by John Read of Horsmonden. A particular advantage of the roundel was that it became possible to create a larger drying area, so that double the amount of hops could be dried at one time. It was also thought at the time that square kilns led to the hops in the corners drying less quickly than the centre, because of restricted air flow. This was later disproved, but the theory led to most Kent oast houses having roundels. Two of the four oast houses drawn on the Tithe Map of 1843 had roundels, one was north of the Green and one stood near Hedgehogs. The others, at Coldrum and Woodgate, are shown as rectangular buildings. Only the one behind the Green is still standing. A double oast was later built at Westfields, but it was demolished in the mid twentieth century. The oasts at Aldon were first in Ryarsh, then in Addington, and are now in Offham. Although hops were never a major crop in the village, the area planted increased during the nineteenth century. The Rectorial Tithe accounts of 1879 state that hops were under cultivation on 67 acres, 2 roods and 22 perches. This mirrors the figure for Kent as a whole. Individual parcels remained small, generally not above three acres.

The heyday for the crop was short-lived. By 1900, hop growing had been virtually abandoned at Addington, and an early twentieth century photograph of the West-fields oast shows it to be in ruins. The situation at Aldon was more robust. Hops were grown there for most of the twentieth century.

Woodland

About 20% of Addington was woodland. This was a larger area than today, mainly because the greatest wooded area, lying under the Downs, is no longer part of the parish. Much of the woodland was in very small strips and pieces, known as shaws and clumps. All woodland was vitally important and even these small pieces were regularly coppiced or pollarded for fencing, general repairs and fuel. Many of the shaws were grubbed out during agricultural improvements, but other areas have become more wooded. One of these is Campions Wood. At the beginning of the nineteenth century, the northern part of this was open farmland, and the southern part was a sandpit. It was still used this way at the time of the tithe schedule. When the 1907 Ordnance Survey was undertaken, however, Campions was an extensive wood. The northern area had been planted with chestnut but, where the sandpit had been, national regeneration seems to have occurred. Although there are some oak and beech, many of the trees are sycamore, an effective colonizer. Much of the chestnut plantation in Campions Wood vanished beneath the motorway during the 1970's.

Coppicing at St Vincents Wood, March 2010

Addington Great Wood, to the north of the parish, provided timber, i.e. the trees were periodically thinned or clear felled as standards. This was both hard and soft wood. It is now all called Ryarsh Wood, but on the tithe map it covered about 58 acres and was separately named.

Chestnut and pine were planted during the early nineteenth century, and these areas are noted as new plantations in the tithe document. In St. Vincents Wood the ditches that formed the divisions of the parcels can still be seen and the areas of pine and chestnut are clearly separate. A fourteen acre chestnut plantation was established beside Park Road, called on the tithe map "The Chesnuts". Pines were planted on Addington Common, this area being known as the Common Plantation. It is now called The Pineys. The Common Plantation, like Campions Wood, has now virtually all disappeared beneath the motorway. The pine softwood was used for the construction and furniture industries.

The hop industry generated a great need for chestnut, because, through coppicing, it produced such long straight poles, but much was also used for fencing. Strong thick straining posts are produced from the base, and the middle and tops of the poles are used for the intermediate stakes or split into pales, for chestnut paling. These are thin strips of chestnut, bound with wire, used to protect woodland, and now gardens. Chestnut was also the preferred local fuel for making charcoal. This was an ancient industry that increased because of the supply of wood from plantations. Charcoal was the principal fuel used in forges. The charcoal burners would camp beside their kilns to oversee the slow process.. A few alder plantations were created near to the stream, as this wood was used for broom handles and other household goods. Hazel and cob nuts were grown in small quantity, for their fruit but also for making the hurdles needed in sheep rearing. Opposite the village hall was an osier bed, the willow being used for basket making. Overblown willow trees still line the rivulet there. Willows were pollarded, i.e. the main trunk was cut at chest height and the regrowth harvested annually. Pollarded trees were easy to identify as boundary markers on such maps.

The chestnut and cob-nut plantations beside Sandy Lane were not planted until later in the century. They appear under the name of Sandy Wood on the 1907 Ordnance Survey map.

Fruit

Because of the gault clay, Aldon was planted heavily with fruit, but most of this was not part of the parish in 1843. At that time, little fruit was cultivated in the rest of the village, presumably because the soil was not suitable. Although the tithe survey counts 20 acres of orchards and fruit, only about seven of these are recorded specifically as producing fruit or nuts, three being in the kitchen garden of Addington Park. The other four acres lay north of the Green, near to the remaining oast house. The rest of the orchards were marked as pasture. Perhaps the fruit harvest was considered of little significance. The fruit would have been apples, pears, plums and cherries. The acreage increased during the second half of the century, as the 1907 Ordnance Survey map shows the whole area between East Street and Woodgate planted with fruit trees. More grew at Westfields Farm. These orchards were managed until the Second World War, but afterwards they fell out of use and most were grubbed out. A cherry orchard was still harvested next to Woodgate in the 1980's. The remnants of another lingers at the bottom of Aldon Lane.

Remnants of the Osier bed near Park Road. Photograph: Lucy Richardson

detached portions of Ryarsh parish. These anomalies were sorted out later in the century, though the current boundaries of Addington were fixed as recently as the 1980's.

Ownership of land in 1843

The tithe schedule shows that Col. Wingfield-Stratford's holdings had increased considerably since 1810, when he and his wife inherited the manor. He now owned approximately 581 acres, of which just over 340 were in hand. The rest was leased to tenant farmers, or consisted of service and rented cottages or substantial leased houses. His farming tenants were

- William Brown, land agent, held 54 acres of Westfields Farm in Addington parish, and more of this in Trottiscliffe.
- Thomas Woodger, farmed 55 acres at Hernewell. His main farm was at Aldon.
- Thomas Whiting, farmed 78 acres at the Mill, East Street and Woodgate. Held further land in Ryarsh.
- William Ledger, held 20 acres adjacent to St. Vincents Lane in the Park. His farms were Ford Farm, in Wrotham and Hedgehogs.

Three major landowners lived outside the parish. They were

- Sir William Geary, 2nd Bart., of Oxonhoath, whose tenant at Ford and Hedgehogs was William Ledger, (111 acres). William Ledger lived at Ford Farm, as Ford Place was then known.
- Charles Augustus Whittaker, of Barming, whose tenant at Coldrum was John Luxford (93 acres).
- George Addison of Offham, whose tenant on land at Teston Road was Jeremiah Fremlin (53 acres).

Col. Wingfield-Stratford also held land in surrounding parishes. Apart from the 94 acres of Westfields Farm that lay in Trottiscliffe, he held three large pieces of land in the then vast parish of Wrotham. The first of these was 110 acres at Roughway, near Plaxtol, the second was 173 acres at Burton's Bourne and the third was 242 acres at Old Soar. He owned 20 acres of Offham Wood, a detached part of Leybourne Parish. Other small pieces of land within the Park were

The church and its Rectors

The church was one of the largest buildings and remained a dominant social force in the lives of the villagers. The manor house gave employment, but the two were closely aligned. Church attendance was high. This may have been a reflection of the control exercised by the estate over the economic lives of the residents. Addington had been, since time immemorial, a part of Rochester Diocese. However, in 1846, because of the eastwards growth of London, diocesan boundaries were changed, and the deanery in which the village stood, North Malling, was transferred to Canterbury. The parish returned to Rochester Diocese in 1905, when, due to the further increase in population, Southwark Diocese was created.

Rev. Daniel Hill, the long serving vicar of East Malling and rector of Addington, died in 1805. He had lived at East Malling, whilst the care of Addington was undertaken by his curate, James Thurston, the vicar of Ryarsh. When Rev. Peter Elers (1758-1820) was installed by Leonard Bartholomew, he was the first rector to take up residence at the Rectory on Aldon Lane for over sixty years. Rev. Elers had been rector of Rishangles, Suffolk, of which he also held the patronage. He had been curate of Trottiscliffe and Birling, and also of Addington after Thurston's death in 1802. His elder brother, Rev. Carew Elers, lived nearby at Oldbury, in Ightham and the two were close companions. They were the sons of a lawyer, George Elers of Chelsea, whose family had come from Germany.

Rev. Elers' rectorial tithe book shows that his income in his first year at Addington was £171 17s 9d, plus some pew rents. It was fortunate that he had private funds,[19] as, otherwise, this was the amount on which he had to live, pay a curate and keep his large rectory and the chancel in the church in good repair. For instance, the tithe dinner at the Angel cost £4 1s 8d in 1806, quite a chunk out of his parochial income. The glebe was an important element of a rector's income. This was the land he farmed himself. Collecting the tithes, especially when some were still in kind, was not that easy. Some landholders moved away, leaving debts, others became paupers. In 1808, Rev. Elers recorded that *"Mr. Sutton's fruit sold for £15 15s 0d."* This must have been very welcome.

Maddan noted that Rev. Elers was a businesslike parish priest, who took steps to repair omissions in the parish registers, as these had been badly neglected under the long tenure of his predecessor. He reaffirmed the bounds of the parish. He redeemed the Land Tax on the rectorial house, which he substantially rebuilt at the start of his incumbency. From his tithe book, it can been seen that in July and August 1805 he employed Stephen Capon and Thomas Woodger, both local farmers, for nine days just clearing rubbish. This work took three horses three days, whilst two men filled carts for four days. The total clean-up cost was £5 19s 0d. Mr. Skinner, a bricklayer, and his assistant, Mr. Carpenter, were then paid £20 15s 0d for pulling down the back part of the old house. Mr. Skinner and his men then rebuilt and enlarged the house. The extent of the works can be seen from his final account, as it came to £558. A feast was given to the workmen at the start of works in September that year, and another when the work was completed a year later. The last payment was made on 11th September 1806. Rev. Elers must have been happy with his new home, as he spent the rest of his life there. He was buried in Addington churchyard on 14th November 1820. By his will he left a substantial annuity of £150 to his sister, a further £50 to three friends and the residual personal and real estate to his brother, Rev. Carew Elers.

Rev. Elers was followed by Rev. Thomas Bowdler, who was presented to the living by Col. Wingfield-Stratford on 6th March 1821. Rev. Bowdler came from Ash-cum-Ridley. Three years after his arrival he fell quite seriously ill, and was non-resident for a while, perhaps recuperating abroad. Rev. Edward Heawood, a master at the Grant School, Maidstone, acted as officiating minister during his absence.

Baptisms and burials are recorded, but no marriages took place at St. Margaret's between 1822 and 1832. Banns were called on a few occasions, but the marriages took place elsewhere.

Like his predecessor, Rev. Bowdler undertook major alterations to the Rectory, borrowing money for them. His successor wrote of being burdened by this debt in years to come. Rev. Bowdler was reputed to have enthusiastically maximised his income by pressing debtors for the tithes due to him. He was the strong character who stood up to the squire when Col. Wingfield-Stratford proposed to stop up paths across his land and enclose it as a park. In this, he was unsuccessful, but he worked tirelessly to improve the lot of others. Rev. Thomas Bowdler was a practical man, who was concerned about the material, as well as the spiritual life of his parishioners. On 9th November 1830 he wrote to the Maidstone Journal advocating that labourers should be *"[allotted] a piece of land, not less than a quarter of an acre, for the growth of potatoes, or of these and some other crop alternately."* His desire for this was not only practical, but also religious, as he believed that by such allotment a man's comfort would *"absolutely depend upon sound principles, good morals and active industry."* He also advocated that wages should be paid on a Friday evening, stating: *"If the wages are received on the Friday, the wife can lay out to the best advantage on the Saturday, and the village shop can be closed on the very morning of the Lord's Day."*

Rev. Bowdler left Addington when he was appointed rector of Sydenham in early 1835. In his later life he became the Secretary of the Church Building Society and an active opponent of the Tractarian (Oxford) Movement. In 1849 he was appointed a prebend (a type of canon) of St. Paul's Cathedral. He published a number of sermons, including those from his time at Addington. One notable sermon from this period was preached at the Archdeacon's Visitation at West Malling. He also wrote memoirs of both his father and uncle's lives. The latter, also named Thomas, had produced a revised edition of Shakespeare which gave the English language the new verb "to bowdlerise". Uncle Bowdler expunged some of the juicier bits from Shakespeare to make it more suitable for family reading. Thus, it seems, Ophelia's death in Hamlet was caused by accidental drowning, rather than suicide. Rev. Thomas Bowdler published his uncle's second "bowdlerism" of the works of Gibbon. He was a man of industry, with strong opinions on events of his day. Perhaps Addington was too small a place for him.

Rev. George Paulson, (1799-1869) on the other hand, remained rector of Addington for 35 years, his tenure ending only with his death. Like Rev. Elers, he had connections with the continent as he had been born in Russia. He and his young wife, Fanny, whom he married in the early 1840's, filled the rectory with a family of seven children. He was a punctilious man. In the rectorial tithe book he recorded the troubles he faced over the care of, and the need for repairs to the Rectory. He complained of the difficulty of keeping both his and his curate's families on an inadequate income. When he arrived in the parish, he had difficulty in agreeing a price for the purchase of the glebe field, which had not been relinquished by Rev. Bowdler. The business, though finally completed, was acrimonious. Rev. Paulson was frequently frustrated by the non-payment of his rectorial tithes, on which he depended so heavily.

The church fabric

The early nineteenth century saw a significant spiritual revival of the Anglican church, which led eventually to the physical rearrangement of its places of worship. The Oxford Movement, as it became known, began in the 1830's and was led by John Newman. Adherents felt that the church had become too plain and wished to return to the rituals of the past, whilst remaining true to the 39 articles of the Church of England. In particular, they advocated a greater emphasis on the communion mass, and less on preaching. They were also called Tractarians, because of the tracts they published from 1833 onwards. These led to heated debate. As has been noted, Addington's rector, Rev. Thomas Bowdler, was determinedly against the movement, but it eventually triumphed in most parishes. Even before 1850, a number of churches gave their preaching

pulpit less emphasis and moved their altar to the east wall of the church. Vibrant images began to be installed in windows. St. Margaret's was slow to adopt the new format, as Col. Wingfield-Stratford appears to have resisted the arguments. It was not until after his death in 1850 that the parish church was redesigned. Rev. Paulson may have been constrained by his patron. Biblical texts replaced the Snayth coat of arms in the east window during this half century, suggesting that, at Addington, preaching remained of paramount importance.

However, towards the end of the period, the first of the stained glass windows was installed. In 1848, Mrs. Harriette Wingfield-Stratford paid for a depiction of St. Peter and St. Paul to be placed in the south window of the Watton Chapel. This is an early work by Warrington and Company, whose use of primary colours had met with some criticism to begin with. She paid later for the repairs, reorganisation and extension that took place during the 1850's.

Rather than major alterations, during the first half of the century money was spent on protection and comfort. Major repairs were made to the roof and heating was installed. At a vestry meeting held on 11th November 1840, it was announced that Col. Wingfield-Stratford had given £52 18s for the heating pipes. The parish raised its assessment to six pence in the pound to cover the payments to masons and carpenters for their installation. This could not have been a very onerous bill, though, as the total income from the assessment still amounted to only £21 5s 1^{1}/$_{2}$d. Rev. Paulson contributed £4 towards the work.

The organisation of the parish

The rector was assisted by the churchwarden, the parish clerk, and the sexton. The last two were paid positions, but the churchwarden had to make up any shortfall in the rates from his own pocket, whilst leaving any surplus for his successor. The churchwarden was appointed by the vestry, which authorised other members to be the overseer for the poor, the way-warden and the constable. The term of duty for the churchwarden was nominally one year. All the wealthier householders were expected to undertake this duty in turn, but, by the 1820's, it became difficult to rotate the office. Thomas Whiting, the miller and a substantial farmer, held the post for a number of years. On the whole the disbursements were small, but regular–the clerk's salary, the bread and wine for the few communion services, washing the surplice, oiling the bells and replacing the bell-ropes, payments to the bell-ringers and to poor vagrants and the annual dinner for the rector at his "visitation". Cleaning the church steeple cost only a shilling in 1800. However, rope appears to have been expensive as, in 1805-6, £1 6s 0d had to be laid out for bell-ropes, and a further three shillings for coffin ropes. The bell ropes did not last long, as they appear as an almost annual payment to a Mr. Dorrington. Some work at the church the following year entailed the need for a horse and cart for four days, costing £1. Payments were still made to boys for hedgehogs and sparrows. Occasionally the outside world intruded. In 1815, thanksgiving books were purchased following the victory at Waterloo and later that year, when peace in Europe was finally achieved, prayer books were bought.

William Smith, the parish clerk and farmer, was paid £1 11s 6d half yearly. He and his wife, Elizabeth Luxford, were both from local farming families and lived on the Green. His payment for 1800 was £3 19s 1d, implying that he had also claimed some expenses. He was buried at Addington on 2nd September 1810 at the age of 64, by which time he had been parish clerk for 31 years. During the 1830's, the post was held by the local carpenter and builder, Thomas Millhouse. At that time, he was living on East Street, but he moved to Lane Farmhouse after John Wells's death in 1848, so it is possible he had already used the old man's yard for his business. The parish clerk's fee had, by then, risen to four guineas, but even in the twentieth century it was only £8 8s. Later in the century, another long serving parish clerk was William Wells (d. 1883) who held the post for 26 years. He and his

wife, Lucy, came to Addington from Hadlow in 1821 and lived at the School House on the Green, owned by the Rev. Edward Holmes Charity Trust until it became part of the manor holdings. They had a family of seven children. Their daughter, Kezia, became the first school-mistress. A memorial plaque to William Wells is in the church.

At the start of the nineteenth century, poor relief was still given to strangers passing through the village, sometimes on their enforced return to their parish of settlement. In 1810 a record was made that the warden *"Gave to a Woman with 8 children and a pass from Maidstone to Shoreham – 2 shillings."* It remained a cruel and inhumane system, in which one imagines a newly widowed woman being forcibly driven from Maidstone after her husband's death to fend for herself and her family on her way back to a village she might have left twenty years earlier. Pregnant and nursing women were sometimes found dead beside the road as a result of hunger and exhaustion. Sadly, the new regime that was put in place from 1834 housed poor people in grim workhouses, serving a number of communities. This tore families apart by refusing to let wives stay with their husbands or brothers with their sisters.

In 1812, the churchwarden's income for running the parish, known as the assessment, brought in £20. Twenty years later, this had risen to over £30. This was in addition to the Land Tax, the rectorial tithes and a rate to maintain the poor, so the inhabitants were fairly comprehensively taxed. The poor rate,

Addington Green as at the beginning of the 19th century. Photograph taken 1930's but, except for the school, how it would have looked in 1800.

administered by the overseers for the poor, was enforced by the parish constable. He was selected by the vestry, but was sworn in by a Justice of the Peace. The overseers' accounts for Addington do not survive for the period. However, Cornelius Kettle was the constable at Offham during the early nineteenth century. His account books survive, and were analysed by Frank Johns for the Archaeologica Cantiana in 1987.[20] He was unpaid, but was allowed to claim expenses, and his account book for 1818 contains a total expenditure of £18 5s 9d, giving an idea of the burden on the parish. Addington must have had a similar office holder, and similar expenses. The Constable's position was fairly onerous, though the holder would also have had a "day job". Some cases had to be taken to the Petty Sessions, others, more rarely, to the Quarter Sessions at Maidstone. The constable was required to accompany persons with a pass. Before 1814, this was to their parish of settlement, but later simply off the boundary and on to that of the next door parish. Kettle seems to have regularly gone as far as Ightham, Kingsdown and Farningham. An active magistrate living at Addington was Rev. J.B. Polhill, of St. Vincents. Kettle's records show that he brought a number of offenders or vagrants to Rev. Polhill at his home, for judgement. On 3rd December 1820, Kettle took William Golding "by Warrant" to Bridewell, where he would serve three months' imprisonment on a charge of *"pulling up ash plants belonging to Col. Stratford".* These ash plants could well have been fencing a piece of land within Offham's boundaries bought by Col. Wingfield-Stratford in 1818 from Lord Thanet, to enlarge his park. Other crimes were stealing coal, assault upon a wife, stealing hops, distraint for not paying poor rates and rioting. Did Addington's residents behave in a similar manner?

1   His papers relevant to these estates are lodged at the Northern Ireland record office under the title: "Verner Wingfield Papers". The catalogue is available on line. Ref: PRONI D2538/D/6 refers to accounts and correspondence with his solicitors, Messrs. Nesbit and Stewart, including about his wife's estates at Addington. Due to the distance, I have not been able to examine them.

2   Stratford was founded in 1775 by Edward Stratford, 2nd Earl of Aldeborough, as a textile centre in West Wicklow. Despite huge investment the industrial venture failed and Stratford practically disappeared. In 1837, before the Great Famine, the village had a population of 952. Despite some recent development, in 2002, the population was only 900. (source: Wikipedia)

3   Now the Oriental Club. The property was sold in the late 19th century. It was taken over by the Oriental Club in 1962.

4   John Larking was a self made man, paper maker and banker. He was married to Dorothy Style, a family connection of the Wingfield-Stratfords, and was the father of Rev. Lambert Larking. He built Clare House, East Malling, and bought up its surrounding park from the Twisden family of Bradbourne Place. In 1807 his bank in Maidstone failed, and he was forced to live abroad for some years, leasing and finally selling Clare House to the Wigan family.

5   His father, Admiral Sir Francis Geary had married Leonard's first cousin, Mary Bartholomew. Sir William Geary (1756-1925) was M.P. For Kent from 1796-1806 and from 1812-1818

6   Kent History and Library Centre, Whatman Way, Maidstone (K.H.L.C.), Addington Parish, P/2/3/1

7   A two sided single manuscript document now at the K.H.L.C., Addington Parish papers, P2/3/5

8   The date when Rev. Davis died. The Land Tax records do not start until 1780.

9   Rev. Style was the younger son of Sir Thomas Style, and had been the vicar of that parish. He was also the Rector of Mereworth, where the couple had lived.

10   Twysden, William *A Plain Statement of Facts*, 1832, printed by N.F. Mullin, London – quoted in "The Family of Twysden and Twisden", p 327

11   In fact she left him, but they were later reconciled and were then legally married in a second ceremony. Sadly for her, Sir William did manage to go through this wife's money, and she spent her old age in penury. (from "The Family of Twysden and Twisden")

12   Rev. Paulson recorded this in his rectorial tithe book.

13   Lemmey was declared bankrupt. Westfields was then acquired by Col. Wingfield-Stratford. William Brown (1805-1887), farmed there and acted as his steward. Brown was a useful and committed member of the community. He was born at Strood, near Rochester, but married Susannah, from Ryarsh, who probably encouraged him to settle here. He was a trustee of the highways board, which shows his standing in the community. On retirement, the couple moved to Bexley.

14   This information comes from the obituary of his widow, Frances (Wingfield-Stratford). Isle of Man Times of 9 June 1888.

15   Stephen West was the shepherd. William Barnden and James Baldwin were agricultural labourers. Thomas Millhouse was a carpenter. Thomas Pankhurst, (1801-1899), was born at Addington (bapt. 1803) and lived all his life in the parish. He worked as a gardener and was recorded as being 98 at his death in December 1899.

16   Their first child, Isabella, was born at Stratford Place, but the parents' abode at her baptism at St. Margaret's was given as St. Vincents. Frances and Edward John were both born at the house. In 1850 the family moved into Addington Park. I do not believe that Col. Grant ever lived at St. Vincents, but his lease gave him the right to vote at Kent elections.

17   Lambert Larking's mother was born Dorothy Style. Her brother was married to John Wingfield-Stratford's aunt. Rev. Larking was married to Frances Twysden, the sister of the 8th Baronet, then husband of Mrs. Polhill. These local family interconnections were quite common during the 19th century.

18   Addington parish records held at Kent History and Library Centre. Ref: P/2/27/1

19   By his will (Prob 11/1636), he left an annuity of £150 to his sister, Measuring worth gives the value in terms of average earnings as being £110,000. He left three further bequests of £50 and the residue of his estate went to his brother, Rev. Carew Elers.

20   Johns, F.D., *A Petty Constable's Accounts Book*, Arch. Cant, 104, pp 9-24

6

1851 to 1899 - VICTORIAN ADDINGTON

The census of 1851 gives a detailed picture of the village and its inhabitants. 220 people were living in 44 houses and cottages, less than half of which stood on the Green. The great majority of the residents had been born within a five-mile radius of the village, 89 in Addington itself. Only 41 were born outside Kent, eleven of these being servants at Addington Park. The rector, Rev. George Paulson, was born the furthest away, at St. Petersbourg.

Average occupancy was five, though a few cottages housed seven or eight, despite having only four rooms. 27 households, over half the total, contained children, and a few had three generations living together. 40 boys and 49 girls were aged less than 18, but only five sons and one daughter over the age of 16 remained at home. All of these had occupations. The young men were employed as labourers. The young woman was Sarah Ann Brown, the farmer's daughter at Westfields.

The squire was now Mr. John Wingfield-Stratford, aged 40. At the census, he was at the manor house with his wife, three children, his stepmother and fourteen servants. The other two substantial homes, St. Vincents and the Vale were both occupied by caretakers. Nine homes held servants, mainly female, and a number of the cottagers had lodgers. Eighteen

residents were over 60, the eldest being Thomas Broad, aged 81. He was recorded as "infirm", but would survive for a further nine years. Thomas was born at Offham but had moved to Addington by 1809.[1] His wife, Ellen, had died in 1849, so when the census was taken he was in the care of his son, John, also a widower. Two of his grandchildren lived with them at the cottage at Woodgate. Only one resident was categorised as a "pauper". Thomas Walton, another elderly man, lived in the cottage next to the new school.

Agriculture was the main occupation, but there were now only two resident farmers, William Brown of Westfields Farm and Thomas Whiting, the miller, who also farmed at East Street. Together with non-resident landowners, they employed 30 agricultural or general labourers and a further 21 skilled outdoor workers, such as bailiff, shepherd, carter, gardener, gamekeeper, cowman and bricklayer. The grocer was Charles Millhouse. His father, Thomas Millhouse, the builder, and his stepmother were at nearby Lane Farmhouse with four children, whilst his younger brother, Thomas, was an apprentice at the Mill. The publican at The Angel was George Smith, who would remain the victualler until his death in 1866. Mrs. Frances Smith had been born in Addington. They spent their entire married life in the village, living firstly at The Laurels before moving to the Angel.

Wives generally did not work for money. Just one, Mrs. Elizabeth Pankhurst, gave her occupation as dressmaker, whilst Mrs. Susan Brown at Westfields said that she was a farmer's wife, no doubt asserting that she worked extremely hard for her husband's business. It is most probable that this was the case with Frances Smith at the Angel as well.

John Wingfield-Stratford Esquire

John Wingfield-Stratford, the new squire of Addington, was the only son of John and Frances Wingfield-Stratford. His inheritance included a village where well over half the farmland and most of the homes were in his ownership. The churchwarden's accounts for 1851 show that his church rates that year were £431 2s 6d. William Brown, his steward, was the only other resident to pay over £50. Mr. Wingfield-Stratford's property included land in Ireland, London, a number of local parishes and more distantly in Kent, as he had a property in Rainham.[2] During his tenure, he would acquire more land and houses in Addington.

Mr. Wingfield-Stratford was educated at Eton, but did not attend university or follow his father into the regular army. He served with the Oxonhoath Troop of the West Kent Yeomanry, being promoted to Captain on 1st August 1848. It is probable that even before his marriage he was assisting his father with the administration of the estate, as he was a voter at Addington through owning property in the village. His main home, when a bachelor, was Addington Park. He was 34 when he married Jane Elizabeth Guise on 10th December 1844, at her home in the Forest of Dean, Gloucestershire. The marriage took place on his birthday, adding an extra happy note to the occasion. Jane was 21. She was the daughter of Sir John Wright Guise, 3rd Bart., of Elmore Court.[3] Her mother was Charlotte Diana Vernon, but she had died before Jane's marriage.

Their family, with the exception of their eldest child,

were all born in Addington, and eventually numbered thirteen children. All survived to adulthood, and only the eldest son, Edward John Wingfield-Stratford, remained unmarried. Below is a family table giving the outline of three generations of Wingfield-Stratfords, their marriages and offspring. The names in bold were the heads of the family. The table shows that John and Jane Wingfield-Stratford had thirteen children and thirty eight grandchildren, most of whom left descendants.

Hon. John Wingfield-Stratford (1772-1850)
married firstly Frances Bartholomew (1775-1827). They had three children:
1. Frances Amelia (1808-1844)
   married Rev. John Cecil Hall (1804-1862) (no children)
2. Isabella Harriet (1809-1858)
   married John Malcolm (1806-1893) (four sons, one daughter)
3. **John Wingfield-Stratford** (1810-1881)
   married Jane Elizabeth Guise (1825-1897)
   1. Isabella Margaret (1845-1933)
      married Rev. James Newton Heale (nine children)
   2. Frances Charlotte (1847-1926)
      married Rev. Sir Henry Michael Hawley, 5th Baronet (three sons)
   3. **Edward John Wingfield-Stratford** (1849-1903),
      unmarried.
      He sold Addington estate in 1887.
   4. Henry Verner (1851-1923)
      married Grace Hopecroft, widow of James Atkinson (no children)
   5. Cecil Vernon (1853-1939)
      married Rosalind Vesey Bligh, daughter of vicar of Birling, (two sons and a daughter)
   6. Emily Rose (1855-1904)
      married Henry Renny-Tailyour (four children)
   7. Leonard Guise (1856-1941)
      married Alethe Montgomery (five children)
   8. Florence Mary (1857-1948)
      married Henry Lawrence Daly (one son)
   9. Howard (1859-1940)
      married Christian Margaret Scot Duncan (no children)

10. Richard Nevill (1861-1942)
     married Grace Dorothea Montgomery
     (a son and a daughter)
11. Georgiana Maud (1862-1945)
     married Howard Guise [her first cousin]
     (one daughter)
12. Francis Mervyn (1864-1932)
     married Norah Mathey (a son and a
     daughter)
13. Violet Alice Ethel (1868-1916)
     married Bertie Angelo Cator (2 sons and a
     daughter)

Col. Hon. John Wingfield-Stratford married
secondly
Miss Harriette Grant, (1783-1863). They had no
children, and she survived her husband.

Mr. Wingfield-Stratford was involved in his local and
countywide community, as were his father and
grandfather before him. He was a magistrate and an
assiduous trustee on the local highways trust.
Meetings of the latter were poorly attended and very
few of the numerous trustees served as chairman. John
Wingfield-Stratford served in this capacity more than
once, and was chairman when it was dissolved in 1861.
He was High Sheriff in 1873 and a Deputy Lieutenant
for Kent. His major contribution to Addington itself
was to build a school for the children of the village,
which was also used as a village meeting room. As this
was already standing on the Green at the 1851 census,
it is probable that he and his father had jointly
commenced the project. Its full history
is described below.

Jane Wingfield-Stratford was a caring
"squire's wife", who took a particular
interest in the children of the village.
The church magazines that survive
record the parties and entertainments she hosted, for both young
and old, and she was clearly much
appreciated. Although the couple
spent time in London, they were at
Addington for each of the ten-yearly
censuses, as well as spending the
summer months and Christmastime
at their country home. Cricket was a
favourite family pastime. The cricket

pitch was then beside Trottiscliffe Road, near
Plowenders Bridge. The Addington Park Cricket Club
played against other country house teams such as St.
Clere House at Kemsing and the Mote at Maidstone,
as well as against local village teams. A cricket brake
took them to the fixtures. The 1879 season included
matches against Plaxtol, Farningham and Bexley and
a fixture with the Royal Engineers took place at
Addington. Their son-in-law, Henry Renny-Tailyour,
served with the Royal Engineers, and was a proficient
cricketer, who played for Kent, as well as for his
regiment. Renny-Tailyour was also a talented
footballer, who played for Scotland. He was a
member of the Royal Engineers Team that won the
third FA cup in 1874.

The Vale came on to the market shortly after John
Wingfield-Stratford's succession to the manor. It then
became one of the leased properties of the manor.
After his stepmother's death in 1863, St. Vincents also
came back into the estate. John made further
purchases when possible. He bought Hedgehogs
Farm and part of Ford Farm from Sir William Geary,
3rd Baronet. In 1891, William Juniper, a dairyman, was
the resident. It is possible that Hedgehogs had been
a dairy for some years, though the census records
show only agricultural labourers at the farm. During
the mid 1850's, John Wingfield-Stratford built Stone
Cottages on the Green for his estate workers. These
were to a design known as model cottages, and were
attractively faced with Kentish ragstone.

Stone Cottages, Addington Green, built in the mid 1850's

During the 1860's, agriculture was booming, and rents were resilient but, as the 1870's dawned, the situation began to deteriorate. The weather became consistently bad, with atrocious winters and wet summers. This led to poor harvests but, worse still, the price of hops dropped, as cheaper imports began to flood the market. For land-holders and farmers in Kent, who had relied on this high value crop, the loss of income was particularly severe. The Addington estate ceased to be economic, and the last few years of John Wingfield-Stratford's life must have been stressful.

John Wingfield-Stratford was aged 70 when he died at Addington Park on 8th May 1881. Due to the large size of his family, some of his children were still at home. He appointed three executors and trustees. These were two of his brothers-in-law, Francis Edward Guise and John Malcolm, and his nephew, John Wingfield Malcolm. His will left the bulk of his estate in trust to his eldest son, Edward John Wingfield-Stratford. Should Edward leave no heir, which proved the case, the estate

Memorial Window to Mrs. Wingfield-Stratford (detail)

would pass to each of his sons in turn, by seniority. His will indicates that, under the terms of his marriage settlement, he was required to provide settlements of between £7,000 and £9,000 to each of his children. As the estate was valued for probate at only £73,000, such settlements would have been a great burden.[4] Only the two eldest daughters were by then married, and four of the children were aged less than 21 years. The youngest, Violet, was only twelve when her father died. By a codicil written shortly before his death, John Wingfield-Stratford directed that no land should be sold to raise the capital for these portions for twelve years. Interest alone would be paid to the legatees during this period. However, in comparison with the inventory following Edmund Watton's death in 1716, his goods and furniture, as specified in the will, were sumptuous. They included not only pictures and prints but also statues, marbles, bronzes, articles of vertu and china. He directed that these should be counted as heirlooms for whoever received the manor.

Mrs. Wingfield-Stratford remained at the manor house for a year, and then left the village for a while before returning in the summer of 1886, when St. Vincents became vacant. She lived there with her daughters, Georgiana and Violet, though Edward and his unmarried brothers were recorded in residence there at the 1891 census. Georgiana and Violet both married in the early 1890's. Violet received her proposal of marriage at St. Vincents from Bertie Cator,[5] a young naval officer, and the couple married at St. Margaret's church on 25th January 1893. Mrs. Wingfield-Stratford then returned to her home county of Gloucestershire. She died at

Mrs. Jane Wingfield-Stratford (1821-1897)

Cheltenham on 20th February 1897. Her memorials at St. Margaret's were a new lych-gate and a stained glass window on the North Wall of the nave.

The entrance to Addington church, early 20th century. Photograph by Freda Barton © The Malling Society

The three Rectors

By 1851, Rev. George Paulson had been rector of Addington for fifteen years. On 30th March, a unique religious census was recorded in England. Each place of worship was asked to state how many people had attended services that day. It transpired that 40% of the population of England attended a religious service, of which 51% went to an Anglican one, but these numbers included many variations. The figures recorded those who went twice that Sunday, but not regular worshippers who were unable to get to a service, especially as the weather was very bad. Further questions were asked, such as the name and description of the church, how funding was obtained, whether by tithes, charges or pew rents, how many "sittings" the building would hold and the average attendance during the year.

Rev. Paulson's entry for Addington shows a remarkable lack of knowledge about the church he had served since 1835. He stated, *"I dont know in*

memory or to the honour of what saint it was built." Rev. Paulson had consulted Hasted, as he quoted Hasted's incorrect assertion that the church was built in 1403. He could not say who built the church *"but no doubt very proper."* The tithe rent charge in 1850 was £243, but netted only £143 after parish rates and expenses. Its glebe was 27 acres, and fees were only about 10s. All but six of the pews were free, and he stated, *"200 may sit not uncomfortably."* This seems a little optimistic. This statement confirms that there were pews in the church, though the present ones are of a later date. The census took place on Sunday, 30th March 1851, a cold, wet and blustery day. The attendance at Addington's two morning services was 39 + 30 at Sunday school, and in the afternoon 66 + 23. This would imply that 158 people, young and old had attended. In this case it was a very high proportion of the population of the village, which was given as only 220 at the national census that year. In reality, a number of worshippers came to more than one service. Rev. Paulson alleged that in the summer months, and in fine weather, the congregation would have been 120. For comparison, in nearby Trottiscliffe attendances were Morning 25 + 25 and afternoon 80 + 25 (out of a population of 283). Rev. Paulson wrote one of the fuller entries. Some of his fellow priests were clearly irritated by being asked anything about their work. Rev. Lambert Larking at Ryarsh complained that, as some of his parishioners lived in outlying hamlets, they attended churches closer to their homes, especially in wet weather. He refused to fill in most of the sections. He was probably referring partly to Aldon, possibly explaining the reasonable turnout at St. Margaret's that day.

Mrs. Pickering was the tenant at the Vale during the latter part of Rev. Paulson's life. Her daughter wrote a memoir of her childhood in Addington. She wrote of Rev. Paulson: *"He was quite old with white hair. Extraordinarily like the portraits of the Russian Emperor Paul. Every summer he disappeared, never telling his wife he was going away, he was absent about 6 weeks, and she had to provide for the Sunday services! One summer he never returned; her brother Canon Elwyn saw a notice of his death in Russia. It was discovered he was an illegitimate son of the Emperor and went yearly to report himself and receive his salary for the year.*[6] The only problem with this story is that Rev. Paulson was an assiduous minister, who signed all the burial notices throughout his incumbency, including through the summer months. He died in Addington rectory on 20th August 1869 aged 71, and is buried in the churchyard here. This anecdote demonstrates the imagination of children, and shows the care one must take over oral history.

Paulson had not been a wealthy man, and his estate's value for probate was less than £1,500. His wife, Fanny, left the parish, but died only four months later, aged 50. In 1882, the next rector of Addington, Rev. Heale noted in the parish magazine that only the youngest of their seven children remained alive.

The last two rectors of the nineteenth century were connections of the Wingfield-Stratfords. The Rev. James Newton Heale (1837-1921) was the only son of a doctor and had been previously vicar of Swindon. He married Isabella, the eldest daughter of the squire, on 14th January 1868 in Addington. He and Isabella stayed in the parish from 1869 until 1882, during which time they had eight children. Unlike Thomas Bowdler, Rev. Heale was an ardent advocate of the Oxford Movement and introduced their liturgy and ceremony to St. Margaret's church. This meant a great emphasis on ceremony, use of vestments and the revival of the Eucharist as the centre for Christian worship. Addington's congregation would remain "High Church" until the second half of the twentieth century. He was an enthusiastic and energetic man in other ways as well. He arranged for musical services to be held at the church on Friday afternoons and readings of religious material at the schoolroom on weekday evenings. This was a period when many new hymns were being written. Rev. Heale placed an emphasis on choral music. The choir grew in numbers, so that by 1879 it had about twenty members. In late July that year, eighteen of the choir travelled in the Wingfield-Stratford's cricket brake to the Wildernesse at Seal, then owned by Marquis of Camden.[7] There they were given refreshments, after

which they moved to Seal church, where they took part in a choral festival with 300 other singers.

Rev. Heale particularly encouraged young people to prepare themselves for confirmation. On Sunday, 25th June 1879, sixteen were confirmed at the morning service by the Bishop of Dover, a very high number for such a small parish.

Towards the end of his incumbency, he introduced the first parish magazine. To begin with, he wrote a page of local input for "The Household", but the printing arrangements were very unwieldy. In 1879, he moved to "The Dawn of the Day", published by the Society for Promoting Christian Knowledge, having agreed with a local printer at West Malling to provide Addington's input. This was a subscription service and throughout its history, and that of most of its successors, ran at a loss. Even in 1879, he was advocating selling advertising space, to begin with of "situations wanted". Rev. Newton Heale's successor used "The Banner of Faith", a national church magazine produced by the Christian Extension Association.

These magazines give a snapshot of village life beyond church services and upkeep. Rev. Heale

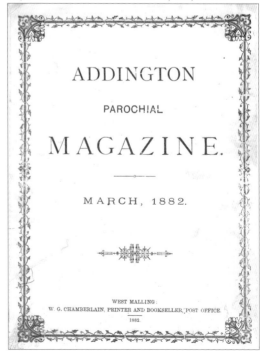

ADDINGTON

PAROCHIAL

MAGAZINE.

MARCH, 1882.

WEST MALLING:
W. G. CHAMBERLAIN, PRINTER AND BOOKSELLER, POST OFFICE.
1882.

commented on the weather, reporting that the sharp and bitter frosts had meant little out-door work, and no entertainment (even fox hunting!). However, stag hounds had met at Wrotham Water on 13th February 1879. They ran through Trottiscliffe to Addington, capturing their first stag at East Street. Were red deer prevalent in the area at the time? Alternatively, was a stag released for the hunt, as was the practice in other areas? Whatever the case, it was a different world, in which the rector closely identified himself with his patron.

A parish entertainment had been planned in the Hall at Addington Park for 1st January 1879, but this had been horrendously affected by a deluge of rain. People had to wade through ankle deep water to come. It raised only 16 shillings and 2 pence, owing to the scarcity of attendance. Rev. Heale reported that, a few days later, Mrs. Wingfield-Stratford royally entertained the Sunday School. She organised *"a good Hare and Hounds Paper Chase"* for the boys *"while the girls had games in the Hall until it was time for all to collect in a large room upstairs to see a capital magic lantern, which Mrs. Stratford had also engaged for their entertainment."* On a sadder note, he wrote of *"the great depression of all trades, and especially that of hopes"* as there had been much hardship and suffering.

He introduced mid week services to complement those on Sundays, and the choir was an important part of these. The choir master came from as far as Maidstone. Mr. Malins gave lessons on Thursday evenings at Addington Park. The number of communicants increased to 306 in 1878, against 284 in 1877, with an average of 18 at each celebration. The offertory collected £41 0s 3d, of which £25 3s 2d was given to charitable societies.

In 1881, Rev. Heale's patron and father-in-law, John Wingfield-Stratford, died. 1882 was a very worrying year for the village, as the Wingfield-Stratford family left their ancestral home for ever. The mansion would be let for five years, until a new owner was eventually found. Despite the uncertainty, Rev. Heale still actively tried to increase

the spiritual life of his congregation. He wrote in the January edition of the parish magazine that he had greatly increased the number of communion services, including some in the early morning. He introduced these as *"he has regard to the convenience of as many as possible, but he is especially guided always by consideration for those employed in labour of any kind."* He was as good as his word in caring for all sections of the community, as his next two ministries were in urban areas. He became the vicar of Orpington in 1883, and later moved to Bethnal Green.[8] On his retirement he and his wife returned to Kent. They lived at Nettlestead Court, where he died in 1921.

The Rev. Julian Guise, nephew of Mrs. Wingfield-Stratford was installed as rector by his cousin, Edward John Wingfield-Stratford, on 18th October 1883. Rev.

Rev. Julian Guise, M.A., Rector of Addington 1883-1928

Guise would be the incumbent for the next 45 years. He was born at Longhope, Gloucestershire in 1856, and was the second son of a clergyman. Between 1880 and 1883, he was vicar of Lea, Gloucestershire. His widowed mother joined him in Addington, where she died on 19th August 1886. Within two months, on 5th October that year, he married Miss Elizabeth Lucy Master, who also came from Gloucestershire, at St. Jude's, Chelsea.[9] Rev. and Mrs. Guise were of similar ages, and must have known each other for some years. Sadly, they were to have no children. Rev. Guise was a kind and popular man, who virtually ran the village during his long incumbency, which extended well into the twentieth century. Like his predecessor, he adjusted the church furniture. He removed a simple oak altar rail and replaced it with one made of brass. Alfred Chapman, Senior, preserved this oak rail at Woodgate, and it was reinstalled in the church during the 1930's.

The lives and service of these rectors shows how the reality of life as a nineteenth century minister differed from earlier times. They were no longer allowed to hold more than one living, leading some to a straightened financial position. However, it meant that they lived amongst their congregation and shared their lives. Rectors were not now wealthy. Their financial position would force Addington into a joint ministry with the century..

The village and its families as seen through census records

Between 1850 and 1900, a number of new homes were added to the village. These were the terrace of four stone cottages on the Green and others at Hernewell (1850's), The Mount on Teston Road (c. 1870), Aldon House, (mid 1880's), Shaw Hill House (c. 1888), and Keepers (1895). Meanwhile, some homes were abandoned, such as

the Mill and in East Street. In 1883, an area around Aldon was transferred from Ryarsh civil parish to Addington civil parish, bringing with it nine properties. (The ecclesiastical boundaries remained the same) However, as there were losses, the number of homes only rose to 56 at the 1901 census. The acreage of the civil parish was now 1,117 acres.

Some of the cottages became very overcrowded, as most had only four rooms. This reflected improvements in childbirth and a better awareness of hygiene, resulting in greater infant survival. William and Sarah Barnden had reared eleven children between 1816 and 1839, but only half had survived. Benjamin and Harriet Barnden, the next generation, had seven between 1870 and 1882 and only one died in infancy. In 1871, a number of cottages housed five or six offspring. Even then, this was not necessarily the total size of the family, as young people left home early. In 1841, William and Ellen Baldwin lived at Woodgate with their seven-year-old daughter, Ann. She had already left home by the 1851 census.

Some couples kept their families with them. Between 1861 and 1881, William and Elizabeth Saker lived in one of the central two cottages in School Row, now a single house. At the 1871 census, William was 54 and Elizabeth was ten years his junior. In the cottage with them were George, 23, Frank, 15, Caroline, 13, Mary Anne, 10, Jessie, 7, Edward, 5 and a grandchild, Emma aged 3, who had been born in London. Even in 1881, their son, George, was still an occupant.

In 1871, Philip and Harriet Fry at the Post Office had four children, the oldest of whom, Ada, was aged seven. Six children were with them at the 1881 census, though Ada had already left home. Elizabeth

From 218 inhabitants in 1851, the population rose to 272 at the 1891 census.

Census	No. of homes	Total	Male	Female	Under 15	Over 60	Born at Addington	Average occupancy
1861	46	226	118	144	78	21	94	4.91
1871	52 (2 uninh)	262	115	146	80	24	83	5.24
1881	50 (2 uninh)	264	114	150	88	25	90	5.45
1891	55	272	123	145	87	12	71	4.94

and Edith remained with their parents, right up until the 1911 census, by which time Philip was a widower, aged 81. John and Anne Sparkes' family of seven in 1871 had risen to eight by 1881, but Anne was by then a widow. She worked as a laundress, firstly to support her family, and then on her own behalf and lived in East Sreet until her death many years later.

Another large family was that of James and Anne Baldwin. James had been born in Addington and married in Snodland. The couple returned to the village in about 1839 with a baby daughter. Nine more children were born in the next twenty years. However, five died in childhood. James and his wife lived first at East Street and then moved to one of Overlea Cottages, on the Green. He died in Addington in 1886, aged 74.

In 1871, fourteen women and twelve men were still in their parents' home. Three of the women were in work, Kezia Wells, the schoolmistress, and two dressmakers. All the men were employed except Edward John Wingfield-Stratford, who was then aged 24. At the 1891 census, the number of unmarried adult daughters at home was 22. That year, 118 children and adults lived with their parents out of a population of 228, well over half the inhabitants. The figure must reflect availability of local work and little independent accommodation. Very few homes were now owner-occupied. Most of the large houses were leased, their tenants being mainly widows.

Agricultural labour and personal service remained the principal means of employment in Addington throughout the latter half of the century. Most jobs were provided by the manor house and estate and this stranglehold increased as the century ended. Although later censuses show slightly more diverse employment, personal service remained high. A significant number of men earned their living as domestic gardeners, despite the emergent market gardening industry in the area. The 1871 census recorded 45 domestic servants, their posts ranged from kitchen maids to cooks to butlers, and included a number of nursery and personal maids. In 1891 nine domestic servants were living at Addington Park, and a further three men, a coachman and two grooms were housed at the stables.

Poverty and wealth

One family story, gleaned from census records, is very sad. At the time of the 1881 census Mrs. Eliza Paddick was visiting her widowed mother, Lydia West, who lived in one of the stone cottages on the Green. Eliza had six children with her, aged from one to eleven. Although pregnant, she seems to have left her husband. Eliza had been born in Addington, and was herself one of a family of seven. Samuel Paddick was a London coachman and the children had been born in Marylebone. Eliza's death was recorded at Malling in 1890. Her older children were by then working, or were quickly sent to work, as Edith, born in late 1876, was a general servant in London at the 1891 census. Her three youngest children: Alice, Leonard and Minnie were separated from each other and put into orphanages. Leonard was in Lewisham, Alice was in a small school in Merrow, near Guildford and Minnie was at St. Michael's Home for Motherless Girls at Shalborne, Berkshire. Their father, Samuel, died in the Marylebone Workhouse in 1926, having, it seems, lost contact with all his large family. On the positive side, Leonard emigrated to Montreal in 1905 and then moved to New York State, where he was working as a paper maker at the 1910 U.S. census.

However, Eliza's story is rare. Very few Addington residents were forced to live in the Malling Union House. Not one was registered there in either 1851 or 1861, although, at the 1871 census, Thomas Chapman, brother to Alfred Chapman of Woodgate, was an inmate, aged then 49. He was unmarried and may have suffered an injury that prevented him from working, as he spent the rest of his life in the workhouse. He died in 1898, aged 76. At the 1881 census, William Barnden, the brother of the local shepherd, Benjamin Barnden, was also at the Union House. He was born at Alfriston in Sussex and had been with his parents in Addington during the 1820s. He would remain at the Malling Union until he died in 1893.

In 1891, four erstwhile Addington residents were housed there, out of 213 inmates. These were William Barnden, Thomas Chapman, Stephen Hodges and David Pankhurst. Pankhurst was the oldest. He had worked as a general labourer and was later one of the gamekeepers on the estate. David had been born in Addington in 1809. He and his wife, Elizabeth, lived firstly at Woodgate then moved to East Street, before settling in the wooden cottage next to the shop. They lost all four of their children at an early age and, when Elizabeth Pankhurst died in 1879, he could no longer manage on his own. He survived at the Union House into the new century, and was buried in Addington on 2nd November 1901. Stephen Hodges worked as a farm waggoner and was aged only 53. He was a married man so, like Thomas Chapman, may well have suffered an injury or debilitating illness. His wife, Maria, was the head of the household at Hernewell at the same census. She had four children with her, the youngest being only two and gave her occupation as "field worker". Stephen died at West Malling the following year. The workhouse was a grim place to live, but many of its residents were disabled or frail.

Overall, villagers were cared for within the community when they fell sick. Although there was no National Health Service, the health needs of residents were now better met. The West Kent General Hospital had opened in Maidstone and contributions were made to this charitable institution by the parishioners. In the case of serious illness, operations at London hospitals were sometimes paid for. These contributions, which also supported a cottage hospital at Wrotham, continued for many years.

In 1858, the new National Probate Office became responsible for the execution of wills. It recorded the value of estates for which administration had been sought. These probate records confirm that the yeoman class had completely vanished from Addington, a fact also borne out by the burial records for the parish. Not one administration was granted after 1858 for this type of estate. In fact, only nine wills from village residents exist for the whole fifty year period, confirming that wealth was now concentrated in very few hands. Three of these were

written by the Wingfield-Stratford family. Two dealt with the estates of the Rev. George Paulson and his wife. The remaining four were those of Mrs. Pickering of the Vale, Mr. Henry Gay Hewlett of Shaw Hill House, Mrs. Harriet Guise, mother of the rector, and Alfred Lankstead, the publican, who died in 1884, leaving an estate valued at £241 7s 2^{1}/2d. The only substantial estates were those of Mr. John Wingfield-Stratford (1881, £73,362 8s) and his aunt by marriage, Mrs. Guise (1883, £11,064 7s 2d).

Church records

The parish records of christenings, banns, marriages, and funerals show a stable community, whose relationships in general were locally based. 62 marriages were celebrated during the second half of the century, slightly more than during the first half. Only seven of the grooms and two of the brides came from outside Kent, and most were still from either Addington or neighbouring villages. In 18 marriages both bride and groom gave Addington as their parish, though sometimes this was because the young man or woman was working here when they met. Six marriages were of widowers. The eldest of these were Stephen Lepper, the shepherd, and Mary Anne Hackett, aged 64 and 50 respectively at their marriage on 26th January 1867. Mary Anne was a widow. She had come from London to work at Addington Place, probably as a laundress. Stephen was born at Hastings, but had been living in Addington since 1831. Seven of his eight children were baptised here. His first wife, Elizabeth Ann, died at the end of 1865. His second marriage would last ten years, ending with his death. The couple lived in a cottage behind the Green that was later demolished. By the time of the 1871 Census it appears that he had suffered a devastating stroke, as he was noted as "paralytic". Mary Anne took in laundry to support her elderly and disabled husband, perhaps continuing to work for the mansion house. She was sixty when Stephen died, and moved back to London. In 1881 she was still working as a laundress, lodging at Greenwich. She died in 1893 at the Greenwich Union

Infirmary. Mary Ann's life spanned almost the entire nineteenth century and reflected the changes and hardships that women endured.

374 christenings were recorded for this fifty year period. The high number might reflect enthusiastic rectors, who were assiduous in persuading parents to bring their children to church for baptism. Later in the century, Rev. Julian Guise ensured that hop-pickers and their children joined the Church of England, conducting joint and multi-aged christening sessions. The 374 christenings were not all of Addington residents. 144 children were born to fathers who gave their occupation as labourer. Other fathers worked as bailiff, gamekeeper, coachman or gardener, but new occupations were given. These were: plumber, glazier, house decorator, stonemason and platelayer.

Addington seems to have been a moral society, or one that was fearful of censure. Only 26 christenings were recorded for children born out of wedlock during the whole century. Most of these children, sadly, were not supported by the community, and moved away from the village.

The number of burials, 202, was much lower than that of baptisms. The census returns confirm a bulge in the population, and infant mortality was about average for Kent. 38 children are known to have been aged less than five at death, 22 failed to reach their first birthday.[10] 76 were burials of people who had been baptised in Addington. 15 of these had been aged over 60 at death, emphasising the stability of housing tenure.

Social life

Although life would have been tough for families in the village cottages, they had a number of entertainments. Addington and Ryarsh Village Cricket Club staged popular and regular fixtures, until the Wingfield-Stratfords left the village. It was revived as the Addington Cricket Club in 1887, with Mr. Spooner Hardy as captain, and Mr. F.

Chapman as secretary. Subscriptions were set at half a crown per year. Luckily there were some funds in the savings bank to kick-start the revival by purchasing equipment for play. The first fixture was a little disappointing! It was played against Birling on Saturday, June 4th 1887. The team members came from all sections of the village and were Messrs. Goodale, Howe, M[ervyn] Wingfield-Stratford, Lancaster, Shrubsole, Lovel, Hawley, Waghorn, Groves and Columbine, plus the rector, Rev. Guise, who achieved no runs in the first innings, but seven in the second. Rev. Guise's main talents seem to have been as a bowler. Addington's score was 16 runs in their first innings and 28 in their second. Birling, on the other hand, achieved 74 and 64 respectively. At a match played against Offham the following month their score was a more respectable 168, but play had to end before their second innings finished, and Offham had made 194 in their first innings.

There was a club room in the village, used for social events. I believe this was above the stables adjoining the Angel, and it was in use well into the twentieth century. It could not have been a licensed room in the Angel, as it was used by women, as well as by men. It was close to the Green, as after a children's tea in the club room the participants were "herded" into the school room for the performance of a conjuror, who had been brought from London for the occasion.

Rev. Guise, writing in the parish magazine of December 1887, described the long standing Men's Club. He wrote, "*The Men's Club goes steadily on in the even tenor of its way; it never changes; it plays the same old game in the quiet contentment one evening every week in the year. The room the club meets in has become more and more changed, as various improvements have been made in it, but its members dont want to be improved; they are perfectly content with their game of cards or tip-it' (how does the word spell itself?), and the pipe that soothes.*" A piano had been donated, and played for a while, but once out of tune it had been ignored by the old men, who also did not welcome new, younger, members, as they were too noisy. The Mothers' Union was formed in 1876 as a Christian organisation. The club room was the venue of the Mothers' Meeting, which was active during the early 1880's, though it then struggled to attract members *"to work and be read to."* When Miss Boys relaunched the meetings at the end of 1886, she introduced bread and butter and cake, to encourage more to attend. A banner shown in a photograph of the church taken in about 1905 by the West Malling photographer, Freda Barton, depicts St. Margaret, but the logo beneath is of an S and an M intertwined, rather than M and U. The Mothers' Union was an active organisation in the village during the twentieth century, and a new banner was designed for it by the local artist Alfred Rushton. During the 1880's Addington ran a subscription lending library, as readers of the church magazine were urged to donate books for it. This was probably also housed in the club room.

The Addington Bell-ringers Association was formally dissolved in 1887, but this did not mean abandoning ringing the four bells in the tower. The association was reconstituted, without its *'many offices of high-sounding title, which if all filled up must have largely drawn on the male population of Addington; and its many rules, which were often more 'honoured in the breach' than in the observance."* The bell-ringers were Alfred Chapman, Harry Chapman, William Barnden, Henry Howe, Alfred Skinner, Frank Sparkes, Senior and Frank Sparkes, Junior. A payment of ten shillings was made to each man annually, out of the offertory fund.

Ryarsh and Addington collaborated in the Cottage Gardeners' Mutual Improvement Society, which was inaugurated in 1869. Alfred Chapman, senior, was its long-serving secretary, having connections with both villages. Entries were welcomed at annual shows from any cottager residing in Addington, Offham, Ryarsh or Trottiscliffe. The society ran for many years, and frequently staged more than one show per year.

The St. Margaret's Banner, probably worked by a member of the Mothers' Union at the end of the nineteenth century.

In 1887, Addington celebrated Queen Victoria's 50th Jubilee in style. A stained glass window for the church was commissioned, and installed in the south wall of the nave. The day started very early, with young men climbing the oak tree on the Green to hang bunting, and a peal of the church bells. A special service was held in the early afternoon at which 200 Jubilee Medals were distributed. This was followed by a cricket match and dinner for the men at eight o'clock. While the cricket was taking place the children were entertained with tea and games at four o'clock and the women's tea was at 5.30 in the coach house at Addington Park. Finally, a great bonfire was lit on the Green, supervised by Philip Fry. The report in the magazine concluded that *"the bonfire proved quite fiery enough to satisfy all beholders. With the addition of a few fire balloons, some behaved properly, and some gave as much excitement by behaving improperly and the explosion of sundry squibs, etc. purchased at the last minute, the Addington Jubilee Celebration came to an end."* It had been hoped to finish the evening with a firework display, but these did not arrive in time. Instead the display was held on 20th July as part of St. Margaret's Day, the dedication festival of the church. One rocket landed on Mr. Elwin's hayrick at East Street Farm, but luckily, by the sacrifice of a coat the fire was put out. The cost of the festivities and fireworks had been £16 5s and the memorial window in the church cost £31 17s. This was quite an expense, but donations of £46 12s 3d had been received, leaving only a small deficit of £1 4s 9d.

Politics

For the first three quarters of the nineteenth century, Addington had very few electors, between eight and thirteen. Some of these did not even live in the village, their right to vote being established by ownership or occupation of land, or of a house on which they paid substantial rates. Although the Reform Act of 1867 introduced the entitlement of all male householders to vote, in effect it still barred those who did not pay rates from this right. This was particularly relevant at Addington, as the squire's properties were "compounded" and he paid one set of rates for all the service and tenanted cottages. The electoral roll of 1884 contained only nine names. These were James Bellingham, at the Mill, John Elwin, East Street Farm, Philip Fry, the Shop and Post Office, John Reynolds Hammond, Westfields Farm, John Spooner Hardy, Addington Vale, Rev. James Newton Heale, The Rectory, Henry Gay Hewlett, Shaw Hill House and Alfred Lankstead, the Angel Public House. Addington Park was untenanted, and the other large properties in the village were occupied by women.

The Representation of the People Act of 1884 gave the vote to male periodic tenants, as this compounding was abolished. 40% of the adult population were still unenfranchised, including service tenants, domestic servants, sons, lodgers and, of course, all women, but it greatly enlarged voter numbers in Addington. In 1885, the number of electors rose to 39. The new electors were able to exercise their right to vote as early as January 1886. The General Election was won by the Liberal Party, but a second, seven months later, returned a Conservative government. Addington was then in the Sevenoaks constituency. Universal suffrage, on an equal basis for all men and women, would not be introduced until 1929.

A Conservative Association was inaugurated in Addington on 16th March 1885. Rev. Guise recorded this in the magazine and appears to have been sympathetic, despite professing to remain independent. He wrote: *"There was a downright good muster."* Edward Wingfield-Stratford was its first president, and his new tenant at Addington Park, Col. George Arbuthnott, was appointed vice president. Mr. J. Spooner Hardy, was its Hon. Secretary. The executive council was Messrs. James Baldwin, John Elwin, Philip Fry, Alfred Hoppe, William Howe, Charles Millhouse, Thomas Parris, Henry Wells and David West, the groom at The Mount.

The new Association provoked the indignation of the Liberal party supporters in the parish. A lively political meeting was held in support of the Liberal Association at Mr. George Phillips' home in St. Leonard's Street, West Malling, under the presidency of Mr. Hewlett of Shaw Hill House. Rev. Guise reported that the meeting was infiltrated by Conservatives, including Col. Arbuthnot and Mr. Hardy, and some heated speeches were made.

Four residents

Thomas Pankhurst (1803-1899) was the eldest child of Thomas and Jane (born Fissenden) and was baptised at St. Margaret's church on 21st July 1803. He was married at Ryarsh in about 1824, and he and his wife, Elizabeth, lived there until moving to Addington in 1829-1830, by which time they had two children. Thomas worked as a gardener for the Wingfield-Stratfords and the family lived in the Lodge on the Green. This seems amazing, as at both the 1841 and the 1851 census, they had six children with them in the tiny cottage. They had nine children in all. Thomas was widowed in 1875 and his youngest daughter, Emily, then cared for him. Some years later, in 1887, Emily married Frederick Wooden and the couple continued to look after Thomas until he died at the age of 96. He was buried on 28th December 1899, just as the century ended. Emily Wooden remained in the village until she died in 1923 and her husband survived her until 1939.

Alfred Chapman (1841-1906) was the sixth child of John and Sarah Chapman. He was born in East Street in 1841. John Chapman worked as a gardener, and the family moved between Addington and Ryarsh. Mrs. Chapman died in Addington in 1842, but John then returned to Roughetts Road, Ryarsh. John Chapman was an extremely talented gardener, and his son, Alfred, inherited this skill. As a young man, Alfred Chapman was employed at Callis Court, London Road, Ryarsh by Mr. George Phillips. Phillips noted his competence and promoted him to farm bailiff, even though he was only 25. He served the family for the rest of his life, at both Ryarsh and Addington. He married Mary Anne Harris in 1867, shortly after obtaining his promotion. The couple first lived at Roughetts Road, and their family of six children were born there. In 1882, he moved as bailiff to Woodgate Farm, Addington. He and Mary Anne spent the rest of their lives at the house called Woodgate, which was then divided into two cottages. One of his long term interests and duties was the Cottage Gardeners' Society, of which, as has been said, he was the secretary. Alfred Chapman served as sexton. His son, Harry, who lived at Heatherview, East Street, followed him in this position. Another son, of his own name, Alfred, followed him as bailiff at Woodgate Farm, though, by this time, Mr. Lionel Hardy, of the Vale, was his employer.

Charles Millhouse (1825-1909) lived at Lane Farmhouse. He was born in London and was in his teens when he arrived in the village with his father, Thomas Millhouse, and his stepmother. He was the grocer at the shop for a few years, before taking over his father's carpentry and building business at Lane Farmhouse. Thomas Millhouse had probably acquired this in 1848 from the executors of John Wells, the previous owner. Wells had been the village carpenter. Charles Millhouse remained unmarried and was active on village committees all his life. His youngest brother, John Cecil Millhouse, lived with him, and their sister, Charlotte, acted as their housekeeper. Millhouse served on the church vestry, as churchwarden, school manager and on the parish meeting. He was well educated and translated the Latin inscriptions on the Watton memorial into English, so that all could understand them. The Lane, as it was then called, was later renamed Millhouse Lane. In their retirement the two brothers were fruit farmers. The family's connection with Addington ceased in 1922, with the death of John Cecil. This was eighty years after their father had arrived in the village.

Another active member of the community was Philip Fry (1830-1911). He was born at Charlton, Wiltshire and, after arriving in Addington in the late 1850's, worked as a gardener. He married in 1863 and he and his wife Harriet moved into the shop, where she became the shop-keeper. They had eight children, of whom seven survived to adulthood. Philip Fry was later appointed the first sub-postmaster, but he mainly worked as a farm bailiff. He served as the census enumerator and Overseer of

the Poor. He collected the weekly rents from the cottagers and was a founder member of Addington Conservatives. Both he and his wife survived into the twentieth century, she dying in 1909 and he in 1911. Their daughter, Miss Elizabeth Fry, took over the grocery business and post office. . The shop was sold at the auction of 1924. Elizabeth and her younger sister, Edith, then left the village to live near family in Edenbridge.

The Angel

During the second half of the nineteenth century, the Angel public house was a stable business, overseen by only three publicans. George Smith was married to Frances Smith, who was the daughter of John and Mary Norton, of Addington.[11] John Norton was widowed in 1829 and lived and worked at the pub for many years. George and Frances Smith moved to Addington in about 1840 and first lived at the Laurels. They had three children. George gave his occupation as "manservant" at the 1841 census, so may have already started working at the public house. In 1846, the previous publican, Thomas Capon, died, aged 86. George then took over the tenancy. Norton continued to work at the Angel until his death in 1861, aged 82. Frances died in 1864, and George was only 54 at his death two years later.

The next publican was Alfred Lankstead, who came from Wateringbury. He had been working as an agricultural labourer before he came to Addington in 1862 with his first wife, Esther, and three children. Their fourth child, Henry, was born at the end of that year. He may have worked for George Smith. Esther Lankstead died in 1879 and two years later, like his predecessor, he married a young woman from the village. This was Eliza Jane Hollands, the daughter of the local policeman, who lived in one of Stone Cottages. Alfred and Eliza had two children together but Lankstead died in 1884. She moved away from the village and remarried in London. She and her new husband, Alfred Lancaster, then returned to the Angel and took over the tenancy. Like his predecessor, Lancaster was not an experienced victualler. He was working as a poultry man when he and Eliza met.[12] However, once settled, the couple ran the Angel for over twenty years. They had four children, three sons and a daughter. Alfred and Eliza died within six weeks of each other, she in February and he in March 1918. Their youngest son, Sydney, served throughout the First World War with the R.A.M.C. and survived, but they did not see him return home safely.

The Victorian extension to the Vale. Note the difference in the glazing bars. From 1923 Auction catalogue. © Knight Frank LLP.

Addington Vale

When the Vale came onto the market in 1851, John Wingfield-Stratford purchased the property. After renovation, it was leased to Mrs. Anna Pickering, the widow of Rev. Edward Pickering, a master at Eton and an excellent cricketer. Pickering had played for Cambridge, the MCC, Surrey and other gentlemen's teams. Just before his early death, he was told he would be appointed the next headmaster of Eton. His father was a successful London lawyer who continued to support his son's family.

Mrs. Pickering lived at the Vale with her daughters, two of whom were married at St. Margaret's. Her father had been a Russia merchant, but had lost his fortune. Her mother became part of the household. A new wing, altered front door and bay windows were added to the Vale during the Victorian period. It seems likely that this was on Mrs. Pickering's instructions. She always wore black, except at weddings, when she assumed violet. She was an excellent singer and musician and took control of the choir at St. Margaret's. She also supervised crowded adult education lessons at the school. Mrs. Pickering died at the end of 1872, aged 59. Her unmarried daughter, Anna Frances Pickering then became a nun at Clewer, near Windsor. Mrs. Pickering is commemorated by a plaque set into the south wall of the church, near to where the family had their pew.

The Vale's next tenants were Mr. and Mrs. Capel Hanbury, who took a five-year lease on the property. He was a fireworks and ammunitions manufacturer. Their three youngest children (of six) were born in Addington. When they left, in 1880, Mr. John Spooner Hardy, (1848-1901), a former West India merchant, brought his family to the village. He is recorded at the property in the 1881 census with his wife, Henrietta, and four children, Katherine, Norah, Lionel and Ralph, then just nine months old. Ralph was born in Addington. Cyril Henry was born three years later, in 1884.

Hardy was born in Ireland, but brought up in Lancashire. He was a particularly talented singer, who performed at a number of prestigious venues, including the new Albert Hall. He sang there in 1873 with the Amateur Orchestral Society, raising money for baths and washhouses in the East End. In 1874, he married Henrietta Hamilton, the daughter of a naval officer, and their first daughter was born in Belgravia. Mrs. Hardy's brother was a business associate of her husband. In 1878, Hardy's businesses, Simeon Hardy & Sons, of London and Hardy Brothers of Barbados, failed. There were, however, substantial assets and, by mid 1880, he was able to satisfy his creditors, but this failure brought the family to Addington.[13] It was a happy choice, especially for the village, as they gave such service to the community. He became Secretary to the West Kent Hospital in Maidstone and to the Central Conservative Association in London.

Even after moving to the village, Hardy continued to sing in London and elsewhere, travelling on occasion as far as Chester. He was a member of the Guild of Amateur Musicians and a soloist with the London Musical Society. A number of the concerts at which he performed were attended by royalty.[14] Not surprisingly, he was the driving force in reinvigorating the musical output at Addington, which seems to have slipped in standard after Mrs. Pickering's death. He spearheaded the fund-raising for the organ that still performs at St. Margaret's. He was a member of the school board, and the first chairman of the Parish Meeting that was established in 1895. Sadly, his life was marred by illness at the end of the century, and he died in 1901, aged only 53. His family continued to support causes in Addington throughout the first half of the twentieth century. The youngest child, Cyril, died as a young adult. Ralph was the only one of the family who left the village and married. Mrs. Hardy, Lionel, Katherine and Norah spent the rest of their lives in Addington.

Park Cottage

Mr. William Stedman, the pharmacist at West Malling, was the son-in-law of Thomas Whiting, through whom he came to own land at Woodgate. When Sarah Stedman was widowed in 1850, she came to Addington and lived for a few years at Park Cottage. When she returned to West Malling, the house was leased to a succession of tenants. The tenant who gave most to the community was Miss Mary Boys, who moved to Park Cottage at the end of the 1870's with a companion who was also a cousin, Mrs. Ellen Elizabeth Boys. Miss Boys revived the Mothers' Meeting in the mid 1880's and donated an alms dish to the church that is still in regular use. When her cousin died in 1886, Miss Boys installed a window dedicated to her memory in the north wall of St. Margaret's. This shows St. Margaret,

and is a companion to the Jubilee window opposite. Miss Boys then left Addington and the property was vacant at the time of the 1891 census. In 1901, the occupant was Mrs. Lillian Warde, widow of Frederick Warde, the fruit farmer. She and her husband had lived at Aldon House.

St. Vincents

St. Vincents was occupied by caretakers at the 1851 census. It was the dower house of the Hon. Mrs. Wingfield-Stratford, but she was then living at the manor house. It was tenanted until nearly the end of the century. According to Kelly's Directory, in 1855 its tenant was Captain Frederick Montresor, R.N. He returned to sea in 1857, served in the East Indies and eventually rose to the rank of Admiral. Charles Devon, a record agent and magistrate, had taken the property by 1859 and was still resident in 1867. At the 1871 census Mrs. Elisa May, wife of Walter Horatio May of Hadlow Castle, was living there. Her husband's great aunt, Mrs. Polhill, had owned St. Vincents at the turn of the century.

During the 1870's, a helpful and popular couple were Mr. and Mrs. Brigstocke who lived with their young family at St. Vincents. When they left, in 1879, it was much to the regret of the rector, Rev. Newton Heale. However, the next tenant, Lady Login, was also an active supporter of village life. She was a very doughty Scotswoman, who spent her early married life with her husband in India. Sir John Login, was a surgeon and the couple immersed themselves in Indian culture. After the Sikh wars Sir John became guardian to the child Maharajah, Duleep Singh, youngest son of the "Lion of the Punjab" Ranjit Singh, and owner of the Koh-in-Noor diamond. This was confiscated by the British Crown and became part of the Crown Jewels. Duleep Singh was brought to England under the guardianship of Sir John Login. He remained in England for the rest of his life, living as a country squire in Suffolk. Queen Victoria took a great interest in Maharajah Singh, even though her ministers refused to return the fabulous jewel to him. In his early manhood, the Maharajah was engaged to an Indian princess, but for some reason the marriage did not proceed. The young woman became the wife of Lady Login's widowed brother. She had a daughter, Victoria Campbell, before dying early. Victoria, then aged 18, was living with her aunt at St. Vincents when the 1881 census was taken. Two Login daughters were also members of the household.

Duleep Singh came to visit Lady Login at St. Vincents at about that time. He was by then a very portly forty-year-old. Despite his bulk, he danced on the gravel drive of the house, accompanied by lively Scottish music played by Lady Login's elderly sister, heard through the drawing room windows. Lady Login felt that he had been very badly treated by the British Crown, and wrote many letters on his behalf, but he did not succeed in recovering his inheritance.[15] Lady Login became very involved in the village, and was generous to its causes. Her daughters assisted Mr. Hardy as organ players at church services. After leaving St. Vincents in 1886, Lady Login moved to the Cedars, Aylesford and died there in 1904.

St. Vincents as it looked at the end of the nineteenth century. The library extension was added by Mrs. Wingfield-Stratford. Photograph: private collection

After John Wingfield-Stratford's death, St. Vincents became the dower house once again. After Lady Login had moved to Aylesford, Mrs. Wingfield-Stratford spent some years there with her youngest daughters. She added a single story wing to the property to house her library. She undertook landscaping works to the stream, installing two waterfalls, then added a tennis court in the grounds.

The original stable block was replaced with stalls for three horses and accommodation for the groom. A three bay coach house was built opposite this, with extensive glasshouses behind it. However, as soon as the last of her daughters married, Mrs. Wingfield-Stratford moved back to her home county of Gloucestershire. She died there in 1897. The house continued to be tenanted and, after her death, the property became part of the Whitburn estate.

The Mount, Teston Road

The land where Mount Offham stands was owned by the Addison family of Offham. It was tenanted from the 1840's by the Fremlins, local farmers. By the mid century, the land became part of David Mucklestone Allen's extensive holdings in Offham and surrounding villages. Allen, who lived in London and Caernarvon, was married to Frances Hodges of West Malling. She may well have been connected to the Addisons. Although the house now lies in Offham parish, its land was part of Addington when it was constructed in about 1870. The 1871 census noted that it was newly built, but unoccupied. After Mr. and Mrs. Allen's deaths, both in 1874, the property came into the possession of George Friend of Maidstone, another connection of the Addisons.[16] His tenant for a few years was Mr. Joseph Hartley but, by the time of the 1881 census, Mrs. Charlotte Madden, a widow, was living there with three daughters. When she left the Mount in late 1886, she moved to Hythe, where she hosted an Addington village outing but, when she died in 1889, she was living at Eltham. These movements were not unusual for women who had been widowed.

Mrs. Hawley, widow of Rev. Henry Charles Hawley, rector of Leybourne, took a lease on the property and a number of her adult children were living with her there at the time of the 1891 census. Her son, Rev. Sir Henry Michael Hawley, was married to Frances Wingfield-Stratford, of Addington Park. He inherited the baronetcy from his uncle, and the couple then moved to Leybourne Castle.

Shaw Hill House

Shaw Hill House was built in the 1880's, on land formerly known as Holly Hill. During the mid century, its site was part of David Mucklestone Allen's holdings. Mr. Henry Gay Hewlett purchased the plot beside Aldon Lane, probably from Mr. Friend. Mr. and Mrs. Hewlett were living at Farningham at the time of the purchase. He built a substantial red brick property there and the couple, who were by then middle aged, moved to Addington in 1884. At the 1891 census, five of their eight children were with them, ranging from Eleanor, aged 31 to Henry, aged 12. Their eldest son, Maurice, was visiting, with his new wife.

Hewlett was the Keeper of the Land Revenue Records and a keen amateur poet. Maurice Hewlett was also a poet, and much admired. Although he succeeded his father as Keeper of the Land Revenue Records, Maurice Hewlett published a number of poems, compositions, novels, and short stories. According to the Dictionary of National Biography, by 1901 he was able to keep himself entirely by his writings.

When the Wingfield-Stratfords left Addington, Hewlett acquired at least one painting from the sale of contents of the manor house. This was the small oil painting of St. Vincents by Dominic Serres that is shown in Chapter Four. The painting had probably remained at St. Vincents ever since Captain Locker commissioned it in 1779, and had thus come into the possession of the Wingfield-Stratfords. Hewlett kindly returned the painting to the Locker family, but during the mid twentieth century it was sold at auction. It is now at the Yale Center for British Art in Connecticut.

H.G. Hewlett died in 1897. His widow remained in Addington with her daughter, Julia, until her own death in October 1921. Julia was a very much loved and respected teacher at Sunday School. After her mother's death, she arranged for a small wooden cottage in the grounds of Shaw Hill House to be moved further up Aldon Lane, where it became her new home.

The depression in agriculture of the 1870's

Rev. James Newton Heale began a new account book for his rectorial tithes when he arrived in the parish in 1869. This was at the beginning of a prolonged agricultural depression, exacerbated by bad weather and poor harvests. In particular, the price of hops dropped significantly, due to cheaper continental imports. From the accounts, it is possible to see the decline in farm profits as the century entered its last quarter. 1869 shows no arrears whatsoever, the following year (1870) only £6 2s 0d, and this had been paid up by the following year. In 1872, Rev. Heale had only a six shilling deficit. However, the accounts for 1879 show a completely different picture. The amount payable for the half year was £180 11s 1d, but eight of the nineteen rate payers had amassed £40 14s 5d arrears from the previous accounts. Although Rev. Heale was quite successful in bringing in his dues, he was still £25 7s 3d out of pocket at the end of the year. His entries in the village magazine confirm the difficulties that his parishioners endured. He noted that hardship came to the village during bad winters. There were a number of these during the late 1870's and early 1880's. He recorded in January 1879 that *"although the harvest was plentiful the great depression in all trades, and especially that in hops, has caused a great deal of hardship and suffering."* That winter saw sustained bad weather. A snow storm struck as late as Easter Day, April 13th. Cold weather continued into May. The harvest was poor that year and, due to wet weather, the hops were late to ripen and the yield was very low.

The uncertain economic conditions continued and the death of the squire in 1881 led to further loss of employment. His coachman, John Herbert, left the village, as did his groom, George Bell, who had been a member of the choir. In 1881, an amended tithe schedule was drawn up, noting the changes to ownership and to the agricultural crops grown in the village compared to 1843.[17] Edward John Wingfield-

Stratford, the new squire, was now in charge of just over 671 acres, almost 70% of the land in Addington. He held 157 parcels of land, as opposed to the 133 of his grandfather. However, he now leased out the greater portion of these. Just 281 acres were kept "in hand".

Mr. John Hammond had become the tenant at Westfields Farm. He held 178 acres, in Addington and Trottiscliffe, and employed six men on a permanent basis, according to the census return. His son, Frederick, aged 21, also assisted him, so this was a major enterprise. A young man of thirty, John Elwin, farmed 80 acres at East Street Farm. He would work hard for the village over many years. He was appointed the Assessor and Collector of Income Tax at the 1879 Vestry Meeting, and later served as Overseer of the Poor. On his retirement at the end of the First World War, he and his wife returned to his native Dover.[18]

The Addington estate now included a portion of the previous Ford and Hedgehogs Farms. John Thomas Ledger was now the tenant there. William Wells had taken over Mr. Woodger's holding of 55 acres at Hernewell.

Very few changes had been made to land use. Although during the mid century a greater proportion of land had been planted with hops, this acreage was already diminishing again. Perhaps this explains the struggle to compete in a difficult world situation, the ground still being light and infertile. Another challenge was that, with the introduction of refrigeration during the 1880's, Australia and New Zealand were now able to export their agricultural produce to Britain and Europe. Cheap food was also imported from Canada and Argentina. This further depressed prices of meat and dairy products.

The village shop

Overall, families were self-sufficient and even the smallest cottage had a large garden to grow a few vegetables. However, this was the century when the village acquired a permanent shop, rather than being served only by itinerant traders. This had been in operation since at least 1819, as it was recorded in Peter Elers' rectorial tithe statement for that year. It operated for over one hundred and sixty years from a cottage on the Green, originally owned by Richard Luxford. The tithe statement of 1843 names the shopkeeper as John Fitness. Fitness quickly moved to Sevenoaks where he was recorded at the 1851 census as a "Master Grocer". In 1847, the tenant was Mr. Thomas Millhouse. However, as Millhouse was a carpenter, it is probable that Mrs. Millhouse was the shopkeeper. Charles Millhouse, then aged 26, called himself "grocer" at the 1851 census.

The shop, cottage and Laurels were probably bought by the Addington Park estate after Mrs Luxford's death in 1855. Kelly's Directory for 1855 gives the name of the grocer as Henry Miller.

By 1861, a post office had been established at the shop alongside the grocery business. The postmistress was then Mrs. Louisa Browning, a young widow. When she left the village in 1863 the shop found long serving tenants, Philip and Harriet Fry. Harriet ran the shop and post office. Mrs. Fry was later assisted by her daughters.

The school

John Wingfield-Stratford built and financed this school twenty years before the Elementary Education Act of 1870 came into force, introducing state run education. This was an important charitable act. He may have planned its establishment with his father, as the school was already open by the time of the 1851 census. Mr. Wingfield-Stratford was not unique amongst landowners in establishing an elementary school in his parish, though not all his contemporaries were as keen to do so. Many landowners were apparently afraid that the children of their labourers might learn to think for themselves! However, this little school was established and it would bring great benefits to the village. It appears that the parish workhouse had stood on the site where the school was built on the Green, as the Tithe Map of 1843 shows a substantial cottage beside the terrace of cottages now called School Row. At that time it housed an agricultural labourer, as the Union House at Malling had by then opened. The school was designed as a double fronted cottage. The two ground floor rooms at the front were used for the school and there was upstairs accommodation for the schoolteacher.

Addington School. Photograph taken c. 1908. Note the original windows on the ground floor. Photograph by Freda Barton. ©The Malling Society

The first schoolmistress was Kezia Wells, (1817-1888). She was one of the numerous children of William and Lucy Wells. Kezia was brought up in the house next door to the school that is now called the Old Schoolhouse. This building had never been a school. Instead, its rental income had provided funds for the Rev. Edward Holmes Education Trust of East Malling, which ran a school for local children, though not for those from Addington. Kezia's father was the Parish Clerk for many years.

Rev. James Newton Heale, even though he had left the parish five years earlier, gave her eulogy in the parish magazine of August 1888. He wrote that she was born in Hadlow and moved with her family to Addington in the early 1820's. Kezia had always been religious. Rev. Heale wrote that during her childhood she had been inspired by Rev. Thomas Bowdler, rector of Addington. Although congenitally lame, she longed to become a missionary. In her early adulthood, she spent some time in a London parish as a bible worker, but poor health forced her to return to Addington. She was in her thirties and living at East Street when she was offered the post of schoolmistress. She was reluctant to accept, as she had no qualifications, but once in post she became *"the model of a good, old-fashioned Village School Mistress, who valued good manners and morals above mere scholastic attainments, and yet never neglected the imparting of a simple and sound education to the children whom she taught, to be modest in dress and behaviour, above all to show reverence to all sacred things, to value their Bible and church, to be helpful at home, and respectful of their elders; and in doing this she taught them to love herself."*

Kezia Wells presided over the school for more than twenty-five years until *"age, infirmity and government regulations"* persuaded her to retire. Mr. Wingfield-Stratford funded the school throughout her tenure. A few years before his death in 1881, he reluctantly handed it over to the new Schools Inspectorate. Kezia Wells returned to her parents' cottage beside her school. There she cared for her widowed father, who lived to be 93. She survived him for five years, and continued to perform charitable acts around the village until her last months. In recognition of this service, her name was added to the plaque on the north wall of the church that she had dedicated to her father.

The Elementary Education Act of 1870 set the framework for teaching children between the ages of five and twelve. The Act established school boards, who were empowered to set up schools where there was no provision and to fund parish or church schools that were already in existence. Not surprisingly, those running existing schools were unenthusiastic to begin with, resisting state interference, and continued to run their schools independently. Compulsory education was not established until a decade later, owing to opposition from vested interests. Addington school joined the system in the late 1870's, after Miss Wells' retirement. The schoolteachers that followed her were young women who stayed for a short time. They had to resign if they married. The first teacher, Miss Jessop, left in mid 1879 for this reason and the turnover remained quite swift. The local directories produced in the nineteenth and early twentieth centuries, give the name of the schoolmistress, and each is different.

As a board school, the school year continued much as it had been established by Mr. Wingfield-Stratford. Holidays were tied to religious festivals and harvest time. Two weeks were given at Christmas, a week at Easter and a longer break in the summer. The church magazine for 1886, called Addington Banner of Faith, notes that the school holidays that Christmas had been limited to a week because the hop harvest had taken longer than usual, owing to bad weather. This had delayed the children's return to school in the autumn.

Reward was given for regular attendance. In one year, ten of the children received prizes for full weekly attendance over the previous twelve weeks. Once under the auspices of the local School Board, an important annual event was the visit of Her Majesty's Inspector of Schools. This was a worrying time, as the inspector would listen to each child reading and reciting. He would then quiz the class on the scriptures, examine their writing and test their

spelling. It seems that even needlework had to be shown and that criticism was doled out without any scruples for the child's feelings. If the children's work in any of the categories was deemed to have failed the standard required, funding for this subject would be withheld for the following year. However, it was not all hard grind.

The parish magazine of January 1882 records an entertainment put on by the children just before Christmas. This was an ambitious programme for such a small school. Under the direction of their schoolmistress, Miss Macnamara, they performed scenes from Shakespeare's "Merchant of Venice". *"Immense pains and efforts had been made for the preparation of dresses, scenery, and decoration, and these were most effective; and except for a little nervousness on account of some rather rashly placed Chinese lanterns, one of which took fire, all went off most successfully, and the children deserve much praise for the accuracy with which they had learnt their parts, and the spirit with which in most cases they delivered them."* wrote the rector, James Newton Heale. This cameo shows a surprising level of literacy and comprehension amongst what were essentially the children of agricultural labourers, though it is possible to picture the faces and stance of the few children who did not quite enter into the spirit of the performance! Miss Macnamara then went on to pastures new and Miss Huntley joined the village community in early January 1883. It seems that the new teacher was a particular asset, as shortly after she arrived she obtained a *"first"* class certificate, in addition to the one she already held.

Miss Huntley was congratulated by the inspector that year and the grant was increased by £5 10s above the year before, bringing a total of £39 6s 8d for 1884. The Inspector wrote that *"This little school is in good order and has passed, on the whole, a fair or pretty good examination in elementary subjects. Reading is pretty good above the Third Standard. Writing is generally legible but papers are not particularly neat. Spelling is not strong in any class. Needlework is satisfactory."* However in another year boys were criticised as being *"very poor at speaking up and answering the questions."* The rector made a comment on this point in the magazine *"with regard to the difficulty the examiner experienced in getting the children to answer, a little more energetic use of those powers of speech, which are so loud on the Green, in School and at the Children's Services is to be desired."*

The last point refers to the children having to attend church on Sundays, though it would appear that their parents did not feel quite so committed. A note at the bottom of the February 1879 edition of the Parish magazine states: *"The Rector is obliged again to urge parents to make an effort to come to church and sit with the children.......He would greatly regret to be obliged to call public attention by name to any child whose behaviour was disturbing the service."*

From the parish magazine it seems that, in 1887, the school running costs were £71 6s 0d. The teacher's salary was £51 18s 8d, the rent was £6 10s 0d (2/6d per week). Other costs were fuel, light, cleaning, books and stationery, replacement and repairs to the furniture and building. £5 0s 1d was given to the children as prizes for attendance. There was a balance in the bank. The school received a grant of £33 17s 3d from the Committee of the Council of Education, plus voluntary contributions of £26 6s. "School Pence", which was paid by each scholar, amounted to £13 9s 7d. A sale of needlework had raised 15 shillings and 16s 6d came from the Guardians.

Communications

Addington has always had reasonable communications with the outside world. These had been improved during the mid to late eighteenth century by the introduction of turnpiked roads. During the early nineteenth century there were 50 active turnpike trusts in Kent, controlling over 650 miles of road. Since 1820, these roads had been hard rolled with "tar macadam". Its inventor, John Loudon MacAdam, served as the principal officer or surveyor of a number of trusts throughout Britain, including the Wrotham to Maidstone turnpike. This was the turnpike that ran through Addington and each Wingfield-Stratford followed Leonard Bartholomew as trustee and chairman. The income from travellers

gradually decreased but the trust was not disbanded until 1861. Income was lost to the new railways, even though goods still arrived at Addington by road. The line from Victoria reached Otford in 1862, but the South Eastern Railway Company did not construct the link between Otford and Maidstone until 1874. Its continuation to Ashford had to wait until 1884. What was installed on the boundary with Seven Mile Lane was a freight siding. The land beside the siding was used a refuse dump. Rubbish was brought down from London, unloaded at the siding and deposited in a long strip on the adjacent fields. Although this was used to fertilise the land, many objects also found their way on to the fields. Addington gained little from this railway. Residents joined with neighbouring villages and petitioned for a station near Harpwood, but the area was never provided with even a "halt".

In January 1899 the siding was used for a sad purpose. Humphrey John Cator, the three year old grand-son of John and Jane Wingfield-Stratford, died at Paddock Wood shortly after Christmas. His small body was brought by train to this siding for burial at St. Margaret's.[19] A stained glass window was later installed in the North Transept in his memory. This suggests that heavy goods may also have reached Addington via this siding. Personal access to Addington continued to be by horse-drawn vehicles, though by the end of the century it is very likely that the Sofer-Whitburns owned one of the first motor vehicles. From the church magazine it seems that cricket teams continued to be taken to fixtures by horse drawn vehicles into the twentieth century and the carrier's carts would still have been a necessary means of transport for most residents.

Major changes to the fabric of the church

Following the death of Col. Wingfield-Stratford in 1850, his widow set in train substantial alterations, additions and repairs to St. Margaret's church. In 1846 Mrs. Wingfield-Stratford had received a lifetime annuity of £5,000 per annum from her brother, Col. Turner Grant. It was, perhaps, this legacy that enabled her to undertake this work. It seems that she may have given most of her income to the work as her effects after her death were valued at less than £3,000.[20]

The church was almost entirely renovated. The roof of the nave was given new oak beams and the Watton Chapel was restored. The barrel vaulted roof of the chapel was painted with vibrant colours, turquoise, soft pink, black, red and white. Gilded metal stars were placed in lozenges of two different designs and the ribs of the barrel vault were painted with a tracery in white and red. Below the barrel a frieze with swags of fruit and embossed, rampant, red lions ties the ceiling to the motifs in the Watton Memorial, though these lions are facing left, rather than the correct way for the family arms.

The Ceiling of the Watton Chapel painted in 1858. Photograph: Lucy Richardson

Under her late husband's instructions, Mrs. Wingfield-Stratford then placed memorial plaques to the Bartholomew and Wingfield-Stratford families on the south wall of the chapel. She left a space on the right hand plaque and her own inscription was added after her death. The change in the engraving can be clearly discerned.

The North Transept was enlarged and given a hipped roof. The servants from Addington Park sat here, behind the choir and a harmonium, according to the reminiscences of Mrs. Pickering's daughter. The residents from St. Vincents and the Vale sat on the south side of the chancel. This is confirmed by the position of memorial plaques to Admiral Parry and to Mrs. Pickering. The rest of the congregation were arranged from front to rear, according to their status! The children were in the West Gallery with their teacher. Unfortunately, despite making comments in his tithe book, Rev. Paulson did not mention these works. This is to be regretted as he might have given helpful insight and confirmed the date of the installations. Mr. Maddan maintained that Rev. Newton Heale reordered the church during the 1870's to follow the tenets of the Oxford Movement and the pews appear to be of that date. .

In 1881, following Mr. John Wingfield-Stratford's death, his widow set in train further alterations. To complement the new liturgy, she erected a reredos of Caen stone, created from designs by A.W. Blomfield, the prolific church architect. The reredos depicts the crucifixion, with statues on each side. On the left of the cross are the Virgin Mary and St. Peter and on the right St. James and St. John. The work required the removal of texts of the creed and the Lord's Prayer. Its dedication took place at the Christmas Service of 1881, showing how quickly new furniture could be installed in a church in those days. Once the reredos

Sketch of Addington Church, 1880's. Used as the cover of the parish magazine for twenty years.

had been installed, more alterations to the church layout took place. The chancel was opened up. Rev. Heale was delighted with the effect that the new reredos made and wrote in the March edition of the Addington Parochial Magazine *"The centre compartment runs up into an angle to the greatest height of the whole, and contains a representation of the Crucifixion, exquisitely carved in full relief out of a single block of alabaster."* He continued that the east end of the church had been *"thrown open with good effect by taking away the reading desk, and by reducing the size of the pulpit. One seat too in the Choir has been removed."* [21]

The parishioners then paid for paving stones to be removed from the choir. These were replaced with Minton tiles. Mrs. Wingfield-Stratford wished for tiles to be fitted on either side of the reredos as well, but the cost of installing them in the choir proved more expensive than planned, as hot water pipes had to be

The reredos at St. Margaret's church, designed by A.W. Blomfield, 1881

moved.[22] Eventually just the floor within the altar rails was tiled. Nine sponsors were named in the parish magazine of March 1882 as funders for this work, whilst others were still being exhorted to come forward. With one exception these were women, Lady Login and three of her family, Mrs. Hawley of Leybourne Rectory, her daughter-in-law, Mrs. Hawley, (formerly Miss Wingfield-Stratford), Mrs. Hewlett of Shaw Hill House and Mrs Madden of The Mount.

It had been hoped to install an organ to replace the harmonium in the North Transept, but shortage of funds prevented this. Instead, Spooner Hardy, the churchwarden and organist, suggested a fund raising campaign. It was through his efforts that the organ was installed in 1883. This was built by Messrs. Forster and Andrews of Hull. With its enhanced sound capabilities, Hardy was better able to develop the choral music for the church services.[23] After his death in 1901, his daughter, Norah, took his place as organist.

In 1885, the pulpit and prayer desk were exchanged, the pulpit being placed on the north side of the nave, where it remains. The vestry was renovated with match-boarding at that time, the work being undertaken by Messrs. Pryer & Co. of Maidstone.

Apart from the window in the south wall of the Watton chapel, all the other windows were still plain, at the most containing the ancient family arms. In 1887, three stained glass windows were created, all designed by Messrs. Warrington & Co.[24] The first was installed in the east window, the arms in this glass being transferred to the other end of the church. The design was the Ascension of Christ. It was dedicated to the memory of Mrs. Vernon Guise, the rector's mother, who had died the previous year. It is a fitting design to have above the crucifixion on the reredos.

The second window, on the north wall, was erected by Miss Mary Boys of Park Cottage in memory of her companion, Mrs. Ellen Elizabeth Boys. It represents St. Margaret's patron saint in one panel and St. Augustine, who brought Christianity to Kent, in the other. The third window of 1887 is opposite this, on the south wall. This was paid for by the donations of

Addington's parishioners in honour of Queen Victoria's Golden Jubilee. This window represents St. Alphège of Greenwich and St. Frances of Rome. St. Alphège was one of the last Saxon Archbishops of Canterbury, at the turn of the 11th century. This was a time of Viking incursions and he was a mediator for King Aethelred the Unready. He was murdered at Greenwich, and a parish church was built where he died. St. Frances was a gentlewoman who had longed to be a nun. She was renowned for her generosity to the poor and hungry.

Two gilded life sized angels were later painted on the east wall, flanking the window. One held a harp and the other a staff. Further motifs covered the stone work round and above the window, reaching to the ceiling. These included decorative columns and fleurs de lis. The effect must have been stunning when first revealed to the congregation.

Lavish altar frontals were commissioned during the mid to late 1880s. One of these was worked in 1885 by the tenant at the manor house, Mrs. Arbuthnott. She was assisted by Mrs. Whitfield Hewlett. In February 1888, Mrs. Wingfield-Stratford donated a violet frontal to be used during Lent. This was executed by the Sisters of St. James' Home, Fulham. The church, lit by oil lamps, must have glowed. In the early twentieth century Mrs. Freda Barton visited St. Margaret's church. A photograph she took is shown below.

As the century drew to a close, further stained glass windows were added. These were designed by Messrs. Curtis, Ward and Hughes, another prolific designing team of the nineteenth century. At Eastertide 1891, Miss Fanny Sofer-Whitburn died, aged only eighteen. Her parents placed a window on the south wall in her memory showing the scene at the sepulchre.

Mrs. Jane Wingfield-Stratford's memorials were a window on the north wall entitled "I was hungry and ye gave me food, naked and ye clothed me," and two small windows in the porch.

St. Margaret's Church as it looked at the end of the nineteenth century. Mrs. Arbuthnott's altar frontal is shown. Photograph by Freda Barton. © The Malling Society

Church administration

During the second half of the century, parish administration followed very much the same pattern until 1895. The Rector was the main administrator, supported by a churchwarden, the Vestry Meeting and the Parish Clerk. The Vestry Meeting remained responsible for the appointment of the village officers. From the magazines that survive, some of the men that undertook these duties can be identified. On Lady Day, 25th March 1879, the following appointments were made:

Guardian of the Poor – Rev. J.N. Heale
Overseers of the Poor – Mr. Philip Fry, (gardener and shop-keeper), Mr. Thomas Fry (miller)
Assessors and Collectors of the Income Tax – Mr. Charles Millhouse (builder), Mr. John Elwin (farmer, East Street)
Churchwarden – Mr. Charles Millhouse (builder)
Waywarden – Mr. Thomas White (farmer, Westfields)

In 1868, the churchwarden's rate was 4d in the £ and raised £24 7s 7d. This was sufficient for the expenditure. The items were insurance of two guineas, a bill for the visitation, a new vestry book, flint and coals for heating, a few repair bills and new bell ropes. There were 22 ratepayers, the identical number as had paid the Land Tax sixty years earlier. However, only two years later, the tax burden fell on only fourteen men as John Wingfield-Stratford had added to his estate.

The village was fortunate to have a long serving clerk in the third quarter of the century. The gardener, William Wells, served in this post for 24 years. He was replaced by Henry Barnes, who left the village in early 1886. The names of later parish clerks are not known.

Church attendance was high. Rev. Guise inserted the following table for December 1885 in the Addington Banner of Faith of January 1886:

"The number of persons attending Church Service on Sundays in the month of December (not including celebration of the Holy Communion):

	A.M.	P.M.	P.M.
Dec.	11.00	3.30	6.00
6th	78	62	83
13th	84	64	75
20th	83	55	76
27th	97	53	76

There were seven celebrations of the Holy Communion during the month, the total number of communicants at which were 73."

In addition, 41 people took communion at two celebrations on Christmas Day. Considering that people would have walked to the church in the cold and dark, the attendance at Evensong is particularly striking for such a small congregation. However, the offertories were extremely small, amounting to £5 6s 9d for the month. The Christmas offertories, from services held at 8.15 a.m. and 12.15 p.m., amounted to £1 4s 8d and £1 18s 11d respectively, or 60 per cent of the total. However, the following month the general services were more productive and brought in £3 5s 3$\frac{1}{2}$d.

The Sale of Addington Manor

After the death of John Wingfield-Stratford, his son, Edward John (1849-1903), realised that the family could no longer afford to live at Addington Park. He was a 42 year old bachelor when he inherited the estate in 1881. As soon as his mother left the mansion house, he leased it to Sir Sydney Waterlow, the printer.[25] When he left, the tenants were Col. and Mrs. George Arbuthnott. After they ended their lease at the beginning of 1886, the property remained empty until, in the summer of 1887, a buyer was found for the entire estate. As the property does not seem to have been advertised in the press, it is likely that the purchase was by private treaty. The conveyance took place on 21st October 1887[26] and Mr. Charles Joseph Sofer Whitburn, a City of London financier and bill broker, brought his family to Addington in the summer of 1888. He retained his London home at 16 Ennismore Gardens, Kensington.

The couple quickly introduced themselves to the village. They provided the children's School Treat on 1st September that year. This included swings, a coconut shy, competitions such as sack races, a huge tea and prizes donated by Mr. Whitburn's sister, Miss Juliana Whitburn. At the 1891 census, the household was Mr. and Mrs. Sofer Whitburn (without a hyphen), their son, Charles William Sofer-Whitburn, 24, their daughter, Fanny Juliana Sofer-Whitburn, 18, and Miss Whitburn. Sadly, Fanny Juliana died shortly after the census was taken. Their elder daughter, Mary Florence, had married an army officer, Robert Bonham Bax Christie, and their baby daughter, Elsie Christie, was also at Addington Place. Captain and

Mrs. Christie had moved to Birling House by the time the 1901 census was taken.

Charles Joseph Sofer Whitburn (1836-1911)

Mr. Whitburn was a self-made man. When only thirteen, he started work as an office boy at Sanderson and Co., a firm of bill brokers, in order to support his mother and sister. Ten years later, with a colleague from Sandersons, he established his own firm, Messrs. Reeves, Whitburn & Co., in St. Clement's Lane, City of London. Through a cautious approach to business, he survived two major financial crashes—the collapse of Messrs. Overend and Gurney in 1866 and that of the City of Glasgow Bank eleven years later. Even after senior partners began to have their own private office, Whitburn continued the old practice of sitting at a desk amongst his clerks. He maintained, *"I am more at the centre of things, and in touch with the stir and details of business."* He took no holidays, had barely a day off for sickness and worked almost to the day of his death.[27] By the end of his life, Sofer Whitburn had made an immense fortune. His son, Charles William, who used the hyphenated form of surname, joined him in the business. C.W. had a more flamboyant character. It may have been he who encouraged his father to buy Addington Place. The older man had little interest in entertainment and spent most of his time in London. The younger Mr. (later Colonel) Sofer-Whitburn enjoyed country pleasures such as the shoot at Addington, and was an enthusiastic breeder of farm animals, winning many prizes. The family were granted a coat of arms in 1884. As with the Wingfield-Stratfords, there is a link in these with those of the Watton family, as the main theme is a rampant lion, though in this case the lion is holding a bezant, a golden roundel, representing, no doubt, their wealth. The description is: *"Az. a lion rampant, arg., holding between the paws a bezant, on a chief or, between two mullets of six points of the first, a pale gu. thereon two swords in saltire ppr"* A blue field, on which is a rampant lion holding a gold coin, the top portion is gold, the centre portion, in scarlet, holds purple crossed swords and on either side are two six pointed stars. The six pointed star is also on the crest, of an eagle's head holding another bezant. Their motto was *"Virtue overcomes difficulties."* With so many different colours in these arms, the effect must have been bright and cheerful.[28]

Arms granted to C.J. Sofer Whitburn in 1884

Mr. Whitburn began a major redesign and enlargement of Addington Place. Towards the end of the century, he commissioned Edward Lutyens, (1869-1944), the celebrated architect of the period, to modernise the seventeenth century mansion house. Lutyens added a south facing extension where glass-houses had stood, but the enlarged mansion was not greatly admired. Lutyens added a somewhat pompous porch to the entrance, and crenulations to the roof. He attempted to match the extension to the original structure but photographs show the result to have been bland and somewhat "tacked on". However, internally Lutyens appears to have achieved his patron's aims. Having contained thirty rooms in 1716, when Edmund Watton died, the mansion house now boasted sixty. These included fifteen principal and secondary bedrooms, with dressing rooms, bathrooms, etc. The mansion had an impressive stairway and open, galleried hall, off which was a grandiose suite of reception rooms on the ground floor. Electricity was installed, operated from a generator in the disused mill, powered by its water wheel. A boiler in the basement supplied hot water to all floors and central heating to the ground floor reception rooms.[29] There were high hopes for the succession of this financial dynasty when Charles William Sofer-Whitburn married Clarissa Heseltine in 1902.

Addington Manor House, showing the Lutyens Extension.

The Parish Meeting is inaugurated

Towards the end of the century, major changes took place in the civil administration of rural areas. In 1888, County Councils were created, mainly to take over the administration of county courts and quarter sessions. Most of their current functions were not granted to them until the twentieth century. County councils did not become responsible for education until 1902, or highways until 1929. During the nineteenth century these continued to be administered by independent boards.

Of greater significance to Addington was the Local Government Act of 1894 that created district, town and parish councils. The new Malling Rural District Council assumed the powers of the local sanitary and highways boards. The Act removed civic powers from church vestry meetings, and transferred these to the newly created parish councils. If a community was less than 300, it could decide instead to have a parish meeting. The powers of the vestry meeting were restricted to church affairs and its main function became to appoint the churchwarden(s).

Addington was not required to form a parish council and chose not to do so. Instead, the Parish Meeting, which was required to meet at least once a year, was authorised to set a precept, the total amount needed to pay work in the coming year. Parish councils and meetings could borrow money, but only with the permission of the County Council.

A parish council elected a set number of councillors to speak at its meetings. A parish meeting, on the other hand, was, and is open to all electors. Both were given specific, but limited powers. In 1894, these were:

- to appoint overseers to the poor (a former Vestry requirement),
- to hold and maintain parish owned property, including allotments, village greens and public buildings,
- to acquire buildings for the parish or land for allotments, public walks or recreational purposes,
- to manage closed cemeteries (not applicable in Addington's case).

In future, no footpath would be diverted without reference to the Parish Meeting.

The precept was levied on householders as part of the rates they paid to the higher authorities. In 1894, a maximum rate of 3d in the £ was set for parish councils, unless a poll had been taken, which could agree up to 6d.

Addington's first Parish Meeting was held in the Schoolroom on the Green, on Tuesday, 4th December, 1894. The Meeting elected Mr. J. Spooner Hardy as its Chairman. Mr. Warde, of Aldon House and Mr. Lancaster, the publican, were appointed the Overseers for the Poor.

Those present were:
- Mr. J. Spooner Hardy, 46, The Vale
- Rev. Julian Guise, 38, the rector
- Mr. Philip Fry, 64, gardener, the Post Office
- Mr. Harry Chapman, 35, groom and gardener, Heather View, East Street
- Mr. William Gregory, 35, domestic gardener, Aldon Lane
- Mr. Frederick Warde, 43, hop and fruit farmer, Aldon House
- Mr. John Elwin, 44, farmer, East Street Farmhouse
- Mr. Alfred Chapman, 54, Harry's father, farm bailiff and sexton, Woodgate
- Mr. Benjamin Barnden, 68, gardener, The Green (cottage now demolished)
- Mr. Alfred Lancaster, 38, publican, the Angel

The occupations of these men show the rural economy of the parish. A number had already served on the Church Vestry. Women were not present as, being barred from voting, they were not eligible to attend the meeting.

At this first meeting Mr. Hardy read a paper explaining the Local Government Act and the new powers given to parish meetings and councils. Those present then resolved to form a committee of the Chairman, Mr. Elwin, Mr. Chapman, Mr. Gregory and Mr. Pratt (not present) to look into the question of allotments. The Parish Meeting then established its rules of procedure. These would be formal, the order of proceedings was to be announced by public notice, standard rules of debate were to be used, and reports of all meetings were to be presented in writing. A second general meeting would be held each year on 29th September or seven days thereafter. The 1895/6 precept was set at £2 8s 0d, to

be administered by the overseers, Frederick Warde and Alfred Lancaster.

Allotments were successfully created on Dalton's Field, next to East Street, the land having been donated by Mr. Whitburn. The 1899 meeting discussed the proposed diversion of a footpath from the parish of Offham that ran beside the railway–the proposal would add 47 yards to the journey, but would do away with two stiles and a railway level crossing. The new route would also avoid a portion *"regularly abused by hop pickers."* The meeting therefore had no objections, but had now exercised the power granted to them by the Act. Apart from these two decisions, life went on very much as usual.

These Government regulations were bringing the village into modern life. However, despite the new civil administration, decision making remained in the hands of churchgoers. The family at the mansion house was now supported by City of London money, rather than the rural economy, but local employment was still tied to the land.

1   Their son, James, was baptised at Addington that year. James Broad lived at Addington all his life, working as a gardener. He died at Woodgate in November 1881, aged 72. His son, Henry Broad was also a long term Addington resident. Henry was buried in 1929, aged 81, having worked as a carpenter and joiner, probably for the manor house.

2   Through which he exercised his vote during elections held in the 1860's. This property may have come to him through his grandmother, born Frances Wildash.

3   The Guise family had lived at Elmore since 1260, even longer than the Watton's had owned Addington.

4   For comparison, when his future daughter in law, Grace Atkinson was widowed in 1891 her soldier husband's estate was valued for probate at £130,000.

5   There was a local connection to this marriage, as Bertie's mother, born Mary Akers, had been brought up at West Malling Abbey.

6   This memoir was quoted to me by Anthony Nicholson, who had researched the life of Mrs. Pickering's sister, Frances. Frances Hutchinson, born Stephenson, had lived in Mr. Nicholson's home in north Yorkshire, but regularly visited Addington.

7   The Marquis of Camden also owned Bayham Abbey estate in Lamberhurst. In 1884, Wildernesse Park was sold to Sir Charles Mills, 2nd Bart., and M.P. for West Kent. Mills was later created 1st Baron Hillingdon. The title is now extinct. Wildernesse House later became Dorton House School for the Blind..

8   1901 census shows him aged 63 at St. Thomas's Vicarage, Bethnal Green. Other information comes from Ancestry.co.uk, Memories of Malling, Mr. Maddan's book, etc.

9   The incumbent was Rev. Francis C. Masters, probably her brother. Her father had also been a clergyman, Rector of Stratton, where Elizabeth was born. The nineteenth century saw an explosion of clergy numbers in England as a whole.

10   The Economy of Kent, 1640-1914, p.38. Kent's figure for 1851-5 was 132 deaths for children under the age of one per 1,000 live births. This fell to 114 in the 1880's but rose again to 135 between 1896-1900. This was lower than England and Wales as a whole, at a ratio of

85.   Sources: Registrar General, Annual Reports. Mitchell & Deane (Abstract of British Historical Statistic, pp 36-7)

11   John & Mary married at Addington in 1814. Mary was a young widow, her first husband, John Sparkes died in 1812.

12   This is the occupation he gave at their marriage at St. Matthews's church, Bayswater on 1st May 1886.

13   The information about Mr. Hardy's business life comes from the Times Newspaper archives.

14   Gale Digital Vault, *19th Century British Newspapers, Parts I and II*. Also the Times Digital Archive.

15   From Lady Login's memoirs, published by her daughter under the title "Lady Login's recollections, court life and camp life, 1820-1904", first borrowed by the author through KCC Library in the 1980's, but now digitised by the California Digital Library at www.archive.org.

16   One of the Addisons a Mr. Friend Addison, was liable for Land Tax during the eighteenth century.

17   Addington Parish Records P/2/27/2

18   He was still farming at East Street at the outbreak of the Great War, as he is recorded there in the 1913 Kelly's Directory for Kent..

19   From private correspondence.

20   Probate proved 4th May 1863 by her son-in-law, John Wingfield-Stratford, her sole executor.

21   The faculty for the works has the catalogue number DCb/E/F/Addington, St Margaret (Kent)/1, and was held at Canterbury City archives, as Addington was then in that diocese.

22   Addington Parochial Magazine, March 1882 The tiles cost about £40 (estimate was £38 13s), plus £20 to alter the pipes. The additional tiles within the rails cost a further £20.

23   These notes are taken from his obituary in the Kent Messenger of 15th June 1901, probably written by Rev. J. Guise.

24   Attributed to them by the Builder (August 1887) and The Guardian (September 1887)

25   Sir Sydney Waterlow moved to Addington after remarrying. His son inherited the home at Fairseat that he had married shared with his first wife, as it had been her property. Sir Sydney was building Trosley Towers (which stood just inside Stansted parish), whilst occupying Addington Park.

26   According to J. G. Maddan

27   Obituary in the Bankers' Magazine. Extracts produced by the Hawera and Normanby Star, New Zealand, Vol. LXII, 4 April 1912.

28   Charles Sofer Whitburn was granted the arms on 19 March 1884. [Coll. Arms Gts. 62.208]

29   An electrician is recorded living in one of the Addington Park cottages at the 1901 census.

7

1900 to 1925 - The GREAT WAR and sale of ADDINGTON MANOR

The size of the village in 1900 was nearly a hundred acres more than it had been a century earlier. Addington's boundaries now contained 1, 119 acres (just under 453 hectares). All of Aldon was now within the civil parish, though the ecclesiastic one remained as before. An extremely rich financier owned the manor house and the property had become a recreational base. The economic viability of its farmland was of less significance to its owner, Mr. Sofer Whitburn. However, most villagers continued to have an economic relationship with the "big house". Although of a similar age to Leonard Bartholomew, the squire of 1800, Sofer Whitburn came from a less privileged background. He had made his fortune through his own skills and effort, rather than through inheritance and marriage. He had lavished some of this fortune enlarging and modernising his manor house and this was now lit by electricity and centrally heated by a coal-fired boiler. Both men, however, had reached their sixties without a guaranteed succession of male heirs.

The number of houses, 44 in the main village area, had not increased in sixty years. Nor had there been significant building at Aldon, only another 12 properties stood there. Many homes were small. 28 cottages within the village boundaries contained less than five rooms. The substantial buildings were Addington Park, The Vale, St. Vincents, The Mount, (Teston Road), Aldon House, Shaw Hill House and the Rectory, where Julian Guise was now into his eighteenth year of a long incumbency. The pre-war era saw little development. Breinton Cottage (now Breinton Lodge) and Appledene, both on Trottiscliffe Road, were built for the land agent and for the head gardener at Addington Park respectively. Col. Sofer-Whitburn, on behalf of his mother, also built a block of four "New Model Cottages" on East Street for the use of estate workers.[1] All these properties had substantial gardens. A house named Quarrenden was built just after the end of the Great War on the Teston Road. Mrs. Gilead Smith and her daughters were recorded as electors there in 1922. The property was later renamed White Ladies. It is now used as an office by the adjacent quarry company.

In the pre-war period much, but not all, of the farmland was part of Addington estate. Some of this was kept in hand and some leased. The two main tenant farmers were John Elwin, who celebrated his fiftieth birthday in 1901 at East Street, and Daniel Thomson, a Scotsman, at Westfields Farm, who was slightly older. Both these farms were mixed, with grain, pasture, hops and fruit. Daniel and Jeannie Thomson had a family of four boys, William, Douglas, Frank and Ronald. The children were all born in Addington.

Wheeled access to Addington Park was by three gates, though the parkland was crossed by a number of footpaths. Two gates had manned lodges. One of these was on the London Road and the other stood beside the Green. The third gate, near to the modern recreation ground, was one that visitors opened themselves. This gate was still in operation until the mid century.

The village was far more wooded than it is today. St. Vincents Wood remains, but Campions Wood was later bisected by the M20, as were the Chestnuts Plantation and the Common Plantation at the end of East Street. Contemporary postcards show how the narrow lanes and roads were bordered by trees. Fields still had small clumps and shaws at their edges and the manor house was approached by an avenue. The megaliths stood in a wood, as can be seen from the comparative photographs below. Addington Wood, then in the north of the village, is no longer part of the parish.

A photograph of one of the stones of Addington Long barrow, showing how much woodland has been lost from Park Road since the 1920's.

Beside Campions Wood, in the extensive grounds of the gamekeeper's home, were pheasant pens for the estate shoot and a number of dog kennels. The fine avenue in the park was no longer the main access to the mansion house, but families continued to walk down it to reach the church.

Woodgate and Coldrum Farms, Shaw Hill House, Lane Farmhouse, The Mount, Aldon House, Aldon Farm and the Rectory were independent of the manor. The farm bailiffs during the Edwardian era were Frederick Capon, at Coldrum Lodge, Alfred Chapman, senior, followed by Alfred Chapman, junior, at Woodgate and Thomas Pattenden, at Aldon Farm. Capon died in 1910, aged 88, and was followed at Coldrum by James Reader, who had come to Kent from Essex. His son-in-law, Jabez Wise, would later farm at Hedgehogs. William Juniper was then a dairyman at Hedgehogs. He was the tenant of the Whitburns. The heavy work was still undertaken by horses, as can be seen from this photograph taken at East Street Farm during the Edwardian period. The ploughman is one of the Fissenden brothers of East Street.

Working horses in Addington before the Great War. By kind permission of Mr. Louis Fissenden

The working farms in the village grew a significant amount of fruit, particularly in the area bounded by the Green, Woodgate Road and East Street. Fruit and hops were also grown extensively from Aldon up to the Teston Road. These were apple, pear and cherry orchards. Soft fruit was also grown. New, independently run, market gardens concentrated on vegetables and flowers.

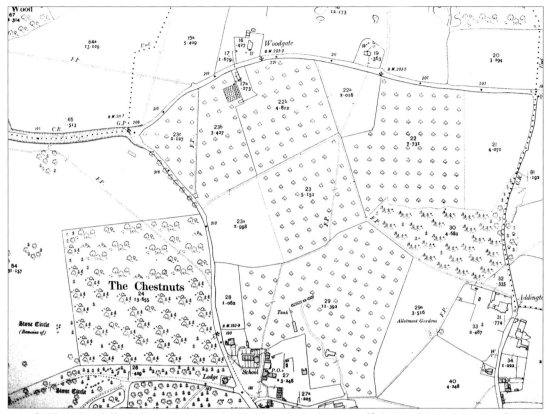

Area of Addington bounded by the Green, Woodgate Road and East Street showing the amount of fruit grown. Ordnance Survey Map of 1907, 6" to the mile.

In the Edwardian era, there were still six oasts within the village boundaries, but most were falling out of use. That at Westfields Farm was derelict by the time of the 1923 auction. Only one at Aldon, a second next to Teston Road and a third near to the Green are still standing. All are now private homes and only the last is still within the civil parish.

In 1997, Alan Chapman, grandson of the bailiff at Woodgate Farm, wrote a memoir of his childhood memories. The farm lay on the southern side of Woodgate Road and stretched to East Street, adjoining the Vale. Alfred Chapman, junior, was bailiff first to Mr. Phillips and later to Mr. Lionel Hardy. Alan wrote that the farm *"grew mainly apples and cherries, but there were cob-nuts on the East Street side and a little meadow opposite. Originally, and until the 1930's there were also four or five long heated glass houses which grew tomatoes, cucumbers and such. These were next to farm buildings which have now been converted to houses. There were gooseberries grown between the*

glass houses and the apple orchard on the corner of Trosley (SIC) Road and Woodgate Road, with a slightly larger area of raspberries which were put into large wooden tubs and sent to a jam factory. To avoid winter shrinkage, the tubs would be soaked in a large concrete water tank." This tank can be seen on the 1907 Ordnance Survey map, near to Overlea Cottage.

Alan Chapman remembered that, by the 1930's, hops were no longer grown on Woodgate Farm, but the old "copper", in which hop-poles had been dunked in tar in the past, still existed. Sheep were run beneath the tall apple and cherry trees. This practice continued until the end of the 1980's, when the old standard cherry trees beside the Trottiscliffe Road were grubbed out. Modern fruit trees are too short to permit sheep to graze beneath them. Woodgate (the house), where the Chapman family lived, was not part of the farm, as it was owned by the Nevills of Birling Place, as part of their holdings near Coldrum. It came on the market during the 1950's.

The farm crew at East Street farm. The young man third from the left is one of the Fissenden brothers. By kind permission of Mr. Louis Fissenden

the community also died during the first decade of the century. Alfred Chapman, senior, the bailiff at Woodgate Farm, died in 1906. Charles Millhouse, the retired builder, and Benjamin Barnden, the shepherd, both died in 1909. Chapman and Barnden had both been born in the village. In 1911, a further loss was of Philip Fry, at the shop, where he had lived for nearly fifty years.

During the Edwardian era, all farms had large workforces. In 1902, John and Jane Fissenden brought their large family to Addington from Trottiscliffe to benefit from the employment opportunities here. Mrs. Fissenden died in 1907, and their eldest daughter, Gertie, returned home from service to act as housekeeper for the family. By the 1911 census, Mr. Fissenden had retired and some of the family had left home. However, in their cottage at East Street Bernard Fissenden, aged 29, was a carter, Thomas a groom, Richard a farm labourer, Jack a waggoner, Harry a gardener and the two youngest, Sidney and Fred (aged 14) were houseboys, probably working for the Whitburn family at Addington Place.

Losses to the community

The early years of the twentieth century saw the coronation of a new King and the passing of a number of residents who had been committed members of the community during his mother's reign. In 1901, the death of Spooner Hardy, aged only 53, was particularly regretted. He had given good service to the church and village, serving as churchwarden, on the school board and the new Parish Meeting, of which he was the first chairman. Three others who had played an active role within

There would be continuity from all these families. Lionel Hardy followed his father in serving the church and civil parish. Alfred Chapman, junior, became the bailiff at Woodgate. He worked for Lionel Hardy, who had purchased the farm from the Phillips family. John Cecil Millhouse assumed his older brother's responsibilities, though he did not serve as churchwarden. By the time John died, in 1922, just two generations of this family had spent eighty years in the village. The Lane where they lived was renamed after them.

Benjamin Barnden's son, William, who worked as a gardener, remained in the village and died here, aged 80, in 1949. Philip Fry's daughters, the Elizabeth and Edith Fry ran the shop until 1924, when it was sold with the estate.

The last of the Watton dynasty, Edward John Wingfield-Stratford, died at Clifton, Bedfordshire, in 1903, at the age of 53. He was buried in Addington. Mr. C.J. Sofer Whitburn died at his London home, aged 74, on 2nd November 1911. His obituary in the Times recorded that he left an estate worth £1,481,219, over £112m in modern value.[2] Mr. Whitburn had remained the senior partner and an active member of his banking firm until his final illness. His will directed that his wife should have use of the mansion house until her death, after which his estate would pass to his son, Charles William Sofer-Whitburn. Should he have no children, the remainder would go in trust to the eldest son of Charles's sister, Mary Christie.

Residents

The population of Addington was shrinking. From a peak of 272 in 1891, it dropped by 44, to 228, in 1901 and then fell to 214 in 1911. Although neither of the figures below include the household of the Whitburns, who were in London on both occasions, the main reason for this was smaller family size. The average occupancy had been 5.46 in 1891, but in 1901 it was 4.07 and 1911 it fell lower still, to 3.82—quite a considerable drop. The ratio of males to females was 101:127 and 99:115 respectively. Less than a quarter of the population were under 15 in 1911, as opposed to 40% in 1841. The table below shows the number of those born in Addington. In 1891, the figure had been 71. There were also fewer homes, as accommodation at the stables of the manor house was abandoned and a cottage allowed to fall down.

carter on a fruit farm, and his brother, Archie, was a market gardener, as opposed to working for a private individual. Three other men were also market gardeners. All these were still, however, connected with agriculture. Two different occupations were those of John Bonwick, at Hernewell, a stone quarryman and John King, the electrician at Addington Park. The estate also gave employment to bricklayers, carpenters, gardeners, grooms, a park keeper and a gamekeeper. Men who had left the village were still employed in similar occupations. A number lived locally and continued to earn their living from the land. However, one of the former miller's sons was a baker's assistant in Wandsworth, and another was a groom at Belvoir Castle.

The 1911 census resembled the earlier one. Sixteen heads of household gave their occupation as agricultural labourer and most other occupations were land based or connected to domestic service. At both censuses, there were domestic gardeners, grooms, cooks, housemaids, table maids, parlour maids, kitchen maids and general domestic servants.

Census	Homes	Total	Male	Female	Under 15	Over 60	Born in Addington	Average occupancy
1901	58 (of which 4 uninhabited)	228	101	127	68	16	49	4.07
1911	54 (of which 2 uninhabited)	214	99	115	52	26	34	3.82

Poverty does not seem to have been a major issue. No head of household was a pauper, though two veterans had been given light employment as caretakers. In 1901, the Malling Union Workhouse on King Hill housed only one former resident. This was David Pankhurst, who by then had lived there for over twenty years. He died in November that year, aged 91. This was the last burial of a member of the Pankhurst family in Addington. The first had taken place in 1789. The Fissendens arrived in 1902.

The average age rose in this ten-year period, from 26.82 to 31.91 years for females, and from 28.75 to 32.88 for males. 28 couples with children lived in Addington at each census, but these were not the same families. Nearly half of the homes changed occupants. This was not the golden age of stability portrayed in nostalgic memoirs. Despite the modern perception that in the past there was generational continuity within country communities, not one family present at the 1901 census was still resident in the year 2000.

Although, in 1901, sixteen men gave their occupation as agricultural or farm labourers, others had specific skills. They were carters and waggoners, a shepherd and a traction engine driver. Albert Chapman was a

Just a few houses at each census were headed by a woman. Mrs. Hardy of the Vale, Mrs. Hewlett of Shaw Hill House and Mrs. Warde of Aldon House were each of independent means, the schoolteacher, Miss Knight, lived with her assistant. Mrs. Annie Sparks of East Street, an elderly widow, gave her occupation as laundress at both censuses. She would live through one more, and was 86 at her death in

1922. The last Sparks burial was that of Annie's daughter, Emily Sparks, in 1939.

The Vale 1900-1970

In 1903, Mrs. Hardy negotiated a new, 21-year lease on the Vale from Mr. Whitburn. Lionel Hardy, her eldest son, modernised The Vale and installed an electric generator, one of very few in the village.

Shortly before the end of the lease, the Addington estate came on the market. At the first auction, the Vale failed to reach its reserve, but the family purchased the property by private treaty. Lionel Hardy continued to play an important role in the village. He joined the Parish Meeting after his father died in 1901 and remained a member for the rest of his life. During most of this period, the chairman was the rector, but Hardy took over in 1928, on Rev. Guise's retirement. Hardy was the voluntary almoner at the West Kent Hospital, Maidstone. He did not marry and was aged 54 when he died on 23rd May 1933. His mother survived him for only five weeks. Whilst both her husband and son died in their fifties, Mrs. Hardy lived to 87.

Katherine and Norah Hardy remained at the Vale for the rest of their lives. Village fêtes were held in its grounds and both sisters played a major role in church, parish and district life. Katherine was Addington Rural District Councillor during the 1930's and 1940's and Norah was the church organist. The two sisters were close friends of May and Aline Cholmeley, of St. Vincents. Katherine Hardy died in 1946, aged 70. Norah died in 1963. The Vale then entered a period of decline. The motorway was planned, and this put a heavy blight on the property. By then it had been placed on the supplementary list of buildings of historic value, but only at Grade III. After falling into decay, it was bought by a developer, Mr. G.F. Baker, of Chart Sutton, near Maidstone. When he applied for demolition, consideration was given to applying for a preservation order. However, as its frontage was mainly Victorian, and its state was by then described as "shambolic", permission was given for its demolition, which took place in 1970. A row of eight family houses was built on the site.

The Vale, photographed shortly before its demolition. © KLHC CC/C-PL/2/AHI-50/85

St. Vincents 1900-1960

St. Vincents was leased to a succession of tenants during the Edwardian period. These were Miss Mount (1899-1903), Mr. George Wilson (1904-1905) and Mr. and Mrs. David Meiklejohn, who came to the parish that year and stayed until early 1912. Meiklejohn was a retired India civil service officer. His younger children were born during their residence in Addington.

When the family moved back to London the house was empty for a period, but in June 1914 May and Aline Cholmeley took a ten-year lease on the property. Like the Hardy family, they purchased their home privately after it failed to find a buyer at the auctions of the manor. The sisters were two of four daughters of Sir Hugh Cholmeley, 3rd Bart., of Easton Park, near Grantham, Lincolnshire, where the family had lived since 1580. Their sister, Winifred Calvert, was my grandmother.

At the outbreak of the First World War, the younger sister, Aline, trained with the Red Cross at West Kent Hospital. She then served as a trauma nurse in Belgium. Her service is described below. As their only brother was killed on Christmas Eve, 1914, leaving young children, she must have had strong motivation. They spent the rest of their lives in Addington. Both sisters became very committed to their community and church. During the inter-war period, they kept horses for hunting and both were keen bee-keepers, dog lovers and gardeners. May Cholmeley died in 1952 and her younger sister in 1960.

Shaw Hill House 1900-1947

Mrs. Emmeline Hewlett remained at Shaw Hill House during her widowhood and died in 1921. Her daughter, Julia, moved to Shaw Hill Cottage, slightly further up Aldon Lane. Miss Hewlett taught the Sunday school children until her own death in 1940. Shaw Hill House was sold to an elderly gentleman farmer, Jonathan May (1860-1939). He increased his land holdings at the 1920's auctions. Mr. May was the son of a farmer, and was born at Cheriton Fitzpaine, near Crediton, Devon. He took up a career as a grocer, before later turning to farming. He and his wife, Abigail, lived at a number of locations before coming to Addington—West Hoathley and Ticehurst in Sussex, then Cricketts Farm, Ightham, Kent. Jonathan May died in Addington just before the outbreak of the Second World War, at the age of 79. His widow survived him until 1947. Their son, John, served as a PCC Member and was briefly the District Councillor for Addington (1946-1947), but he moved away after his mother's death.

St. Vincents kitchen garden as it looked during the first half of the twentieth century.

Communications and services

With the advent of the combustion engine, communications became easier for the wealthy, and bicycles were becoming a popular means of getting about for a wider section of society. During the Edwardian era, John Larking & Co., of Pudding Lane, Maidstone undertook a daily carrier service to Addington and two other Maidstone carriers also regularly delivered to the village, as the nearest railway stations remained, as now, either West Malling or Borough Green and Wrotham. Motor buses did not stop at the village until the 1920's, when the Maidstone and District Bus Company began a service along the London Road. The service became more frequent during the 1930's, as the customer base grew. Despite these advances, walking remained the principal means of personal transport within the village. The network of footpaths was extremely important and was more extensive than in the twenty-first century.

Private telephones were still scarce, but were installed in some of the larger homes. The post was important, and deliveries were far more frequent than today. Kelly's Directory for Kent for 1903 gives three collection times for letters from the Post Office on the Green, and two for deliveries. There was also a Sunday collection and delivery. Aldon had its own collection box, cleared at 8.10 a.m. and 6.20 p.m. each day and once on Sunday. Postal orders could be purchased at the village shop, but not paid out there. The nearest money and telegraph office was at Wrotham Heath.

The village was now supplied with gas by the Mid Kent Gas and Coke Company. However, the church was still lit by oil lamps. Electricity required a personal generator. It would be thirty years before overhead lines were installed.

Village Administration

Civil administration had been removed from the Church in 1894, but the membership of the Parish Meeting still closely resembled that of the previous Vestry. All were still men. This was the normal pattern for small villages. The rateable value of Addington in 1903/4, was £2,096, whereas Ryarsh and Birling, each with a considerably larger population, had a rateable value of £2,709 and £2,760 respectively. Trottiscliffe, with slightly fewer households than Addington, was valued at £1,206. The precept for 1910/11 was set at 2s 6d in the pound. After the war, the parish rates fluctuated. They were 5s 8d in 1920 and 6s 10d in 1921, but dropped back to 4s 8d in 1924.

The Parish Meeting met twice a year. The Annual Meeting was held in March, and a second would usually be held in September. By 1901/2, there were already changes to the original personnel. Frederick Warde, the fruit farmer at Aldon, had died. John Millhouse assumed his place as Overseer for the Poor. Another member, William Gregory, had left the village. The first chairman, Mr. Spooner Hardy, was gravely ill at the beginning of 1901. After his death the chairmanship was taken by Mr. Whitburn, owner of Addington Park. However, this was a nominal position as neither he, nor his son, Col. Sofer-Whitburn, who accepted the post in 1908, would ever take the chair. In their absence, each Parish Meeting was presided over by the Rev. Guise until, in 1919 he was officially appointed chairman. Lionel Hardy followed when Rev. Guise retired in 1928.

The most pressing issue that the Parish Meeting addressed in the new century was the provision of piped water to the village. A special meeting was convened on 19th August 1902 to discuss the guarantee required by the Mid Kent Water Company to bring their pipes to the Green. Although the cost would be offset by rates charged to house-holders, the parish was required to guarantee up to £20 per annum to cover the potential shortfall to the Company. The minutes imply that the parish was already charged a small fee by the Gas Company. They enlisted the help of Mr. Allison, Clerk to Malling Rural District Council, to ensure that the parish was not overcharged. Some areas of the village would continue be without mains water for some years to come.

The Church

At the turn of the century, the Rev. Guise was a driving force within Addington's community. He was also a link with the past, being the first cousin and contemporary of the last Watton squire, Edward John Wingfield-Stratford. Rev. Guise began his long ministry in 1883 and was very much a hands-on rector, renowned for crossing and re-crossing the Park as he passed from his home at Aldon to the village three or four times a day, to attend to his duties or visit parishioners. He ran the church, the school and, once up and running, the Parish Meeting. At the beginning of his Ministry, he had no parochial church council to assist him. These were set up by Parochial Church Councils (Powers) Measure 1921 Act to replace vestries, which from henceforth simply appointed the churchwardens. During the Edwardian period, Rev. Guise was supported by the churchwarden and the vestry, though this had already lost its civil functions. The membership of the new parochial church councils (PCCs) was set as the incumbent, one or two churchwardens and elected members of the congregation. In practice, PCCs were about twelve strong. Until the end of the 1920's, Addington PCC was led by a single churchwarden. The post was later divided into the rector's warden and the people's warden.

However, although civil duties were now the responsibility of the Parish Meeting, in 1912, poor relief of £5 12s 6d was still distributed within the village by the church, from its income of £66 10s 6d. Covenanting was already in force. In addition to the general offertories, eleven parishioners made regular gifts totalling £21 5s 0d. The churchwarden kept accounts that recorded that the income paid mainly for coal, repairs to the fabric and the Sexton's salary of eight guineas (which was never raised).

The church co-ordinated two "Clubs" which promoted self-help. In 1912, the Addington Clothing Club collected £20 17s 0d. The subscriptions included "Payments of women" of £12 7s and "Payments of children" amounting to £3 5s. The Sunday school, it seems, raised the modern day equivalent of £247.19. The fund was topped up by five guineas from Mrs. Whitburn (Addington Park), Mrs. Hardy (The Vale), Mrs. Meiklejohn (St. Vincents), Mrs. Phillips (Aldon House), Mrs. Hewlett (Shaw Hill) and Mrs. Guise (The Rectory). The clothes were bought from Mr. Viner's shop in West Malling, which remained in operation until the early 1980's. The second club was the Addington Coal Club, which had been running since the 1870's. It was referred to in the Dawn of the Day, the parish magazine of 1879. Members subscribed £13 and, again, the fund was topped up by wealthier householders. Subscribers were entitled to five distributions of coal each year. The congregation also supported local health institutions such as the West Kent Hospital and the Kent Nursing Association, both of which were vital before the National Health Service was set up. Other donations were given to mission work; locally to the Church of England mission to hop-pickers and further afield to Melanesia and Calcutta.

Although the church played such a significant role in the village, church attendance was now generally low, judging from the registers of services. Rev. Guise recorded an average of five to six communicants each week at the turn of the century and about 40 to 60 at the major festivals, when communion would be celebrated at 7 a.m. and 12 noon. Three services were held each Sunday; Holy Communion at 8, Matins at 11 and Evensong at either 3 or 6 o'clock. Sunday School was held regularly and, when the children came to church, they sat in the west gallery with their teacher—and made far too much noise. Rev. Guise recorded the names of those who came to the Christmas services, showing that more women than men attended church, and that there was a wide social range amongst the worshippers.

Externally the church was much as it is today, except for the addition of the recent extension. The interior was far more highly decorated. Services were "High Anglican" and the music at Matins was led by a choir of men and boys. Even during the Second World War, the rector was assisted by a boy server.[3]

Mr. Whitburn, the squire, had the patronage of both Addington and Ryarsh churches. He was not called upon to exercise this right to appoint a new rector for Addington but, in 1906, he appointed a new vicar at Ryarsh, Rev. Albert William Stockley, in succession to Rev. Edward Vesey Bligh.[4] In 1911, both "livings" passed to his son. In 1923, Rev. Guise celebrated forty years' service at St. Margarets. He was by then a widower, as his beloved wife Elizabeth, known as Elsie, had died in 1915. The patronage of the church was advertised for sale in the auction particulars that year, but the new owners did not wish to take on this duty. Rev. Guise resigned through ill health in 1928, and died in 1932 at Bournemouth. Col. Sofer-Whitburn appointed his successor to the living of Addington. This was Rev. Edward Ernest Hill, another connection of the Wingfield-Stratfords.[5] When Rev. Hill moved to another parish in 1933, the Bishop of Rochester appointed the next rector.

The Great War

The photograph right shows a carefree outing to the seaside taken just before the outbreak of hostilities. George, Bernard and Richard (far left) Fissenden are seen with three friends. The brothers would shortly be serving their counttry.

Though only a small village, Addington was very deeply affected by the First World War. As with other communities, many of its young men fought in the conflict, and seven died. Its squire, Charles Sofer-Whitburn, was appointed Hon. Lieutenant-

Colonel of the Royal West Kent Yeomanry at its outbreak. The Yeomanry were a branch of what is now called the Territorial Army. They were raised during the mid nineteenth century and were cavalry. Col. Sofer-Whitburn was a keen and long-serving yeomanry officer. He was their commander from 1914-1921. This was a prestigious position. His predecessors had been Charles Warde, M.P., of Barham Court, Teston and Viscount Hythe, son of 1st Earl Brassey, and grandson of Thomas Brassey, the railway tycoon. During the war, Col. Sofer-Whitburn was the chairman of the War Office's Cinematography Committee. He would have had oversight of some of the iconic photography of the conflict. By the time the unit was wound up in 1919, it had amassed earnings of £72,000, which were then distributed to charity.

1914 brought new challenges for the Addington Parish Meeting. On Tuesday, 11th August, a special meeting was called, on instructions from the County Council. This was *"with a view to providing in each Parish Special Constables, employed for the protection of life and property, to act unpaid, under direct orders and control and instruction of the Superintendent of the Police Division in which the Parish is situated to appoint*

The Fissenden family at the seaside just before the outbreak of the Great War. By kind permission of Mr. Louis Fissenden.

special constables." There was a considerable turnout of the men in the parish. Those present were: the Rev. J. Guise, Messrs. P. Philips, H.P. Stevens, L.H. Hardy, D. Thomson, W. Thomson, T. Pattenden, T. Thomson, G. Costin, W. Howe, H. Chapman, A. Chapman, W. Barnden, H. Fissenden, J. Fissenden, S. Fissenden, T. Bolton, W. Johnson, G. Peters, J. Denn, F. Cheeseman, T. Goodhew and E. Page.

The duties of the special constables were

- to protect telegraph and telephone wires, culverts and bridges,
- to instantly arrest any suspicious foreigners found tampering with the above,
- to protect women and children and
- to keep general order.

There was to be a committee, with a leader who would act under the control of the police. The special constables would be formed into two patrols, so that there was a succession of protection, and the patrols would wear armlets for identification.

The men sworn in by Major General Cecil Wingfield Stratford[6] and HG. Wood were *L.H. Hardy, *H.P. Stevens, F. Cheeseman, *P. Phillips, W.R. Thomson, T. Pattenden, *D. Thomson, W. Barnden, J. Denn, *T. Thomson, G. Peters, A. Chapman, H. Chapman and A. Botten. (* denotes committee member)

Strangely, at the following four annual Parish Meetings, little of relevance to the war was discussed even though so many young men and women of the village were giving service to their country.

Some of the young men from the village were already serving soldiers or mariners, and others enlisted, either voluntarily or, later, by conscription. The local regiment was the Queen's Own (Royal West Kent Regiment). A number of new battalions were formed to meet the need and to cope with the response to arms. A third of the men whose service is outlined below served with the Queen's Own, their recruiting stations being at Maidstone and Chatham. Men who had left the district enlisted at recruiting stations nearer to their employment, so were enrolled into other regiments. Some may have enrolled with the Royal West Kent but been sent elsewhere. During the first months of the War, the response to arms in Kent was outstanding, so some recruits transferred to other county regiments because there was no space in the local training programmes. If possible, these transfers were done by company (about 70-120 men), but even so it must have been quite a blow.

The War Memorial

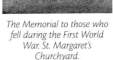

The Memorial to those who fell during the First World War. St. Margaret's Churchyard.

It seems fitting to first honour those who died for the country. During the 1920's, people in Britain felt a great need to honour those who had given their lives during the appalling conflict. Memorials were erected in the mid decade in communities throughout Britain. Seven casualties are commemorated on Addington's War Memorial. Their names are given in the sequence that they died:

1. **James Edward Hood**, Leading Stoker, was born in Trottiscliffe on 5th June 1888. He was the son of Edward John and Rhoda (Bristow) Hood of Addington Green, and grandson of Edward and Ellen Hood, who also lived on the Green. James was a regular mariner, already in service at the time of the 1911 census. He was aged 26 when, on 1st January 1915, his ship, HMS "Formidable", an elderly pre-dreadnought battleship, was torpedoed and sunk. The battleship was based at Portland, as part of the Channel Fleet assigned to defend the English Channel. It was the third naval casualty of the war. After a day of gunnery exercises, the Formidable had remained at sea in choppy weather, believing that this would protect her from submarine attack. This was not to be the case. She was torpedoed twice and sank very quickly, with the loss of 512 men from a complement of 780. Captain Loxley remained on the bridge with his fox terrier, Bruce, and oversaw

the evacuation of his ship. Both perished. The body of Bruce was washed ashore and buried in a marked grave in Abbotsbury Gardens, Dorset.[7]

2. **Sydney William Fissenden**, Private, was born on 3rd December 1893 in Trottiscliffe. He was the eighth of nine sons of John and Jane Fissenden. He enlisted at Chatham, on 30th March 1915 and served with "C" Company, 2nd Battalion of the Queen's Own (Royal West Kent Regiment). On 15th October 1915, he was posted to the Balkans. He died there less than two months later, on 7th December 1915. He is commemorated on the Doiran Memorial. The Salonika Campaign of 1915-1918, in Greece and Macedonia, was, an attempt by the Allies to open a second front, to relieve pressure on British and French forces in Belgium and France, but achieved few successes for the Allies. The Commonwealth forces were hampered by disease, diplomatic wrangling between the Allies and difficult relations with the Greeks, who were ostensibly neutral. From October 1915 to the end of the war in 1918, the British Salonika Force suffered 2,800 deaths in action, 1,400 from wounds, and 4,200 from sickness. As Sydney is not buried in the cemetery, it is likely that he died in action and his body was not recovered.

3. **Percy Pattenden**, Gunner, was born on 17th November 1888 in East Malling. Percy was the eighth of twelve children of Thomas and Eleanor Pattenden. His father was bailiff at Aldon. He became a groom, and was at Halstead Hall, Leicestershire at the 1911 census. He enrolled in the Royal Horse Artillery and

served in Mesopotamia with the 6th Cavalry Ammunition Column. He died at Amara, a town on the left bank of the Tigris, on 15th May 1916. Amara was a hospital centre. By April 1917, seven general hospitals and some smaller units were positioned there. The War Cemetery contains 4,621 burials, of which more than 3,000 were interred after the Armistice.

4. **Harry Fissenden**, Lance Corporal and Sydney's elder brother by a year, was born in Trottiscliffe in 6th June 1892. Harry was a gardener when he enlisted at Maidstone on 4th September 1914. He carried out his basic training with the 3rd (Reserve) Battalion, Queen's Own (Royal West Kent Regiment). He was then posted to the 9th (Reserve) Battalion but on 7th September 1915 was transferred to the 7th (Service) Battalion, and posted to France. On 19th August 1916, Harry was promoted to Lance Corporal but only just over a month later, on 30th September 1916, he was killed in action at Thiepval, during the Battle for the Somme. Captain C.T. Atkinson, chronicler of the Royal West Kent Regiments during the First World War, recorded that there had been hard fighting during July that year, but later that summer the 7th Battalion's stay in Flanders had been uneventful, with trenches in excellent condition.[8]

The action in which Harry died was described by Atkinson a *"regular soldier's battle"*, in which *"all depended on the courage and tenacity of individual N.C.O.'s and men"*, one of whom would have been Harry Fissenden. By the end of September, only one of the officers who had gone into battle on the first day was still on duty, and he had been wounded three times. Of the "other ranks", 70 were killed or missing and 200 wounded. The Seventh Battalion was not required to fight again for many weeks.

Harry's name is on the Thiepval Memorial, Pier and Face 11 C. Again, this suggests that he was killed in action and that his body was not recovered. He was awarded the Victory Medal, the British Medal and the 1915 Star.

5. **George Thomas William Martin**, Private, was born in 1893 in Wrotham. He was a son

Photograph of Belgium but showing the general use of horses during WW1.

of Thomas and Ellen Martin of Woodgate Cottage, and the older brother of Fred Martin, who later gave exceptional service to Addington. George enlisted at Woolwich on 3rd March 1916 into the 20th London Regiment. He was transferred into the Gordon Highlanders. One wonders whether he had difficulty understanding his companions' Scottish brogue. George also died on the Somme, in northern France. He was killed on 29th November 1916, at Miraumont, and is buried at the Adanac Cemetery nearby, with nine regimental companions who died that day.

6. **Bertie John Masters**, Private. He was born in Maidstone in 1887 and was the son of James Masters, a paper maker. I have not been able to establish his connection with Addington, but he may have been working here before the war. Bertie served with the 10th (Service) Battalion, Yorkshire Regiment. He died on 6th October 1917, in the run up to the First Battle of Passchendaele. He was buried at Godewarsvelde British Cemetery, on the French/Belgian border. The cemetery served three casualty-clearing stations, so Bertie Masters may have died of wounds.

7. **Charles White**, Unfortunately, it has been impossible to trace this casualty amongst men of that name who died.[9]

Other casualties

Two further casualties had been born in Addington, but no longer lived in the village at the time of their death, so are honoured elsewhere.

● **Walter Frederick Wells**, Private, was baptised in Addington on 23rd February 1887. He was the son of Thomas and Theresa Wells. His mother had also been born in the village, but the family later moved to West Malling. Walter joined the Grenadier Guards and served with the 4th Battalion. He died on 1st December 1917 on the French/Belgian border. He was married man and lived at Barming Heath, so he is commemorated on the Barming War Memorial.

● **Leonard Gregory**, Private, was born in Addington on 3rd July 1896. He was the son of William and Sarah Gregory of Aldon. Leonard gave his occupation as gardener when he enlisted at Sittingbourne on 27th August 1914. He joined the Buffs (East Kent Regiment). His parents had moved to Penshurst, where their oldest son, Frederick, ran the Bridge Tavern. Leonard was only 20 when he died on 8th March 1916. He is buried at the Abbeville Communal Cemetery. Abbeville, near to Boulogne, was a hospital centre. This would imply that Leonard died of wounds. He is commemorated on the Penshurst War Memorial.

Other war service

Not all who fought or served were casualties. Addington's parents endured years of worry as their sons fought on the continent, but some came home. Edgar Sydney, the youngest son of Alfred and Eliza Lancaster, of the Angel, had enrolled with the Territorial Army in November 1914, served through the whole war and returned home safely. Sadly, both his parents died at the beginning of 1918 and were unable to celebrate with him. Twenty other youths and young men were recorded as resident in Addington at the 1911 census, so many of these must have served in the forces.

The photograph below was found in a book kept by Aline Cholmeley, who served as a nurse in Belgium. It shows the appalling conditions under which the men

Photograph taken in Northern Belgium in January 1916 showing the devastation to communities that shelling caused.

fought during the winter months in Northern France and Flanders.

The 1918 voters' list gives the names of nineteen absent voters, of whom seven were noted as being on military service. Four others are marked with an "R", which may have meant they were in reserved occupations, away from home.

The serving men, who included a prisoner of war, were (in alphabetical order):

● **Ernest Allen Allman**, (1898-1979) 3rd Battalion. Grenadier Guards, B.E.F. Ernest was the son of John James and Elizabeth Allman. His father, a mechanic in the lace industry, lived for some years in Addington with his second wife, Rose. The family later returned to their home village of Shardlow, Derbyshire. Ernest also returned to Shardlow. He married in 1922 and lived the rest of his life in Derbyshire where he died in 1979, aged 81.

● **Walter Sydney Bennett**, (1896-1978), was born in 1896 in Offham. He was the younger son of James and Francis Bennett, of Kiln Cottages, Aldon. He enlisted on 27th October 1915 at Maidstone, giving his occupation as a farm labourer. He later moved from the Royal West Kent Regiment to the Suffolk Regiment. He was a prisoner of war in Germany in 1918. His marriage to Rose Sutton was registered at Malling in 1920. He died at Coalville, Leicestershire, in 1978, aged 82.

● **Percy Henry Broad**, (1887-1951), was born in Addington in 1887 and was the second son of Henry and Eliza Broad of Woodgate. He was a mariner and served on HMS "Lancaster", a Monmouth Class Cruiser. These cruisers were lightly armoured and, before the war, were mainly used in home waters. However, between September 1913 and August 1915, the ship was stationed at Bermuda and then sailed to the Pacific. She returned home in June 1919, after which she was scrapped. Percy would have been on his way home when the election took place. His death was registered at Woolwich in 1951.

● **Frederick Fissenden**, (1896-1990), Private, Machine Gun Corps. Fred was the youngest brother of Harry and Sydney Fissenden, honoured above. He enlisted on 30th March 1915, joining, like his brothers the Queen's Own (Royal West Kent Regiment). He later transferred to the Machine Gun Corps. and received the Victory Medal and the British Medal. Discharged on 9th May 1918. He married Amy Bristow in 1927 and lived at Hawthorns, Addington until the end of his very long life.

A photograph sent to Jack Fissenden at Coldrum Lodge Farm, showing a group from the Machine Gun Corrps.

● **Jack Fissenden**, (1890-1957) He served with the 572 Company (Agriculture). He was the sixth son of John and Jane Fissenden, brother of Harry and Sydney. He married Susan Watts in 1927. His death was registered at Maidstone 1957.

● **Lionel Hamilton Hardy**, (1879-1933) Lance-Sergeant, Queens Own (Royal West Kent Regiment). He lived at The Vale, East Street. He was 37 when he enlisted on 25th March 1916. He remained the rest of his life in Addington.[10]

● **Christopher Pattenden**, (1897-1966), Queen's Own (Royal West Kent Regiment) He received the Victory

Medal and the British Medal. He was a younger brother of Percy, whose name is on the war memorial. He served in France with the British Expeditionary Force. He married Marion Costan in Offham in 1921. His death was registered at Chatham 1966.

Even after the Armistice, demobilisation took some time, and some battalions remained for more than a year in Europe before coming home. During the Great War, the whole village had played its part. Some served as emergency officers; women wrapped bandages or knitted for the troops. The church accounts emphasise the response of the congregation. In 1914-15, £8 was donated to the National Relief Fund for sick and wounded, £8 18s 3^1/2d to the Belgian Refugees and £10 10s 0d to the British Red Cross Society. In 1917-18, a special collection was taken for Kentish Prisoners of War. This raised £5.

Aline Cholmeley was in her late thirties when she trained as a nurse at Maidstone Hospital in 1914. She

The nursing complement at L'Océan Hospital, La Panne, Belgium. 1915 From "Elsie Fenwick in Flanders" © Spiegl Press, Stamford, Lincolnshire

The passport photograph of Miss Aline Cholmely obtained for her service at La Panne.

and a family connection, Mrs. Elsie Fenwick,[11] set out on Tuesday, 16th February 1915 for La Panne, on the Belgian coast. (This town is now spelt the Flemish way, as De Panne). Mrs. Fenwick kept a diary during her time at the front, which was later published by her adopted daughter as "Elsie Fenwick in Flanders".[12] They worked in a Belgian field hospital to which the British Red Cross sent a number of trained nurses. Belgium was particularly short of such women, as the profession was con-sidered a religious vocation, and specialist training had been sorely lacking.

At the outbreak of war, Dr. Antoine Depage established the military hospital, L'Océan, at La Panne. Prior to this, he was one of the founders of the International Surgical Society. In 1903, he established a surgical institute for nurses of which Edith Cavell was the head nurse. He was a hard taskmaster, but one whose outstanding abilities saved the lives of many soldiers and civilians. He used the Carrell treatment, a new method of sterilizing wounds invented by the French surgeon, Dr. Alexis Carrell. At La Panne more than 50,000 casualties, with wounds, fractures, cerebral trauma, nitrous gas intoxication, and infectious diseases were treated by Dr. Depage. The results that he and his team obtained were excellent and mortality was low.[13]

Aline nursed with Mrs. Fenwick until November 1916. The work was intense, the men, women and children brought into the hospital had suffered dreadful injuries. It was frightening and dangerous, as the battle raged nearby and aeroplanes conducted dogfights overhead. However, the British Navy commanded the Channel so the women were able to return home for short breaks, and they received food parcels from Harrods! The diaries show two resilient women, who met the challenges they encountered, whilst still seizing opportunities in their rare free time. The following extract, dated Saturday, 2nd October 1915 gives a flavour of their lives:

"The shooting all night was terrible, the guns booming every few minutes the whole night through and in the morning towards Dixmude and Pervys. We heard the Germans were attacking hard with gas to help them. We soon had ambulances rolling up, and about 3.30 we had three brought up one after another, all bad – one shot through the hip and abdomen, another head, but

not bad, and another with the whole of the back of his neck shot away and a splinter of the vertebra of his spine, and his arms are useless and, poor fellow, he's so swollen and so patient. I had a real hard day of work and thoroughly enjoyed it, though there doesn't seem to be a medium! ! As to the Carrol (SIC) treatment[14] *it's driving me wild and giving us plenty of extra work. About 50 wounded came in. Such a lovely day. The ships bombarded. The ships were hard at work about 5 o'clock, shaking the house."*[15]

Aline had kept a photograph book since her teenage years, that mainly recorded parties she had been to and homes of friends that she had visited. Well before I knew that she had served in the Great War, I had found some small, but intriguing photographs of damaged buildings, clearly of the period. One had the date and place noted on it – "28 Janv 1916 Loo". Loo was a hamlet in Belgian now known as Lo Reningen and part of a large commune. It seems that Aline kept these photographs to remind her of her time at the front, though she never spoke of her experiences to her nephews. On Saturday, 31st July 1915, Elsie and Aline visited Loo. The following extract describes their "joy ride", as they called it.

"The Mission told us we might go where we liked as long as we didnt go into French lines, so we got a pass from Dr. Depage to Pollincave, and hoped to get on from there, which we did with the greatest success; in fact we did the whole of the Belgian lines. We started through Furnes down the Ypres road to Pollincave, from there we got to Loo, which has a lovely church spire, and up we proceeded and climbed and climbed as far as we dared and saw a lovely view over the whole

Ruins in Northern Belgium. Photograph kept by Aline Cholmeley.

Elsie Fenwick and Aline Cholmeley visit the trenches. Still in hats.
© *Spiegl Press*

country between Dixmude and Ypres. The whole of Loo has been shelled and any amount of huge shell holes. All the houses deserted except for soldiers, and they looked at us as if we were wild beasts! Some guns were shooting close by, but we couldnt see them."[16]

They continued down the road, seeing nothing but ruins. When they were near the German lines their *"chauffeur went as hard as he could, which was difficult because of the shell holes."* The soldiers along the road, sheltering in *"little dug outs and bomb proof shelters"*, gave them a welcome but the villages were devastated, with just a few children peeping out. They considered their trip a tremendous privilege and excitement. In August that year, they took the same direction, as by then a third line of trenches had been established on the road that led through Vieurne, towards Ypres. There they had their photograph taken before driving through Reninge (now a part of a commune that includes Lo, Reninge, Noordshoote and Pollincove). Elsie Fenwick wrote *"Renninghe is just a shell of a village and the Church stands out at the end of the deserted street, just the front wall of the tower standing with huge shell holes through, all the churchyard turned up with bomb holes and small holes; it really is awful and it's so sad to go into some of the houses, all deserted and knocked down and just bits of broken furniture about."*[17]

That day they crept within 500 yards of the German lines and watched their soldiers shooting, *"just the 'ping' of their rifles"* before returning to Renninge where their driver pointed to a shell hole and said *"Tiens, tiens, that has fallen since we left."*

In 1916, Aline returned to Addington. The reason for her return before the end of hostilities is unclear, but the British Red Cross sent nurses to Belgium for specific terms of duty, and this may have been the reason. She and her sister lived through another world war, during which they were prolific knitters for the troops.

Meanwhile, life and death continued in the village. During the war, there were 13 civilian burials, but only two baptisms. This was not only because the men were at war. It was a reflection of the ageing population in the village. About two thirds of the heads of household were over the age of 45, and baptisms had already declined sharply since 1910.

The Post-war Period

There is no evidence that Addington suffered from the flu epidemic that ravaged the country in 1919. The number of burials did not deviate from the average of three a year, and there is no oral history to suggest this. The soldiers returned to their homes and tried to build a new life.

However, they would now all be enfranchised. In 1900, there had been just 41 electors for Addington, and some of these did not live in the village, being qualified by leasing or owning land in the parish. Thus before and during the Great War, Mr. Tom Davies, who owned The Mount, but lived in London, was entitled to vote in Addington, and Daniel Gurr and Percy Lovell had this right because they leased land at Hernewell. These property entitlements were abolished in 1918, but exclusions and inclusions would remain until 1928.

On 28th March 1917, the House of Commons voted 341 to 62 that women over the age of 30 who were householders, the wives of householders, occupiers of property with an annual rent of £5 or graduates of British universities, should be enfranchised. Parliament had not, however, granted the vote to women on the same terms as men. The Act provided that all men over the age of 21 could now vote in the constituency in which they lived. One driver for change had been the need to give soldiers returning from war, many of whom were unmarried sons, the right to vote. Nationally, the number of voters increased from 7.7 million in 1912 to 21.4 million in 1918. The number of electors for Addington jumped to 127, but only 24 were women. Considering that females outnumbered males in the parish, this was still an injustice. Parliamentary boundaries were altered and Addington was moved again, this time from the Mid Kent to the Sevenoaks Parliamentary Division. The first opportunity to vote for these new electors was at the General Election held in December, 1918. Thomas Jewell Bennett, the Conservative candidate, was returned as the Member of Parliament for Sevenoaks.[18]

Ten years later women gained equality with men, as property and age restrictions for women were removed, making 21 years the eligible age for all to vote. The 1928 measures gave votes to a greater proportion of the male population as well. The number of electors had grown to 214 by 1933. At the eve of the Second World War, development along the London Road ensured that the number rose to 321.

Not only could women now vote, but they could be called as jurors. However, the property qualification barriers and age limits proved a barrier to women serving in this capacity. They were also restricted in the cases they were permitted to judge, in case they were upset! Under legislation introduced in 1825, a property had to be rated at £20 or more before its head of household could be called as a juror. This was to ensure that people on a daily or weekly wage were exempt, as they were likely to lose pay if they had to serve. There were two categories of juror. A common juror was eligible under the above rules but a special juror did not have to own property. He or she was categorised as "Esquire, banker or merchant (import/export)" and did not sit on criminal trials. Addington during 1924 had four common jurors,

Daniel Thomson of Westfields, Frederick Reader of Coldrum, Jonathan May of Shaw Hill and Richard Bagenal of Breinton Lodge. In addition, there was one special juror, May Cholmeley of St. Vincents. One can only assume that as she was not a banker or a merchant she was considered an "Esquire"!

A first Village Hall

In the early 1920's, the squire, Col. Sofer-Whitburn presented the parishioners with a very useful gift, a village hall. The actual building was a former army hut, made of wood and roofed in corrugated iron. It is probable that he obtained this as surplus to the requirements of the yeomanry regiment that he had led. He also donated the land on which it was erected. This was a plot behind the Angel, on the right hand side of Millhouse Lane, adjacent to Lane Farmhouse. Many social events took place there: meetings, coffee mornings, parties and weddings. There was an active Women's Institute, which was part of the original management committee, and the Mothers' Union. Surprisingly, the Parish Meetings continued to be held at the School until the mid 1930's. The hall did not have electric light until 1940, when the railways were electrified and overhead electricity was brought to the village. During the 1960's, theatre productions were staged at the hall. This small building served the needs of the village for nearly fifty years, and was not demolished until 1972, after which a home was built on the site.

Colonel Charles William Sofer-Whitburn

Charles William Sofer-Whitburn, who gave the village hall, was born at Kennington in the summer of 1867. He was educated at Eton and Trinity Hall, Cambridge, and joined his father's firm in 1889. This was a year after the family moved to Addington. He was a Justice of the Peace for the

Malling division of the county. In 1902, when he was 35, he married Clarissa Heseltine, the daughter of a stockbroker. Sadly, the couple would have no children. At the census the year before, he was with his parents at their London home, 16 Ennismore Gardens, Kensington. After their marriage, Col. and Mrs. Sofer-Whitburn lived at 38 Grosvenor Place, Belgravia. Both Whitburn couples were in their respective London homes at the 1911 census. When his father died, in November 1911, his mother resided for longer periods in Addington Park, though she retained her London home. Col. Sofer-Whitburn seems to have taken full charge of the estate during her widowhood, and it was most likely on his instructions that the estate cottages and houses were built. Although Col. Sofer-Whitburn sold the manor shortly after his mother's death in 1921, this building work suggests that this had not been his intention before the First World War. He was a keen competitive breeder of farm animals, specialising in sheep and pigs.

In 1919, Col. Sofer-Whitburn returned to his firm, Messrs. Reeves, Whitburn & Co. The financial environment had changed so, in 1925, he reconstituted the partnership into a limited company. He was its chairman until his retirement in 1931, at the age of 64. By then, he had given 42 years of service to the firm. Col. Sofer-Whitburn had other financial interests, including acting as director of the Colonial Bank, whose chairman was Max Aitken, 1st Lord Beaverbrook. The bank was active in the West Indies, the United States and Canada. It later merged with Barclays.

In 1922, a year after Mrs. Whitburn's death, Amport House, near Andover, came on the market. Col. Sofer-Whitburn bought this property and put Addington Park and its substantial estate up for sale. The details of the sale are given below. Mrs. Sofer-Whitburn had an exceptional eye for a good horse. She probably influenced her husband in his decision to sell the estate, as Andover is much closer to the racing industry around Lambourn. There he would also have better facilities to develop his prize herds. The newspapers of the day record that he spent significant sums to obtain the right breeding stock.

At Amport House, Col. and Mrs. Sofer-Whitburn

became enthusiastic and high profile racehorse owners. She started to raise horses before the Great War, but now developed her special talent of breeding and bringing on young hunters and thoroughbreds. She won a number of important races during the 1920's. The National Horse-racing Museum at Newmarket records that most of her winning horses ran under her own colours. These included Chivalrous, which won two Chester Cups, Drake, D'Orsay and Jennie Deans. Her most important win, however, ran under her husband's colours. In 1923, the year that the Addington estate was put on the market, they bought a mare in foal for 860 guineas. The foal, Adam's Apple, was trained by Harry Cottrell of Lambourn and, as a three year old, won the 1927 2000 Guineas at Newmarket, beating the favourite by a short head, at odds of twenty to one.[19] The owners of the other runners read like the Debrett's of racing. They included the Aga Khan, Sir Victor Sassoon, Lord Derby, Lord Beaverbrook, Mr. Anthony de Rothschild and Sir Malcolm MacAlpine. Adam's Apple was sold to an Argentine breeder for a five figure sum and stood there at stud. Mrs. Sofer-Whitburn also had an interest in coursing and two of her greyhounds won the Waterloo Cup. This was the most prestigious coursing event in the calendar. From 1836 to 2005, it was run at Great Altcar, Lancashire as a three-day meeting. It was a knock-out tournament between 64 coursing greyhounds.

Mrs. Clarissa Sofer-Whitburn on one of her hunters. © National Horse-Racing Museum, Newmarket

Although based in Andover, the couple spent most of their time in London whilst Col. Sofer-Whitburn

continued in business. Amport House was the place where they entertained. They commissioned Edward Lutyens a second time. He redesigned the gardens at Amport, in partnership with Gertrude Jekyll. There was a derelict private golf course on the land and Mrs. Sofer-Whitburn arranged for this to be renovated for the use of her guests. By coincidence, the parkland they sold in Addington has become a golf course. In another parallel, both houses were used by the Royal Air Force during the Second World War. Amport House was requisitioned by the Royal Air Force Maintenance Command. In 1962, it became the Royal Air Force Chaplaincy Centre, known, since 1996, as the British Forces Chaplaincy Centre.

Charles Sofer-Whitburn passed the last years of his life abroad. He died at Villa Noby, near Cap-Martin in southern France on 6th March 1955, aged 87. Mrs. Sofer-Whitburn survived her husband for eight years.

The Breakup of Addington Estate

In early December 1921, Mrs. Fanny Whitburn died at her London home. She was buried in Addington on 8th December. This event meant that her son, Col. Sofer-Whitburn, came into full possession of the manor and its estate, which covered over 2,400 acres. The land was not only in Addington, but also in Trottiscliffe (over 900 acres), Wrotham, Offham and West Malling. 1,250 acres were in hand (farmed by the Sofer-Whitburns). The rest was leased on tenancies of up to fourteen years. As has been described, the farming was mixed. Addington was also a sporting estate. 90 per cent of homes were owned by the estate, but a lower percentage of the land. Farms outside the control of the estate were Coldrum, Woodgate and Aldon. The only other trading enterprises were the public house on the Green and a beer house at Mayhill.

In late 1922, Col. Sofer-Whitburn instructed Messrs. Knight, Frank and Rutley to market Addington Park as a manor and estate. As the news circulated, it is difficult to underestimate the impact that this would have had on residents and tenants. Although the new squire and his wife had spent little time in the village, the close relationship between villagers and their "big house" would now be severed. The mansion would no longer be its centre of privilege, employment, shelter and deference, involving both work and home life. The houses, cottages and land holdings within the village and the wider area would from henceforth be in diverse ownership. Numerous new homes would be built for people who previously had no connection with Addington. These new families would bring fresh ideas, occupations and businesses to the village. The manor house and its park would be separated from the estate and would pass through two more private hands, before being acquired by a Trust. It finally left individual ownership in 1933. Some residents gained autonomy under the new arrangements, but it must have been a very daunting prospect that spring. Others, in particular those living in service cottages, faced the imminent prospect of losing their homes and livelihoods.

The first auction

On Thursday, 14th June 1923, Addington Park and its estate were auctioned by Messrs. Knight Frank and Rutley at the Concert Hall in the Corn Exchange, Maidstone. It had been heavily advertised, both locally and nationally, and the estate was offered as a whole, or in lots. The solicitors were Bischoff, Cox, Bischoff and Thompson, London E.C.2 and the resident agent was H.P. (Harry) Stevens. The photograph of the mansion taken from the auction brochure shows the well-maintained grounds. Recent tree planting can be seen, confirming that the availability of Amport House influenced the decision to sell Addington Park. Within ten years, the house and grounds would have deteriorated, as will be seen from a photograph in the next chapter.

The lots in Addington covered well over 500 acres and included the mansion house, its park and

Addington Park in 1922/3. From the auction brochure. © Knight Frank LLP.

shooting estate, St. Vincents and the Vale. The farms and small holdings were Westfields Farm (155 acres, including land in Trottiscliffe), land at Hernewell, Hedgehogs Farm and East Street Farm. The cottages on the Green were all for sale, plus Addington Post Office and shop, the school, the Angel pub and Park Cottage. In East Street stood the four New Model Cottages, and on Trottiscliffe Road, Breinton Lodge and Appledene.

942 acres more farmland came under the hammer in Trottiscliffe, including West Park Farm, Court Lodge Farm, Walnut Tree Farm and Miller's Farm. The Georgian residence, Trottiscliffe House, was then part of Addington estate, as was Trottiscliffe Post Office and shop, the White House, the forge, garden land, cottages, allotments and woodland. In Wrotham parish, 630 acres of farmland came under the hammer, including Moat, Nepicar Meadow, Wrotham Water, Ford and Little Wrotham Farms. Ford Place and its farm fetched one of the highest sums, £5,200. The buyer was a Mr. Kilpatrick of Kingston-upon-Thames. Godwell, Durrell's and Church Farms in Offham stretched over a further 350 acres. The estate owned more cottages in that village, yet another Post Office and shop, Offham House, which sold for £1,000, and a beer house and off-licence on the north side of the London Road near Mayhill. This site has become part of Addington civil parish and is now a car showroom and small business estate. Houses and cottages on Norman Road, West Malling, then called New Town, were offered, together with shops and business premises in and near the High Street.

The auction brochure confirms that the Mid Kent Water Company was by then supplying most of Addington, but that overhead electricity had not yet arrived. Mechanisation of farming was patchy and farms still relied mainly on

horse power for traction. A note to the holding at Westfields Farm stated, *"The Petrol Gas Plant and Fittings are the property of the tenant."* This suggests that the Sofer-Whitburns had not helped their tenant farmers to modernise. Many animals were still kept. Each farm had stables, cow sheds, pig pens etc.

The brochure gives us the names of cottage and house tenants. Their tenancy terms were relatively short, showing the vulnerability of agricultural businesses and insecurity of housing tenure. Most cottages were on weekly tenancies, though Miss Fry's tenancy on the shop, as a business, was on a semi-annual basis. The property was offered in a joint lot that included the wooden cottage beside it and the Laurels at the rear, so she was not in a position to buy it. The lot did not achieve its reserve, but was sold the following year at a second auction. Miss Fry and her sister then left the village to live near members of

Two photographs from the 1923 auction brochure, showing properties outside Addington. The first is Court Lodge Farm, Trottiscliffe and the second is Offham House and Post Office, © Knight Frank LLP.

their family at Mark Beech, Edenbridge. Many of the properties were let as service tenancies, meaning that if the worker lost his job, he also lost his home. The substantial houses were on leases of up to 21 years.

The mansion house was offered with a park of 179 acres, home farm, and two lodges. It was described as having fifteen principal and secondary bedrooms, five bath-rooms, six dressing rooms, a panelled outer hall and galleried lounge hall (54 feet long), a suite of four reception rooms, a billiard room and *"commodious domestic offices and staff accommodation".* The property had electric light, which was generated by a 10-hp Tangye engine in the old water mill at the stream, and mains water. A furnace in the basement supplied hot water by pipes to all floors and heat by hot air to the lounge, hall, dining room and billiard room.

The Kent Messenger gave an extremely full report of the auction, including prices paid and by whom. They reported that Col. Sofer-Whitburn himself was present. The first lot was for the whole estate but,

although a bid was received for £75,000, this was below the reserve set by the owner. The properties were therefore offered individually. The mansion and its park failed to find a buyer and not all the farms and homes were sold either. The Times of 15th June 1923 stated that the house had been bought in, and that land and properties totalling 1,326 acres had achieved £58,000 (equivalent about £2.8 million using the retail price index).[20] 40 of the 122 lots received a bid that was below the reserve, or failed to attract a buyer.

The cottages mainly went to "buy to let" purchasers from Sevenoaks, Maidstone and from as far afield as Eastbourne. The 65 cottages that came under the hammer achieved an average price of £105, though a significant number went for less than £70. Higher prices were achieved where land was attached, so the model cottages in East Street fetched good prices. Breinton Cottage reached £1,300 and was bought by Mr. Richard Bagenal of East Malling, who then moved into the property. If these four homes are removed from the calculation, the average price for a

The galleried hall of Addington Place, showing the Edwardian style of furnishing. © Knight Frank LLP.

cottage drops to £94. Most were not, of course, offered with vacant possession. On 1st December 1926, just three years later, the contents of Addington Park were offered at another auction. At this, a set of twelve Queen Anne dining chairs sold for £300, the price of four cottages![21]

Farms were on leases of up to fourteen years, though Hernewell was let on only a yearly tenancy. For tenants to find the money to purchase their farms proved quite difficult, and arranging a mortgage seems to have taken some time. A number of farms failed to sell at the first auction, but were purchased privately during the following year. Those that found immediate buyers were all sold to existing tenants. These were Church Farm, Offham, (£27 per acre, Mr. J.R. Betts), 57 acres and pair of cottages, part of Durrells Farm (£71 per acre, the Kent Hop, Fruit and Stock Farms Ltd), Wrotham Water farm, Little Wrotham Farm and Moat Farm (Mr. Henry Poore, who added Nepicar Meadows Farm after the auction, bringing his holding up to 377 acres) and Godwell Farm, Mayhill, Offham (£44 per acre, Mr. Sedgwick). Mr. Daniel Thomson's bid of £3,750 for 155 acres at Westfields Farm (c £24 per acre) was initially rejected. He did not complete the deal until after the second auction.

The average price paid for mixed farmland (including the farmhouses and outbuildings) was in the region of £34 per acre, though hop gardens and fruit orchards commanded higher prices. General farmland fetched only about £20-24 per acre. Although the farms were bought by their tenants, parcels of arable land fronting the London Road at Addington were purchased by speculators. This started the gradual development of housing in that area.

Shops, businesses and large private houses fetched the highest prices. The Angel Public House sold for £2,000 to its tenants, the brewers Messrs. Style and Winch. The company, through its successors, continued in ownership until the twenty-first century. Messrs. Style and Winch were acquired in 1929 by Barclay Perkins Brewery, who merged with Courage's in 1955. When Courage's sold the Angel, it became a free house.

The second auction of 12th June 1924

In April 1924, Col. Sofer-Whitburn accepted an offer for Addington Place and its parkland from Sr. and Sra. Alfredo de Peña. He was from Argentina and she from Colombia. They were newlyweds.[22] By then, a further nineteen of the forty unsold lots had found buyers, including The Vale and Trottiscliffe House, farmland at Wrotham, Court Lodge Farm, Trottiscliffe, which had been withdrawn after a bid of only £4,750 at the first auction(£12 per acre) and Walnut Tree farm also in Trottiscliffe. 524 acres had therefore been sold privately.

The *"Remaining Portions of the Addington Park Estate extending to an area of about 373 acres"* were offered by Messrs. Knight, Frank and Rutley at a second auction, held at the Star Hotel, Maidstone on Thursday, 12th June 1924. Harry Stevens, the agent, had by then moved with the Sofer-Whitburns to Hampshire, as his address was given as the Estate Office, Amport St. Mary, Andover. The remaining properties were Westfields and Hernewell Farms, St. Vincents, Keepers, Campions Wood, adjacent parkland (now a sandpit), the four Stone Cottages on the Green, the Post Office with three cottages, the smithy in Trottiscliffe, four houses on Norman Road, West Malling and a house, shop and cottage on the High Street there. The de Peñas acquired another parcel in Addington Park at this auction, paying £600 for 25 acres. This was a piece beside St. Vincents Lane that had been outside the estate during the late nineteenth century.[23]

By the end of the afternoon, virtually all the properties had sold. The exceptions were Westfields Farm and St. Vincents. These were both acquired privately after this auction by their respective tenants, Daniel Thomson and the Misses Cholmeley.

1   Dates are difficult to establish, as following the 1884 Act some employee tenants were still ineligible to vote. This seems to have included those living at the New Model Cottages, as the first elector registered there was Alfred Rushton in 1933, and Appledene is not included until that year.

2   Calculated from RPI on the website MeasuringWorth.com.

3   Harry Thynne, one of the evacuees, tells me he filled this position for Mr. Phillips when at Addington.

4   Rev. Bligh was married to Isabel Nevill of Birling and lived at Fartherwell, West Malling. Their daughter married Cecil Wingfield-Stratford, son of John and Jane W-S.

5   Rev. Hill's wife was Elizabeth Cator. Her parents were Bertie Cator and Violet Wingfield-Stratford, so she was the sister of the child commemorated in the window in the north transept.

6   Brother of the Edward John Wingfield-Stratford, the last squire of the Watton line.

7   See the entry for HMS "Formidable" in Wikipedia, including bibliography.

8   The Queen's Own Royal West Kent Regiment 1914-1919, Captain C.T. Atkinson, London 1924 pp 211-216

9   Neither Charles, nor his family, can be traced to Addington, despite searching through census records and voting lists. There was one family called White, living here at the end of the 19th century, but despite extensive checks, Charles cannot be connected to this.

10 Alan Chapman, grandson of Lionel Hardy's bailiff, told me that Hardy had to be sent home before the end of hostilities as unfit, due to a violent allergy to the khaki dye used in his uniform. I have not been able to verify this, and as he was absent at the time of the 1918 elections, it seems he was still then a serving man.

11 Aline's sister, Rita, was married to Elsie's brother, Jack Robarts, a London banker. Mrs. Fenwick lived at Luffenham Hall, Rutland. Her husband was Major Guy Fenwick. Major Fenwick was in America during much of the time his wife was serving in Belgium.

12 Butler-Henderson, Una, ed., *"Elsie Fenwick in Flanders, the Dairies of a Nurse, 1915-1918"*, Spiegl Press, Stamford, Lincs., 1980,

13 World Journal of Surgery, Springer, New York, Vol. 26, No. 10 October 2002

14 The Carrell treatment was a new method of sterilizing wounds invented by the distinguished French surgeon, Dr. Alexis Carrell.

15 "Elsie Fenwick in Flanders", p. 82 Her spelling of the Belgian villages is Anglicised.

16 As above, p. 60

17 "Elsie Fenwick in Flanders", p. 69

18 Bennett, MP for Sevenoaks from 1918-1923, was knighted in 1921. He was a journalist, the principal proprietor and editor of the Times of India. From Wikipedia.

19 Her successes were recorded in the Times newspaper, where she is also noted buying young stock at the sales, bringing them on and reselling them. The figures are quite substantial. Col. Sofer-Whitburn is recorded as spending £300 on a stud boar, whilst his rams were leased out for £250 per year. Adam's Apple was sold to a breeder in the Argentine for a five-figure sum, according to the National Horse-racing Museum.

20 www.measuringworth.com. The calculations can be made as standard of living, economic status or economic power. The lowest is the first, £2,580,000 to 2010, the highest, economic power, gives a figure of over £19m.

21 The Times, Issue 44446. Saturday 4th December 1926, p. 10, Col. C

22 Brief announcement by Messrs. Knight Frank and Rutley in the Times of 1st May 1924, p. 32 that Addington Park had been sold with 179 acres.

23 In Miss Cholmeley's copy of the auction brochure, she marked this price against the lot. Perhaps she had hoped to buy it, as it lies beside St. Vincents' Land.

8

1926 to 1959 - NEW FAMILIES and ANOTHER WAR

Following the Great War there was a great need for new housing. The slogan was "Homes for Heroes". The Housing Act of 1923 empowered and instructed district councils to administer grants of £50 to people who fulfilled certain criteria to construct homes for themselves or for sale. The farmland on the both sides of London Road, that had been sold to outsiders at the 1923 and 1924 auctions, was now gradually developed. The number of families living in Addington would double by 1934 and the breadwinners of the new families were in a much wider range of occupations than those of the past. Addington Park remained open grazing land, but its parkland north of St. Vincents Lane was sold to a sand extraction company during the 1930's.

The first new home on London Road was on its southern side, almost opposite the old lodge into the Park. This was Rosemount. It was built by Sydney Bates, who was a local builder and decorator, in 1928. In 1929, Herbert King built a second home nearby and named this West Bank. The third bungalow, Bonheure, was built by Ernest Cook, who grew soft fruit, particularly strawberries and raspberries, on its substantial plot of land. During the 1930's, more bungalows then followed on this section of road. On the north side of the London Road, because of Addington Park, development took place closer to Wrotham Heath. A wooden bungalow still known as The Bungalow was built in 1929 on the corner with St. Vincents Lane. This was four years before the start of the Clearway estate.

That same year Mr. Cook, of Bonheure, applied for a subsidy under the Housing Act above to construct a bungalow opposite Offham Crossing, where the service station now stands. Due to lack of funds, he was unable to start work within the time period allowed. It was the beginning of the Depression, and development slowed down. By 1930, only eight new homes were in occupation within the village boundaries. The major development drive took place during the next decade.

Addington Place as it looked in the 1930's. The creeper then covered most of its frontage.

Between 1927 and 1934, planning permission was granted for twenty-eight homes on London Road, Sandy Lane and St. Vincents Lane. Another small developer was Mr. John Carden, who built and lived in The Foss, on London Road. He also constructed the semi-detached pair of homes next to the Foss, known as Hawthorn and The Chestnuts, Cartref, and the Lattices on Sandy Lane. Vehicular access to all these properties was then via Sandy Lane. Unlike the homes on the southern side of London Road, which were all bungalows, Carden built two-storey houses. In 1929, Mr. Reginald Brice built a house he named Kippenkop on Sandy Lane. This is now called The Mount. Four years later, he built Fiddling (now Brookfield House) on St. Vincents Lane and this was where he and his family lived. In 1934, Southfields was constructed further down the lane, for Mr. and Mrs. Roger Hine.

Commercial development also began on the London Road in the 1920's. The Jubilee Tea Rooms, opposite Addington Park, were already open by 1927/8, run firstly by Mr. and Mrs. Charles Gilbert. A bakery was established that delivered to local families. By 1927, Mr. Glenn was trading as a motor engineer on the London Road, according to Kelly's directory of that year. His business was later known as the Regent Service Station but is now the Offham Service Station. Mr. and Mrs. Glenn lived in a bungalow on a rise above the business. Their son continued their business as a filling station into the 1980's.

The eastern part of London Road, beyond Addington Crossroads, was also being developed. Part of this land had also been sold when Addington manor was broken up. This area then lay in Offham, but became part of Addington at the end of the century. As early as 1926, the off-licence and beer-house at Mayhill that had been owned by the Sofer-Whitburns became a petrol filling station, with motor engineers. This was one of the first of such businesses in mid-Kent. The Winsor café opened next door and traded for over sixty years.

By the end of the 1930's, a number of catering establishments were thriving on the London Road from Mayhill to Seven Mile Lane. These served both the commercial and private trade. There were also a bakery, grocer's shop, butchers shop, tobacconist, motor engineers and two filling stations. Many of the potential housing and commercial plots had been

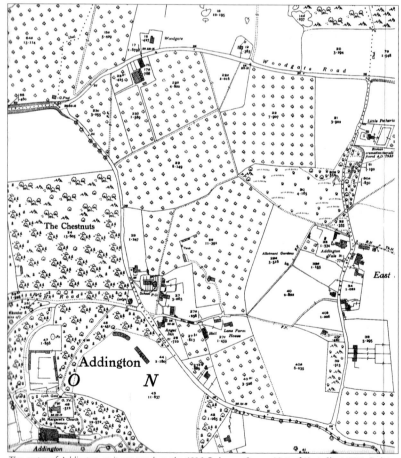

The centre of Addington as it appeared on the 1936 Ordnance Survey Map of Kent, Sheet 30.11. Breinton Cottage and Appledene can be seen on Trottiscliffe Road, and the New Model Cottages and Frenchay had by then been built on East Street, but other frontages are unchanged from 1907 © Crown Copyright

filled, though some homes were not constructed until after the war. As Sandy Lane was a rural, wooded area, during the 1930's new homes were given substantial plots and planning permission was denied for an application for four homes on a single plot. The reason given for refusal was that this was over development, because the site was only eight acres! By 1953 planning guidance for Sandy Lane had eased, as least on the southern side. Mr. Dunckley of Trottiscliffe built a terrace of houses, which he called Dunckley Villas, behind a small holding attached to Miline.

As the twentieth century ended, a number of these 1920's and 1930's homes were rebuilt, and the process continues. A number of plots were subdivided and now hold two or more houses. The accesses via Sandy Lane to houses fronting the London Road were closed, allowing new homes to be built in their long back gardens.

Clearway

The Local Government Act of 1929 directed district councils to develop a planning scheme. These were the forerunners of the district, county and metropolitan plans that now control planning in England. These development schemes came into being against a background of extreme housing shortage, both in towns and villages. Development was to be encouraged. In an urbanised environment, homes were allowed at a density of eight to twelve houses to the acre. In an agricultural situation, each house had to have four to five acres of land attached. Each council drew a loose line around communities, both villages and towns and development would be permitted within this. The word later used was "envelope". The district was zoned for different purposes: residential, industrial or commercial. Proprietors of land were invited to submit an "Owner's Scheme" and the general assumption was that this

would be accepted. This opened up possibilities to owners and purchasers of blocks of land, but district schemes were slow to beset up. The Malling Rural District Council Scheme, with zoning proposals and map, was put to the council in early 1935 but, during the prior two years planning generally followed its principles.

The Malling Scheme brought about the Clearway Estate. Mr. Alfred Clear, who created this, was the son of a bricklayer. He was born in Holmwood, Dorking, in 1874. He gave his occupation as builder at the 1901 census, when he was living with his family at his father-in-law's public house in Holmwood. His wife died as a young woman, leaving two small daughters, who were obliged to live with their aunt whilst Clear found work at Lewisham.[1] He later moved to Malling, where he worked on his own account.

At the end of 1933, Clear seized the opportunity that the new District Scheme presented. He purchased a block of land bounded by the London Road, St. Vincents Lane and Sandy Lane and submitted the layout of his development to the Malling Rural District Plans Committee of 1st July 1934. He quickly obtained permission to construct four bungalows.

The first homes built as Clearway. Numbers 1 to 6 were constructed during 1934-5.

The Bungalow already stood on the corner of St. Vincents Lane. Clear constructed his show house, No. 1 Clearway, next door. Mr. and Mrs. George Goodwin, who had been living at Wrotham Heath, bought the property and named it Rose Bank. Numbers one to six all face the London Road. They are Rosebank, Sunny Ridge, Hazelpear, Hillview, Angley and Poynings. Plans for two shops were then submitted. There would eventually be four, two on each side of the access road. By the end of 1935, eleven buildings were occupied, some fronting the London Road and others on St. Vincents Lane.

At this stage, the development of the estate ran into difficulties. Further plans had been approved on the inside of the block, but the Council was concerned with access and safety, and inserted a condition relating to paving. Sadly, the strain had taken a toll on Alfred Clear's health. He received approval for two garages at the planning meeting held on 31st December 1935 but died in Malling in early 1936, aged 63. The remaining plots on the estate were acquired by others and a few more homes were built on the estate before the outbreak of war, but it was not completed until the 1950's. Access remained a problem. In 1936, when the District Council gave approval for two houses submitted by a Mr. Willcocks, they included a condition that this was *"subject to the Estate road being made up to the satisfaction of the Council on the houses being completed."* The private roadway was metalled but not tarmacked and a pavement was built around the inside section. This reflected the standard of the day, as local lanes were not black-topped until after the war. With growing car ownership, later applications were mainly for garages to the properties.[2]

Clear had intended that this new community should be well serviced, but the shops were slow to open. The post box remained on the southern side of the main road, opposite St. Vincents Lane, until after the war, thus forcing people to cross a busy road to post a letter. A fire hydrant was installed only due to the threat of war. However, by the end of the thirties, a butchers, grocers and tobacconist, by this time run by a second owner, were operation. There was a café and the estate was served by two bus services. The Maidstone and District No. 25 bus ran from Wrotham along the A20 to Maidstone and the No. 9 ran from West Malling to Borough Green, via Offham and Platt. This

was used by the schoolchildren, especially after Addington Village School closed. The arrival of new families revitalised the village, but they did not bring enough children with them to save the school on Addington Green.

The Addington Park changes hands

Ownership of the manor house and its park underwent two more changes during the ten years following the breakup of the estate. Sr. de Peña, who had bought the house and its park from Col. Sofer-Whitburn, was a skilled polo player. Judging from press reports, he and his wife led an extremely social life in England, though he was often in South America, as he bred polo ponies there. They did not remain long in Addington. The marriage failed and, on 13th January 1927, Addington Park was auctioned yet again by Knight Frank and Rutley, on behalf of Sra. de Peña. The couple had bought extra land, as it was advertised with 263 acres, rather than the 179 offered in the auction catalogue of 1923.

The auction details stated, *"The Estate has over a Mile of IMPORTANT BUILDING FRONTAGE to the main London-Maidstone road and additional frontages in the village of Addington"*, but again, the property failed

The Lodge, London Road, from the auction catalogue, 1923. Courtesy of Knight Frank, LLP

to attract a buyer. The building stood empty until June 1927, when it was re-offered for sale *"at a very much reduced price".*[3] It was sold by private treaty to Mr. Henry Gurney Aggs, a banker, who had lived in Dorking. It seems that he and Mrs. Aggs came to Addington on his retirement from business. The splendid 1927 Standard "Pall Mall" saloon illustrated below must have belonged to Mr. Aggs. The chauffeur standing beside it is Edward Ebdon, whose son still lives in Addington. Mr. Ebdon was then living at his parents' home, the Lodge on London Road.

Mr. Aggs was able to enjoy his purchase and retirement for less than two years, as he died at Addington Park on 21st May 1929, aged 63. From a memoir given in 1970 by Fred Martin, of Overlea Cottage, Aggs contracted tetanus in the garden at the Park and died within twenty-four hours. Mrs. Aggs retained the property for a while, but put the mansion and park up for sale by auction on 19th July 1932, this time through Hamptons. The park had been enlarged once more. The mansion was offered with two lodges, the gardener's house and 286 acres. Given its chequered history, it is not surprising that a sale was not achieved. The Seekers' Guild of Prayer and Spiritual Healing, a community led by Charles Adams Simpson, acquired it privately in 1933. Mr. Simpson was a New Zealander. He had founded the community that was later called the Seekers' Trust some years earlier in London. The Seekers' Trust remains in Addington to this day, and their history is told more fully below.

The Parish Meeting between the wars

During the 1920's, the Parish Meeting took on a more defined role as the representative of villagers' rights and expectations. In 1925, a complaint was made to the new owner of Addington Park, Sr. de Peña, after he erected stiles across the Park, requesting gates instead. The elderly rector, Rev. Guise, may have been one of those who did not appreciate the installation. Cars were now more common and, during the same year, the Meeting discussed repairs to the road to the church, as motor vehicles were creating problems for pedestrians. It seems that no action was taken. Two years later the matter was an urgent necessity, as the surface had been badly cut up by vehicles.

Other changes were happening. The Local Government Act of 1929 abolished the poor law unions, thus ending the role of parish overseers. The Act also sought to consolidate or redefine the boundaries of smaller urban and rural district councils, to ensure their viability. The Ministry of Health, which was then responsible for local government, recommended that Addington should be removed from Malling Rural District and included in Wrotham Urban District, especially as the boundary with Wrotham parish crossed Sandy Lane. There was real concern and 43 residents came to a special meeting on 30th May 1929 to discuss this. Thirteen were women, showing that, once given the vote, women took an active role in public life.

The response agreed by the meeting is of interest, because it shows how the villagers saw themselves. It is pragmatic and reads as follows in the minutes:

1. Addington is a purely rural parish of 252 people
(figure from the 1921 census). Its rateable value is £1,786, with a penny rate of £8[4] *– it*

Edward Ebdon, chauffeur at Addington Park, with 1927 Standard "Pall Mall" saloon. Printed with kind permission of Mr. Bryan Ebdon.

would not be worth anything significant to Wrotham.

2. We are naturally connected to our current neighbours.

3. Our needs have always been sympathetically considered by Malling Rural District Council who have always administered us efficiently.

4. Our rates for 1930 will be 8s 10d in the £ - in Wrotham the rate is set at 13s 1d in the £, so what benefit would we get for this?

The village succeeded in remaining within the Malling Rural District Council area. In 1934, Wrotham Urban District Council was abolished and the area it covered was merged into Malling.

Addington's councillor on the Malling District Council that year was Col. Trant Luard, of Park Cottage, The Green. Col. Luard joined the Royal Marines prior to World War I and held the rank of Major in 1914. He served in Egypt during the conflict. He and Mrs. Luard moved to the village in 1925, having purchased the property from a Mr. Pilcher, who had acquired a number of properties at the 1923 auction of the estate. Col. Luard enlarged Park Cottage, adding a wing on the north side of the front door. Although he only spent nine years in the village, he gave great service to the community. He was on the Parish Meeting, serving as chairman from 1932 to 1934, and acted as a school manager as well as being the District Councillor. He and his wife left the village at the end of 1934. He lived to an immense age, being 103 at his death at Richmond in 1976.

During 1931, Col. Luard raised a matter at the Parish Meeting that would trouble the village for many years to come, until they took matters into their own hands. He drew attention to the state of the path around the Green, which was greatly in need of repair, due to the proliferation of trade vans. The path was becoming a public highway. The Meeting resolved that, as they paid rates for the upkeep of highways and the road was meeting the wider trading needs of the district, including access to the market garden behind the Green, Malling Rural District Council should be expected to help with this matter. The reply read to the Meeting the following

year (events moved very slowly!) was unsatisfactory, as the District Council ruled that the path would continue to be treated as a private road until the frontagers were willing to bring it up to a satisfactory standard. The 1932 meeting decided that no action would be taken to speak to them about such a great expense. The track was finally tarmacked in 1967, but only through the personal efforts of the frontagers.

Col. Luard's successor on the District Council was Miss Katherine Hardy. She served for eleven years and throughout her tenure was the only woman on the Plans Committee of twelve councillors. Miss Hardy and her fellow councillors had to consider planning applications that could totally change the character of the village. Her lifelong knowledge of the area must have been a great boon to her fellow residents. She served throughout the Second World War, despite failing health. She passed away in February 1946, aged 70.

Mr. Ronald Thomson of Westfields Farm took over Col. Luard's position as chairman of the Parish Meeting. Thomson, the youngest son of the Scottish farmer who came to Addington at the turn of the century, was only 30 when he took up the reins. Like Miss Hardy, he steered his community through the Second World War. The main discussion in his first year of chairmanship, 1935, was how to celebrate King George V's Silver Jubilee. It was decided that the children would be taken to a film show at the Granada Theatre, Maidstone and that a tea and entertainment would be put on for them in the village.

Twenty-five people came to the 1936 meeting, when a proposal was put that residents, who up until then had disposed of their own rubbish, should have this collected by the District Council. The motion was defeated by 13 votes to 10 (with two abstentions). However, an amendment was agreed as follows: *"Refuse should be collected provided that the M.R.D.C. figure of a 3d rate be not exceeded."* Miss Hardy, as District Councillor, was also requested to put to the council that *"prominent notices be placed to deter the public for littering rubbish in public places such as Addington Green and St. Vincents Lane opposite the new bungalows."* Disposal of garden waste in the strip of woodland opposite the homes in St. Vincents Lane continued for many years more.

The Parish Meeting had to address a number of footpath issues. The parkland that lay north of St. Vincents Lane was developed into a sandpit, necessitating the diversion of a footpath. The Parish Council did not submit an objection, as the employment generated by the pit was much welcomed. A number of other footpaths, however, were in poor condition and needed repair and clearance. 1937 saw happier times. After

The children of Addington School during the Edwardian period. By courtesy of Mr. Louis Fissenden.

the national trauma of his elder brother's abdication, this was the coronation year for King George VI and Queen Elizabeth. As for the jubilee celebrations of two years earlier, The Parish Meeting paid for the children to go to the cinema. They also agreed to present them with a souvenir coronation mug. A tea and sports event was held on Coronation Day at the chairman's home, Westfields Farm, followed by supper and entertainment in the village hall. A two pence rate was set, but voluntary subscriptions were also raised.

As early as 1937, Britain was fearful of war with Germany. The Annual Parish Meeting considered air raid precautions, and Mr. James Madden, of Aldon House, took on the post of Air Raid Warden in the village. 49 people came to the 1938 Meeting. They were very concerned about the danger of fire from a bombing raid and it was agreed to provide an extra fire hydrant at Offham Crossing, opposite Clearway. The Mid Kent Water Company had already agreed that those already in the village could be used in the event of an emergency. The amounts raised and spent by the Parish Meeting between the wars were, however, very small and were carefully spent. In 1939 the accounts showed a balance of just £9 7s 3d to be carried forward.

Addington School in the twentieth century

This was a church school, but funded by the County Council. In 1900, the building and the adjacent School House, where the teachers lodged, were both in the ownership of the Addington estate, leased to Rev. Guise on behalf of the church. On the 28th May that year, a memorandum noted the agreement made between Miss Evelyn B. Knight, the Rev. J. Guise, Mr. C.J. Sofer Whitburn and Mr. J. Spooner Hardy when she took up the post of head teacher. The essence of their agreement was that she should teach her pupils in accordance with the requirements of the Board of Education and instruct the pupil-teachers in the school. Her salary would be £70 per annum, paid monthly. The teacher would have the use of the teacher's house, which stood next to the school and a reasonable supply of coal. The managers would keep the house in good repair and pay all rates and charges.

School holidays would be not less than seven weeks in each year, to be agreed with the managers. In 1902, the school was closed from 7th September to 10th October for hop picking, Christmas Eve, and one week over the New Year, one week at Easter and one more at Whitsun. The infants' teacher hired that year was paid £40 p.a., and lodged with the headmistress. A third teacher was Miss Florence Bishop, who required no lodging as she lived at Birling. In 1902, the School Board consisted of the Rev. Guise as chairman, C. J. and C. W. Sofer-Whitburn, Canon Capes and Charles Millhouse, who had just been appointed the representative of the Parish Meeting. The school roll was well over fifty.

During the first years of the century, the head teacher of Addington School was invariably a single woman. The reason for this was budgetary, as the salary for a woman teacher was fixed at two thirds that of a man. In 1903, according to Kelly's Directory, the teacher was Miss Ada Fry, the eldest daughter of Philip and Harriet Fry, who ran the Post Office. The number of children enrolled was noted as 60, with attendance in the region of 50. As there were only 39 children aged between five and thirteen in the village at the 1901 census, it is clear that some were toddlers, or came from neighbouring parishes. In 1906, a decision was taken not to admit three year olds, as the head teacher insisted that this was an educational establishment, not a babysitting service. She wrote that young children were a distraction to good teaching, and that in future no child would be admitted before the age of five. The managers also refused at this time to install a crèche, even though parents, notwithstanding attendance laws, were likely to keep older children at home to supervise their infants. Kelly's directory for 1913 gives the roll as 64, with an average attendance of 38. Again, this number is surprising as the 1911 census, like that of ten years earlier, gives a much lower number of elementary school children living here—just 37.

The meetings of the school board were not held in the schoolroom. Instead, they took place either at the church or in private houses. The pool from which the members of the School Board were drawn was very small. Two residents of St. Vincents served as

"Correspondent", the term for the Hon. Secretary. The first was David Meiklejohn and the second was Aline Cholmeley, who joined the Board in 1922 and remained on it until it closed. Other members were Col. Luard, who also acted as Correspondent and both Mr. Whitburn and his son, Charles. The Parish Meeting had the right to send a representative and for the first twenty years of the century this was one of the Millhouse family. Charles was followed by his youngest brother, John, who served until his own death in 1922. Sunday School was also held in the village school. Fred Martin, speaking in 1970 to Ronnie Blair, then chairman of the Parish Council, said that the children were afterwards "herded" by their teachers to church for Matins. Sunday School attendance was good and needed three teachers: the Rector, Miss Hardy and Miss Hewlett, who taught the infants.

The only long serving head teacher was Miss Bertha Webster Finch who was already fifty when she came to the village in 1918. She served as headmistress for nine years, so was able to give a sense of stability to the village. Miss Finch, the daughter of a schoolmaster, was born in 1867 in Caverswall, Staffordshire and was already teaching at her father's elementary school at the age of thirteen. She lived at the School House until 1924. When it was sold she moved to White Cottage, East Street. After her retirement she moved to Hemel Hempstead, where she died in 1932, aged 65.

In 1923, when the estate was put on the market, the School was offered for sale in the auction brochure. It failed to attract a buyer, so Col. Sofer-Whitburn transferred the freehold of both the School and the School House to Rev. Guise and the school managers for the Parish. In a kind and regretful letter, he wrote that he must do this, as he would not return to Addington. Following the severance with the Sofer-Whitburns, foundation governors were appointed. These were Col. Trant Luard, Jonathan May, the new owner of Shaw Hill House, Mrs. Hardy and Miss Hewlett. Surprisingly, given that the Parish Meeting met in the schoolroom, meetings were held at The Vale, but they transferred to the new Village Hall in 1926. Rev. Guise served as chairman until his retirement, after which Col. Luard took over this position.

In 1927, when Miss Finch made her report to the Board, she was concerned about the low number of pupils. The school roll had shrunk to 21, possibly due to the family profile in the village. The development on London Road had barely begun. The attendance record, however, was 96%, and many children had attended every session. As she also stated that the school opened 415 times, this implies that children would come in the morning, but some would not be seen after returning home for lunch. The Diocesan Inspector had spoken in pleasing terms, as reiterated in his report. The children had collected money for "war savings", the Lenten Box and the N.S.P.C.C. Miss Finch then went on to report that it was rumoured that *"some Trosley parents are eager for their boys to attend Addington School. For my part I am not in favour of importation from neighbouring villages and am hoping that the incident may be settled amicably, nevertheless it is not my prerogative to refuse admission."* These children may have been those living in cottages between the two villages, as Fred Martin had attended Addington School in the Edwardian period whilst living in one of them.

By the 1930's the pinafores and formal clothes had been abandoned. This photograph was taken at some time during the 1930's, and shows children in casual clothes relaxing on the village green

This postcard shows the schoolchildren on the Green. Behind can be seen a number of trade vans outside the Shop.

Despite development on the London Road, the school roll remained low. Families were now small. Alec Carden lived with his family at the Foss, built, as has been said, by his father. Writing in the 1990's he

gave the village his reminiscences of a childhood in Addington before and during the Second World War. He included a ten-year roll call of the children who attended the school between 1933 and 1943. It runs to only 33 names. He was only four years old when he started school. He recalled walking down St. Vincents Lane with his six-year-old sister to reach the Green. If they met a farm cart going the same way, they would hitch a ride, whether or not the driver knew he had children on board. Carden wrote that the postman was a veteran of the Great War, who rode his bike with one hand and carried the letters beneath the stump of his other arm. During the autumn season, his bike would often have a brace of pheasants across its handlebars and, in the summer, a basket of live crabs would be in the front carrier, with just a label tied to it.

He described the school building as appearing tall and imposing to his young eyes. Inside was an entrance hall where coats were hung. Off this were two classrooms, lit by oil lamps. The younger group went up to nine and were taught by the assistant, with the older children helping the infants. The ten to fourteen year olds were taught by the head teacher, Mrs. Hughes. A fire burned in the grate during the winter, surrounded by a brass fender. On this stood $\frac{1}{3}$ pint bottles of milk waiting to take the chill off. Carden wrote that at times this was so successful that the milk was almost boiling hot. The rear of the school had a play yard, beyond which were rudimentary toilets. These consisted of a gulley leading to a soak-away and an additional plank with two holes in it over a pit. The children played mostly on the Green at the front, perhaps not surprisingly, given the proximity of the somewhat primitive "plumbing" to the schoolyard.

Holidays were Easter and Christmas, plus two weeks in June for fruit picking and a similar period for hop picking. These were working holidays, as the children accompanied their mothers into the fields, either to pick strawberries and other soft fruit, or to fill the "bins" during the hop picking. The money earned bought winter coats and shoes. As a church school, the rector was a regular visitor, but the pencils and all the equipment were firmly marked with the words Kent County Council, to stress who paid the bills!

The last meeting of the school board was held in 1939. Aline Cholmeley, as Correspondent, recorded that, for financial reasons, Addington School would no longer be a church school. The Kent County Council signed a lease to run the school until 1947 and took over its administration. During the war, the building was heavily used. Local pupils were taught in the mornings and evacuee boys from Woolwich Central School were taught by their own teachers in the afternoons—though they later used the Village Hall for their lessons. In the closing months of the War, despite the lease it had signed, the Kent County Council decided that the school was no longer viable. Its closure took place on 28th February 1945.[5] Pupils thereafter attended the local primary school that was most convenient to the part of the village where they lived. This was Platt School for those on the London Road and either Trottiscliffe or Ryarsh for those in the centre or east of the village.

The loss of the school diminished interaction between residents and community spirit now had to be actively fostered, but economics overruled objections. Kent County Council continued to pay rent to the church until its lease ran out. The building was then sold and converted into a private house. The proceeds of about £1,000 were given to St. Margaret's Parochial Church Council.

Farming

Between the two wars, farms continued to be intensively cultivated, with fruit and hops in abundance at Aldon and cattle, grain and fruit on the northern side of the London Road. Fruit growing was of paramount importance, not only for the London market, but also for

canning, jam making, bottling and juice making. The 1936 revision of the Ordnance Survey Map (1:2500 or 25 inches to the mile)[6] shows little change from that of 1907. Although petrol driven farm vehicles were now more common, horses were still of great importance. Alec Carden remembered cadging lifts on the farm waggons as they came home from work.

The Seekers' Trust

The Seekers' Trust was, and is a spiritual healing community. In early 1933, when Charles Simpson brought his community to Addington, they moved into the mansion house. Seventeen names appear on that year's electoral roll under that address. The members immediately converted some of the stables into small chapels where they could hold prayer meetings, seeking healing and consolation for their members and for those who contacted them for help. The mansion house was converted into flats, and members ran it as a country house hotel for some years. However, they quickly identified a need for private accommodation for married couples, some of whom had dependent children. An accommodation block, called Churchfields, was built on land near to the Trottiscliffe Road, called Troop Field on the 1843 Tithe Map. A second block was later built beside this.

The Seekers' Trust Cloister Garden during the 1930's

The Trust then began to plan how to use the land that was surplus to their immediate needs. Their agent began to write an Owner's Scheme, through discussions with Mr. Culpin, the Planning Adviser at Malling Rural District Council. He submitted this on behalf of the Trust. The Scheme's proposals included 272 homes in the Park, which included the land on which the megalithic monuments stand, stretched to Campions Wood and northwards to where the motorway now runs. Without access to the accompanying plan, I have not been able to judge the area where these homes were to be built, but they were unlikely to have been directly below the mansion house.

The District Council approved the Owner's Scheme but, when trees began to be felled in preparation for construction, there was a great outcry in the village. By this time the ancient avenue to the mansion had already been felled, a particular sadness to villagers. As the early postcard in Chapter Seven showed a wooded environment around the Neolithic graves, it is likely that these trees were also felled at that time. Members of the Seekers' Trust were also having misgivings; perhaps some had not been fully involved in the discussions. In the event, the Trust withdrew the proposals, and agreed with the timber contractors and Addington residents a limited further felling of trees. Although revised proposals were later put to the Council, these were refused and an appeal was not successful. The peaceful community at the Seekers' Trust, with the conversion of the stables, two residential blocks, an office, the Lilacs and the Woodhouse were all that were eventually constructed.

The mansion house was requisitioned during the Second World War, for use as a rest home for pilots from West Malling Airfield. After the war, much work was needed to bring the house back into productive use and it proved impossible to recreate the hotel without these works. The Trust tried to sell the building but failed to find a buyer. Although repair work started, a devastating fire occurred that gutted its central core. The County and District Councils became concerned over safety aspects and the

mansion was deemed unsafe. It was demolished in 1950. The fire had not damaged the whole building, so a sale was held for local people to bid for salvage. Items were sold "standing", so if a purchaser had successfully bid for three window frames, he had to go and remove them himself. Strangely, there are no reports of injuries during this process.

Having withdrawn its development plans, the Seekers' Trust leased the parkland to Mr. and Mrs. John Sterrett, who were then living at Callis Court, Ryarsh. This was sold to the lessee in about 1949. Mr. Sterrett later acquired the site of the former mansion and built a modern home where it had stood. After his death in 1968, his home was sold and the parkland was leased for use as a golf course.

The Seekers' Trust in its peaceful setting, taken from the church tower in 2012.

The two sand pit companies

In September 1935, the Addington (Kent) Sand Company was granted permission to extract sand on Addington Lane, within Trottiscliffe Parish, but with access through the village. The following year, also in September, and possibly consequent on the failure of the appeal for housing, the Seekers' Trust sold the northern part of Addington park to the Ace Sand and Gravel Company. They obtained permission to extract sand on the land that lay directly opposite the first company's holding. They were invited to decide how to exit from these workings. Both St. Vincents Lane and Addington Lane were approved, but the company decided to use only the latter.

One of the reasons for the need for sand was the fast expanding motor industry. The sand in Addington contains silica, some is of extremely high grade, and suitable for foundry work. The two sandpits were welcome as they gave employment at a time of recession in the country. As I have mentioned above, when one of the companies applied to alter the line of footpaths, the Parish Meeting did not object. Contracts with the Ford Motor Company at Dagenham were in place for many years, and only ended when the foundry closed in the 1980's. The very high quality sand produced in Addington still has a specialist market. It is transported all over the country.

When the motorway was built during the early 1970's it bisected the second sandpit, so that it now sits on either side of the road, with a haul tunnel beneath the traffic. The impact of the motorway on the sandpit is described in the next chapter.

The church from 1920 to 1945

Parochial Church Councils (PCCs) were set up in 1921 by the Parochial Church Councils (Powers) Measure 1921 Act. However, the surviving minutes for Addington commence on 12th November 1931. This does not mean that Addington church did not have a PCC before then, but that the first minute book was unfortunately lost. Fred Martin, the longest serving member of all time, started his service on the Council in 1924.

PCC meetings took place at the schoolroom until March 1940, after which they moved to the newly electrified village hall on Millhouse Lane. The rector in 1931 was Rev. Ernest Hill, his churchwarden was Lionel Hardy and the other eleven members were Mr. F. Cheeseman, Mr. H. Chapman (verger), Miss Cholmeley,[7]

Miss Fissenden, Miss Hardy (Hon. Secretary), Miss Hewlett, Mr. F. Martin, Mrs. A. Rushton, Mr. Speechley, Mrs. Speechley and Miss White.

1933 was a disastrous and worrying year. Rev. Hill left the parish that spring and, in May, Lionel Hardy died. The parish was left without a rector or churchwarden. An emergency meeting was held on 25th August and Lionel's sister, Katherine, was appointed churchwarden but she took over at a particularly stressful time. Firstly, she was required to oversee obtaining the faculty for a memorial to Rev. Guise, who had died a year earlier. This was not an easy task. The parish wanted a brass plaque, but the Diocesan Advisory Committee insisted on the memorial being in wood. The compromise was to remove the tablets from beside the reredos and replace them with specially commissioned oak panelling.

Secondly, the Bishop of Rochester, Rt. Rev. Christopher Chavasse, proposed that as there was a vacancy, the benefices of Addington and Offham should be combined. This was despite the rapid development that was taking place in Addington. Miss Hardy and the PCC managed to ensure that Rev. Donald Band was inducted into the parish in January 1934, before the final decision had been taken. It may have been at Miss Hardy's insistence that one of Rev. Band's first proposals was that in future two churchwardens should be appointed. At the AGM held in April 1934, Miss Hardy took on the role of Rector's Warden, while Mr. Francis Withers, of Aldon, became People's Warden. When Miss Hardy died in February 1946, nearly 62 years had passed since her father had first joined the Vestry.

In August 1934, the proposals for a merger with Offham were dropped. However, boundary changes were made. Addington ecclesiastic parish lost Coldrum Lodge and its surrounding area to Trottiscliffe, but three detached pieces from Ryarsh parish that had been transferred to the civil parish in the 1880's now became part of the ecclesiastic benefice as well.[8]

Rev. Band was a young man and a moderniser, who wished to integrate church and village life. He added a section of village news to the parish magazine, to encourage people to take out a subscription and perhaps become interested in attending church. This meant that the cost had to rise from $1^1/_2$ pence to two pence a copy and, after a few issues, the village insert was abandoned due to lack of sales. During his two-year tenure a number of issues arose. A Diocesan inspection in 1934 indicated that the Tower needed repairs costing £150, and that the inside of the church was also in bad repair, requiring over £450 to be spent on it. This was a huge challenge for such a small parish, but by running fund-raising events, at least the tower repairs were finished in 1936.

The PCC had begun negotiations with the owners of Addington Park, the Aggs family, to extend the churchyard. Delays occurred and the Seekers' Trust had bought the land in question before agreement was reached. Despite strenuous efforts by Rev. Band, negotiations with the Trust broke down, and he had left the parish before the extension was finally acquired in 1938. The land was generously donated to the parish at no cost except legal fees. In thanks, the church agreed to reopen a path and gateway that had been closed and to fence the area. An envelope collection raised £54 1s 0d, but the legal fees for Messrs Arnold and Grimwade, the Diocesan solicitors, came to only £33 9s 6d, so there was a surplus to use for the fencing. The new piece was then landscaped and paths laid before the first burial in 1940.

Perhaps the transfer of the patronage to the Bishop of Rochester prompted the sale of the large rectory on Aldon Lane. The cost of its upkeep would have been a major factor in the decision. In October 1934, Rev. Band called an extraordinary meeting of the PCC, at which it was agreed that the rectory should be sold and a more suitable home be built for the rector. A site was found in Addington Park, to the south east of the churchyard, with vehicular access from the Trottiscliffe Road. However, the sale of the old rectory took some time during these years of depression. Mr. and Mrs. Edward Wanostrocht eventually purchased the property in 1937. Once the sale had been achieved, construction started on the new building. Rev. Band's successor, Rev. Phillips moved into the new rectory, now called The Warren, in 1939.

By assiduous visiting, Rev. Band had built up the church electoral roll to 134 within a year of his arriving in the parish, a significant increase. It was 128 when he moved to the larger parish of St. Mary's, Strood, in May 1936. Rev. Band's whole ministry was in Kent and he continued to have a great affection for his first parish. He was buried here in 1972, aged 74.

Rev. John Timothy Phillips, known to his family as Tim, came to the parish in the summer of 1936. His first years were dominated by fund-raising, as repairs to the tower and lych-gate were achieved. Once the rectory had been sold, he oversaw the building of his new home. He was the rector throughout the War years. He was fortunate in his churchwardens. When Mr. Withers, the first People's Warden, left the parish, Mr. Bert Pattenden, of Aldon Farm, assumed this role. Pattenden served in this position until the end of the war and then succeeded Miss Hardy as Rector's Warden until 1954, when he resigned through ill health. He moved to Otford, but died the next year. He was another stalwart in service to St. Margaret's.

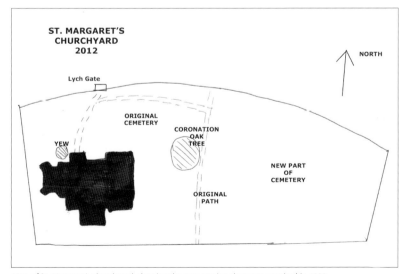

ST. MARGARET'S
CHURCHYARD
2012

NORTH

Lych Gate

ORIGINAL
CEMETERY

CORONATION
OAK
TREE

YEW

NEW PART
OF
CEMETERY

ORIGINAL
PATH

Map of St. Margaret's churchyard, showing the new portion that was acquired in 1939.

There were other changes. Miss Julia Hewlett died in September 1940, aged 68, at the height of the Battle of Britain. One of her former pupils, Alec Carden was disappointed when electricity came to the church that year, as he was no longer allowed to work the organ bellows for Miss Norah Hardy. Because of the low stipend, Revs. Hill, Band and Phillips each stayed in the village for a relatively short period before moving to a larger parish. They made efforts to reach out to the new community living along the London Road, some of whom had little experience of village life. Even though the roof had been repaired, the church needed substantial internal repairs, almost out of reach of the small congregation. However, church attendance rose during the thirties. In 1931, the church electoral roll was 72, but it had nearly doubled by 1935, as families from the new homes became part of the congregation. The figure dropped back during the 1940's but averaged about 120. Even with a lively and committed congregation, the roll today is only about 80.

I have already mentioned a long serving PCC Member, Fred Martin (1900-1978). He was born at Northfleet and his family came to Trottiscliffe when he was about four. He began to attend Addington School and church when they lived in one of Bullshole Cottages, between the two villages. His parents moved to part of Woodgate Cottage in about 1911. His older brother, George, was killed in the First World War, and is commemorated on the war memorial. Fred Martin's first job was as under gardener to Col. Sofer-Whitburn. He joined the PCC in 1924 and gave 47 years service, to nine rectors. He preferred to be a "foot soldier" but was persuaded to act as People's Warden between 1968 and 1971, after which he retired from the council. He married Elizabeth Glover at St. Margaret's in 1930. She was the adopted daughter of Mr. and Mrs. Edward Hood and had been brought up on the Green. Fred and Elizabeth lived at 2 Overlea Cottages. Mrs. Martin died in 1955, so Fred was a widower for 23 years. After his death a small brass plaque was put in the pew where he sat.

Other members of the PCC also lived in the old cottages of the village, Miss (Gertrude) Fissenden, was at Carolcot, East Street and Fred Cheeseman at Rectory Cottage, Aldon. However, it was not until 1946 that any of the new families living on or near the London Road came onto the council. The first PCC members from London Road were Mrs. Calladene and Mrs. Forsey.

Village life during the 1930's

Although a number of garages were being added to the homes in the village, car ownership was not universal and the husband was overwhelmingly the sole car driver. Milk, bread, newspaper and groceries were delivered to people's homes from local shops. It was a long day for shopkeepers such as Mr. Jack Gower, at Clearway, as he would carry out these deliveries after closing in the evening.

From about 1919, Addington cricketers had used a pitch on land near Roughetts Road, on the boundary with Ryarsh, but a few years later they returned to the nineteenth century site in Addington Park, opposite the entrance to East Street. Reg Humphrey, a founder member of the revived club of the late 1950's, understood that it had a "faggot" wicket. This was bundles of willow withies buried four feet into the ground to give a bouncing wicket and to improve the drainage. The club fell into abeyance during the war, because the Park and mansion had been requisitioned and the ground was no longer available. It would not be revived until 1958.

Social life took place in the Angel, the church, the village hall, the schoolroom and the cricket club. The publican at the Angel in 1926 was Thomas Bristow, who had taken over the tenancy after Alfred Lancaster's death in 1918. However, Bristow left in 1928 and was replaced by Arthur Bedford. At this period a second couple occupied the former club house next door. Bedford was the publican during the Second World War, but Mr. Bennett had taken the tenancy by 1948. He was then replaced by Alf Allwright. As can be seen, the turnover of publicans was much higher during the twentieth century than in the past.

Although the photograph here is from the 1950's, it

could have been taken at the Angel at any time during the mid century. George Fissenden and a friend were visiting the Angel after a Remembrance Day service at St. Margaret's church. The pub was a popular watering hole on the way home from a church service. It had three bars, the public bar, the saloon bar (with comfortable seats and where the beer was more expensive), and the snug. When indoor toilets were installed, the snug vanished and the other two bars were amalgamated. The publican in the photograph, Alf Allwright, was a leading force in the formation of the new cricket club at the end of the decade.

George Fissenden and friend with publican Alf Allwright on Remembrance Day. By kind permission of Louis Fissenden

Women belonged to either or both the Mothers' Union and the Women's Institute. Both institutions organised many gatherings and outings. The meetings took place mainly in the village hall, and included fund-raising events. During the 1930's,

The Mothers' Union banner designed by Alfred Rushton, A.R.C.A., during the 1930s

Alfred Rushton, an excellent water colour artist who lived in East Street, designed and executed a Mother's Union banner for the church. He is also known to have painted a number of watercolours of the church and village, but these have now dispersed.[9]

The thirties were a decade of travel,

particularly by motor bus (known as a charabanc) and train. Just beyond Addington's bound-aries, the Royal Oak Hotel at Wrotham Heath was rebuilt for large parties and Messrs. Rootes opened a saleroom, repair workshop and garage next door to cater for those with private cars. By 1936, Greenways Hotel had opened just east of the village boundary with Offham, a site that is now The Links. This is shown on the 1936 Ordnance Survey map with an extra freestanding hall and swimming pool. A further hall was built later, as the business expanded. The swimming pool was very popular with Addington residents. The dances and activities were also enjoyed by young and old.

However, the thirties were still a place of the past. Alec Carden described the abundant flowers in the woodlands and the charcoal burning that took place in the chestnut coppices throughout the village. The men had to be on hand 24 hours a day to prevent any fire escaping from the mound and ruining the charcoal, so were a fascination for young boys. At lambing time, the local shepherd lived in a moveable hut in the Park, to be near his sheep. Young Carden and his friends could see his billycan bubbling away on a fire outside this. They loved to paddle in the clear stream next to St. Vincents, to hang from the low branches of beech trees and to stroke the three gentle shire horses at Westfields Farm, whose names were Polly, Daisy and Bob. They were sometimes lucky enough to ride on their backs as the horses were led home from work. In those days, the track around the Green was soft and sandy. It ran right round past School Row, then down the slope to rejoin the lane to Trottiscliffe. Another path led to Woodgate, but this was closed when the motorway was built. From contemporary photographs, it can be seen how these paths were deeply etched into the grass of the Green. It was still a time of mainly pedestrian journeys. Trottiscliffe Road was narrow and winding, and trees hung down over it.

Allotments had been established near to The Vale by the end of the nineteenth century, accessed by Millhouse Lane. However, as many gardens were substantial, it seems that these were not well patronised until the war brought a pressing need to grow extra food. The schoolchildren were then given their own allotment and encouraged to participate in the war effort by growing food.

The interwar years saw intense change and development. Older residents had endured one devastating world war and, at the end of the period faced another. The village was no longer under the control of a single landowner and the influx of new families brought new life to the community. The number of homes more than doubled during the period. Modern services came to the village, the most dramatic being overhead electricity. People learned new ways of administration in an increasingly bureaucratic world. Despite the depression of the thirties, it was a period of hope, as breadwinners and their families seized the greater opportunities in both work and leisure.

But as the thirties ended, the country was once more at war with Germany, and the next five years would again tear young men, and now women, away from Addington.

The Second World War

The village had anticipated the outbreak of war two years earlier, so air raid wardens for the village were already in place. The chairman of the Parish Meeting, Mr. Ronald Thomson, the farmer at Westfields, had been appointed the chief air raid warden for the village in 1938. Discussion had also taken place about the location and accessibility of fire hydrants in the village. The announcement of war on 3rd September 1939 was still a profound shock. The rector, Rev. Phillips, who had been an army chaplain during the Great War, noted in the margin of his Register of Services book "WAR DECLARED". That very day he also recorded an air raid warning. He became chaplain to the Royal Air Force at West Malling. The village was fortunate to have an energetic rector during these years. Rev. Phillips was an engineer by profession and a practical man, who

personally repaired the footpath across the park for the benefit of his parishioners. He was an amateur musician and wrote a "Hymn to Airmen" in honour of the brave pilots at West Malling Airfield. To the tune of AM 316 (Alleluia sing to Jesus, his the sceptre his the throne). The final verse went:

> "When they scale the heights of glory,
>   Battling with the alien throng,
> When the strife is grim and gory,
>   and the night is drear and long,
> May the Angel-host watch o'er them
>   Until terror's reign be past,
> Then let smiling peace restore them
>   To their loving friends, at last."

Mr. Thomson chaired the Parish Meeting throughout the war. Its minutes are surprisingly bare of references to the conflict or to the difficulties and privations that residents faced. As during the First World War, the subjects discussed remained strictly parochial and were mainly to do with footpaths. By reading the minutes, one would not be able to tell that there was a war on! However the Meeting gave a donation of £5 to the Village Hall in 1943, acknowledging its importance as a community meeting point. The annual meeting of 1944 attracted an attendance of only eleven people. A two pence rate was set to repair stiles and footpaths and a further £2 was donated to the Village Hall. Even more surprisingly, no meeting at all was held in 1945.

This was despite the development of the airfield at West Malling, an influx of evacuees into the village and the requisitioning of Addington Place as a rest home for pilots. Park Cottage was requisitioned for officers and the evacuees lived in homes throughout the village. Addington Park was a battery station and, at times, was disguised as a decoy for the airfield. Lights were set out to confuse enemy bombers.[10] Forty years later quite substantial anti-aircraft shells, which had misfired, were still being dug up around the village, including two in the author's garden. The village was lucky to escape lightly as only a few bombs fell here. The first was before the end of 1939. Mr. Jack Gower, who with his wife had returned to his childhood locality to run the grocery shop at Clearway, very vividly described to me hearing this first bomb whistling past his head as he was making a late delivery. Luckily, it failed to explode, instead burying itself deep into the field behind Fiddling (Brookfield House), where it no doubt remains to this day. It may have been that night that another bomb blew tiles off the roof of St. Vincents. The plaster fell from the ceiling of the sitting room, but when Roy Goodwin, then a teenager, helped Sydney Bates, the builder at Rosemount, to repair the damage, he found the two Miss Cholmeleys quite unfazed. The bomb crater can still be discerned at the bottom of the garden.

At the outbreak of war, Jack Gower was also an air raid warden, but he joined the R.A.F. and trained as an aircraft fitter. He was first seconded to Short Brothers at Rochester, then served alongside Canadians at Northolt, later being posted to Bahrain, where he spent the rest of the war. His sister was Mrs. Glenn, whose husband ran the Regent Service Station. Mrs. Glenn and Mrs. Gower ran the shop in his absence.

During 1940, shells dropped in a line from Offham to Wrotham Heath. One landed at the Royal Oak and, sadly, killed one person. This was Mr. Frederick Heine of Heathfield, on the London Road, who was on duty as air raid warden that evening. A third raid was recorded by Rev. Phillips on Trinity Sunday, August 1944, when he jotted in the margin of his service book, "BOMBS FELL!" A casualty on that occasion was the glass in the west window of the church, which had to be boarded up for the rest of the war.

An air-raid shelter was built near Addington Green behind the school.[11] This was for the benefit of the schoolchildren. Alec Carden's reminiscences also covered the war years. He wrote that food actually improved with the introduction of rations. Some young men from the village went straight to war, especially if they were already serving in the Territorial or Regular Services. His elder brother was one of these, as were two of the Wise brothers from Hedgehogs. Albert Wise, their younger brother, would lose his life. Other young men joined up quickly and left for France, whilst the older men served as air raid wardens or in the fire-watching service. Mr. Carden, who was 61 at the outbreak in 1939, became a firewatcher. Alec wrote that his father

The West end of the church showing the boarded up window. Electric lighting had by then been installed.

had little time for the Chief Warden, who made them practice putting out a candle the other side of the room using a stirrup pump and a bucket of water.

One air raid siren was based at Borough Green and another was at West Malling. The children were told that at the sound of the siren they must find the nearest tree, lie down underneath it face down and cover the backs of their heads with their hands until they heard the "all clear". To start with they were frightened and obeyed, but they quickly became unconcerned and during raids would watch the skies for contrails, parachutes etc., whilst listening to the sound of cannon fire. Mr. Marshall, who as a sixteen year old spent his holidays with his parents at the Seekers' Trust, recalled lying on his back on the tennis court there in August 1940, watching a daylight raid over London being driven back through Kent by the Royal Air Force. It was fortunate that there was only one local casualty, as large pieces of shrapnel were regularly picked up on the roadside verges, the railway line being the probable target.

In late 1939, the village welcomed over thirty boys into its homes. My correspondent, the late Ray Huson, who was one of these, said that these children were aged between eleven and fifteen and came from the Woolwich Central School for Boys.

More were sent to Watering-bury, including Huson, as were all the pupils from the Woolwich Central School for Girls. They came with their teachers. School lessons for the village children took place in the mornings under Addington's head teacher, and the lessons in the afternoon were for the boys, conducted by their own teachers. The Seekers' Trust played its part and about five boys lived in The Close. The evacuees were fed in the servants' hall at Addington Place, so the

The Evacuees from Woolwich Central School photographed with their teachers and the Rev. JT. Phillips in 1939 Courtesy the late Ray Huson.

Seekers' Trust seems to have retained part of the building for their own use. St. Vincents and the Vale took in about four evacuees each and smaller homes were allocated one or two. Although the compulsory billeting was viewed with uncertainty to start with, the boys settled in well. From reminiscences, it seems that some were able to treat their stay as an adventure, though the younger pupils were much more susceptible to home-sickness. However, at least one of the group lost his mother through a bombing raid on his London home whilst he was living in Kent. The boys were expected to attend the village church whilst in Addington, and the village was fortunate to have Rev. Phillips as rector. The older boys did not stay long, being already fifteen in 1939. Some later served in the armed forces.

To give them some freedom, parents put bicycles on the train to Maidstone and the boys took the bus there to collect them. During the summer months, some of the boys, against all rules, would get on their bicycles at 4.30 on a Friday evening, cycle back to their homes in southeast London and return to their billets on Sunday evening. Although this was very much frowned on, it meant that they were able to keep in touch with their families (who were also, on occasion, able to visit Kent, as it was not too far away.) During the summer holidays, the boys found work on local farms, fruit and hop picking. They had quite a lot of freedom, and Ray Huson lost the sight of an eye when

he found the detonator to a shell. He spent five weeks recovering in Maidstone hospital . The children, whose classes later moved to the Village Hall, became part of the village. However, they were evacuated to the West Country in 1944, as there was then a very real threat from doodlebugs to homes in the South East of England.

Local pupils remained at Addington School until they were nearly fourteen, after which some attended secondary school. Alec Carden was a pupil at the Central School at Ham Hill, Snodland (now Holmesdale Technology College) and spent a year there before leaving in 1943 to work in the office at Walter Smiths' Quarries at Leybourne. To get to school he had to walk from Clearway to the Green to catch the bus run by F.A. Brooks of Ryarsh, a company that is still in operation. If he was late he had to walk on through Ryarsh and Birling, as he wrote *"with plenty of time to think up an excuse"* for his lateness.

The church played an integral part in the social fabric of the village, despite low attendance at services. It administered a sick fund, out of which donations were given to the Red Cross and to Maidstone Hospital. Some improvements continued to be made to the church, despite the hostilities. In 1941, electric cables were installed to feed the bellows for the organ, and a fund successfully installed electric lighting in 1944.

The Plaque in Memory of those who died in the Second World War

Rather than add the names of those who had died in the War to the existing war memorial in the churchyard, at its meeting in August 1946 the PCC decided to place a plaque within the church itself. Mr. and Mrs. Wanostrocht had lost their son, Hugh, during the War and they offered to help pay for this. Their offer was gratefully accepted. The original design was in the form of a cross, but the Diocesan Advisory Committee rejected this and the accepted form was a simple stone rectangle. The memorial cost £31 and was made by Messrs. Witcombe and Sons, a firm of monumental masons in Maidstone. It was not until 1949 that it was finally installed in the alcove on the South wall, opposite the entrance to the church. When the church extension was built, this was re-opened as a door, so the memorial was moved closer to the chancel. The following four men lost their lives in the conflict and are commemorated on the plaque.

John James Robert Ware, (1904-1940) was born in Rainham. He was the son of Ebenezer Ware, a market gardener, and his wife, Alice. John married Grace Shaw in 1927, and the couple came to live at St. Michael's, 19 Clearway, with their two children. Ware was a Sapper in the 100 Army Field Company, Royal Engineers. He died on 29th May 1940, during the evacuation from northern France. He is buried at Oudezeele churchyard, 24 kilometres from Dunkirk, one of only five British soldiers in the cemetery. After his death, Grace and the children left the village and moved to Gillingham, Kent.

Hugh Nicholas Wanostrocht (1917-1942) was born in Canterbury. He was the son of Edward and Kathleen Wanostrocht, of the Old Rectory, Aldon. He was a Sergeant in the No.9 Squadron, Royal Air Force Volunteer Reserve. He died on 7th May 1942, site unknown, and his name is recorded on the Runnymede Memorial.

Albert Wise (1923-1943) was born in Hollingbourne. Albert was a younger son of Jabez and Constance (Reader) Wise, who moved to Hedgehogs when he was an infant. His mother's family were tenant farmers at Coldrum. Constance Wise died in 1932, leaving four sons and a daughter. Albert served with No. 40 R.M. Commando, Royal Marines. He was only 20, and Addington's youngest casualty, when he died on 1st September 1943, during the expulsion of the Germans from Sicily. His younger brother, Robert, also served in World War II. Albert is buried in the Catania War Cemetery.

Bruce A. Simpson (1914-1944) was born in New Zealand, but came to England as a child. He was the son of Charles Simpson of the Seekers' Trust, Addington, by his first wife, Grace Agnes. Bruce married Madeline Giometti in 1934, when he was only 20. He was a Lance Corporal in the 3rd Divisional Signals, Royal Corps of Signals.[12] He died on 2nd July 1944 during the push after the Normandy landings. He was buried in Hermanville cemetery, just behind Sword Beach.

Other service men and women

The service register for the electoral roll of 1945 contained the names of sixteen Addington men: James Camber, Alfred Clarke, Moorcroft Cooper, Maurice Day, Arthur Gardiner, Jack Gower, Keith Hanson, Leonard Harmsworth, Ronald Hickmott, Roger Hine, Guy Hughes, John Hughes, Geoffrey King, Robert Lovell, George Maddan and William Maddan. The list also contained one woman, Hilda Beatrice Davey of Poynings, London Road. This may not have been a complete picture though, as others such as Fred Marsh were still on war service, and the list does not include those in reserved occupations. However, it must have been with relief and gratitude that they were eventually welcomed home by their parents, wives and children.

Peacetime

In the closing months of the war, Rev. Phillips took on the extra responsibility of Trottiscliffe parish, but he resigned both benefices shortly afterwards. Another loss to the village was Miss Katherine Hardy, who was greatly missed for the exceptional service she had given to her community. She was active to the last. As Hon. Secretary, she had taken notes at the PCC meeting held in November 1945, but then suffered her terminal illness. She died in February 1946 and had not been able to write her notes up in the minute book. Rev. (later Canon) John Rahe-Hughes (1907-1982) had just replaced Rev. Phillips. When he took the next meeting in March 1946, he made a note that he had relied on his memory as to what had passed at the meeting. At the annual meeting in April that year, Mr. Pattenden assumed Miss Hardy's role of Rector's Warden, whilst Mr. Wanostrocht was elected People's Warden. Another death was mourned that spring. This was of Harry Chapman, the verger, son of the Alfred Chapman, Senior. Chapman had been sexton since just

after the turn of the century at the unchanging salary of £8 a year. He was the last paid sexton and verger.

The 1946 Annual Parish Meeting was attended by 46 parishioners, who elected Mr. Wanostrocht as their chairman. The main discussion was about the Victory celebrations. A motion was put forward for a supplementary rate of two pence in the pound to be levied, but this was rejected. Instead, it was agreed that public subscriptions should be sought. This second motion was passed by 27 votes to 8. The Village Hall Committee were asked to organise this, and Mrs. Rickard, Mrs. Hughes (the head teacher) and Mrs. Gower offered to assist them and to give a tea and sports party for the children.[13]

The village slowly recovered after the war. Most homes had avoided bomb damage. However, two cottages on Addington Lane, Trottiscliffe, known as Leney Cottages, were hit and badly damaged by enemy action. The cottages were then part of Westfields Farm and repairing them was a financial worry for Ronald Thomson. It was universally recognised that living conditions in workers' homes must be improved, and he wished to install a new scullery, indoor plumbing and a bathroom in these cottages. This raised the cost substantially and the extra work was not necessarily covered by Government provisions. With the help of the District Council, Thomson was able to find an acceptable estimate from a contractor. With some difficulty, he then obtained a grant of £750 from the War Damage Commission to undertake the work for both war damage and improvements.

With Britain at peace once more, the 1946 Parish Meeting was able to concentrate on the poor bus service to the village. Not only was it infrequent, but the timetable was not adhered to. It was also unpleasant to wait for the buses. The Maidstone and District Bus Company was lobbied to erect a shelter at Addington Crossroads, as older children had to use buses to get to secondary school. Three years passed before this was achieved.

Mr. and Mrs. Wanostrocht left the village in 1949 and Col. L.D. Scott assumed the chair. In 1950, the Parish Meeting joined with that of Trottiscliffe to petition for a rail passenger "halt" at Offham Crossing. Despite strenuous efforts, this was still not achieved.

Three notice boards were placed around the village, as the Parish Meeting wished to communicate better with residents. The footpaths in the village continued to be of vital importance and two concrete bridges were built on those that crossed the park, linking the London Road and Aldon to the village centre.

Two sandpits were already operating within Addington. In 1949, proposals came forward for a third pit to be opened on the south side of St. Vincents Lane, where the recreation ground and golf course now lie. Parishioners were very concerned about the detriment to their environment, but recognised the pressing need for new aggregates, so did not entirely oppose the plans. Instead, they proposed that Malling Rural District Council should ensure *that the amenity of the countryside would be safeguarded and the land left after excavation of the sand in a tidy condition with the sides sloped down to the bottom of the excavation.* They also asked that the Long Barrow be protected, as it lay so close to the proposed sand workings. Fortunately, the application was withdrawn.

Addington's historian

In my introduction I acknowledged the inspiration that James Gracie Maddan gave to my own researches into the history of Addington. As he was living in the village during this period I felt it right to present a short biography of his life.

J.G. Maddan was born in Lanarkshire in 1874, the eldest of six children of William and Anna Maddan. His father was an accountant who worked for the British Linen Bank in Berwick-upon-Tweed. James Maddan, then aged 17, was with him at the bank when the 1891 census was taken. Maddan came south and, in late 1914, married Dorothy Tuke at Dartford. The couple lived in Croydon, where their first two children were born. They had moved to Lancashire by 1920 as their third son was born there. Maddan worked for the Post Office for many years. He was awarded a C.B.E. in 1933 for his work as Postmaster-Surveyor at Manchester.[14] Shortly before the

war he and his wife returned to Kent with their sons, two of whom were still based in Addington when they fought in the Second World War. They lived at Aldon House. It was probably after 1946 that he did his research into the village where he was living, as he published his articles in the church magazine in the early 1950's. Mrs. Maddan died in 1962, after which he moved away. He died in Surrey in 1966 and his ashes were interred in his wife's grave in Addington churchyard.

Population growth after the War

Private house building very slowly got under way again, but the late 1940's were a time of austerity and shortages, particularly of building materials. There were still some substantial empty plots on the London Road. Immediately after the war, on one of these, Mr. Hayes built Miline, using scavenged materials from bombsites in the Chatham area. Its site, like others built prior to the war, stretched down to Sandy Lane. Mr. Hayes worked the land as a smallholding, and built a substantial glasshouse. The plot included a "dip" which has the appearance of having been a quarry but, if so, it had not been worked for many years. It is possible that stone was extracted from the area when London to Folkestone turnpike was constructed as long ago as the eighteenth century.

By 1948, there were 137 homes in the village and the electoral roll was 397. 29 homes stood on the London Road. Clearway and St. Vincents Lane now held 33, but only four stood on Sandy Lane, mainly because the extensive gardens of those on the London Road. East Street held fifteen homes, but only one of these had been built since 1925. The Green and Millhouse Lane were also unchanged since the First World War.

A number of the post war applications were for the addition of garages to existing homes as private car ownership increased. However, these were still for a single car. Not all plans for new homes were approved. Mr. E.A. Langridge was refused permission for a bungalow with four further building plots on an 8½ - acre site on Sandy Lane. He was asked to resubmit plans for just the bungalow. The reason given was that *"the erection of further houses at the density proposed would be likely to cause danger or injury to health."* How times have changed.

Council Housing for Addington

There was a great need to house the families of returning servicemen and women. As early as 1944, Malling Rural District Council was discussing the allocation of funds for council housing to be built in the district, but parishes as small as Addington were excluded from the first allocations. Miss Cholmeley raised a petition for council homes in the village and this went to the Plans Committee of 28th February 1947, but their response was that the homes to be built at West Malling would cover the needs of Addington's residents. The Parish Meeting that year took up the cudgel and passed a resolution as follows: *"Owing to the urgent need for more houses, The Meeting agreed to urge the Rural District Council to give early attention to the provision of new houses in the Parish."*

District Councillor J. C. Wells undertook to pursue the matter and the Building Surveyor agreed to meet him to look at a number of sites, both in the village centre and the London Road area, though there was little enthusiasm for this amongst Clearway residents. The first site to be identified was on the corner of East Street and Trottis-cliffe Road, near to Plowenders Bridge, but this site was rejected. It was not until January 1949 that the Ministry of Health approved a scheme for eight houses, to be built as four semi-detached

pairs on a site on Park Road. These were built in 1951 under Malling's Additional Schemes Programme.

Chestnuts Wood stood where these new homes were planned and trees had to be grubbed out. Addington Park Estates Ltd., who owned the site, were opposed, not because of the loss of productive woodland, but mainly because it was so near to their members' homes. They suggested that the entrance should be on the Trottiscliffe Road, but this was rejected, owing to the steep bank. Instead, the entrance was moved further along Park Road. A compulsory purchase order was made for the site. The District Valuer set a price of £105, plus 14 guineas for the surveyor's fees and extra for the vendor's legal costs. Clearance was given by the Ancient Monuments Officer that the site would not affect the megalithic monuments close by. More problems arose when the Sanitary Inspector insisted that a full sewage scheme should be constructed, and more land was needed for this. After further negotiations with the landowners, the price for this was agreed at £25. The site was cleared in 1950 and levels taken, but the project still moved forward very slowly. It was not until early 1951 that the contract was awarded to Messrs W.H. Benstead & Son (Contractors) Ltd., of Maidstone, for eight houses, in four pairs, to be built, at a price of £11,330, plus site works of £910 19s 0d.

Things suddenly went ahead at a cracking pace. The work started on 8th March 1951. By April, the foundations and concrete slabs had been laid to

The Chestnuts, Park Road, were built in 1951 and originally had long front gardens. This picture shows how a parking area was created twenty years later, when four bungalows for senior citizens were also built.

all four pairs of houses and one pair was ready for roofing. By May, three pairs had been roofed and tiled, two had been plastered and one was ready for decoration. By then the drains and the septic tank were completed. All eight houses were finished on 17th July, only nineteen weeks after construction began. Each home had large front and rear gardens, the latter being necessary for growing vegetables. The first seven tenants were already in occupation by the Plans Meeting of 23rd August 1951. Of these, two families were already village residents, two moved from Trottiscliffe, two from Ryarsh and one from Birling. The new homes were given the name The Chestnuts.

Trottiscliffe Road and East Street

Both Trottiscliffe Road and East Street had remained largely undeveloped until the late 1950's. A single home, Frenchay, had been built on East Street in 1934.[15] In the late 1950's more homes were built nearby but, even then, progress was slow. The substantial agricultural plot beside Fairview, one of the New Model Cottages built by Col. Sofer-Whitburn, was sold and two homes were constructed on this, each with an acre of garden. These were named Franklin and Elmwood. Franklin was built for Mr. and Mrs. Reeves and was constructed by the building firm for which their son, Frank, was then working.[16] East Street was then gradually developed during the 1950's.

During the 1950's Miss Norah Hardy continued to host village fêtes in her garden at the Vale. The annual show of the Addington and Trottiscliffe Gardeners' Society was also held in her grounds. A marquee would be erected and these events were well patronised. After her death in 1963 the Vale came under blight, due to the proposed motorway. It was never occupied again. The house was demolished in 1970 and a row of eight substantial family homes was built on its site.

Bungalows and houses later began to appear on Trottiscliffe Road. The first three to be built were

Blackmans, Beechview and Orchard Rise (later renamed Clematis Cottage), all constructed in 1954. Again, the original plots on Trottiscliffe Road were large, and their gardens were later divided for more housing. Six four-bedroomed houses, named Plowenders Close, were constructed on part of Blackman's land just after 1960. Merridene was also built in the early 1960's next to Orchard Rise and Squirrels Keep was built next to Beech View. By 1965, the northern side of Trottiscliffe Road to the east of Breinton Lodge had been developed. More House, then a wooden cottage in a large hilly plot, and Cherington stood on the southern side. Trottiscliffe Road, however, remained a narrow country lane, reached by a sharp bend and the single track Plowenders Bridge.

Land use and business development

In the immediate post war period, agriculture still provided employment for many residents. Arable farming and animal husbandry had become uneconomical and farmers and smallholders were keen to diversify. Addington became an important market garden centre for fruit, flowers and vegetables. Flowers were grown at Lane Farm by Messrs. Harry Mills (Florist) Ltd. They continued until the late 1980's. More flowers were grown on the field next to the Angel Pub and beside the London Road. Those on London Road were specialists, one grew chrysanthemums and another dahlias.

Both soft and top fruit remained the principal industry at Aldon, though land laid down to hops was shrinking fast. Strawberries and raspberries were grown in the substantial gardens of Lane Farmhouse and Southfields, St. Vincents Lane. Their owners had moved to the village after the war. Both Mr. and Mrs. Keith Wagstaffe and Col. and Mrs. John Tomlinson grew fruit specifically for the luxury trade. Raspberries went to Fortnum and Mason's in punnets lined with doilies and Addington's strawberries were served at Wimbledon. Chicken meat was a luxury item until the development of battery farming. There was a chicken farm at More House, Trottiscliffe Road. Sheep and cattle still grazed in Addington Park and elsewhere in the village. Jock Terry was a smallholder at East Street, Addington who grew fruit and also grazed sheep. His ram was not always obedient. The animal was prone to roam if he could find the smallest break in his fencing. Frank Reeves, who by then had moved to Merridene, told me that Terry would set out in his Austin 7 to retrieve the solid beast from garden foraging. It must have been somewhat strange to see the animal being bundled into the front seat. Luckily this was a time before seat belts became compulsory.

The planning permission for mineral extraction held by the Ace Sand and Gravel Company expired but, after a number of adjournments, a further period was granted in February 1948. With subsequent extensions and changes of ownership, this is still extant. Ford Sandpit, run by Olley & Company, was in operation nearby, in Trottiscliffe parish. The two pits merged in the early 1970's.

A number of new businesses were founded along the London Road. In 1946, the garage and workshops on a site that became Astran and then Endeavour Park, was established by Mr J. C. Wells. The business was called Hill View Garage and Mr. Wells lived on the site. A barrel-making factory, owned by W. Titterell & Son, was nearby, but the dominant industry remained catering. At one time there were four transport cafés in business along the London Road within a mile of each other, though two were then in Offham parish. The Baldock family continued their bakery. Mr. Andrews, Mr. Gower and Mr. Cherington all ran shops at Clearway up to and beyond 1960.

The Mount

The Mount, later known as Mount Offham, was owned during the early part of the twentieth century by Mr. Tom Jones Davies, but he did not live there. Instead, it was occupied by a succession of tenants, most of whom stayed for only a year or so. In the late 1930's, Major Arthur Tahu

Gravenor Rhodes, K.V.O., a New Zealander, bought the property. Mrs. Helen Rhodes was the daughter of the 5th Lord Plunket, Governor of New Zealand between 1904 and 1910. As owner-occupiers, they became very much involved in the community. Between the wars, Mrs. Rhodes ran a Sunday School at her home for the children living in the Clearway area of the village. On 24th February 1938, her brother and his wife, the 6th Lord and Lady Plunket, were killed in an air crash on the ranch in California owned by the American tycoon, Howard Hughes. Major and Mrs. Rhodes gave a home to their three teenage sons, Patrick (7th Lord Plunket), Hon. Robin and Hon. Shaun Plunket. Major Rhodes died in 1947 and his eldest nephew, Lord Plunket, began to develop the economic potential of the Mount's estate. He created a market garden business and built cottages for some of his workers. He served as equerry to Her Majesty the Queen from 1954 until his death in 1975. He was Deputy Master of the Royal Household and a close and valued friend of the Royal Family, whom he hosted at Addington on a number of occasions. With his younger brother, Captain the Hon. Robin Plunket, who moved to the Old Rectory, Lord Plunket was a founding member of the revived Addington Village Cricket Club.

The church faces amalgamation with other parishes

Between 1945 and 1960, three rectors served Addington. Rev. John Rahe-Hughes was installed in late 1945 and spent about two and a half years in the parish before becoming the vicar of Kemsing. He, was the last rector whose ministry covered solely Addington. Rev. Rahe-Hughes was much supported by his congregation, who bought a motorbike for him to get around.

His replacement, Rev. J.H. Boothroyd was particularly keen to develop the choral singing, and attracted a number of teenagers into the choir, as the photograph shows. He was a rector of the old style,

Addington church choir. Reproduced by kind permission of Mrs. Sylvia Baker, who is seen at the right of the front row

non-stipendiary curate would assist the rector. Bishop Chavasse even pre-empted the two parishes' agreement by purchasing, for £5,000, *"a small house with nine acres of orchard land"* for the curate (though I can find no record of where this was). This was bitterly resented as Addington was given the duty of raising an extra £1,000 per year to pay for a shortfall in the rector's stipend and was also charged £30 interest on the mortgage of the property. Rev. Boothroyd served both parishes for less than a year. During this time he realised that the new chancel arrangement could not go ahead, even though the faculty had been approved. In the end only part of the work was undertaken. This was to reinstate the original oak altar rail that had been conserved at Woodgate by the Chapman family. Sadly, the plan to rejoin the memorial stones was shelved. As a result, any residual legibility of the lettering has been lost in the intervening years, and the pieces remain separated from each other.

as can be seen from his clothing. Rev. Boothroyd proposed an ambitious rearrangement of the chancel area. An Omnibus Faculty was obtained that included uniting once again the broken memorial stone and setting it in the wall under the south window, then removing the wooden flooring and rear choir stalls to enable the North Transept to be used as a Lady Chapel. The new Lady Chapel would then have had a movable communion table for use midweek, an electricity point so that it could be heated, better lighting and the font situated there. This last would have entailed moving it from the west end of the church. The faculty also involved removing the step at the altar rail and dropping the level of the Sanctuary floor, lengthening the communion table by eighteen inches (45 cm) and providing a straight communion rail in place of the brass rail that Rev. Guise had installed.

The financial viability for small parishes was deteriorating quickly and the Bishop of Rochester, Rt. Rev. Christopher Chavasse, whose ministry lasted from 1940 to 1961, worked hard to find a solution. He had the difficult task of combining a number of parishes under a single clergyman, and he approached Rev. Boothroyd in 1948 about taking on a second parish. However, it was not until the summer of 1952 that a merger was agreed with Trottiscliffe. Each parish would retain its PCC and a

When Rev. Boothroyd resigned within a year of taking on the extra responsibilities, this provoked yet another crisis in ministry. The livings of Offham, Addington and Trottiscliffe each had an income of less than £400 per annum and, even in 1952, it was expected that a clergyman's minimum income should be £500. This was resolved by Bishop Chavasse placing the parish under the care of the rector of Offham, Rev. R.D. Johnson, assisted by a curate living at Addington rectory. Members of Addington PCC were not much pleased, especially as they already interviewed a prospective rector. At the Annual Meeting of 1953, several parishioners spoke, and a statement was recorded that *"Offham is a Low Church and has not an active congregation, and it might happen the Curate in Charge at Addington might depart from traditional arrangements wanted by*

Church goers." In addition, they had been told that the proposed curate, H.W. Howe had not yet been ordained and the parish could be left with no one to celebrate Holy Communion for six months.

The parish capitulated, welcomed the by now Rev. Howe in 1953 and found him very satisfactory. The young curate made a particular point of reaching out to young people and continued to develop the choir. He seems to have done much good. It was whilst he was in post that a term "parochial evangelisation" was used, and he tried to encourage lay involvement in visiting and holding prayer meetings in private houses. This reflected the views of the congregation. The annual report of 1955 stressed the need for the *"extension and deepening of the spiritual life of the parish"* through more visiting by members of the congregation, by increasing the numbers coming to Sunday School and by founding youth groups. Regular freewill giving was also promoted to strengthen the financial position and encourage commitment. In 1955, regular donors through this scheme increased from 30 to 100, but the numbers were not maintained, and within a year or so had dropped back to 47 donors. It is not clear whether house meetings started, as the first report of one was not given to the PCC until some twenty years later.

Services still followed the traditional pattern of 8 o'clock Communion, mid morning Matins and afternoon Evensong, but a proposal was put forward for a mid morning Family Communion. Rev. Johnson, the rector, is recorded as saying that *"It needs careful preparation over some time."* Although the congregation were stalwart and regular worshippers, an opportunity may have been missed to reach those who rarely came to church. Looking back from a twenty first century perspective, it seems a very different world. Even the work undertaken by Rev. Howe with the youth of the village was not fully supported. Rev. Johnson was concerned that a youth club in Addington might diminish activities in Offham.

Rev. Howe's replacement was another young man, Rev. Palmer, who was also popular. When Rev. Johnson retired in 1960, Rev. Palmer was made

temporary Priest in Charge, but his appointment was not confirmed and Rev. Victor Callow came to the parish in 1961. For financial reasons he was not assisted by a curate, even though his ministry still covered both Addington and Offham. He decided to live at the rectory in Addington because it was the more comfortable and economic property.

Those who served as churchwardens during this period were Mr. E. Wanostrocht (1946–8, left the village), Mr. B. Pattenden (1938–54, retired through ill health), Colonel L.D. Scott (1948–55, retired through pressure of work), Mr. P Young (1951–54, left the village), Mr. R. Brown (1954, left the village), Mr. F. Marsh (1954–68) and Mr. G. North (1955–61).

In 1948, Mr. Mander, the organ repairer, reported that the very restricted position where the organ stood had resulted in substantial water damage. It was removed from the North Transept, repaired and reinstalled in the West Gallery. The work was completed by mid 1949, but it had been necessary to adapt some of the pipes and shorten others, as it proved impossible to lower the floor of the gallery. The cost for the work was £392.

A second change in the church was the removal of the gilded paintings of angels and other decorations surrounding the East Window. These must have badly deteriorated since the photograph shown in Chapter Six was taken by Freda Barton at the turn of the century. Advice was sought from the Warham Guild[17] who, according to the minute book was the *"acknowledged expert in such matters."* After inspection, the Guild recommended that *"the wall should be thoroughly cleaned and stripped of present decoration. The plaster should be made good and the mullions left as natural stone."* This action was agreed. At one stroke, St. Margaret's eastern wall became simple and unadorned once again.

Church finances continued in a poor state throughout the late forties and fifties. In 1950, the school building, which had been used as a church hall since the closure of the school during the war, was sold and raised £1,000, less costs of £119 4s 5d. The proceeds were invested with the Diocese so that the interest could be used for future maintenance needs. A new church hall was suggested, but the proposal was rejected on financial grounds. A new Sports and Social Club raised funds to build a permanent pathway to the church and levelled the new area of the churchyard but, in 1952, in the middle of yet another financial crisis, the four church bells were identified as being in a sorry state. This was mainly because the ringing chamber ceiling beneath them and the belfry beams were rotting. The whole structure was unsafe. A new belfry floor and beams would have to to be made, if the bells were to be rung again. They fell silent and in 1955 were taken down. The estimate for repair work within the tower was not received until 1958, and came to £1,132. A bell fund was started, but many years would pass before the bells were rehung. Work was carried out to the bells themselves and, for a while, it was hoped to add two more, but this proved unaffordable. They were finally rehung in 1968.

Although the Diocese made inspections and gave advice to parishes, it became clear that a formal, insurance style regime was needed. The Rochester Diocesan Repair Fund was set up in 1956, tied to a quinquennial inspection of each church. This would become an aid, but also a worry for the Parochial Church Council, as major repair needs were now identified in a structured way. The first quinquennial inspection report fortunately identified only minor work such as outside painting and repairs to a copingstone on the tower. However, later ones would prove more of a challenge. The PCC put £250 into the new fund, the first of many annual premiums on which they would eventually be able to draw.

At the end of the fifties, the church electoral roll was still as high as 141 and there were 80 communicants at the Christmas Service. The church remained an integral part of spiritual and communal life in the village. In 1960, it still administered one charity. The nineteenth century Stratford Bequest was distributed that year to ten elderly parishioners, who received baskets of provisions, funded by the interest paid on the Consols. However, inflation and lack of public interest led to this bequest being closed by the end of the century. The Consols were sold and the money was absorbed into general church funds.

The last years of the Parish Meeting

From the late 1940's, the emphasis of the Parish Meeting turned towards community development. A Sports and Social Club was proposed, with the intention of finding a site for a sports ground on which to play cricket and football. Although this was inaugurated, it struggled to find members, and the recreation ground had to wait another ten years before getting off the ground. Its development is described in the next chapter. The Sports and Social Club folded very quickly, as its members became involved in the Village Hall Committee instead. It was this Committee, for instance, that took charge of the celebrations for the Coronation of Queen Elizabeth II.

By the end of the decade, the state of the track around Addington Village Green was becoming deplorable. This was another problem that would take years to resolve. Although asked for help, the District Council replied that this was purely a parish matter, so no assistance would be forthcoming. It was also becoming difficult to find volunteers to mow the grass and maintain the footpaths in the village.

Concern was now expressed about the effectiveness of the Parish Meeting, The few times a year that this met may have had some bearing on this. To gain some outside expertise and to join in solidarity with other small communities, Addington Parish Meeting joined the new Kent Association of Parish Councils in 1948. At a meeting held on 28th November 1950, the Chairman, Col. Scott, forewarned the Meeting that the 1951 census would probably result in Addington being forced to have a Parish Council. He suggested that it might be sensible to apply prior to this as he felt that the parish would be better served by a Council. The Annual Parish Meeting in March the next year was attended by sixty people, but no decision was taken as the results from the census were still awaited.

One of the legacies of the day was that a young oak tree was planted in the churchyard. This came from Windsor Great Park and was obtained for the village by Lord Plunket.

The Coronation of Queen Elizabeth II

In early 1953, the Village Hall Committee was reconstituted to enable each end of the village to send representatives. The new committee proposed that on Coronation Day a television would be set up in the Village Hall so that everyone could view the ceremony. Previous royal celebrations had necessitated a visit to the cinema in Maidstone. There would be fun and games for the children, dancing in the evening and fireworks. However, it was then discovered that families in Clearway were planning their own party. A fund had by then been set up, and Clearway residents asked for some of this. A compromise was reached. The Village Hall would be used for the televised ceremony and the tea party, but an evening party would be held at Mr. Wells' house on the London Road.

Decision to form a Parish Council

Almost immediately after the Coronation, the decision was taken to apply for a Parish Council for Addington. At a special meeting held in the Village Hall on 22nd June 1953,[18] Minute 3 recorded:

"Application for a Parish Council

The Chairman read to the meeting the letter dealing with this subject, dated 19th May 1953, received from the Clerk to the County Council and following a general discussion on this subject the following resolution was passed, 17 votes being in favour and one abstention:

Miss Gertrude Fissenden and Mrs. Elsie Lankstead, representing both parts of the village, planting the Coronation Oak tree in St. Margaret's Churchyard. The second photograph shows the tree sixty years later.

It was proposed by Mr. F.W. Stow and seconded by Mr. E.A. Langridge that application be made to the County Council for an order, under the Local Government Act, 1933, Section 43(2), establishing a Parish Council for the Parish of Addington in the Rural District of Malling."

The first meeting of Addington Parish Council was held in the Village Hall at on Tuesday, 20th October 1953. Subsequent meetings were held on Wednesdays. The newly elected Parish Councillors were all men. They were Messrs. P.H. Martin, F. W. Marsh, J.N. Mills and C.D. Rochez, Hon. R. Plunket and Col. L.D. Scott. Also present were Mr J.C. Wells, the Rural District Councillor for Addington, three members of the public and a press representative. Col. Scott, who lived at Appledene, was elected chairman. The National Provincial Bank was appointed treasurer.

The new Council learned that the balance outstanding from the Parish Meeting accounts was £22 11s 1d at the bank, and that £100 worth of 2¹/₂% consolidated stocks, registered in the name of the representative body of the parish of Addington, would also be vested in them.[19] A note in the margin of the minutes gave the current value of these as approximately £63. £20 9s 10d of the £22 was owed to the Malling R.DC. for election expenses. The cost of declaration was £1 13s 8d. A Parish Councillors' handbook had been purchased for the chairman, costing £1 11s 4d, so the Council would start with a small deficit. It was agreed that an advertisement for a parish clerk would immediately be placed at Addington post office, at Clearway and in West Malling.

The following month, a precept was set for a two pence rate. This would raise approximately £26 10s. A suitable candidate had been interviewed for the post of clerk. This was Mr. B.L. King, of Scotby, London Road. He was appointed in December at a salary of £9 per annum. Mr. King would served as clerk for the next six years.

Planning applications were not shown to the Parish Council for comment, so a close relationship with the District Councillor was important. This was the decade when development was gathering pace on East Street, Clearway and Trottiscliffe Road. By the end of the 1950's most of the plots were full on Clearway, though two significant applications in Addington Park, one from the Seekers' Trust and another from Mr. Sterrett, were both refused. The first was an outline application for ten dwellings with accesses on to Trottiscliffe Road. This was deemed by the District Council to be *"undesirable sporadic development unrelated to the needs of agriculture, and likely to lead to drainage difficulties."* The terminology implies that the application was for land near to Plowenders Bridge. It also failed to meet with approval from either the Kent County Council or the Ministry of Agriculture and Fisheries for reasons of *" ribbon development to rural amenity"* and *"harmful to agricultural interests."* The land was not built on, but nor was the agricultural use of the Park preserved. However, it is still an open space, as it forms part of West Malling Golf Course.

Mr. Sterrett was looking to develop land at the other end of the Park, on the corner of St. Vincents Lane. This was refused as being *"sporadic development adjoining a trunk road."* Both these refusals show the shift in emphasis over planning by the mid 1950's. The Town and Planning Act of 1947 had strengthened the early Metropolitan Green Belt law of 1935, and planners were becoming aware of the need to conserve open land for future generations. Addington's position on the outer fringes of the Metropolitan Green Belt would see the village in good stead as the twentieth century continued. Permission for new homes would continue to be granted and welcomed, but landscape considerations would prevent over development.

1   1911 census records for Dorking and Lewisham. The girls were Annie Elizabeth and Bessie Ethel.

2   The information comes from the council planning minutes held at the K.H.L.C. – RD/Ml/Am3/17 and RD/Ml/Am3/18, plus Ancestry.co.uk

3   Times Newspaper, Issue 44603, 19th June 1927, p26, Col. C. The advertisement, inserted by Messrs. Knight Frank and Rutley, states that the property will be sold, but does not give a date for an auction. The advertisement also indicates that the mansion could be sold with only 93 acres, but Mr. Gurney Aggs bought all 263 acres.

4   The amount that would be raised by asking for an extra penny from £1 rateable value of a property. The rateable value in 1929 was, it seems, lower than it had been in 1902.

5   This was recorded in the PCC minutes of 10th March 1945.

6   Ordnance Survey Map, Revised edition 1936 sheets XXX/11 to 14

7   Miss Cholmeley was Miss May Cholmeley, and Miss Hardy was Miss Katherine Hardy. The convention at the time was that an elder/st sister or single woman was referred simply as Miss, the initial was given for younger sisters.

8   The London Gazette, 17th August 1934, p 5256 There was one anomaly. Harpwood, on Pilgrim's Way, was ommitted and remained within the ecclesiastic boundary until the 1990's.

9   Alfred Rushton, Associate of the Royal College of Art, exhibited at the Royal Academy a number of times. The water colour he painted of the church is in J.G. Maddan's book at the Kent History and Library Centre, but unfortunately, as a photocopy it was not of high enough quality to print here.

10 The author's father-in-law, Douglas Richardson, an officer in the R.A.F., was present at some of the decoy sessions.

11 According to research carried out by a barrister for the Parish Council when researching legal access to the Green, its position was next to the gate of Shelmerdene, opposite Overlea Cottage.

12 3rd Divisional Signals had fought in WW1 – they were reformed in 1939 as a regular division, in 1942 as a mixed division and in 1943 as an infantry division. (Regimental notes). Their first commander in the Second World War was Montgomery.

13 The tea party made a small profit. A donation of £2 6s 4d was made the following year to the new Sports and Social Club.

14 Edinburgh Gazette, 6th January 1933, p 15 London Gazette, 2nd January 1933 p 9

15 At the time of writing, after 78 years of existence, this has been demolished and a modern home is rising on the site.

16 Information supplied by Mr. F. Reeves

17 The Warham Guild was founded in 1912 to carry out "the making of all the 'Ornaments of the Church and of the Ministers thereof' according to the standard of the Ornaments Rubric, and under fair conditions of labour". The Guild's influential Advisory Committee was headed firstly by Percy Dearmer, followed by Jocelyn Perkins, Sacrist of Westminster Abbey. Besides providing vestments, furnishing altars, and acting for craftsmen in wood and metal, the Guild - according to the handbook of 1932 – was "able to offer valuable advice and help, architectural and ecclesiological, in any work connected with the fabric of our churches".

18 Parish Meeting Minute Book 1, p 200

19 These would have come from the Addington Freeholders inaugurated by Col. Wingfield-Stratford in 1840.

9

1960 to 2012 - MODERN TIMES

As the 1960's dawned, the post war period of reconstruction was over, and rationing had finally become a memory. The village had a well established Parish Council that was in the process of acquiring a substantial recreation ground for its residents and there would at last be a playground for the children. Addington was firmly in the modern world. It had about 400 electors, a small village hall, a post office and a number of shops, a much used public house and an active church community. However, traffic was becoming a real nuisance, with unwelcome pollution from heavy traffic along the London Road. At busy times, it could be extremely difficult to join this from the lanes. Addington could no longer stand on its own and depended increasingly on its neighbours, both in civil and church matters. The fragility of the environment was now appreciated, and villages in rural England began a fight to preserve open landscapes.

Addington had grown quickly in the past twenty years and the "old" residents were now very much in the minority. Both Miss Cholmeleys had died by the end of 1960 and their friend, Norah Hardy, passed away in 1963. Shaw Hill House, the Old Rectory and Aldon House had all changed hands. Indeed, most people who were living in Addington in 1960 had been resident for less than fifteen years. Clearway

and the London Road, however, still housed families who had moved to Addington when their homes were first built. New residents often came from an urban setting. They worked in industry, commerce and services, both public and private, rather than in agriculture. From henceforth, farming would play a decreasing role in the village economy until, by the millennium, it had effectively ceased. During the sixties and seventies cattle, sheep and horses still grazed in the local fields and fruit was grown; by the end of the century there would be no working farm in the village and virtually no animals, only a few horses and sheep, in the fields.

In 1958, the electoral roll was 390 but it rose to 569 in 1965. It is now in the region of 620, and there are about 300 homes in the village. New housing projects took place. Plowenders Close was built in 1960. Later in the decade, the terrace of eight homes known as Hazelview was built on East Street. This was half an original proposal for fifteen. In the early 1970's, eight substantial family houses were built further down East Street, on the site of The Vale. Elsewhere, development during the latter part of the twentieth century was mainly along Trottiscliffe Road and Sandy Lane. The long gardens running back from London Road to the latter were gradually sub-divided, though the process did not end until the start of the 21st century. This area was later designated another "village envelope", to protect the open space and woodland to the north of the lane.

Some of the houses that replaced the Vale on East Street.

At the end of 1964, the Malling Rural District Council proposed taking the front gardens from numbers one to eight The Chestnuts, to build four (originally six) senior citizens' bungalows and providing off street parking for all residents. There was a delay in building these, so the first residents moved in during 1968. The rear gardens of numbers one to eight were later extended in compensation, through the Council purchasing more land.

The village lies within the London Metropolitan Green Belt, which extends to the A228. This gave protection from overdevelopment. The eastern side of the A228, without this designation, was comprehensively built up during the sixties and seventies. During the 1960's, at a period of rapid expansion in housing, the Parish Council still had no right to see plans before they were presented to Malling Rural Council or to put forward their views, so any influence depended on collaboration with the local District Councillor. Luckily, the village was then served by the very doughty Mrs. Sally Demeny, of Keepers. Parish councils gained this right after the 1972 Local Government Act, described below.

As the century drew to a close, most planning issues discussed by the Parish Council were for minor infilling, redevelopment, infringements and mineral

extraction. Some of the small bungalow homes of the thirties were enlarged. Businesses on the London Road closed or moved away but their sites were redeveloped. Endeavour Park was built as office buildings and the Big Motor World car showroom first took over a transport depot and then absorbed a redundant café site. Through vigilance, Addington Parish Council was able to prevent inappropriate development, whilst encouraging other proposals that were in keeping with the environment. The Council supported the redevelopment of the Greenways Hotel site in 1993, when 32 four to five bedroomed houses were built round a pleasant green. Other small developments followed, including five homes called the Paddocks, on Woodgate Road.

The Links, with its well matured landscaping.

Housing tenure was markedly different from that of the Edwardian era. Instead of a village of some 55 households, of which at least 90% were rented or held on a service tenancy, in the year 2000, 90% were in owner-occupation. During the 1980's, council house tenants became eligible to buy their homes and a number took advantage of this. In 1991, the remaining council owned homes at The Chestnuts were transferred to Tonbridge and Malling Housing Association (later Russet Homes). Privately rented accommodation is now very scarce in the village, though Shaw Hill House has been converted into flats.

Services

The Parish Council's priorities centred on developing services. A bus shelter already stood at Addington Crossroads but, following a village petition, another was erected on Addington Green. In 1969, a competition was held for its design, as it was important that it should be in keeping with the area. The winning entry was by Bill Rawson, who designed simple brick shelter roofed by Kent peg tiles supported by oak beams.

Despite the growing workload for the Parish Council, the precept was still 2d in the £, bringing in £206 in 1965/6. Ground maintenance work, such as cutting the Village Green and mowing the Recreation Ground, was undertaken on a voluntary basis. However, cleaning the bus shelters was charged to the rates and a small allowance was eventually agreed for the household costs for the clerk, who worked from home. It was not until the late 1980's that a fax machine and computer were purchased. Parish Council chairmen during the 1960's were Col. L.D. Scott and Messrs. Fred Marsh, Charlie Rochez and Ronnie Blair, a Canadian who had taken a lease at St. Vincents.

In 1965, a main drainage scheme was proposed. This was a mammoth undertaking but, even so, it was not possible to connect all the homes in the village. The fall of the land meant that sewers ran from Wrotham Heath down across the field opposite the Royal Oak, over Ford and Hedgehogs land and then under St. Vincents Lane into the woodland by Addington Brook. The line then followed the brook along the parkland until it reached Plowenders. Work was well under way in 1968 but took some time to complete. Connections from properties stretched over many metres of garden and open land. In some areas woodland had to be grubbed out to accommodate the pipes. The supply of running water to outlying homes had also been a problem. Some pipes had run long distances across open land, including Addington Park. A new system was laid down lanes during the early 1970's, again a major undertaking. Despite this, some areas such as Sandy Lane still had low pressure. These pipes had to be replaced in due course. Towards the end of 1965, improvements were made to the A20 and this was widened. A lay-by was suggested at Clearway, but the residents along that part of the trunk road strongly and successfully resisted this.

1967 Laying Tarmac to the Village Green trackway. This was carried out by members of the Addington Green Preservation Society.

During the 1960's, The Addington Green Preservation Society was inaugurated and this was active into the 1970's. Through their voluntary labour, tarmac was laid on the trackway to the village shop on the Green. The Society also strove for the Village Green to be formally registered as such. This was achieved in 1968.

A residents' committee was also active at Clearway. At a Parish Council meeting held on 7th January 1969, they made clear to the Council that they were concerned that the County Council wished to adopt their road. Their representative, Reg Humphrey, said that residents of the estate were not willing to contribute to the cost of making it up to public road standards. They were assured that the decision was entirely in their hands, as residents of a private road, as it remains.

Other organisations in the village during the 1960's were the Addington and Offham Darby and Joan Club, Young Wives and a Youth Club.

The Motorway and its impact on the Sandpits

The first proposals for the M20 Motorway, which would eventually run from Sidcup to Folkestone, were put forward in early 1963. The new road was then called the Ditton By-pass. The route would have a major impact not only on the village, but also on the sandpits operating in the area. At about this time Messrs. Olley acquired Addington Sandpit and began extracting sand from the northern part of Westfields Farm. Instead of selling the sand on the open market, they stockpiled it for use during the construction of the motorway, which began the late 1960's. Once construction got under way better access was vital. The first of many construction vehicles had to reach the site by negotiating the narrow Plowenders Bridge.

The first motorway construction vehicles crossed this little bridge to reach the site.

Trottiscliffe Road was quickly altered and widened to allow better access for these lorries during the motorway's construction. Plowenders Bridge was by-passed, leaving a lay-by and a grassy island on which additional trees were planted. A number of footpaths had to be diverted to accommodate the motorway. An underpass was constructed to allow access for

sand extraction equipment from the works on the southern side, using an altered line for the footpath. A footbridge was installed at East Street as this had been bisected by the motorway. In August 1970, access to the centre of Addington from East Street North was briefly reopened to allow the funeral cortège of Mr. Frank Hooker to cross for his service in St. Margaret's Church. Mr. Hooker, known as "Bobdog" to his friends, had bitterly opposed the closure of East Street, so it was considered a small triumph on his behalf. The motorway was opened to traffic a year later, in December 1971.

The M26 motorway opened at the end of 1980 as a southern link to the M25. This required a new junction which took further local land, but this lay mostly in Trottiscliffe. The land lost from the two villages under both motorways included most of Campion's Wood, farmland, sandpits, private gardens and common land. A tree planting scheme was established to shield the village from the sound of traffic coming down Wrotham Hill. More trees were planted along the south side of the motorway, on the banks of the regraded sandpit next to the remaining portion of Campion's Wood and on East Street Green. Sand was later extracted from a field adjacent to Rose Alba. After extraction, it was restored by regrading the land. Beneath this field lie buried great boulders of iron-rich red sandstone, riddled out during the extraction process.

By the end of the century, Trottiscliffe Road residents were spared sand extraction movements as a haul road was constructed from Addington Sandpit on to Ford Lane. Access to the A20 from Pearson's Pit, Trottiscliffe, remained via Addington Lane and Trottiscliffe Road After the resources of this pit had been exhausted, a lengthy period of infilling with inert materials took place. The Parish Council had to complain on a number of occasions that lorries arrived at the entrance well before the permitted opening time of operation, causing disturbance to residents.

By the end of the 1980's the communications to Addington looked as below:

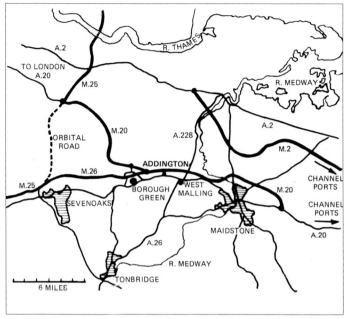

The Road system to and from Addington established by the 1980's. From Addington Village Appraisal 1985. Drawn by John Hawtin.

The Village Environment

The Commons Registration Act of 1965 gave the opportunity to villages to take control of their village greens and commons. The Parish Council registered the Village Green, The Pineys (formerly Common Plantation) and East Street Green. However, part of the Pineys then disappeared beneath the motorway. In 1986, the Parish Council persuaded the Department of Transport to compensate the village for the loss of this common land and for land now under Trottiscliffe Road. The road widening scheme had removed a strip of land 344 yards long by 18 yards wide, previously in parish ownership. Within this an animal pound had existed for many centuries. It was clearly marked on the Tithe Map of 1843. The Parish Council registered this as common land and the Kent County Council then offered compensation of £5, plus legal costs, for its loss. After legal advice, the land was transferred to the K.C.C. by a Deed of Dedication.

With regard to the loss at The Pineys, the land beneath the motorway was de-registered and the Parish was allowed to register an equivalent area in compensation. A field had come on the market next to East Street North, just within Ryarsh parish. This was purchased in September 1987, after a year of negotiations. It was then renamed Pineys Meadow but was not registered as a village green as the Council were advised that this would prevent grazing. An Open Spaces Committee was established to manage the field. Sheep were grazed on the land for a few years but the poor sandy soil could not support this. A mixed hedge was later planted as a visual amenity. It has established well.

A definitive footpath map was drawn up by the District Council. Some of these paths were later designated as part of a long distance walk from Gravesend to Haywards Heath, called the Wealden Way.[1] This enters the village at Woodgate Road and uses the motorway underpass before skirting the motorway to Westfields Farm. It then joins St. Vincents Lane, which it follows to Brookfield House, then it turns towards Wrotham Heath. The path leaves the parish at Ford Lane. A large number of groups use this attractive walk each year.

As early as 1962, safety concerns arose over the ancient oak tree on Addington Green. Advice was taken from a timber merchant, who said that the tree was well past maturity and should be felled. The Parish Council was reluctant to take such drastic action without further advice and approached the County Estates Officer. His report was that the tree *"was seen to be in a very sound and healthy condition, and in spite of its great size could be considered as in its prime of life."* Some remedial work took place, removing dead wood from the crown and treating the wounds where two large limbs had been removed in the past. Later work was undertaken to brace the tree. This was of great benefit when the dreadful hurricane of October 1987 took place. The braces prevented most of the branches from falling. Even so, cars parked beneath its canopy were badly damaged. Emergency work was undertaken in the aftermath of the storm. The braced limbs were removed, leaving a truncated shape. However, over the next twenty years the crown renewed itself. By late 2007 the stumps had regenerated so that the crown of the tree was about the same as in the photograph taken in 1982 by Tonbridge and Malling Borough Council. A management plan was established. During 2008 work was taken to thin and shorten the regrowth, as can be seen from the third photograph, and this process will be repeated each five years. The cuts to the limbs undertaken in late 1987 can still be seen.

Looking to the future, during the final quarter of the century two oak saplings were planted lower down Addington Green and one can be seen in both later photographs. A third tree, a fastigiate beech, was planted in 2010 when the village won the Chairman's Prize in the Kent Men of the Trees annual competition, Trees in your Village.

During the early 1970's, Dutch elm disease ravaged England. Many fine specimens were lost throughout the village and Addington's hedgerows were changed irrevocably. The disease did not affect the quality of the timber, so contractors were willing to take it as long as enough trees stood in one location. This was the case in St. Vincents Wood, where an entire compartment perished. After felling, this was replanted. Where contractors were unwilling to act, a Parish Councillor and tree surgeon, David Reffold, felled individual trees for parishioners, another example of community spirit in the village. This disease still affects the village environment, as each regrowth from elm suckers inevitably succumbs to the beetle after fifteen to twenty years. Periodic felling has to take place, though of much smaller trees.

The long dry summer of 1976, followed by a second drought two years later, killed many plants, shrubs and mature trees. Through replanting, all the gardens within the village envelope contain a wide variety of colourful species. The early 1980's then saw particularly bitter winters. In 1983, heavy snowfall was followed by massive drifting from the sandpits across to the golf course, which severed Clearway from Addington

The first photograph was taken in 1982, and is from "Conservation Studies for Trottiscliffe, Birling, Addington and Fairseat. Reprinted courtesy of Tonbridge and Malling Borough Council. The other two photographs show the tree in November 2007 and during work undertaken in 2008 as part of the management plan for the tree.

Green for some days. To prevent further road closures, the Kent County Council set up arrangements with local farmers to clear the lanes after snowfall, which on the whole has been successful.

Deep snow at Hedgehogs beside Addington Brook. By kind permission of Mrs. Judy Grimes

Apart from the damage to the oak on the Green, Addington lost a great number of other trees in the hurricane of 17th October 1987. Electricity supply was lost to the centre of the village for a week and up to thirteen days in the outlying areas. Many homes were damaged. The telephone service to some of the lanes was not restored for six weeks and this was before widespread use of mobile phones. Local contractors were drafted in to clear the lanes, and the army was later used to re-erect the electricity and telephone poles. The Angel Public House, then run by Peter and Sandy Lucas, was an extremely popular place to visit during the first frightening week. A second severe storm a few years later did

Clearance work next to Addington Brook after the storm of 1987.

further damage. Through natural regeneration and replanting, the village remains wooded, despite the difficulty of establishing trees on sandy soil.

Schooling

The decision to close Addington School at the end of the war was connected to the 1944 Education Act which raised the school leaving age to fifteen. All children were now given secondary education and pupils were assessed to see whether they should attend a grammar school, technical school or secondary modern school. This meant that primary education ceased at eleven and small rural schools became uneconomic to run. Primary schooling provision was now based on a locality, rather than a village.

As all Addington's pupils, whether primary or secondary, now had to travel to school, bus services to and from Addington came under greater scrutiny. A significant number of school-children caught buses from Addington Crossroads, Clearway or Addington Green. From the 1960's, Addington Parish Council had the right to appoint governors to three primary schools, Ryarsh, Platt and Trottiscliffe. At the Annual Parish Meeting of 1971 the governors reported that 25 children were attending Platt school and that 12 went to Trottiscliffe. Ryarsh and Offham remained the choice of other parents. The nearest secondary schools were at Wrotham, East Malling and Snodland. Those who attended grammar schools travelled to Maidstone or Tonbridge. However, as the children now attended schools in so many venues, the village had to work much harder to foster social cohesion.

These journeys involved crossing roads. There was much concern over the safety and comfort of children. It was primarily for their use that the bus shelters were built at Addington Crossroads, Addington Green and Harpwood. The third shelter was delivered in kit form in 1971 and erected by members of the Parish Council. After much lobbying, traffic islands were installed on the A20 to protect children crossing to and from the bus stops. Offham Railway Crossing was closed in 1965 and the junction of the A20 with Seven Mile Lane was altered. This meant that pedestrians, including school-children, coming from Teston Road now had to make a long detour. Mrs. Maureen Fissenden of Hawthorne led a sit down protest in an attempt to have a pedestrian crossing over the railway line but this was not achieved.

By the 1980's, bus use had declined considerably. Fewer children of school age lived in the village, and car use had increased hugely, particularly as women were now drivers. The lack of flexibility and the unreliability of bus services encouraged the switch to the car, though school-children going as far as Maidstone were still bus travellers.

Village facilities

A s has been seen in the last chapter, shortly after the war ended, the Parish Meeting actively began to promote recreational opportunities in the village. The cricket field in Addington Park, opposite East Street, had fallen out of use some years earlier. A Sports and Social Club had been unsuccessful in reviving the sport in the village and there were no facilities to play football.

Well into the 1960's, the Village Hall on Millhouse Lane and the Angel Public House continued as two main social foci in the village. The Angel was now owned by the Courage brewery company. Its publican during the 1950's was Alf Allwright, ably assisted by his wife, Queenie. Its three bars were well frequented, though mostly by men. It did not develop its culinary reputation until later in the century. The Village Hall, although small, was the venue for weddings and dances,

especially barn dances. It hosted jumble sales and many other gatherings, as well as being the place where the Parish Council met monthly. The Village Hall was run by a committee, who appointed a manager. It was funded by bookings and fundraising, though the Parish Council gave some support.

In 1968, following the death of Mr. John Sterrett, owner of Addington Park, planning permission was granted to construct a golf course on this land. A great deal of discussion took place about the location of its club house and its name. Because there was already an established golf course called the Addington Golf Club at Croydon, that name was quickly ruled out. Instead, the new facility was called the West Malling Golf Club.

It was first proposed that the entrance and club house should be built on St. Vincents Lane but this was deemed impracticable because of the narrow road. The club house, which also provided facilities for squash, was constructed opposite Hernewell Farm in 1974, with a long access road from Trottiscliffe Road, near to Addington Crossroads. Further land became available next to East Street later in the century. The eighteen-hole course was then extended by a further nine holes. As well as preserving the fine park trees, more planting took place as the course was constructed. The area is an attractive "green lung" for the village and is crossed by footpaths that people use and enjoy. A complex of storage buildings and workshops was established

West Malling Golf Course in January 2010, showing its importance to the village, even during the winter time.

where the old mill house had stood, giving this site a new purpose. A practice range was also established there, next to the Recreation Ground.

Until its closure in 1992, Greenways Hotel remained a major venue for entertainment. It eventually boasted four large halls that catered for dances, exhibitions and conferences. Smaller rooms were available to hire for private meetings and parties. The hotel had 24 bedrooms and its restaurant was open to the public. Regular activities took place, attracting young people. These included aerobics, roller skating, ballroom and country dancing and discos. The outdoor swimming pool was well patronised. During the late 1970's, a public sports facility opened at Larkfield. Elsewhere, a private cinema was in operation on Norman Road, West Malling until the late 1980's. The Granada Cinema in Maidstone later moved from the centre of town to the Lockmeadow complex, where it has become a multi-screen facility.

When Trust House Forté applied for planning permission to open a hotel near to the M20/M26 motorway interchange, one of the conditions imposed was that its recreational facilities should be open to the public, by subscription. There is now also a major sporting complex at Kings Hill.

Addington Village Cricket Club and the Recreation Ground

These are indisputably linked. In 1952, after only a few years in existence, the Sports and Social Club was disbanded at the final Parish Meeting. Its intention had been to find three to four acres on which to play cricket and football, to have a small playground for children and to build a new Village Hall. It was hoped that a site in Addington Park could be found and, by 1947, three possible sites had been identified but none of these were eventually chosen. The one that found most favour was on the corner of St. Vincents Lane and the London Road, but this site was far from the village

centre, so more land would be needed for a second children's playground near Addington Green. It had proved impossible to take forward the idea of a recreation ground (and especially not two) for the village and the committee members had instead joined the Village Hall Committee. The funds from the Sports and Social Club were transferred to this. They were quite substantial as they included £106 15s 10d from the Addington Home Guard fund and £14 7s 1d belonging to the Club itself.

It was not until the end of the fifties that a second group of residents came together to form a new cricket club. The idea was mooted during a social get together at the Angel in early 1958, the founders being David Miskin who then lived at the Seekers' Trust, Stan Rimmer who ran the village shop and Peter Clark of Blackmans on Trottiscliffe Road. They called a meeting at the Village Hall and founded the first cricket club for many years. They called this the Addington Village Cricket Club. The Hon. Secretary was Don Castle of Miline and the Hon. Treasurer was Stan Wall of Lilistan, East Street. Their first president was Captain, the Hon. Robin Plunket. The imperative was to find a pitch on which to play, although their first fixture was held on Sunday, 21st September 1958 at Key Croft, against Trottiscliffe.

One of the committee members was Alf Allwright. He was friendly with Mr. Richard Boyle, the owner of a piece of land adjacent to the Seekers' Trust. Boyle regularly ate at The Angel as he was then a bachelor. He lived at Rose Alba, a new house that he had built on Park Road, his land including the megalithic monuments. Richard Boyle ran a small holding on the north side of the lane, where he had a number of glasshouses. He also owned land on the south of the lane. Allwright approached him and he generously offered a large plot of land to the nascent Cricket Club, at a reasonable sum. Even so, the members realised that they would struggle to raise the funds quickly, so they approached the Parish Council for help. The Parish Council chairman, Mr. J.N. Mills, called a special meeting of the Council on 20th November 1958. This was attended by nine members of the public, including members of the Addington Village Cricket Club, who had been specifically invited. Mr. Mills informed the meeting that the

Cricket Club was seeking a ground and that an offer of approximately five acres of land abutting St. Vincents Lane had been tentatively made by Mr. Richard Boyle.

Allwright and Clark said that they had no other site to suggest. The Chairman then confirmed that he had received an offer in writing from Boyle, who was present, and that the sum in question was £300. Members of the Cricket Club stressed that they must own a ground, or have a lease for a significant period of years, before they could seek grant assistance for equipment, etc. They were particularly keen to expedite the matter so that they could start playing during the coming season. This was a very steep order, as the matter would have to be put to all electors at a special Parish Meeting, the District Valuer would have to make a report and enquiries would have to be made as to grant aid. Following a discussion, the Parish Council agreed to put the matter to a Parish Meeting, with a recommendation to accept the offer.

Before this took place, however, the Cricket Club decided to negotiate directly with Richard Boyle. They were concerned that delays would mean that they would not obtain the ground in time for the 1959 season. The Parish Council Chairman received a further letter from Boyle, withdrawing his offer. This was met with some dismay as it could have barred the use of the ground by all residents. In the event, the independent negotiations failed to proceed and, on 10th April 1959, the special Parish Meeting took place. Fred Marsh was now the Chairman. Five other Parish Councillors and 42 village electors were also present, showing the interest that a proposed recreation ground for the village had generated. The District Surveyor had made his report and the offer was finalised as 4.35 acres (1.76 hectares) at a purchase price of £275. Further start up funds would be needed—the fencing alone was likely to cost £50 and there would be legal charges of £25. The meeting was slightly concerned that the site, although central, might be too far from both ends of the village for children to use as a playground. However, the fact that it was large enough to contain both a cricket and football pitch was welcomed. Residents were also reassured that footpaths across the ground would be preserved.

The parish electors were also asked whether a 20-year loan should be taken out. If so, an extra penny would be levied on the precept for this period. Maintenance costs could mean a further penny on the rates, though these might be offset by rental income.

Although decisions were not unanimous, the Meeting decided that

> 1. They would like the village to purchase a recreation ground (28 for 8 against)
>
> 2. The site was suitable (25 for 12 against)
>
> 3. The purchase money should be raised by public subscription and not through a loan. (A motion for a loan was defeated)

A Recreation Ground Committee was immediately inaugurated. The founding members were five Parish Councillors plus Messrs. J. Lander, J. Waller, F. Baker and R. Hogwood. Those at the meeting were told that the offer of a short term loan had been received from a parishioner for the whole £350, to speed the purchase. The loan would be repaid once public subscriptions had been received. The legality of this had to be investigated but this generous offer again shows the enthusiasm to get the project quickly under way.

By the May Annual Parish Meeting, £275 had been received from the Recreation Ground Committee. The Parish Council's solicitors had been instructed to proceed with the purchase and planning consent had been granted for the change from agricultural to recreational use. Would that matters could be accomplished as quickly these days. Further funds were later raised by selling a small part of the ground for use as a private house.[2] Grant aid was received from the Kent Education Committee for half the amount required to equip the ground but the Playing Fields Association offered only a loan, so this was rejected. One member of the committee, Frank Baker, had undertaken some exceptional fundraising. He had personally encouraged subscriptions of £100 to the fund, for which he was heartily thanked.

Unlike the fundraising, the conveyance of the land was very protracted, owing to a restrictive covenant on the site that Richard Boyle had given to the Seekers' Trust when he bought the land. This prevented any building being erected on the ground. As it was imperative to have a cricket pavilion, this covenant had to be removed, but negotiations took a considerable amount of time. The ensuing minutes show how steadfast the Parish Council was. They refused to sign the contract before this was done, despite heavy pressure.

The Cricket Club obtained permission to use the ground before the contracts were signed, and threw themselves energetically into preparing the very rough and sloping terrain. In order to accommodate a football pitch, the orientation of the square was originally fixed at East/West, but now is North/South. The first match on the new pitch took place in August 1959, the pavilion being a marquee loaned by Mr. Healey of Hedgehogs, who owned a marquee hire business. There was obviously no running water, so this was brought from Rose Alba in rubbish bins on the back of a trailer. Peter Clark gave the club a hut from which teas were served.

announce the full inauguration of Addington Recreation Ground. By then Richard Boyle had conveyed extra land for the outfield, to make it easier for football to be played in the winter.

The Recreation Ground Committee agreed a constitution whereby the membership would be four members of the Parish Meeting, i.e. all electors, three Parish Councillors and additional members to represent the needs of children. In addition, each organisation using the ground would be permitted to send two representatives each. The first members, all male, were:

* For the parish: Messrs. Boyle, Baker, Marsh and Clark

* For the children: Messrs. Humphrey and Woodger

* For Addington Football Club: Messrs. Waller and Parrott

* For the Parish Council: Messrs Allwright, Rochez and Lander.

The first match of the Addington Village Cricket Club, held at the Recreation Ground in August 1959.

Addington Village Cricket Club agreed to pay a nominal annual rent of £1 per year to the Parish Council, who owned the freehold, the first payment being on 1st June 1961. The club was to own the freehold of the cricket square, to ensure its protection. John Lander convened the first meeting.

Members of the Cricket Club put up the fencing and carried out all the maintenance, as they do still. In 1962, members brought in 8,000 tons of "fill" to

The 1960 Annual Parish Meeting came and went, as did the Annual Meeting of the Parish Council a month later, and still the contract remained unsigned. A further delay incurred when the Seekers' Trust changed their solicitors. It took another year of negotiations until, at a Special Parish Meeting held on Monday, 29th May 1961, Fred Marsh, as Chairman, was able to welcome the press and public and

raise the lower end of the ground, which then sloped sharply down towards the stream and used their own labour for the back breaking task of laying it down. The club then set about obtaining a proper pavilion. Stan Rimmer, who had by then given up the shop and was working on a project at The Mount, spotted a building there that was being used as a hay store. This was a holiday home purchased by Lord

The first cricket pavilion, a holiday home donated by Lord Plunket. In this picture it looks very sad, as it was about to be demolished to make way for its replacement.

Baker, Reg Humphrey and Stan Wall were all active members living in Addington. Fred Marsh took over as President from Robin Plunket. The vital contributions given by wives, girlfriends and families cannot be under-estimated and the Kent Messenger of 30th August 1968 records a memorable match between the sexes. The match ended in a tie, not surprisingly! In 1968, Peter Robinson came to Addington with his family and quickly became involved with the Club. He encouraged and trained young cricketers. The replacement of the old "holiday home" with a new Sports Pavilion at the end of the 1970's gave a real boost to the facilities on the Recreation Ground.

Plunket in kit form a few years earlier at an Ideal Homes Exhibition. Internally it had a sitting room, kitchen, shower room and two bedrooms, with flooring made of mahogany tongue and groove boards. Lord Plunket kindly donated this building for use as a pavilion. It served the club for over ten years. Water was laid on to the Recreation Ground, but the toilet blocks were external. The Pavilion and Ground were officially opened on 21st July 1963 by the well known cricketer Jack Young, whose first class career had stretched from 1933-1956. He played for Middlesex,[3] and was a member of the English team between 1947 and 1949.

A cricket match played between the members of Addington Village Cricket Club against wives and girlfriends. Courtesy of the Kent Messenger.

A children's playground with equipment was installed. This was partly paid for by fundraising organised by the children themselves. They sold an early form of charity "scratch card", although this actually had a flap. The card was based on a cartoon character from the Daily Mirror called Useless Eustace.

By the mid 1960's, the Recreation Ground had a cricket field, a football pitch, a small cricket pavilion and a children's playground. However, although the Cricket Club paid rent, the finances of the Recreation Ground Committee rapidly became quite stretched. By the mid 1970's the Parish Council was giving an annual grant of about £150 as, unlike a village hall, the recreation ground had few sources of income.

Meanwhile, the Addington Village Cricket Club went from strength to strength. Within a few years, the membership had spread far wider than the actual village, though Don Castle, Charlie Rochez, Frank

Addington Dramatic Society and Hedgehog Productions

During the early 1960's, a second group of residents founded the Addington Dramatic Society. Its first president was Peter Rimmer, son of the postmaster. The Hon. Secretary was Enid Coates of Trottiscliffe Road. Other founder members were Arthur Gardiner of Sandy Lane and his daughter, Don and Margaret Castle of London Road, Audrey Reeves of Trottiscliffe Road and George Fenner, owner of The Greenways Hotel. As can be seen, the members came from all areas of the village. Arthur Gardiner had experience of amateur dramatics and supplied the first scenery; Mr. Fenner provided the lighting and sound for the productions. The first performance was staged on 21st and 22nd November 1963. This was "The French Mistress", a new comedy by Sonnie Hall. The producer was Norris Stayton.

Both the cast and backstage personnel were predominantly Addington residents and later also included Bill Rawson, John Hawtin and Meg Robinson. Margaret Castle not only acted but later directed productions. From 1964 to 1972, Addington Dramatic society staged up to two productions a year. These comedies, dramas and thrillers attracted patronage from far beyond the village. The Society attracted excellent amateur players from outside the village and their productions were well reviewed in the local press. The social life in the village was enriched not only by the plays, but also by the associated fundraising, which included dances.

A performance of "I am a Camera" by the Addington Dramatic Society, 1970. Enid Coates, Margaret Rees, John Kennedy and Margaret Castle. Courtesy the Kent Messenger

It was the Addington Dramatic Society's needs and their members' drive which led to the eventual closure of the old hall down Millhouse Lane and the move to a new one on the Recreation Ground in 1974. A stage was built at the new hall specifically for their use. The Society's first production on this was a one act play. After 1975 there was a break of two years before they relaunched in 1977 with "Time and Time Again" by Alan Ayckbourn. Productions continued into the 1980's and early 1990's, but the Society then disbanded. However, almost immediately a new dramatic society was created in Addington.

Hedgehog Productions was formed as part of the fundraising for a new church centre, which began in 1995. Its cast and production crew were and are associated with St. Margaret's church, and live in Addington and surrounding villages. Its first production was "Chimneys" and included a cast of both adults and children. A number have been original works, written by the members. Although the funds for the church centre were raised some years ago, Hedgehog Productions continues to stage at least one play or show a year at Addington Village Hall and other local venues. The proceeds support the church and other charities. Directors have been Martyn Begbey, Jim Hayman and Christine Halliday-Saddler, all of whom act in the productions.

The finale from "Moving with the Times", the 2012 production staged by Hedgehog Productions. Photograph by Colin Bowles

A new Village Hall

In 1966, it was recognised that the aged Village Hall on Millhouse Lane had to be replaced. A site was identified next to the "Plunket" sports pavilion on the Recreation Ground. However, the restrictive nature of the lease between the Parish Council and the Recreation Ground Committee meant that no grant aid could be sought to achieve this. After taking advice from the Kent Association of Parish Councils, the Parish Council agreed a new lease with the Recreation Ground Committee. At the end of 1970, the Village Hall Committee was able to report that they could now apply for grant aid and that that fundraising would start. Kent County Council offered a generous grant, but this would be paid only when the matching funding was raised. Meanwhile, the old hall on Millhouse Lane, which had up to 2,000 personal visits each year, was ordered to improve its toilet facilities to meet new hygiene legislations. This was an unwelcome expense of £300.

The cost of the new hall was £19,544. This was achieved by selling the old site for £10,000, through grant aid of £7,630 and by local fundraising that secured £3,000, giving a small surplus for fixtures and fittings. Building started in the summer of 1973 and the new Addington Village Hall was opened on 4th May 1974 by Ronnie Blair, a past chairman of the Parish Council and a driving force in its build. Bookings came in quickly and one of the first organisations to establish a permanent presence in the hall was a children's playgroup.

The Village Hall Committee set out to attract regular hirers. They did not want to rely on occasional bookings, though events such as weddings, anniversaries, village dances, theatrical performances and fundraising events were encouraged. The Parish Council met in the hall for many years, but later transferred to the Sports Pavilion as it was more compact and therefore warmer in the winter months. During the 1970's, playgroups became increasingly popular as a way of socialising and educating children between the ages of three and five. The new Village Hall on the Recreation ground created an excellent venue. Mrs. Sheila Barber, of Plowenders Close, founded Addington Kindergarten and ran this three mornings a week, until her retirement. The Kindergarten was then acquired by three Lindas: Linda Pearman, Lynda Roots and Linda Lovelock. It is now open on each weekday morning and is the longest running hirer. Although a number of local primary schools now have their own pre-school facilities, the Kindergarten remains a very much appreciated organisation.

Other regular hirers of the hall have been exercise and ballroom dancing classes, Sunday School and the South East Trailer Caravan Club, who pay weekend visits. Club members park outside the hall and use its facilities for their get-togethers, a very popular one being over the Christmas holiday. At the beginning of the 21st century discussions took place

with the Church Council with a view to adding an extension to the hall so that they could use this as their main venue for meetings and for children and youth work. These had to be abandoned due to legal technicalities and permission was later given to extend St. Margaret's church, as can be seen below. The Village Hall, however, remains the main venue for large church social and fundraising events.

A number of building and refurbishment projects have improved the facilities at the Hall. Other changes have been made in response to Government regulations. Maintenance and refurbishment is needed on an ongoing basis to attract hirers. Over £5,000 was spent on indoor and outdoor painting, new chairs, curtains and light fittings in 1995-96. At the end of the century, the toilet facilities were extended and repositioned to provide wheelchair access. The storage facilities for the cleaner's equipment were also improved at this time. The substantial assistance from both the Parish and Borough Council over the years has been much welcomed. The kitchen was redesigned during 2010-11, and now has two ovens, updated storage and washing facilities, a lengthened serving bar and a more convenient access.

A permanent Sports Pavilion

After serving Addington Village Cricket Club well for over ten years, Lord Plunket's pavilion became too small and was also somewhat dilapidated. The drive to replace it was launched at the Annual Parish Meeting of 1974. Like so many projects, achieving a permanent structure took some years. Successful negotiations took place with the new owners of Rose Alba, Mr. and Mrs. Bygrave, to acquire further land to enlarge the car park, but planning permission for the new pavilion was not granted until the autumn of 1977. The holiday home was then demolished. A grant of £1,000 was received from Tonbridge and Malling District Council and a generous private donation was also received. This was the start of very active fundraising, one successful scheme being to "buy a brick". The club members themselves carried out the construction work and the pavilion was formally opened on 4th August 1979 by Mrs. Cynthia Howles of the Seekers' Trust. The new building included changing facilities, a downstairs meeting room with kitchenette and an upstairs bar with a club licence. Over the ensuing years, the pavilion has been extended and more facilities installed, including an extensive viewing gallery.

During the 1980's, the playground facilities adjacent to the field were improved. Outdated equipment was removed and wooden climbing frames were built. Particular emphasis was given to free play through a safe environment with a soft play surface. However, by the end of the century these new facilities were also beginning to show their age. The play area was again redesigned and at the same time extended into the arboretum next door, which had been planted by the chairman of the Recreation Ground Committee, John Hawtin.

The Addington Village Cricket Club was achieving major successes. In 1985, the Addington Village Colts, an under-15 side, became the Kent champions and reached the national semi-final before being defeated by a team from Essex. It was the first cricket club in Kent to achieve Sport England's Clubmark accreditation as a "Safe, Effective and Child Friendly Club". After rigorous, and ongoing, assessment, the club was selected to deliver coaching in the area under the "Chance to Shine" initiative. It is also one of only sixty Focus Clubs in the country. These are responsible for raising the game within their respective counties.

In this capacity, A.V.C.C. was encouraged to improve facilities for practice in the area. In 2004, grant aid of £43,000 was received to install the substantial practice nets which now stand beside the Pavilion. This led to a number of other grants, including from the sand extraction companies in the vicinity, enabling the upgrading of the Pavilion itself.

The Cricket Club now arranges a number of district wide volunteer training sessions, including grounds-manship, child protection, and first aid. Disability sports meetings, planning and community meetings are also held at the Recreation Ground. All the maintenance of the ground is undertaken by volunteers. The qualified coaches run courses in local primary schools and, as the young players reach maturity, many consider becoming coaches themselves.

In 2012, the Recreation Ground was awarded the status of a QEII Fields in Trust challenge site. This provides protection for its recreational status in perpetuity. The scheme was part of Queen Elizabeth's Diamond Jubilee celebrations and is similar to the King George V playing fields designation of 1935. An additional benefit is that it gives better access to sponsorship.

Addington Village Cricket Club has two adult teams and a range of junior teams from under nines up to sixteen year olds. A girls' section was launched in 2011, who took part in their first Girls under-11 and under-13 matches. Even four to seven year olds are helped to develop their ball handling. In 2012, the Club won Division 3 of the Kent League and will be promoted to Division 2 in the 2013 season. Peter Robinson told me that this means that the Club is now in the top thirty of 330 cricket clubs in Kent. They also host South-East based senior and all-age matches, with inter-County matches against Sussex and Hampshire. They hosted a Kent 0-70's match against Sussex in 2012.

The Recreation Ground in 2012 showing the Sports Pavilion with the Village Hall to its left.

Addington Football Club

Addington Football Club had their pitch on the Recreation Ground for fifty years. A founding member of the Addington Dramatic Society, Pete Rimmer, was one of its first members. From the 1970's the organisers were Peter Williamson and Mike Hinton. The Club played in the local Saturday Friendly League. Trottiscliffe Football Club, which belonged to the Sunday Friendly League, also shared the pitch during the 1980's, but then moved to West Malling. In the early years of the 21st century, Addington Football Club undertook a considerable amount of renovation work on their pitch and widened the playing area. The club also started a successful junior team. It later became increasingly difficult to find volunteers to run the organisation. The club terminated its lease and left the ground at the end of the 2010-11 season. Although they played at New Hythe, Larkfield for a season, they have subsequently closed, one reason being that the junior team were now adults and had left home. Some of these young men are now training footballers in the United States.

As can be seen from both this photograph, and the one previous, the ground is particularly attractive. It is fringed with trees and the church tower peeps over these on the eastern side. This is part of the A.V.C.C. logo.

The pavilion accepts outside hirers. The better facilities benefit the other organisations represented on the Recreation Ground management committee, at no expense to rate payers. Double glazing and better upholstered chairs revitalised Addington Bridge Club, which had developed from a Whist Drive started by Mrs. Barbara Dicker in the 1960's. There was a period when both clubs ran in tandem. Addington Bridge Club was founded as an evening duplicate bridge club but, a few years ago, a morning Improvers Group began and the club now has a membership of about 90. The organisation is 'live' on the web as part of "Bridgeweb". Sessions are well attended with up to ten tables being set up on a Tuesday evening. Another organisation that uses the ground and pavilion is the West Malling and District Homing Society, a racing pigeon club that came to the village when their meeting place in Offham closed down. They use the Sports Pavilion for social and business gatherings, their season corresponding with that of the Cricket Club.

The Queen's Jubilees and other village events

In 1977, the village celebrated the Queen's Silver Jubilee with a large village fête, a barbecue, cricket match, sports for the children and a dance in the Village Hall. Commemoration mugs and crowns were given to the children. A tree was donated by Brookfield Garden Centre and planted outside the Chestnuts. A special dinner was staged for the large number of older people then living in the village. This became a regular event and continued for many years as the Senior Citizens' Lunch. A number of fêtes and other village events such as jumble sales and dances were held on the Recreation Ground and in the Village Hall during the 1970's and 1980's, but sadly it became more and more difficult to find the volunteers to run these. They are now less frequent.

The village has gained prizes in Kent Village of the Year and Trees in Your Village. One prize was a seat for the Village Green and others were a brightly variegated maple near to the Village Hall and the fastigiate beech on the Green, mentioned earlier.

The Millennium was marked by a service at St. Margaret's and the planting of a yew tree in the churchyard by the children's group "Oggies". The Queen's Diamond Jubilee in 2012 was celebrated by a musical party in the Village Hall, historical exhibitions in the hall and the church, guided visits at the megaliths and the lighting of a beacon at the Village Hall. A plaque was dedicated on 2nd June 2012 in recognition of the Recreation Ground's new status as a QEII field.

Politics, Planning, Transport and Development

During the early 1960's, proposals were made that some parish councils should be abolished and groups of small villages should be merged as a confederate parish council. As Addington is a small parish, this threat was taken very seriously and the Parish Council initiated talks with their neighbours, who also confirmed their desire for independence. Although some mergers took place, this locality was spared. The threat showed the need for small communities to join in collaborative action

to achieve more influence. Parish councils, through their association, the National Association of Local Councils, began to press for a greater say in planning matters. They demanded the right to see and comment on planning applications themselves, rather than having to rely on their District Councillor as spokesperson. They achieved this right when the Local Government Act of 1972 was passed.

The Act also abolished rural and urban district councils, merging them into larger authorities representing at least twice the number of electors. Malling Rural and Tonbridge Urban districts became Tonbridge and Malling District (later Borough) Council in 1974. At the end of 1973, the Parish Council was addressed by the Information Officer of Tonbridge and Malling District Council, who informed members that the intention from April 1974 was to remove the right of local parish councils to set their own precept and that Tonbridge and Malling District Council would levy a rate and distribute money to parish councils at their discretion. There was an outcry, not only from Addington, but from all its neighbours in the district and the proposal was abandoned. If it had, the ethos of self-sufficiency in the village might have been lost forever.

One anomaly that resulted from the reorganisation was that the third tier of parish and town councils was not uniform across every district. The parish and town councils of Malling Rural District Council had always paid for their own ground maintenance and other facilities through their precept. Tonbridge had been an urban district council and the town decided not to have a separate town council under the new arrangements. This meant that ratepayers in the parishes now became liable, through their district rates, to pay for services in Tonbridge town that were for their residents' benefit alone. An agreement was eventually reached that annual grants would be given to parish councils by the District Council to compensate them for this double taxation. Under a separate scheme, specific grants can be applied for to enhance village facilities. In addition, the church receives a grant for maintaining a public burial ground.

In 1974, new Parliamentary divisions were created and Addington left the Sevenoaks Constituency and

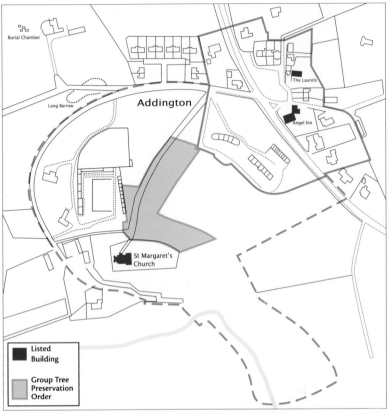

The original and enlarged Conservation area of Addington and the wider Group Tree Preservation Order. Drawn by John Hawtin.

became part of Tonbridge and Malling (later Tonbridge, Edenbridge and Malling). Parliamentary boundaries may change again in the near future.

On 16th April 1971 the central portion of the village, including the Village Green and Churchfields, was designated a Conservation Area. At the end of the century, a wider line was drawn, so that all of the land owned by the Seekers' Trust, the churchyard and a "tongue" of woodland stretching down from the churchyard, that includes a stretch

of Addington Brook, were also included in the Conservation Area. At that time a group tree preservation order was put on the trees within the Seekers' Trust grounds. Despite these protective measures, Addington's environment continued to change. The motorway, although it relieved pressure on the A20, caused noise and light pollution closer to the centre of the village. Addington Park became a golf course. Active farming came to an end. Cherry and fruit growing were abandoned and the orchards were grubbed out. During the 1980's the last flower growers became businesses of the past as they ceded dominance to Holland.

When, in 1986, the village boundaries changed once again, the only remaining working farms at Aldon transferred to Offham. The southern border

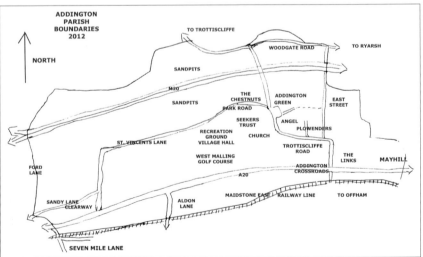

The modern civil parish boundaries of Addington, set in 1986, drawn by Patricia Richardson. The ecclesiastic boundaries were not changed.

retreated from the Teston Road to run along the line of the railway from Seven Mile Lane to Mayhill. It then turns north, skirting the eastern side of Mayhill, the last home being Stubblesdown, and then turns back west to a point behind the industrial complex that includes metal working. The boundary line then runs north again along the boundary between the golf course and Roughetts, before heading west to join East Street just beyond of Bumblebee Barn, north along East Street across the motorway to Woodgate Road and westwards just north of the road itself, to include Woodgate Cottage and Woodgate. On reaching Addington Lane the boundary runs briefly towards Trottiscliffe but turns left off this road at the sandpits and uses footpath 177 on the northern part of Campions Wood. It skirts the western part of the sand pit area (formerly Ford Sandpit) joins Ford Lane, and heads south to join the A20. The boundary then runs east for a short distance along the A20 then south until it meets the railway line at Seven Mile Lane, where it started.

These changes meant that homes and land south of the railway line became part of Offham parish, but homes on the western edge of Sandy Lane and two cottages on Ford Lane, south of Ford Place, joined Addington, as did Greenways and homes at Mayhill, as far as Stubblesdown Cottage. The only house north of Woodgate within the old boundary had been the most eastern house on Pilgrims Way called Harpwood. This was transferred to Trottiscliffe. The parish now covers 284 hectares (700 acres) much less than in previous centuries. Of these, only 40 hectares are built up. Thirty are used for sand extraction, and more lie beneath the concrete of the two motorways and their junction. The golf course stretches over previous pasture land, a few fields have animals grazing on them but others lie uncultivated.

The Local Government Commission of 1992 was charged with investigating whether to recommend that Kent should be a single unitary authority or a larger number of unitary authorities made up of two or more of the district councils. Some district councils welcomed the latter proposals, and there was much lobbying. Maidstone Borough Council was particularly keen for the Malling area to be transferred to them. After taking soundings from its

electorate, Addington Parish Council put forward their firm rejection of either proposal, fearing that its influence would diminish sharply under both structures. Luckily, as Kent was amongst one of the later tranches that the Commission visited, a groundswell of similar opinion had arisen throughout rural England by the time they arrived. The Kent Association of Parish Councils played a key role in consulting parishes throughout Kent, and represented their views to the Commission. The overwhelming opinion in all communities was similar to that in Addington. This was for the status quo to be maintained. Although the Medway towns merged with Dartford to become the Medway Unitary Authority in 1998, the rest of Kent retained its dual structure.

It would have been impossible for Addington to influence any of these decisions without the work of its Parish, District and County Councillors. The Parish Council, in particular, has been strengthened by some people spending a few years on the Council, bringing fresh ideas, and some very long serving members of the community, who have given stability and continuity. Two of these have been Philip Wilson and Patricia Garrett. Between them, they have given over fifty years service to the Council, both also serving in the chair. The Council was fortunate to have two long serving clerks in the last thirty years, Barbara Earl and Patricia Hughes, and has recently welcomed Louise Goldsmith to the post.

St. Margaret's Church

Rev. Callow, who came to the parish in 1961, remained only three years. Unlike in the past, when a new rector would arrive within a few weeks, a lengthy interregnum took place. The burden of running the church fell heavily on to the churchwarden, Fred Marsh, though services were taken by a previous curate, Rev. Palmer. The link with Offham was severed and in June 1965 Rev. John MacDonald became Priest in Charge of Addington as well as serving Trottiscliffe. Finances were tight, though, so he was on a part-time basis, retaining a teaching post.. The following year the two benefices were united. The rectory in Trottiscliffe was sold and Rev. and Mrs. MacDonald lived in Addington. Despite a surge in new housing along East Street and the Trottiscliffe Road, the church electoral roll was falling. Newcomers to the parish were less likely to be regular churchgoers, and many fundraising events had to be held to cope with the difficult financial situation. Rev. MacDonald was an active and much loved rector who gave his two parishes a period of stability, but he could not fight the general trend away from regular churchgoing. Sadly, he became unwell and, after a long fight with cancer, died in 1975.

Once again, the financial situation in the local parishes came into sharp focus. The Bishop of Rochester, the Rt. Rev. David Say, searched for a viable solution. The decision was taken to appoint the vicar of Ryarsh and Birling, the Rev. Malcolm Bury, as Priest in Charge of Addington and Trottiscliffe, meaning that he would have the pastoral care of four parishes. It was in this way that the BART (Birling, Addington, Ryarsh, Trottiscliffe) parishes came together. Rev. Bury attended his first meeting of Addington PCC on 17th November 1975. The arrangement ran for five years, after which the congregation was strongly in favour of this continuing. Further temporary periods ensued though, before the joint ministry was formally created as a united benefice. Despite his original reluctance to take on two extra parishes, Rev. Bury remained in post until 1983. He then moved to Halstead, near Sevenoaks. His successor was Rev. Struan Dunn, who came to BART from Barcelona, where he had been the Anglican chaplain. One of his first innovations was to publish a four parish magazine. This came to be known as Pilgrims. This began to attract local advertisers, and has become fully self-funding.

In 1990, following Rev. Dunn's move to Gillingham, Christopher and Julia Miles came to the Vicarage at Ryarsh from Leigh, near Tonbridge. Rev. Miles had been an engineer before being ordained and he became the Diocesan advisor to parishes installing lightning conductors. It was during his incumbency that the main fundraising for the church centre was undertaken, described in the next section and he steered the parish through the strains of such a major

undertaking. He was the joint vicar when the four parishes "produced" new ordinands, Revs. Brenda Hurd, Paul Filmer and Andrew Balfour. He also encouraged the laity to take a central role in services. A number of people from all four parishes became lay readers. After Rev. Miles' retirement in 2001, Rev. Hurd played a major role during the year long interregnum, after which she moved to Wrotham as its rector.

The United Benefice of Birling, Addington, Ryarsh and Trottiscliffe was finally confirmed and Rev. Jeremy Cross was appointed its first vicar. His previous parish had been at St. Leonards, Hastings. He also remained until his retirement, in July 2010. The BART Ministry welcomed its first woman vicar, Rev. Dr. Linda Shuker, in July 2011. Dr. Shuker is by profession a chemist. BART is her first parish, her curacy having been at Rothley, Leicester. The parish has therefore been served by seven incumbents since 1960. All have had a supportive wife or husband. In particular, Charmian Bury and Julia Miles developed children's outreach and Suzanne Cross enriched the music at services. Mrs. Cross developed the BART choir, and staged appreciated and well attended concerts at Birling Church. David Shuker also leads the choral work.

Surprisingly, during the same period, St. Margaret's has had only twelve churchwardens, nine men and three women. The men were, in order of date, Messrs. Fred Marsh and Ronnie Blair, Cdr. Stockbridge, Messrs. Fred Martin, John Lander, John Noble, Eric de Banzie, John Humphrey and Steve Hodges. The women have been Mrs. Rhoda Ainscouth, Joan Scott and Wendy Gardner. Joan Scott and John Humphrey, with breaks in service, were the longest serving. Whilst Joan oversaw the services and fabrics, John took overall charge of the construction of the new room, both very mighty burdens. There have been very few Hon. Secretaries and Hon. Treasurers, Mrs. Brenda Humphrey and Mrs. Jean Ebdon each giving sterling service.

During the latter part of the twentieth century, the congregation in Addington began to grow again, though the church electoral roll has remained between 80 and 90. The number of worshippers at main services on a Sunday was frequently over one hundred. This revival was mainly through the partnership of active vicars, energetic lay people, the introduction of new services and modern music. In 1973, Geoffrey and Judy Grimes moved to Hedgehogs, on St. Vincents Lane. Geoffrey was a partner in a major firm of London solicitors. They had been involved in a Christian youth organisation in south east London. They quickly opened their new home and began to develop child and youth work in Addington.

They were supported by the Parochial Church Council, which also began to look forward. Modern services were introduced that attracted young families. These used the revised liturgy that had recently been introduced. Isabel de Banzie led an excellent group of singers and musicians and services began to include visual and dramatic presentations. These new ways of worship brought people to St. Margaret's from the wider locality and the church "family" grew. Activities covered all ages of children and some grew up to be youth leaders themselves. The young children met at the Village Hall and the older ones at Hedgehogs, where there was teaching, indoor and outside games and sports. Oggies later progressed to be Soggies (Senior Oggies) and later attended a group known as F.A.C.T. (Friday for Addington Christian Teenagers). Missions were held and the children began to attend summer camps. Geoffrey Grimes was the first to be trained as a lay reader and, after his retirement, he gained a theology degree.

Addington's chief bell ringer, Bryan Ebdon.

Prayer and discussion groups for adults started, including women's groups and a men's breakfast, all aimed at the four parish community. Some were held in homes and others in local halls. Eric and Isabel de Banzie were the first leaders in this adult outreach in Addington. The bells were rehung and brought back into use. A new group of bell ringers was trained, led by Bryan Ebdon.

In late 1983, when minor repairs to the inside of the bell tower were being costed, the Church Council was advised that within the next five years the stonework of the tower would need a major overhaul. This was deteriorating badly and the cost would be substantial. Geoffrey Grimes set out to obtain grant aid for the work and the Tower Repair Fund was opened with a £25 donation from the Senior Citizens' Lunch. The main problems were associated with the dressed stonework, much of which needed replacing. In June 1984, the architects, Purcell, Miller, Tritton and Partners, of Sevenoaks, gave the following specification. 100%, of the stair turret and the creasing course above the nave roof would need to be replaced, as would 75% of the merlons and embrasures (the solid parts and spaces) of the parapets, the middle window openings, the main west window and the buttresses. Work was also needed to renew the string courses (the projecting horizontal lines of stone), the belfry window openings and the former west door. 30% of the tower walls needed repointing.

An Oggies camp at Hedgehogs during the late 1980's. Courtesy of Judy Grimes.

The tower of St. Margaret's under repair. Detail of one of the new gargoyles. As in the past, this is said to have been modelled on one of the workmen!

Early in 1985, fundraising got under way in earnest. The substantial problems noted above indicated that £95,000 would have to be found to carry out the work. The local community was extremely generous in both freewill giving and fundraising, but grant aid was desperately needed. In less than two years, Mrs. Jean Ebdon, as the Hon. Treasurer of St. Margaret's, was able to report that the fund stood at £45,714.20, but it took longer before the whole amount was raised. Grants were received from the Friends of Kent Churches, the McFarlane Trust, Colyer Ferguson Trust, St. Judas Trust, Marshall's Charity, the Historic Churches Charity, English Heritage, the Kent County Council and the Diocese of Rochester. Work finally got under way and was completed in early 1989. The dedication service took place on 14th May.

The fundraising had been so successful that it was possible to retile the church roof. A concurrent appeal was made to repair the obelisk memorial in the churchyard dedicated to Captain Locker and his wife. By fundraising and with further grants, including a donation from the National Maritime Museum Charitable Trust, the repairs were rapidly effected. By 1990, all stone and tiling work had been completed and the church fabric was in excellent condition. Sound and security systems were installed, so that St. Margaret's was ready to meet the new millennium.

Further work was undertaken at the start of the 21st century. The chancel, the north transept and the south chapel were all reordered. Pews and screens were removed and matching tiles and reclaimed stone were laid where the floor was now bare. Handmade oak storage cupboards were placed in the north transept. Another fundraising campaign ensured that the painted ceiling and monuments in the Watton Chapel were cleaned. The vibrant colours on the barrel vaulted ceiling had lain hidden beneath dark varnish for many decades and this had been a long hoped for project. It was first proposed in the 1960's. A generous bequest allowed the stonework of the reredos to be cleaned and modern lighting installed. The church now has a flexible and well lit space that gives room to move for musicians and singers.

Although the civil parish boundaries were changed in 1985, those of the ecclesiastic parish remained largely unchanged. They continue to stretch from south of Teston Road to north of the old site of Coldrum Lodge. A small northern portion of Pilgrim's Way, containing Harpwood, was transferred to Trottiscliffe, at the request of the resident. The last few homes on Sandy Lane have not become part of St. Margaret's, nor have those in the Links or further along the London Road, at Mayhill. Residents in these areas are, however, heartily welcomed as members of the church family and a number are regular worshippers and on the church electoral roll.

A new church room

By 1993, it was apparent that the church needed extra room to cope with congregational needs and activities. Geoffrey and Judy Grimes warned that Hedgehogs could never be a permanent home for youth work and the congregation needed a venue for church meetings and social events. The first suggestion was to reinstate the gallery at the west end of the church, by moving the organ back to the north transept. This was rejected as impractical. The PCC then had to decide whether to build an extension to the church or to construct a new building. The Diocese was approached on the first proposal and at the same time the Seekers' Trust were asked whether they would sell or lease a piece of land on which to build a church hall. The Diocesan Advisory Committee rejected the idea of a church extension but preliminary discussions with the Trust went well. The church was offered a lease on land next to the lych-gate.

Geoffrey Grimes led the new project. Tonbridge and Malling Planning Department was supportive of the plans and a fundraising committee met for the first time in 1995. The appeal was launched in March 1996 and very substantial funds were raised, by planned giving, grants and activities. This was why the drama group, Hedgehog Productions, was founded. It seemed that construction would shortly go ahead. Unfortunately, it was then discovered that church law insisted that a building must be owned on a freehold basis if services were to be held in it.

The Geoffrey Grimes Room at St. Margaret's church. The photograph shows how the south wall of the church has been conserved and the landscape view from the room. Photograph by Lucy Richardson

After taking legal advice, the proposal had to be abandoned. The funds were invested whilst alternative solutions were explored. Geoffrey Grimes died but the leadership was assumed by Paul Drayson, who moved to Hedgehogs with his wife, Rita, and their children. They continued the youth work there to give the parish time to achieve the new centre. After their return to live at Trottiscliffe, the Village Hall became the base for Sunday School but, as has been mentioned earlier, proposals to extend the hall and to stay there permanently fell through.

The PCC approached the Diocese of Rochester once again and this time it favoured an extension to St. Margaret's church on its southern side. Work got under way in 2010. The extension is faced with stone and the original exterior wall of the church has been retained as a feature within the room. The ancient south door was re-opened as access from the nave and skylights enable light to come into this through the existing stained glass windows. Fully glazed double doors give an attractive outlook over parkland. The room was dedicated at a service held at the church in September 2011, eighteen years after the project was first conceived. Because of Geoffrey Grimes' inspiration, drive, enthusiasm and skills, the extension was named after him as the Geoffrey Grimes Room. This now provides a teaching and play-space for children during services. The room is also used for gatherings and as a meeting room. It has a small catering area and internal plumbing.

The Village Appraisal of 1985 and the Parish Plan Survey of 2009

In 1984, questionnaires were delivered to all homes in the village. The stated intention was *"To enable the Parish Council to make sure when taking decisions concerning the present and future development of the parish, that these are based on sound knowledge of all aspects of village life, and of the wishes of Addington residents."* 114 replies were received from approximately 260 households and the eventual report, published in

1985,[4] stated that the residents were generally happy with their village, though they disliked the volume of traffic they had to endure. The decision to stage an appraisal was prompted by the realignment of the parish boundaries recorded above. The electoral roll had reduced to 530, so the population was then about 700. The census of 1981, though it covered the larger parish before it was reduced in size, showed that only 4% of residents were less than five years old, 16% were of school age and 22% were aged 65 or older. The respondents to the 1984 survey tended to be the older, long term residents. However, as the mean age of residents in Addington was slightly higher than in similar communities, the answers were probably representative.

Although close to London, Addington could not then, or now, be judged as a dormitory town. Most employment was undertaken locally, no further than the Medway Towns, Maidstone or Sevenoaks. Although some respondents complained about local bus services, few were concerned about rail travel. Car ownership was high. A significant proportion of respondents' households owned three or more cars, all used on a daily basis. Eleven people stated that they did not have a telephone in their home. The variations in wealth appear to have been quite stark thirty years ago.

Community spirit seemed to be waning. A number of suggestions were made for new clubs and recreational facilities, as well as dances and get-togethers, but it was clear that only a very small proportion of residents actually organised such events and clubs. This trend would accelerate as the century drew to a close. No particular plan was made from the village appraisal. It was always intended as a document to present to the planning authority, so that residents' opinions would be taken into account. But it did emphasize the strength of feeling for continuity and organic growth rather than rapid change.

It was then expected that the volume of traffic from sand extraction and infilling would come to an end within two years but lorry movements to and from the pits still continue to some extent. In 1985, house building was in abeyance and the assumption was that future permissions would be mainly for single homes, rather than estates. This has been borne out, with the exception of the two developments known as The Links and The Paddocks. The hope that new homes would be built in materials in keeping with their environment has been achieved. The report was correct in foreseeing that little agriculture would return to the fields. The appraisal concluded: *"It is, when all is said and done, the villagers who will fashion the village and village life for the future."* Has this indeed happened?

Twenty-five years later a second survey was undertaken, from which a Parish Plan is currently being actioned. This was undertaken with the help of Action for Communities in Rural Kent, who analysed the responses. A series of open days was held at which people could interact with the survey committee, led by Parish Councillor, Peter Robinson. In 2009 there was a lower ratio of respondents, only 65 replies from a possible 300 homes but over the intervening years, responses to surveys nationally had dropped away. The replies came mainly from long term residents, as in the earlier case. Nearly 25% of respondents had lived in the village for more than thirty years, whilst only 8% had been resident for five years or less. However, it is likely that the average age in Addington has risen over the past thirty years. Many who replied stated that it was the "attractive area" that had brought them to the village. Others had sought "suitable and affordable housing" or had family connections in the area. Ten respondents had bought a home here after retirement.

Responses to the survey reiterated residents' concerns about the volume and speed of traffic through the village. There were also safety concerns about Addington Crossroads, despite the introduction of a 50 m.p.h. speed limit in the area. Although the layout where Seven Mile Lane meets the A20 had been altered, it was clear that this junction was still giving cause for concern.

Maintenance and repair of footpaths, roads and pavements was criticised. It is clear that these are still frequently used, as respondents complained that they should in better condition and free of obstructions. There was little demand for new housing. This was a similar response to the earlier questionnaire. The Parish Plan aims to tackle issues such as communication with residents and improvements to services, both those run by the Parish Council and those organised by the local authorities. Other issues to be addressed are traffic problems, activities for children and young people, environmental issues and ways to rebuild a sense of community.

Present and future

Although the major development in the village has slowed, in 2012 Addington has just over 300 households, an increase of over 20% since 1980. There are about 620 electors, indicating a population of over 800 people. The occupancy level per dwelling is far lower than during earlier centuries, particularly the nineteenth.

Gas had long been available along the London Road, but was finally laid to the centre of the village in 1992 and to Sandy Lane a few years later. Homes in other outlying areas still rely on oil, gas cylinders or electricity for cooking, heating and lighting. The Angel public house is now a free house that hosts a restaurant and bed and breakfast establishment in addition to its bar. Other businesses have vanished from the village. The Post Office on the Green and the shop at Clearway had both closed by 1990, two transport cafés traded for some time longer, but the 1990's saw the demise of Greenways Hotel, whilst Addington Motors and Astran transport moved away from the village. A number of independent businesses operate within the boundaries. These are an antiques centre, a golf club, two printing works, an agricultural contractor, scaffolding, machine works and transport services firms, a plumbing business, a filling station, sandpits, a scrapyard, a car showroom and one remaining transport café. In addition, "intellectual" businesses operate from peoples' homes. Boot fairs take place regularly during the summer in fields adjacent to the London Road and these are well patronised. Addington's public facilities, the Village Hall, Recreation Ground, Sports Pavilion and St. Margaret's Church, have all seen improvements during the past quarter century. The public open spaces are well maintained by the Parish Council and the public footpaths are much walked.

Although the filling station at Offham Crossing has a small convenience shop, residents must go elsewhere for necessities and have to rely on cars, infrequent buses or taxis. Children attend a number of local primary schools and must travel further for secondary education. Some attend private schools, though there are none within ten miles. Addington is still not a village of commuters to London, but many workers have long journey times. For those who work at home, general broadband speeds are still very slow, considering how close the village is to a major conurbation.

Addington has not been allowed to grow uncontrollably and its green and open aspect has so far been retained. The golf course, sandpit, grazing land, village greens, woodland and substantial garden plots all play a part in this. However, even as I was completing this life history, things continue to change. Some village organisations close, whilst others open. The Parish Council is lobbied for improvements and some will come about. Developers are constantly on the lookout for opportunities.

The challenge for the future is to revive and foster the community spirit that was so evident in the past. There are excellent facilities in which to meet and interact. The future could look bright.

---

1   Although a long distance path, in Addington the sections are MR164, MR168, MR177A and MR173.
2   This was built for Mr. and Mrs. Charles Simpson, and is now called The Woodhouse.
3   Jack Young, 1912-1993. He was a slow arm bowler who took 150 wickets for his club in each of three seasons, 1947, 1951 and 1952. (Wikipedia).
4   A copy of this appraisal is lodged at the Kent History and Library Centre, Whatman Way, Maidstone, on the open shelves.

BIBLIOGRAPHY

Books

Armstrong, A., *"The Economy of Kent, 1640-1914"*, Kent County Council (K.C.C), 1995

Atkinson, Captain C.T., *"The Queen's Own (Royal West Kent Regiment) 1914-1919"*,
    Simpkin, Marshall, Hamilton Kent & Co. Ltd., London, 1924

Brandon, P., Short, B., *"The South East from AD 1000"*, Longman, 1990

Burgoyne Black, S., *"Farningham Crossroads, A Study of two Kentish Turnpike Roads"*,
    Darenth Valley Publications, 1984

Butler-Henderson, U., *"Elsie Fenwick in Flanders, Diaries of a Nurse, 1915-1918"*,
    Spiegl Press, Stamford, Lincolnshire, 1980

Chalklin, C.W., *"Seventeenth Century Kent, A Social and Economic History"*, Longmans Green, 1965

Charnock, J., *"Biographia Navalis"*, 1801, (Reprint now available in six volumes)

Cheney, C.R., revised Jones, M., *"A Handbook of Dates, New Edition"*, Royal Historical Society, 1945, 2000

Churchill, I.J., *"Calendar of Kent Feet of Fines to the end of Henry III's reign"*,
    Kent Records, Vol. 15, Kent Archaeological Society (K.A.S.), 1956

Councer, C.R., *"Lost Glass from Kent Churches"*, Kent Records, Vol. 22, K.A.S., 1980

De Boulay, F.R.H., ed., *"Medieval Kentish Society"*, Kent Records, Vol. 18, K.A.S, 1964

Everitt, A. *"The Community of Kent and the Great Rebellion 1640-1660"*, Historical Society, 1969, 1986

Fielding, Rev. C.H., *"Memories of Malling"*, H.C.H. Oliver, West Malling, 1891

Gooder, E.A., *"Latin for Local History, an Introduction"*, Longman, 1961, reprinted 1998

Lansberry, F., ed., *"Government and Politics in Kent, 1640-1914"*, K.C.C., 2001

Lawson, T., Killingray, D., ed., *"An Historical Atlas of Kent"*, sponsored by K.A.S., Phillimore, 2004

Morris, J., *"Domesday Book, Kent"*, Phillimore, 1983

Mortimer, I., *"The Time Traveller's Guide to Medieval England"*, Vintage, 2009

Mosley, C., ed., *"Burke's Peerage & Baronetage, 106th Edition"*,
    Burke's Peerage (Genealogical Books) Ltd., Switzerland, 1999

Newton, D., *"Papists and Puritans 1596-1714"*, Cambridge University Press, 1998

Nicolas, Sir N.H., *"The Dispatches and Letters of Lord Nelson"*, Vols. 1-3, of 8,
    Chatham Publishing, 1997 (reprint. Originally published by Henry Coburn in 1844)

Oman, C., *"Nelson"*, Hodder & Stoughton, 1947

Pine, L.G., ed., *"Burke's Landed Gentry 1952"*, Burke's Peerage, London, 1952

Roake, M., ed., *"Religious Worship in Kent, the Census of 1851"*, K.A.S., 1999

Sitwell, S., *"Conversation Pieces"*, Batsford, 1936

Stuart, D., *"Latin for Local and Family Historians"*, Phillimore, 1995

Tate, W.E., *"The Parish Chest"*, 1946, reprinted Phillimore, 1983

Twisden, Sir J.R., completed Dudley Ward, C.H., *"The Family of Twysden and Twisden"*, John Murray, 1939

Walker, R., *"The Nelson Portraits"*, Royal Naval Museum Publications, 1998

Whiteman, A., Clapinson, M., *"The Compton Census of 1676: A Critical Edition"*, British Academy, 1986

Williams, J.H., ed., *"The Archaeology of Kent to AD 800"*, Boydell Press and K.C.C., 2007

Woodcock, T., Robinson, J.M., *"The Oxford Guide to Heraldry"*, Oxford University Press, 1990

Yates. N., Hume, R. and Hastings, P., *"Religion and Society in Kent, 1640-1914"*, K.C.C., 1994

Zell, M., ed., *"Early Modern Kent, 1540-1640"*, K.C.C., 2000

Other Printed Matter

Addington Parish Council, 1985, 2012, *"The Village Appraisal of Addington in the County of Kent"*,
    "Addington Parish Plan"

Alexander, J., 1958, *"The excavation of the Chestnuts Megalithic Tomb at Addington, Kent"*,
    K.A.S., Archaeologica Cantiana (Arch. Cant.), Vol. 72, pp 191-2

Alexander, J., 1961, *"The excavation of the Chestnuts Megalithic Tomb at Addington, Kent"*,
    Arch. Cant., Vol. 76, pp 1-57

Ashbee, P, 1993, *"The Medway Megaliths in Perspective"*, Arch. Cant., Vol. 111, pp 57-111

Ashbee, P., 1999, *"The Medway megaliths in a European Context"*, Arch. Cant., Vol. 119, pp 269-284

Ashbee, P., 2000, *"The Medway Megalithic Long barrows"*, Arch. Cant., Vol. 120, pp 319-345

Bartlett, D., 1966, *"Recent Excavations\: Emergency Excavation at Addington"*,
    Kent. Archaeological Review, Vol. 3, p 41

Coleman, D.C., 1851, *"Thesis on the Economy of Kent under the Later Stuarts"*,
    London Ph.D. Thesis, 1951 (manuscript)

Johns, F.D., 1987, *"A Petty Constable's Account Book"*, Arch. Cant., Vol. 104, pp 9-23

Kent Historic Buildings Committee, 1997, *"The Kent Historic Buildings Index, Tonbridge and Malling Section"*,
    Issue No. 1

Linklater, A, 2010, 2012 *"Archaeological Evaluation at St. Margaret's Church, Addington"*,
    Canterbury Archaeological Trust

Philp, B., 1981, *"A Survey of Medway megaliths"*, Kent Archaeological Review, Vol. 64, pp 78-92

Tonbridge and Malling District Council, 1982, *"Conservation Studies Trottiscliffe, Birling, Addington and Fairseat"*

Zell, M.L., 1977, *"Early Tudor J.P.s at work"*, Arch. Cant., Vol. 93, pp 125-144

Material available on the web

Ancestry.co.uk. Subscription

Kent Archaeological Society: Membership.

Kent County Council Online Reference Library. Library card. www.kent.gov.uk

National Archives. Pay per document.

Times Archive Online. Subscription.

Material at Kent History and Library Centre, Whatman Way, Maidstone

Census records

Electoral Roll information 1900-1970

Historical maps

Kent County and Trade Directories

Knight Frank & Rutley, 1923, Auction brochure for sale of Addington Park, including a map.

Maddan, J.G., 1952, *"Material for a History of Addington"*, manuscript book

Parish records for St. Margaret's church, Addington, CKS/P/2 MSS, some on microfilm

Planning records for Malling Rural District Council

INDEX